STORYTELLING IN THE NEW HOLLYWOOD

STORYTELLING IN THE NEW HOLLYWOOD

Understanding Classical Narrative Technique

Kristin Thompson

HARVARD UNIVERSITY PRESS
CAMBRIDGE, MASSACHUSETTS
LONDON, ENGLAND   1999

Library of Congress Cataloging-in-Publication-Data

Thompson, Kristin, 1950–
  Storytelling in the new Hollywood : understanding classical narrative technique /
  Kristin Thompson.
      p.   cm.
  Includes bibliographical references and index.
  ISBN 0-674-83974-9 (cl.: alk. paper). — ISBN 0-674-83975-7 (pbk.: alk. paper)
  1. Motion picture authorship. 2. Motion picture plays—Technique.
  I. Title.
PN1996.T46   1999
808.2'3—dc21
                                                               99-18427

FOR CHEN MEI

Contents

Preface

In 1985 David Bordwell, Janet Staiger, and I published *The Classical Hollywood Cinema: Film Style and Mode of Production to 1960*, a historical examination of the enduring stylistic and narrative traits of Hollywood filmmaking and their connections to the industry's organization and to the changing technology. Because the breakup of the traditional studio system that had begun after World War II was largely complete by 1960, we ended our study with that date, asserting that "the principles of classical filmmaking still hold sway."

In some ways, *Storytelling in the New Hollywood* is a follow-up to our earlier work. *The Classical Hollywood Cinema* was a large-scale history of several decades of Hollywood practice in which we described many aspects of the studio era and presented brief examples from an extensive survey of films from all years. Given that formidable task, we had no space for detailed analyses of individual films. The present book is a more limited, in-depth study. I propose to lay out contemporary Hollywood's most important and typical narrative strategies (which are in most respects the same as those in use during the earlier studio era) and then to examine closely ten recent films to show how those strategies are used in practice. In particular, I will show how films typically break down into large-scale parts, usually with carefully balanced proportions that help shape the trajectory of the narrative. I will also examine the notion of the "goal-oriented protagonist" so characteristic of classical narratives and will show how character goals often change, helping to shape the plot and indeed often marking the transitions between the large-scale portions of the narrative.

In recent years, some historians have claimed that there is something new at work in American cinema—"post-classical" filmmaking. This claim implies a fundamental shift in Hollywood's basic system of telling stories. As I have suggested, I will contend that modern Hollywood narratives are put together in much the same way as they were in the studio era.

This book is aimed at students and others interested in learning how modern films tell stories. It will also be useful to scriptwriters because it offers a more fine-grained account of how actual films work than do screenplay manuals.

This project originated when I was asked to give a series of lectures to the Summer Sessions for International Cinema Studies, held by the China Film Association in Beijing in 1988. My thanks to Chen Mei and Cheng Jihua for inviting me to this event, as well as to Janet Staiger (a veteran of the Beijing Summer Sessions) for suggesting that something on recent Hollywood cinema would interest our audience.

Many others have subsequently aided me a great deal in fleshing out those lectures into a book. I have delivered versions of several chapters as lectures and received many helpful comments and suggestions during the question sessions. Although I cannot thank all of those people by name, I am grateful to my audiences (and to those who arranged the lectures) at the Université Libre de Bruxelles (Dominique Nasta); the Filminstitut, Hochschule der Künste, Berlin (Carlos Bustamente); the University of Zurich (Noll Brinkmann); the Academy of Media Arts, Cologne (Yvonne Spielmann); the Chicago Film Seminar (Miriam Hansen); the University of Warwick (Ginette Vincendeau); Oxford University (Ian Christie); the Deutsches Filmmusuem, Frankfurt (Kitty Vincke); and the Filmmuseum München (Andreas Rost). I appreciate John Fullerton's friendly assistance. Special thanks go to the participants in the Film Colloquium of the University of Wisconsin–Madison's Department of Communication Arts, and particularly Sally Ross, all of whom patiently sat through three excerpts from this tome, and to the students of David Bordwell's "Critical Film Analysis" class, one of whom cleverly pinpointed the central turning point of *Jurassic Park* for me. Hank Luttrell, Deborah Daemmrich, and Richard West, of the University's Tolkien Society discussion group, offered useful comments on the *Groundhog Day* chapter.

Gabrielle Claes and the staff of the Cinémathèque Royale de Belgique kindly facilitated my research. The Communication Arts Department of the University of Wisconsin–Madison provided facilities for film viewing. Special thanks go to Hideaki Fujiki for his technical assistance with the widescreen frame enlargements. Most of all, I am grateful to my wonderful colleagues at the university, who discussed the issues with me and in some cases critiqued drafts of chapters: Lea Jacobs, Ben Brewster, Vance Kepley, Donald Crafton, Julie D'Acci (*The Silence of the Lambs*), Noël Carroll (*Alien*), and J. J. Murphy (whose faith in the three-act scriptwriting model has kept me on my toes in offering my own alternative). David Bordwell has been his usual helpful and supportive self, luring me into watching Tsui Hark films when I had intended to time large-scale portions of Hollywood classics.

Madison, Wisconsin
January 1999

I'm old-fashioned in this respect, I guess. Linear movies. Movies with some dramatic drive. I want to know what happens next, not what happened last year in Marienbad. If it was last year, if it was Marienbad, if it did happen. That kind of script you can knock out on a rainy afternoon. Critics have a tendency to assume that the more obscure something is, the more profound it must be.

I. A. L. DIAMOND

A note on film timings: Except when otherwise noted, running times for whole films include credit sequences. When story action occurs under the opening or closing credits, the credits are counted as part of the running time of the setup or epilogue. Timings have been rounded off to the nearest half minute and hence do not always add up precisely to the total running time.

1

Modern Classicism

First, the story must be understood.

    —EUGENE VALE, *The Technique of Screenplay Writing*

It's very hard to find any two things the storytelling faculty cannot connect.

    —J. R. R. TOLKIEN, *The Notion Club Papers*

WHAT IS THE "NEW HOLLYWOOD"?

The "old" Hollywood grew up during the 1910s and 1920s, as a group of producer-distributors banded together to form an important new industry with production headquarters in the Los Angeles area. From 1916 on, the United States became the number one supplier of movies in the world market, a position it has held ever since. Hollywood's success was based on telling stories clearly, vividly, and entertainingly. The techniques of continuity editing, set design, and lighting that were developed during this era were designed not only to provide attractive images but also to guide audience attention to salient narrative events from moment to moment.

As the big studios' output grew, with each one producing dozens of features a year, they put most of their personnel under long-term contract. Having a set of clear-cut guidelines of filmmaking could help coordinate the labor of all the people involved in the planning, shooting, and post-production phases. To a considerable degree, the classical Hollywood cinema that had developed by the end of the silent era was standardized—though it was never a "factory" system turning out a string of identical products on an assembly line. Since every story was different, the classical guidelines were crucial, granting filmmakers flexibility in achieving their goals. The classical system of storytelling flourished during the "golden age" of studio filmmaking in the 1930s and 1940s.

Since the late 1940s, the studio system has changed enormously. Forced by antitrust decisions to divest themselves of their theater chains after the war, the major companies increasingly focused on distribution and became more dependent on acquiring films made by large independent producers. Beginning in the 1960s, the studios have become part of increasingly large, horizontally integrated corporations. Were these changes so profound that they caused a radical shift in Hollywood's approach to storytelling?

The term "New Hollywood" is now commonly applied to the American film industry since its financial crisis of the late 1960s and early 1970s. During all these changes, have American filmmakers moved away from narrative clarity and coherence as central values? Just what, if anything, is new about the New Hollywood in terms of what audiences see in theaters?

According to film historians, the short-lived "youthquake" phenomenon that began in 1969 with the unexpected success of *Easy Rider* was the first sign that Hollywood was changing significantly. Then came the mainstream success of the "movie brats"—most centrally, Francis Ford Coppola, Steven Spielberg, George Lucas, Brian DePalma, Martin Scorsese, and Peter Bogdanovich. In addition, the veteran television director Robert Altman moved into features and proved pivotal in the changes to come. Several directors in this generation had film school educations and were well aware of the auteur theory and of film history in general. They aspired to become auteurs themselves, working within the industry but at the same time consciously establishing distinctive artistic personas. Young critics equally familiar with the auteur theory have helped to promote these directors and other film school alumni ever since.

Many people assume that the youthquake and the rise of the first auteurist generation of directors fundamentally changed Hollywood filmmaking. In recent years some film academics have made claims for a "post-classical," "post-Hollywood," or "postmodern" approach to mainstream popular American filmmaking. Those scholars argue that the old Hollywood was in decline by the late 1960s and that after the youthquake/auteurist phase there arose a new type of filmmaking that is still with us today. As early as 1975, the critic Thomas Elsaesser analyzed several of the auteurist films (including *Thieves Like Us, American Graffiti,* and *Five Easy Pieces*), detecting a "new realism" that he hoped indicated a liberalization of Hollywood politics: "The change I think one can detect is that the affirmative-consequential model of narrative is gradually being replaced by another, whose precise nature is yet to be determined. This is why the films I'm interested in have a transitional status."[1]

That particular direction, I think it is safe to say, was even then in the process of being filtered out of the Hollywood system, as the directors of these films either became more marginalized (like Altman) or more mainstream (like Lucas).

How then can we characterize the films that have dominated Hollywood production since the mid-1970s? In his book *High Concept*, the historian Justin Wyatt has offered a thoughtful discussion of "post-classical" filmmaking, which he defines in this way:

> In terms of film history, the period of the "classical Hollywood" is marked by the mature studio system and a style of filmmaking centered around continuity; however, the traits of the "post-classical" period (i.e., after the postwar disintegration of the studio system and the concurrent rise of television) have been suggested, but not formalized. Most frequently, a "post-classical" period is aligned with the "New Hollywood" of the '60s and the '70s, a period characterized by auteurs and the media conglomeration of the film industry. High concept can be considered as one central development—and perhaps *the* central development—within post-classical cinema, a style of filmmaking molded by economic and institutional forces.[2]

The rest of the book discusses the impact on films of such factors as the need to base many films on an easily pitched, pithy idea ("high concept") and the pressures of synergy (necessitating, for example, hit songs and other marketable ingredients). Wyatt's claim is that these developments have changed Hollywood's basic approach to filmmaking, including its stylistic traits.

I would suggest that the phenomena described by Wyatt are best thought of as intensifications of Hollywood's traditional practices. First, many Hollywood films of all eras have been based on ideas that could be simply summarized. Frank Capra derived the narrative of *It's a Wonderful Life* (1946) from a greeting card. (I shall return to this idea in Chapter 5.) As for synergy, the big Hollywood firms have always been driven by market considerations. Marketing and publicity tie-ins go back to the 1910s and have grown steadily in importance.[3]

There is no doubt that the industry changed in many ways in the decades after World War II. In 1948 the federal government won its antitrust proceedings against Paramount, leading to the divorcement decrees that enforced a separation of the exhibition wing of the industry from the main production/distribution firms. There was no longer a guaranteed week-by-week outlet for those films, and film attendance also sank as a result of the competition of other forms of leisure entertainment. Consequently, each studio cut its output. The earlier division of movies into various levels of A and B filmmaking gave way to today's situation: a more hit-or-miss blend of big-budget, superstar-oriented "event" movies with lower-budget fare, including the occasional "sleeper" that hits box-office gold.

Similarly, the Motion Picture Association of America's shift in 1968 from self-regulation based on the old Production Code to a rating system has led to an obvious change in the types of subject matter dealt with in mainstream Hollywood fare. Increasingly high violent and sexual content has been crucial in the rise of the action film, and the popularity of such fare abroad has expanded Hollywood's hold on international markets.

Still, neither the increased obsession with the bottom line brought about by the uncertainties of the market nor the changing subject matter in itself implies that the basic economic system underlying Hollywood storytelling has changed. Rather, the differences are essentially superficial and nonsystemic. In 1983 the industry historian Douglas Gomery concluded that "little changed in the American film industry during the Seventies, despite all the pundits' claims of a 'New Hollywood.'" He pointed out that aside from RKO, the big Hollywood studios were still in charge at the end of the decade and that the same stable oligopoly that had existed since the 1920s was still in force. He credited this to such factors as the major companies' worldwide distribution networks, economies of scale, and product differentiation.[4] At the beginning of 1998, Gomery assured me that the same still holds true, and that the decline of MGM/UA and the passing of the major companies into conglomerates have only consolidated the control enjoyed by a small cluster of older Hollywood firms. It is not my purpose here to examine the changes in the film industry in recent decades. Jim Hillier, however, offers a useful and detailed examination in *The New Hollywood*, where he comes to much the same conclusion: "In spite of all the changes that have taken place, Hollywood in the late 1980s and early 1990s does not look all that different from the Hollywood of the previous forty years."[5]

By the same token, I would suggest that the youthquake/auteurist films of the period from 1969 to 1977 or so were not harbingers of a profound shift in Hollywood storytelling but a brief detour that has had a lingering impact on industry practice. Despite all the critical attention they received, films like *Alice Doesn't Live Here Anymore, McCabe and Mrs. Miller, Sugarland Express,* and *Five Easy Pieces* constituted a tiny portion of the films released by the big Hollywood firms. Certainly such firms proved more open to hiring young or untried directors and scriptwriters after the success of *Easy Rider*, but that was undoubtedly a result of its proportionate rather than its absolute grosses. This film took in $7.2 million on an investment of less than half a million, but it reached only number 11 on the box-office chart in a year when *The Love Bug* was the top grosser with $17 million. Anyone who believes that mainstream Hollywood films went into eclipse during this period would do well to peruse Eddie Dorman Kay's *Box-Office Champs*,[6] which presents its figures in chronological order, revealing a business-as-usual pattern in the era's other number-one grossers: *Patton* (1970), *Love Story* (1971), *The Godfather* (1972), *The Poseidon Adventure* (1973), *The Sting* (1974), *Jaws* (1975), *One Flew Over the Cuckoo's Nest* (1976), and *Star Wars* (1977). Only one of these, *One Flew Over the Cuckoo's Nest*, could be considered to deviate significantly from classical storytelling. *M*A*S*H* was the other most successful of the "auteurist" films, at number three in 1970.

There is no doubt that in the early 1970s the auteurist directors set out deliberately to change Hollywood in what at least some of them perceived as a subversive way. In the ironically titled book *The Movie Brats: How the Film Generation Took Over Hollywood* (published in 1979 but current to 1977), Michael Pye and Lynda Myles helped define the new generation. They quote Francis Ford Coppola on his goals: "'The way to power,' he once said, 'is not always to merely challenge the Establishment, but first make a place in it and then challenge and double-cross the Establishment.'"[7] Indeed, some directors who were Coppola's contemporaries credit him as the leader of this challenge. His formation of the American Zoetrope studio in 1969 led to the production of a number of non-mainstream films, including his own *The Conversation* (1974) and Wim Wenders's *Hammett* (1983).

In interviews with Pye and Myles, some of the young directors expressed a cocky sense that they were succeeding in wresting power away from the studio bosses:

"We're the pigs," George Lucas says. "We are the ones who sniff out the truffles. You can put us on a leash, keep us under control. But we are the guys who dig out the gold. The men in the executive tower cannot do that. The studios are corporations now, and the men who run them are bureaucrats. They know as much about making movies as a banker does. They know about making deals like a real estate agent. They obey corporate law; each man asks himself how any decisions will affect his job. They go to parties and they hire people who know people. But the power lies with us—the ones who actually know how to make movies."[8]

John Milius expresses similar confidence: "Nobody in a studio challenges the final cut of a film now. I think they realize the filmmakers are likely to be around a lot longer than the studio executives. Now, power lies with the filmmakers, and we are the group that is getting the power."[9]

For a brief time, this attitude may have contained a grain of truth. On the whole, however, the auteurists got power for the same reason that any other director would: each made at least one successful film early on. Altman's *M*A*S*H* set the pace, surprising the studio by grossing $12.2 million on a $3 million film with a no-star cast. Coppola's subsequent success was based on *The Godfather*. Brian DePalma built his career on *Carrie*. Peter Bogdanovich seemed golden in 1972, with both *What's Up, Doc?* and *The Last Picture Show* in the year's top-ten box-office list (numbers 4 and 6 respectively). Steven Spielberg's entrée was *Jaws*, which did far better than its producers had dared hope, and Lucas's was *American Graffiti*, which was the tenth top grosser of 1973, flying in the face of a top Universal executive's opinion that it was unreleasable.[10]

The extent to which these and other directors of their generation have been able to keep working within the Hollywood system ultimately depended not on the faltering American Zoetrope but on these directors' continued financial success. Those who pushed too hard to create unusual, personal films became marginalized, with Altman being the most famous example. In fact, the most surprising thing about Altman's career in the 1970s is not that Hollywood could treat a great auteur so shabbily that he finally went into theater, video, and small-scale independent production, but that 20th Century-Fox would undertake to finance his increasingly obscure "art" films like *Three Women* (1977) and *Quintet* (1979). Paul Shrader provides a less extreme instance of a director who has hovered on the fringes of the mainstream with projects like *Mishima* (1985) and *Touch* (1997). Bogdanovich, after his early success, seems now to be largely inactive.

Lucas went in the opposite direction, moving on to bigger hits with the *Star Wars* trilogy and ultimately gaining executive status and his own company through controlling a big share of the merchandising from those films. On a less spectacular level, DePalma has remained a moderately successful commercial director by working largely within the classical tradition, as with *The Untouchables*, the fifth highest grosser of 1987. Like Coppola and other auteurist directors, DePalma has strategically alternated between popular and more personal projects. In 1998, *Newsweek* commented on *Snake Eyes:* "The success of *Mission Impossible* [1996] has freed DePalma to be himself again—to return, that is, to making psychological thrillers in which helicopters stay safely out of railway tunnels."[11]

The most successful creators embraced classical filmmaking, working within a system where studio executives still usually call the shots. At the time *John Grisham's The Rainmaker* (1997) was released, a summary of Coppola's career published in *Entertainment Weekly* demonstrated the director's realization that the heady ambitions of the 1970s had faded:

> More than 25 years ago, Coppola spearheaded a feisty movement of young visionary auteurs (including George Lucas and John Milius) who wanted to remake Hollywood on their own terms. "Ultimately, we didn't succeed," he says, referring to various incarnations of his boutique production company American Zoetrope, "but we made a dent. We wanted to transform the system by showing a love for writers and directors. We're proud of what we did, but it would have been nice if we changed the system a little."[12]

Coppola does not say what that "dent" was, but I think that the auteurist generation did have a significant impact on the Hollywood industry in at least two ways—neither of which seriously changed the basic guidelines for classical storytelling.

First, the considerable success of some of these films probably convinced company executives that the "auteur" label and publicity based on the personalities of the directors could provide another means of product differentiation for marketing. With the proliferation of "infotainment" coverage of movies on television (including regular "behind the scenes" documentaries on cable stations) and the spread of popular show-business-oriented magazines like *Premiere* and *Entertainment Weekly*, there appeared new opportunities to cover not just famous actors but directors as well. Such publicity has bestowed upon some directors a prominence matched in the studio era only by Alfred Hitchcock (whose TV series and popular publications undoubtedly accounted for much of his fame). When I was drafting this chapter in January of 1998, the mail brought a new issue of *Wired*, with a cover portrait of James Cameron; the caption, "Jim Cameron, Obsessed," assumes that readers would be able to recognize Cameron even without a reference to his then-current megahit, *Titanic.*[13] Less prominent directors also get star treatment. In that same week's mail was an issue of *Newsweek* containing a set of interviews with what the lead-in describes as "some of Hollywood's hottest directors": Gus Van Sant *(Good Will Hunting)*, Paul Thomas Anderson *(Boogie Nights)*, Curtis Hanson *(L. A. Confidential)*, and Barry Sonnenfeld *(Men in Black)*.[14]

In the era of film production by package deal, such name recognition undoubtedly enhances the power of directors with track records. Recently, for example, we have seen the phenomenon of big-name actors willing to take reduced sums to work with prestigious directors, as when Bruce Willis acted in *Pulp Fiction* and did a formally crucial cameo in *The Player*. Altman's and Woody Allen's reputations allow them to attract all-star casts on slim budgets. (One of Allen's producers has estimated that his actors' willingness to work for small fees saved around $20 million per film.)[15] Kenneth Branagh agreed to star in *The Gingerbread Man* (1998) only if Polygram hired Altman to direct it.[16]

A second, undoubtedly unintended, effect of auteurism was the "juvenilization" of American cinema. The Movie Brat generation's awareness of Hollywood history led them to inject a "retro" quality into their films, and the tactic proved enormously appealing to the public. Older, minor genres that had previously been designed to attract young audiences were elevated to the level of A pictures: rock-and-roll musicals *(American Graffiti)*, monster movies *(Jaws)*, science fiction tales *(Star Wars)*, and action serials *(Raiders of the Lost Ark)*. These were the kinds of films that the Movie Brat generation had grown up with, and they managed to convey their love of them to young and old audiences alike. Now aging baby boomers go to the same popular sci-fi films that teenagers do. Along these same lines, older films, in terms of both genres and specific movies, proved to be valuable sources of subject matter—hence the growth of the remake and the sequel in the 1970s.

What happened in the mid-1970s was not a shift into some sort of post-classical type of filmmaking. Rather, some of the younger directors helped to revivify classical cinema by directing films that were wildly successful. The three most significant of these were *The Godfather*, *Jaws*, and *Star Wars*, and it is hard to imagine films more classical in their narratives. They perfectly exemplify how Hollywood continues to succeed through its skill in telling strong stories based on fast-paced action and characters with clear psychological traits. The ideal American film still centers around a well-structured, carefully motivated series of events that the spectator can comprehend relatively easily.

This view runs against the grain of some current writing on Hollywood, which claims that the entire trend of Hollywood cinema since the big studios' forced divestiture of their theaters in the late 1940s has been toward a new type of filmmaking. Warren Buckland has succinctly summarized the standard characterization of the post-studio, post-classical, postmodern Hollywood film:

> Many critics argue that, in comparison with Old Hollywood, New Hollywood films are not structured in terms of a psychologically motivated cause-effect narrative logic, but in terms of loosely-linked, self-sustaining action sequences often built around spectacular stunts, stars, and special effects. Complex character traits and character development, they argue, have been replaced by one-dimensional stereotypes, and plot-lines are now devised almost solely to link one action sequence to the next. Narrative complexity is sacrificed on the altar of spectacle. Narration is geared solely to the effective presentation of expensive effects.[17]

Buckland finds this argument "overstated." Admirably, as a counterexample he tackles a film which would seem eminently susceptible to the "postmodern" blockbuster reading, the self-consciously episodic "serial" *Raiders of the Lost Ark* (1981), and demonstrates its classical underpinnings. (It would have been much easier to deal with *Jurassic Park*, which strictly in terms of its causal motivation contains as well-honed a narrative as virtually any film in the history of Hollywood.)

It would take me too far afield here to mount an extensive critique of the position Buckland rebuts. For now, it suffices to say that for a researcher convinced of the appropriateness of a post-classical or postmodern cinema, it is certainly possible to map that model onto a few films and make them conform—especially if the example is chosen precisely because it seems to fit the model (as with Thomas Elsaesser's virtuosic analysis of the wholly atypical *Bram Stoker's Dracula* [1992]).[18] It is quite another thing to account for *Tootsie* and a wide variety of recent popular films using such an approach. In attempting to refute the claim that a post-classical approach is dominant in modern Hollywood storytelling, I present the ten extended analyses in this book as evidence that the classical system is alive and well. In the final chapter, I will offer some suggestions as to why recent arguments for a "post-classical" cinema are unfounded.

In order to demonstrate that the films of the New Hollywood continue to conform to the classical guidelines of the studio era, I will be taking an inductive approach, examining what the industry's artists and craftspeople actually do in creating a wide range of narratives. I will also pay attention to what Hollywood practitioners themselves have said they are doing, both in interviews and in how-to manuals—though I will not always take such statements at face value. I will also present some observations from educated commentators, the journalists who cover industry news; they often see so many films that they can notice and remark upon typical patterns. The most central body of evidence, however, will be the films themselves, both a small number analyzed in detail and a larger, highly varied survey used for local examples. This chapter lays out a set of critical tools that I will use in analyzing a representative group of contemporary films. By paying attention to how the films tell their stories, we can reveal the enduring power of the classical tradition.

BASIC TECHNIQUES OF PROGRESSION, CLARITY, AND UNITY

In any medium, a narrative can be thought of as a chain of events occurring in time and space and linked by cause and effect. The classical Hollywood narrative system is a set of flexible guidelines that was initially developed during the era before 1918. These guidelines have been in use ever since, though they have been expanded through the introduction of influences from other filmmaking practices. Such influences, like the increasing emphasis on character subjectivity in the wake of German Expressionist imports and Murnau's *The Last Laugh* during the 1920s, have typically been adapted to fit the existing system (primarily through the use of a clearer motivation than an "art film" might employ).

The most basic principle of the Hollywood cinema is that a narrative should consist of a chain of causes and effects that is easy for the spectator to follow. This clarity of comprehension is basic to all our other responses to films, particularly emotional ones, and it will be one of the main concerns throughout this book.

In stating that most Hollywood films aim at being relatively easy to understand, I am not implying that they are simple. There is a common assumption that Hollywood films are slight, thin, and lacking in complexity in comparison with, say, works of the European art cinema like Bergman's *Wild Strawberries* or Fassbinder's *The Marriage of Maria Braun*. Yet I would contend that the best Hollywood films of any era, whether a classic of the studio era like Ford's *How Green Was My Valley* (1940) or a more recent film like *The Silence of the Lambs*, are as complex in their own terms as their art-house equivalents. They do tend, though, to be much easier to understand, lacking the ambiguities and symbolism that can make many art films fascinating or pretentious, depending on one's tastes. The glory of the Hollywood system lies in its ability to allow its finest scriptwriters, directors, and other creators to weave an intricate web of character, event, time, and space that can seem transparently obvious. The idea of unobtrusive craftsmanship is one thing that the auteur theory—for all the controversies it has stirred up among screenwriters—has helped to teach us. It would seem also to be one of the most basic factors in the enduring international popularity of mainstream American movies.

This craftsmanship has been so unobtrusive that it has largely gone undocumented. Many stylistic features, such as principles of cutting and camera movement, were seldom discussed in print by studio artisans. In those cases we must infer the craft norms from regularities we detect in the finished products. When we turn to principles of storytelling, however, we are a little more fortunate, for we can get some help from screenwriting manuals. Such manuals date back to the 1910s, when the burgeoning studios still depended heavily upon freelance submissions of scripts and stories. With the growth of the studio system during the 1920s, contract writers became the norm, and far fewer scenario manuals appeared over the next few decades. With the rise of package production since the 1970s, however, freelance scriptwriting has enjoyed a resurgence, and a flood of manuals has appeared to cater to aspiring authors.[19]

I have not attempted to survey such handbooks systematically, since they often repeat the same information with minor variations. Yet, alongside the numerous interviews with scriptwriters that have appeared in recent years, the manuals usefully point up the basic techniques of classical storytelling—or at least what Hollywood practitioners think those techniques are. And these manuals have had an impact on recent classical filmmaking. Indeed, there is some evidence that by the mid-1990s some of the more formulaic advice of such manuals was actually having a negative effect on the films coming out of Hollywood (I will return to this theme in a number of my analyses). At any rate, historians and analysts of music or painting or architecture routinely draw upon practitioners' manuals, and there is no reason for film to be any different. My main body of evidence, however, will be the films themselves, which can be used to reveal the craft assumptions of their makers.

What principles of storytelling govern classical films?[20] In Chapters 2 through 11 I present ten extensive analyses that will trace these principles in action, as they cooperate to shape whole films. Here I will set the stage by sketching out some key strategies and tactics of the mainstream Hollywood movie.

Hollywood favors unified narratives, which means most fundamentally that a cause should lead to an effect and that effect in turn should become a cause for another effect, in an unbroken chain across the film. That is not to say that each effect follows immediately from its cause. On the contrary, one of the main sources of clarity and forward impetus in a plot is the "dangling cause," information or action which leads to no effect or resolution until later in the film. For example, about midway through *Witness* (1985), John Book and his partner Carter agree that Book will stay hidden at the Amish farm guarding young Samuel while Carter tries to enlist the FBI's help. Nearly half an hour of screen time later, Book learns that his partner has been killed and realizes he must save himself and the Amish family from the corrupt cops. Carter's risky investigation serves as a dangling cause that eventually results in his death. That effect in turn causes Book to fly into a violent rage in the town and reveal his whereabouts to the police. Despite the relatively long stretch of action during which he is not mentioned, Carter does not simply drop out of the story or reveal that he has been doing something completely different from what he and Book had discussed. After the phone conversation, the action concentrates on Book's interactions with Rachel and other members of the Amish community, and the line of action initiated by Carter is put on hold until it is needed. Many such dangling causes typically stitch a classical narrative together.

Causes are typically not left dangling at the narrative's end, however. Virtually all Hollywood films achieve closure in all plotlines and subplots. The open, ambiguous endings that often characterize art films like *Bicycle Thieves* (1947) and *The 400 Blows* (1959) are typically avoided. Epilogues often serve to tie up any loose ends, and *American Graffiti* (1973) even launched a vogue for endings that tell what would subsequently happen to the main characters. The main exception to this generalization is the film aimed at generating a sequel, in which a new dangling cause will be introduced late in the narrative. This new cause, however, does not typically generate ambiguity but hints at the direction the sequel's action will take. In *The Silence of the Lambs*, Clarice refuses to promise the escaped Lecter that she will not pursue him, and in the first *Back to the Future* film, Marty and Jennifer depart into the future with Doc to help solve a problem with their children.

Unity and clarity demand that everything in the film should be motivated, whether in advance or in retrospect; that is, each event, object, character trait, and other narrative component should be justified, explicitly or implicitly, by other elements in the film. The lack of such justification is commonly referred to by Hollywood practitioners as a "hole." *Variety*'s review of *Flubber* (1997) provides a good example of an unmotivated device. After praising the inclusion of a "charismatic gizmo," a small flying and talking robot named Weebo, the reviewer adds: "Still, Weebo raises one distracting (and, of course, unanswered) question: If Brainard needs money for his university so desperately, why doesn't he sell the patent for a talking, flying, multifunctional robot?"[21] As this passage suggests, plot holes are "distracting" and hence run counter to narrative linearity and unity.

The motivation may be an impersonal event beyond the control of any character. In the disaster-film genre, cataclysms often precipitate the action, as in *The Poseidon Adventure* (1972) where a tidal wave motivates the inversion of the ship and hence all the adventures that follow. In *Edward Scissorhands* (1990), the fact that the otherwise human-looking hero has elaborate blades on the ends of his arms is motivated in a flashback when it is revealed that the eccentric inventor who had assembled Edward died just before he could replace the blades with hands. Similarly, a social system or large organization of some kind can motivate events. Both *Alien* and *Terminator 2: Judgment Day* are based on the idea of a cold, grasping firm that is willing to tinker with a species *(Alien)* or a technology *(Terminator 2)* that could be fatal to humanity. Genre conventions can also provide motivation. We accept the fact that Judy Garland expresses her joy by breaking into "The Trolley Song" in *Meet Me in St. Louis* (1944) because that's what characters do in musicals.

Ordinarily, as in popular fiction and drama, the characters provide most of the motivations in any given film. Those motivations are based upon the traits of the characters. Even in *The Poseidon Adventure*, the ship's fatal instability is motivated in an early scene when a greedy company representative is blamed for the vessel not having proper ballast and running too fast. In most films, as soon as the characters appear, or even before we see them, they are assigned a set of clear traits, and our first impressions of those traits will last through the film; that is, the characters act consistently. In the opening of *The Bodyguard* (1992), Frank is established as a person who does not take long-term jobs: "I'm no good in a permanent position—my feet go to sleep." This trait resurfaces at the end and motivates the fact that he does not stay with his client Rachel despite his love for her; he goes on living alone, working as a short-term bodyguard. (This trait also, incidentally, allows the filmmakers to sidestep the potential controversy of an interracial marriage.)

If a character behaves in a way that is contrary to his or her traits, the classical narrative will offer some explanation. In *Jaws*, for example, the police chief, Brody, says he is terrified of the water. Yet he goes out as an assistant in Quint's boat, and ultimately he kills the shark. The implication is that he does something uncharacteristic because of his strong desire to protect his family and community. His fear of the water is still present: during the shark hunt, he is more frightened than the shark hunter Quint and the scientist Hooper and does not enter into the chase with the same delight that they express.

Characters with sufficient traits to be interesting and to sustain the causal action remain central to Hollywood filmmaking. Those films which fail to create rounded or consistent characters draw criticism, as in *Variety*'s complaints about *Twilight* (1998): "Yarn becomes even more farfetched when, on a second attempt to deliver Jack's package, this time under the Santa Monica Pier, Harry is attacked by a vengeful Jeff, Mel's former lover, only to be bailed out by Reuben (Giancarlo Esposito), an eager-beaver limo driver who, utterly implausibly, aspires to be Harry's partner and seems willing to do all manner of flunky work to that end; role is strictly a structural convenience, with no human credibility."[22] Big, special-effects-laden action films come in for similar critiques, as with this assessment of *Armageddon* (1998): "The more prominent of the other thesps are given one trait to define their characters: Will Patton has been a bad father but hopes to redeem himself, Ken Campbell is a big man with big fear, and Steve Buscemi likes busty hookers. None of them has any more depth than a character in a 30-second TV commercial."[23] Thus characters are expected not only to motivate causal action but to do so in an engaging way.

In virtually all cases, the main character in a classical Hollywood film desires something, and that desire provides the forward impetus for the narrative. Hollywood protagonists tend to be active, to seek out goals and pursue them rather than having goals simply thrust upon them. Almost invariably, the protagonist's goals define the main lines of action. These lines are usually at least two in number, making the double plotline another distinctive feature of the Hollywood cinema. Romance is central to most Hollywood films, so one line of action involves that; the other line deals with another of the protagonist's goals. These two goals are usually causally linked. In *Tootsie*, for example, Michael Dorsey's first goal is to get work as an actor, which will earn money to produce his friend's play; when he dresses as a woman and gets a job on a soap opera, he then falls in love with one of the other stars. Winning her love then becomes a second goal. But in *The Silence of the Lambs*, Clarice Starling's two goals are both professional: she wants to become a special agent for the FBI, and specifically to work for Jack Crawford; second, she desperately hopes to catch the serial killer before he murders his next victim. These goals are thoroughly intertwined, in that we assume her success in saving the victim will ensure her the job with Crawford.

In discussing momentum in a plot, the scenario adviser Dana Cooper has suggested that goals may not provide the main forward thrust in all films: "When discussed at all, one theory claims that it's created by the hero's desire for a goal. However, there are many compelling films, like *The Graduate* and TV's *The Burning Bed*, in which heroes don't know what they want until far into the story, so what provides momentum then?"[24] The answer, she suggests, is that these films set up a series of questions. There is some truth in what Cooper says, but it is a rare film in which the protagonist does not formulate a goal early on. Indeed, one of the main jokes in *The Graduate* is that Benjamin seems such an unlikely Hollywood protagonist precisely because he has no goal. The whole thrust of the story is for him to find one. Another unusual example of an apathetic protagonist is the hero of Frank Borzage's *Lazybones* (1925). Lazybones has a goal thrust upon him when he decides to save a young woman from the unjust rumor that her child is illegitimate by raising the girl himself. In *American Graffiti*, the Richard Dreyfuss character is indecisive about whether to go to college, and his goal is simply to make a decision; the Ron Howard character thinks he wants to leave for college, yet eventually he decides not to do so. Nevertheless, such protagonists are rare.

Most scenario manuals assume that the protagonist has only one main goal, though most do allow for subplots that presumably involve subsidiary goals. David Howard and Edward Mabley's useful book *The Tools of Screenwriting*, however, asserts baldly: "There can be only one main objective if the film is to have unity. A story with a protagonist who has more than one ultimate aim must invariably dramatize the success or failure of one effort before going on to the other, and this breaks the spine of the work and dissipates our interest."[25] Yet most protagonists have at least two goals, and they may be equally important. In *Back to the Future*, Marty must induce his parents to fall in love at a high school dance in 1955, thus ensuring his and his siblings' existence in 1985. He must also, with Doc's help, arrange to take advantage of the bolt of lightning to return to 1985 in the time machine. That these two goals are distinct is shown by the fact that Doc actually handles most of the arrangements for the time travel. The failure of either goal would be fatal for Marty's future existence. The resolution of the parents' romance goal takes place first, but it hardly dissipates our interest in Marty's return to 1985.

Again, the idea of goal-orientation seems obvious, yet there are some types of films that use quite a different strategy. In the European art cinema, for example, characters often act because they are forced to, not because they want to. Michelangelo Antonioni has made a number of films where the protagonists have goals but seem unable to pursue them actively. *L'Avventura*, for example, involves both a search and a tentative romance, both of which would be the kinds of goals common in Hollywood narratives; yet the film concentrates on the psychological inability of the characters to follow through on these goals. In Jaco van Dormael's *Toto le héros* (1991), the protagonist starts out with a general grudge against the neighboring Kant family, the head of which he blames for his own father's death. He then conceives the idea that he was switched with Alfred at birth, hence the goal of getting his birthright back. Eventually he realizes that his sister is in love with Alfred, the neighbor's son, and later blames Alfred for her death. After a number of plot twists, he conceives the goal of killing Alfred before some terrorists do. And still later he decides to take Alfred's place as a victim of the terrorists. Such a shifting, ambiguous set of goals would be impossible in the classical cinema. In another example, the young sister and brother of Theo Angelopoulos's *Landscape in the Mist* (1988) leave home with the goal of finding their father. Yet they have no clear notion of where he is, and the film deals instead with their adventures on the road. Finally, the heroine of Chantal Akerman's *Jeanne Dielman, 23, Quai du commerce, 1080 Bruxelles* (1975) simply has no goal beyond supporting herself and her son.

One thing that sets art-film narratives apart from classical-style ones is that often the protagonist in the former is under little time pressure to accomplish his or her goal. In many Hollywood films, however, both forward impetus and temporal clarity are provided by the inclusion of one or more deadlines. The deadline may last across the film. In *His Girl Friday* (1940), for example, the opening scene reveals that Walter Burns is under intense pressure to obtain a reprieve for Earl Williams before the execution, scheduled for the next morning. Or a deadline may last only a brief while, as in the situation near the end of *Alien* when Ripley sets the spaceship's self-destruct mechanism and has only ten minutes to escape.

Hollywood films tend to convey information about deadlines, character traits, and indeed any sort of story factors redundantly. Eugene Vale's classical scenario manual, *The Technique of Screenplay Writing*, explains the rationale for redundancy:

The fatigue of concentrated attention during the whole run of a picture is very considerable. Sometimes our ears do not pick up certain parts of the dialog, sometimes our eyes get tired, sometimes we have difficulties in following and understanding the plot. In all these cases we shall be grateful if certain facts are brought back to our attention by duplication. . . . We must keep in mind that the picture moves fast and that the audience has little time to lean back and think to the end what it is being told.[26]

The same event may be mentioned by a character as about to occur, we may then see it occur, and other characters may then discuss it. Or a character trait will be reiterated often. For example, in *The Silence of the Lambs* Clarice Starling gets two emphatic lectures about how dangerous Hannibal Lecter is before she meets him—one from Jack Crawford, the FBI official, and the second from the asylum doctor, Chilton. Barney, the guard, further cautions her about how to behave. By the time we finally see Lecter, we expect him to be terrifying, and indeed he is—though in a different way than we had anticipated.

Similar information is given to Clarice by three different characters, conforming to the "rule of three" commonly used as a guideline for exposition in the filmmaking community. Another example occurs in *The Untouchables* (1987): when the accountant Oscar is assigned to Elliot Ness's team, he mentions that Al Capone has not filed tax returns, thus planting a crucial motif. In a later scene in which an alderman tries to bribe Ness, Oscar is working on some ledgers. Still later, on a plane with Ness, Oscar suggests prosecuting Capone on tax evasion. After these three mentions, the team begins working toward that goal, which will ultimately lead to Capone's conviction.

Keeping the Narrative Progression Clear

One of the potential sources of complexity in Hollywood films—as indeed in any type of filmmaking—is the medium's ability to move about freely in time and space. Intercutting may link characters who are widely separated. The locale may shift halfway around the world in the instantaneous change provided by a cut. An interval of time, whether only a few seconds or many years, may be elided in the same blink of an eye. In the studio era, the average Hollywood film contained over 600 shots. Most modern dramas consist of over 800 shots; many contain over a thousand; and some of the faster action thrillers, like *The Last Boy Scout* (1991), are cut so quickly that they include around two thousand.[27] Such a huge array of different images creates an enormous challenge to Hollywood practitioners who want to maintain clear, comprehensible causality, space, and time. Again Vale summarizes the problem well:

> We must understand that the form of the motion picture is not a continuous entity; instead, it is a conglomeration of blocks, represented by shots and scenes. These blocks have the tendency to fall apart, thereby interrupting the continuity of the story in a decisive manner. In order to overcome these breaks we must search for connecting elements within the story. If the elements of the story overlap the breaks caused by the technical subdivisions, we can achieve connection.[28]

As Vale says, the narrative disruptions can occur either within a scene or at the transitions between scenes.

Within the scene, there is a host of stylistic devices that were created in the early years of Hollywood to achieve clarity. These include placing a distant framing of the action early in a scene to establish the locale and who is present in it. This general view may be preceded by or include a sign further specifying the locale. The analytical editing system of breaking the space into closer framings makes the action more comprehensible by enlarging the salient visual elements. Matches on action at the cuts promote a sense of temporal continuity. Compositions usually center the most important characters or objects, ensuring that the spectator will notice them. In a shot/reverse-shot conversation, the characters are often balanced in a gentle seesaw of slightly off-center framings. Similar emphasis may be provided by design techniques like bright-colored clothing or staging that calls attention to a moving character.

Such clarity is still valued in modern American cinema, as this review of *Air Force One* suggests: "The movie has its bloody jolts, its leaps into explosive, James Bondish hyperbole (the moments in which Ford and company dangle off the end of the plane are truly scary), yet [Wolfgang] Petersen grounds it with scenes of disarming quiet and with the ferocious physical logic of his staging. The plot may be a comic book, but you always know exactly where you are."[29] Taken together, such techniques constitute a film's style. In general, the classical continuity system utilizes style primarily to make the narrative events as clear as possible, though it also sometimes promotes additional values like humor and big production values (splendid sets, elaborate special effects).

It might be argued that Hollywood style has changed too much in recent decades still to be called "classical." No doubt the music-video aesthetic, with its fast cutting and occasional jump cuts, has influenced modern films. Lighting and tonality tend to be darker, even outside the realm of the film noir. Dissolves to soften scene transitions have all but disappeared, and fades are used only to mark the few most important scene changes. Startling sound bridges have become common. Dazzling developments in special effects have made flashy style much more prominent, especially in science-fiction and action films. Yet these techniques have not broken down the principle that style's most fundamental function is to promote narrative clarity. Shot/reverse-shot passages still abound in conversation sequences, and the axis of action is typically obeyed in skillfully made films. The faster editing of modern films has been accompanied by a simultaneous simplification of composition by cinematographers seeking to keep shots easily legible.[30]

Moreover, faster, slightly discontinuous editing arguably has become fashionable not because Hollywood has changed its basic approach to filmmaking but because the action genre has, for a variety of reasons, become so prominent since the 1970s. Quick editing is useful for rendering violence, but the sequences between the moments of high action are again handled for the most part in dependable old shot/reverse shot. A similar phenomenon also occurs occasionally in films not belonging to the action genre. In *Dead Man Walking* (1995), for instance, the flashbacks are rendered with discontinuous, somewhat confusing editing that has clearly been influenced by nonclassical films, especially the documentary *The Thin Blue Line* (1988). Yet there are so many of these flashbacks that we can gradually piece together the original crimes, with the main question being to what extent the Sean Penn character participated in them. Aside from the flashbacks, however, the scenes are handled in insistent shot/reverse shot. It is the stable system of classical storytelling that allows such "avant-garde" devices to be selectively assimilated. For this reason, I will be focusing on narrative form rather than on style in this book, though there will inevitably be some discussion of stylistic devices that perform important storytelling functions.

Spectators are most likely to lose track of time, space, or the causal chain during the progression from one scene to another. This is one reason why the establishing shot is so crucial for maintaining a clear sense of locale. The most basic source of temporal and causal clarity is the dangling cause. One simple technique is to leave a cause open at the end of one scene and immediately pick it up in the next; such a transition is known as a "hook." For instance, a famous transition in *Tootsie* moves Michael Dorsey from his agent's office, where he defiantly vows that he will get a job, to the street, where he appears in drag—thus revealing how he intends to go about achieving his goal.

Frequently at the end of a scene a character will mention what he or she is going to do and then will immediately be seen doing it early in the next scene. Such a line is a "dialogue hook." After Rupert Pupkin, an obsessive fan, is kicked out of talkshow host Jerry Langford's office in *King of Comedy* (1983), he tells a fellow fan, Rita, that he is invited to Jerry's country place for the weekend. A cut leads to a scene of Rita and Rupert dressed up, on a train going to pay an unwanted visit to Jerry. Although dialogue hooks provide a high degree of clarity and redundancy, a too-frequent use of them would soon come to seem mechanical and contrived, and they are used for only some transitions.

Another means of providing temporal clarity from scene to scene and across stretches of the narrative is the appointment. The appointment may act as a dialogue hook that reveals the time interval that the next scene transition will pass over. Thus in *The Elephant Man* (1980), Dr. Treves asks the villainous freak-show proprietor to bring John Merrick to his hospital the next morning. The new scene that then follows shows Merrick's arrival at the hospital, making it clear to us that this new action is taking place the morning after the previous scene. Although theoretically an appointment could extend across a large part of a film, in practice such a lengthy and important anticipated moment will tend to place more at stake and hence to be a deadline, which is often a form of appointment.

All of these methods of achieving scene-to-scene clarity can be supplemented or replaced with a voice-over narration, though that relatively self-conscious narrational device is not common in classical narratives. The story of *To Kill a Mockingbird* (1962) extends over a period of more than a year, and the voice of the grown Scout recalling her childhood minimizes the need for dialogue hooks and such transitional tactics.

Finally, a film can achieve overall unity and clarity by means of motifs. These can be auditory or visual. The phrase "Pop quiz, hotshot" in *Speed* helps to pull the elevator, bus, and subway segments together. It also provides a snappy means of exposition, as when the protagonist's answer to the first pop quiz—"Shoot the hostage"—immediately suggests his recklessness. A visual motif may help add redundancy without the need for heavy-handed dialogue, as when Mozart's move from highly fashionable wigs to messy ones to his natural hair in *Amadeus* reinforces our sense of his decline. Since the earliest days of classical filmmaking, Hollywood has been adept at using visual motifs to add emotional resonance to a narrative, from the teddy-bear good luck charm clutched by a dying protagonist in *Wings* (1927) to the finger-to-finger greetings and farewells in *ET: The Extra-Terrestrial* (1982).

The five yellow barrels that Quint uses to try to control the shark in *Jaws* provide a splendid example of the virtuosity with which modern classical films can handle motifs. The barrels serve a surprising number of functions. Firing the harpoons that attach the barrels to the shark creates moments of excitement. Once the barrels hook into the shark, they provide the viewer with a visual means to track the movements of a creature that would otherwise be invisible most of the time. The attachment of the barrels also helps create a sense of steady progression during the last half of the film, breaking up what could just be a simple lengthy chase. The shark's ability to dive despite having to drag three barrels inspires awe in Quint, even with his long experience, and hence reemphasizes that the team is confronting a sort of supershark. After the fish's long absence, a shot of one barrel popping up signals the beginning of the long battle that will constitute the film's climax. Finally, the two remaining barrels that were never attached to the shark serve as the survivors' life preservers as they paddle ashore in the epilogue. Such apparently simple devices are woven carefully through the action in such a way that much of the story can be told visually.

How, one might wonder, can films displaying this sort of unity and complexity be made by teams of writers, some of whom—especially given the modern system of endless rewriting—may be at odds with each other? I will address this issue in the conclusion to Chapter 2.

STRUCTURING THE ACTION: LARGE-SCALE PROPORTIONS

From the earliest scenario manuals of the silent era to the latest guides, most authors refer at least in passing to Aristotle's observation that a play should have a beginning, middle, and end. In a temporal art like the cinema, the same principle seems self-evident. The questions are what those parts consist of and what their relative proportions should be.

Early scenario manuals frequently referred to action rising and falling at intervals across a narrative consisting of several parts. For example, William Lord Wright, who wrote a regular scenario advice column in *The Moving Picture News*, wrote in 1922: "There must be the opening of the story, the building and the plot development; the big situations and the climax; comedy relief and a happy ending." For a five-reeler, "there must be no deliberate padding of plot, and yet there must be minor climaxes in the action as well as one great major climax."[31] I have found no discussion from this period of fixed proportions or timings of these parts. Since the earliest years of the feature film, however, many Hollywood practitioners have, whether deliberately or instinctively, tailored their narratives into large-scale segments of roughly balanced length. Practitioners of the studio era frequently refer to such segments as the "structure" of a narrative.

Why does a narrative need this type of structure? We might posit that breaking a narrative into parts gives the spectator a sense of the direction in which the action will proceed and thus aids comprehension. Structure can be learned instinctively by watching a great many movies. It also helps prevent any one portion of the story from becoming too long and boring the audience. As we shall see, the scriptwriter's idea of failure is having the viewer go out to the lobby for popcorn.

The Three-Act Model

Similar notions of parts and of rising and falling action have been expressed in more modern scenario manuals as well. Since at least the early 1970s, a long portion of a film has been called an "act." In the late 1970s, a much more specific formulation of a "three-act structure" was introduced. The exact origins of the current notion that the three "acts" of a film should be temporally proportioned at ¼ - ½ - ¼ are unclear. Certainly Syd Field's 1979 manual, *Screenplay*, has popularized this idea, and it has become enormously influential among screenwriters, studio heads, and employees alike—so much so that the book is sometimes referred to as the "Bible" of screenwriters. In fact these proportions had already been offered in 1978 in a far less famous manual by Constance Nash and Virginia Oakey, *The Screenwriter's Handbook*. There they recommend three acts as the preferable breakdown of a script into parts. They characterize the first act as "problems introduced" and give its length as approximately 30 pages. The second act involves "conflict between protagonist and antagonist leading to the seemingly unsolvable problem" and occupies approximately 60 pages; finally, the third act consists of "action providing solution to the problem(s)" and lasts for 30 pages. Nash and Oakey allow for flexibility, saying that the "crisis" that ends each act may come as much as ten pages away from these suggested lengths.[32]

Field, usually credited with this formulation, has recalled teaching a scriptwriting class in 1977 and improvising the concept of scripts having a beginning, middle, and end.[33] As we have seen, these Aristotelian terms were widely used in scenario manuals going back to the pre–World War I era. Still, *Screenplay* inextricably linked the ¼ - ½ - ¼ breakdown with Field's work.

Given its wide influence, the basic assumptions concerning act structure laid out in *Screenplay* are worth looking at closely. According to Field, Act I is the "Beginning" or setup, and it ends with a "plot point."[34] A plot point is "an incident, or event, that hooks into the story and spins it around into another direction." Plot points are also commonly referred to as "turning points" or "curtains." In this book I will use the term "turning point," since it implies a crucial event or change, whereas a plot point would simply seem to imply a significant event that might or might not create a major transition. (Indeed, Field confusingly claims that there are plot points within acts, citing ten in Act II of *Chinatown*.) Act II Field considers the "Confrontation," which contains the conflict and constitutes the bulk of the narrative. Another plot point creates a transition to Act III, the "Resolution." Field claims that this description fits all fiction feature films, including *Last Year at Marienbad*.[35]

Like Nash and Oakey, Field posits large-scale proportions among acts that result in a lengthy "middle." On average, a page of a Hollywood script equals a minute of film. Field specifies that for a two-hour film, the first plot point should begin in the page-25-to-27 range and yield a setup of 30 pages. Act II then occupies a full 60 pages, with the second major plot point falling between pages 85 and 90 and with Act III running from page 90 to page 120. The result is an act proportion of ¼ - ½ - ¼.[36] It is not clear whether Field thinks that in a shorter film of, say, 90 minutes, the second act simply contracts or all three acts shrink to maintain this same proportion, but I suspect it would be the latter.

This three-act model has been repeated by many screenplay advisers. While some declare it to be an absolute rule, others argue that it is simply a set of flexible guidelines.[37] In William Froug's numerous interviews with writers, several claim to follow Field's act structure. An exchange with Anna Hamilton Phelan (scriptwriter of *Mask* and *Gorillas in the Mist*) suggests that she has virtually memorized *Screenplay*:

> *Phelan:* I structure my screenplays in three acts.
> *Froug:* Do you follow a general paradigm? Do you say to yourself, "I need to have a first-act curtain around page twenty or twenty-five"?
> *Phelan:* I do. I think for me it's from coming out of the theater and writing in acts. I wrote plays before I wrote screenplays. I try to find a dramatic event to bring in around page twenty, twenty-five—twenty minutes into the movie—that hooks into the action and swings it around.[38]

Other writers dismiss the idea of acts and page-counts as too rigid or theatrical. Nicholas Kazan (*Frances, Reversal of Fortune*) describes his approach:

I never think about a film's structure in terms of acts. To me, an act is for a playwright and a play because the audience *gets up* and leaves and goes to have something to drink and you've got to have something to bring them back. In a movie, there are different rules. The audience doesn't get up; you *don't want* them to get up for popcorn. You have to keep them in their seats. So the rules are quite different, and I think this emphasis on acts is misleading.

You *do* have to have a novel premise, and it's helpful if the piece can shift one way and then turn another.[39]

The veteran writer Ernest Lehman stressed the importance of structure while questioning the "act" concept:

Walkow: What do you think about screenwriting courses where they stress for example, the three-act structure, plot points, etc.?

Lehman: I have often had the feeling that teaching about formula screenwriting is a little artificial. I have read all the books written by all the well-known teachers of screenwriting and find myself discovering how much I never knew. I must have been doing it without knowing it. Somebody once told me there are 10 acts in "North by Northwest." But don't get me wrong: I truly believe in dramatic structure. . . .

Walkow: You never said, Act I, Act II, Act III, Act IV, but rather, this feels right, this feels wrong?

Lehman: Yes, and I don't know why, but I somehow do have that feeling for what's right and what's not working. I have seen enough Lillian Hellman and Arthur Miller plays. I have seen enough of everything.[40]

Surely the man who wrote *North by Northwest had* seen enough of everything. This is certainly how one would expect a screenwriter to internalize the large-scale pacing of films, and many manuals advise aspiring writers to watch a great number of movies.

Despite the widespread influence of Field's model, there are indications that it has a problem. Manuals, screenwriters, and even reviewers, although they accept Field's timings as correct, consistently refer to the second act as protracted and difficult to write. Linda Seger, author of one of the best manuals, defines the issue clearly:

Act Two can seem interminable. For writers, it means keeping the story moving for forty-five to sixty pages. For movie goers, an unworkable second act is a time to snooze, to buy popcorn, and to vow never to see a film by that filmmaker again.

Most Act Two problems come from insufficient momentum and lack of focus. The movie doesn't move! We're unsure what's happening and why.[41]

Ron Shelton, author/director of *Bull Durham* and *Tin Cup*, was asked in an interview what advice he had for aspiring screenwriters. His reply included this comment: "Second acts are the hardest. Really be ruthless with yourself. We tend to repeat ourselves and not to advance the story. We tend to spin our wheels in the second act."[42] Viki King's manual refers graphically to "the Act II desert."[43]

In the early 1970s, well before the ¼ - ½ - ¼ model came into vogue, William Froug's interview with Buck Henry *(The Graduate, Catch-22)* included this exchange:

> *Froug:* When you're constructing a screenplay, do you consciously have a first-act curtain, a second-act curtain, kind of structure in mind? A beginning, a middle, and end? You talked earlier of a beginning and end. What about the middle? So many films fall apart because they have no middle.
>
> *Henry:* Yeah. I don't know what the middle is. Whether it's really the second act in the theatrical sense, or whether it's just whether you find those changes in gear, which I'm often accused of not finding. When you relax the pace, move back into second gear, give them a breath. If it's just a series of climaxes you can go crazy. You have to find some way to moderate the tempo so that it's not all one crescendo, or one diminuendo. There have to be changes of pace to give the audience time to stop and start again.[44]

Henry has, I think, pinpointed the problem. Whether a writer adheres to Field's model or simply assumes the old beginning-middle-end schema, no one seems to know what "middle" means for a film plot.

What happens in the setup portion is clear to all: the introduction of expository material adding up to an initial situation. Similarly, the end is clearly concerned with bringing the action to its highest pitch and resolving it, leading typically into a short epilogue. No one has figured out specifically what goes on in the long middle stretch, beyond vague claims about protagonists struggling toward goals and encountering strings of obstacles.

I agree with those commentators who claim that an hour or so of narrative action without a major turning point is almost always difficult to sustain. In fact, I think virtually no films even try to do so. Occasionally a writer who comes up with a very strong situation can write a long "Act II." Despite watching hundreds of films, the only example I can think of is *Speed* (1993), which does conform fairly closely to Field's ¼ - ½ - ¼ proportions. The entire film is 116 minutes long, including credits, with the opening elevator section functioning to introduce the villain and the bomb squad partners, the protagonist Jack and his pal Harry. (Timings are rounded off to the nearest half-minute; if the credits are superimposed over significant causal action, they are included as part of the timed action.) The setup lasts 23 minutes, with its final turning point being the revelation that the mad bomber, Howard, is still alive. A brief, quiet scene of Harry drunkenly heading home ends the setup.

The famous bomb-on-a-bus segment begins after the ellipsis to the next morning and lasts an amazing 66 minutes without a turning point. Most viewers would probably agree that there are no dead spots in that entire time. *Speed*'s climax begins with an elliptical cut to Annie and Jack having their cuts and bruises tended to by paramedics. By this point fully 94 minutes have elapsed, yet the narrative cranks up again for the climax in which Howard kidnaps Annie and the two men fight for her aboard a runaway subway train. Since the bus episode had lasted so long and had its own climax portion, the subway section has struck many audiences and reviewers as anticlimactic. Indeed, Howard's line to Jack early in the climax, "I think Harry would be disappointed feeling that we're right back where we started. Huh?" sums up many a viewer's reaction as well. Moreover, the climax, though full of suspenseful action, lasts only about 18 minutes.

Speed's problem is that it has used up an enormous amount of narrative energy in the bus episode without leaving any dangling cause at the end except the simple fact that the villain is still alive and bent on getting his ransom. Even the quirky passengers who had helped sustain the bus episode have departed. Thus while the film as a whole cannot be said to be episodic, the climax portion becomes an isolated episode that suffers by comparison with the lengthy and exciting large-scale parts that precede it.

Perhaps an occasional film like *Speed* can successfully handle a middle hour, but in general many scenarists confess a problem with writing second acts. I suspect such difficulties are traceable to the basic drawbacks of the three-act paradigm. It is too often based on page numbers or timings, not dramatic logic; it does not sufficiently analyze the ways in which characters formulate and change their goals; it does not recognize that Hollywood films incorporate a lot of sheer delay; and it does not take into account that the demand for a beginning, middle, and end need not—indeed, usually does not—result in a three-part structure.[45]

An Inductive Approach to Structure

In breaking narratives down into segments for analysis, one always confronts a problem: a plot can be divided up into an indefinitely large number of parts. Field stops at three, while someone who spoke to Ernest Lehman found ten acts in *North by Northwest*. A minute segmentation of a narrative could run to hundreds of parts. To propose a useful schema that is not capricious, I have to show that some principle governs the division. A plausible structural principle will relate to something about which both filmmakers and audiences intuitively care. Field abided by this constraint in choosing as his principle the story "action," declaring that major changes occurred when it was spun into a new direction. This basic idea seems plausible, and practitioners often refer to action "shifting gears."

We can, however, account more precisely for the structural dynamics of Hollywood storytelling by suggesting that the most frequent reason a narrative changes direction is a shift in the protagonist's goals. We have already seen that such goals are central to plotting in the classical film. If we can account for plot structure by means of these goals, we have a schema that has some initial plausibility. Further, we can then analyze a large body of films to see how these goals are formulated, developed, altered, replaced, furthered, blocked, delayed, and eventually achieved (or not). The regularities we find in films' treatments of the heroes' goals can suggest how large-scale parts are commonly articulated.

Instead of starting with an *a priori* assumption that all films must have three acts, we can instead simply study the plot patterns to be found in a sampling of Hollywood films, both from the studio era and from more recent times. What we find is striking. A great many of these films—indeed, I would contend, the bulk of them—break perspicuously into *four* large-scale parts, with major turning points usually providing the transitions.

Drawing upon what seems to me the most usefully descriptive terminology that has been employed by scenario-manual authors and commentators in other narrative arts, I will refer to the four parts of the average feature as the setup, the complicating action, the development, and the climax. A short epilogue usually follows the climax. This schema points up something I will elaborate shortly: that movies very often present a crucial turning point more or less at dead center.

In the setup, an initial situation is thoroughly established. Often the protagonist conceives one or more goals during this section, though in some cases the setup sticks to introducing the circumstances that will later lead to the formulation of goals. The complicating action then, as Field says, takes the action in a new direction. We can, however, further specify why this happens. That new direction may simply involve the hero pursuing a goal conceived during the setup but having to change tactics dramatically. In many cases, however, the complicating action serves as a sort of counter-setup, building a whole new situation with which the protagonist must cope. *Witness* provides a perfect example. Its setup brings Rachel and her son Samuel from the Amish community into the violent big-city world that John Book inhabits. The first turning point, Samuel's identification of the killer as a cop, forces Book to change tactics completely, and the complicating action consists of his flight to the farm and introduction to the unfamiliar Amish world. Another example occurs in *Top Hat* (1935), where Dale (Ginger Rogers) initially dislikes Jerry (Fred Astaire); the musical number "Isn't It a Lovely Day" ends the setup as Jerry wins Dale's love. Yet this happy, stable situation is reversed early in the complicating action when Dale mistakenly gets the idea that Jerry is her friend Madge's husband. Her belief that Jerry is a married seducer will dictate the many comic cross-purposes at which all the characters operate through much of the rest of the action.

The third large-scale portion of narrative films, the development, often differs distinctly from the complicating action. By now an extensive set of premises, goals, and obstacles has been introduced. This is where the protagonist's struggle toward his or her goals typically occurs, often involving many incidents that create action, suspense, and delay. (That is, the struggle against obstacles that most commentators see as typically constituting a film's central hour seems to me often to be confined primarily to the third quarter.) In *The Miracle Worker* (1962), for example, the development consists of the two weeks Anne spends with Helen in the isolated cabin, trying and failing repeatedly to teach her language. The development ends after the parents have taken Helen back home; the turning point concludes as Anne reiterates her goal: "I know, *one word*, and I can put the world in your hand." That one word, "water," will cause Helen's breakthrough at the end of the climax. As is typical of many development sections, very little progress is actually made in this 27-minute section of *The Miracle Worker*. We shall see this again quite clearly in *The Silence of the Lambs*. In *Witness*, the turning point that ends the complicating action is Book's conversation with Carter in which he agrees to stay hidden on the farm. The development then moves in a direction which suggests that Book might fit into the Amish community through his love for Rachel, renouncing his violent profession. Since this suggestion proves false, again little actual progress toward narrative closure is made during this section of *Witness*.

The development section usually ends at the point where all the premises regarding the goals and the lines of action have been introduced. Here the climax portion begins, and the action shifts into a straightforward progress toward the final resolution, typically building steadily toward a concentrated sequence of high action. The key question now is: will the protagonists' goals be achieved or not? In *Witness*, the call that informs Book that Carter has been killed ends the development. Book realizes that help cannot come from outside and that his staying hidden has forced his partner to assume the risk alone. Nothing more needs to be introduced to move the film toward the final battle at the farm.

I am assuming that the turning points almost invariably relate to the characters' goals. A turning point may occur when a protagonist's goal jells and he or she articulates it. The complicating action of *Amadeus* ends when Salieri burns his crucifix and declares that he will ruin Mozart and thus revenge himself on God. Or a turning point may come when one goal is achieved and another replaces it. During the setup of *Alien*, the crew's goal is to identify the source of a mysterious radio signal. Once the face-hugger attaches itself to Kane at the end of the setup, the goal becomes to determine the nature of this strange creature. (As we shall see in Chapter 10, two further changes of goal occur that divide *Alien* into four major parts.) The turning point may also involve a shift in tactics to achieve a goal. In the musical version of *Little Shop of Horrors* (1986), the song "Feed Me" comes at roughly the halfway point, running from minutes 42 to 44 in an 88-minute film. It changes the premise of the film radically, from Seymour's being willing to sacrifice a few drops of his own blood for the small carnivorous plant Audrey II to his decision to kill the obnoxious dentist in order to keep the plant alive. A turning point may also be a major new premise that will eventually lead to a new goal for the protagonist. In *Back to the Future*, the Libyan attack is a turning point, because it forces Marty to travel back in time and thus reverses the situation of the setup; that time travel eventually leads him to formulate his two goals of using a lightning bolt to return to 1985 and getting his parents to fall in love at a dance.

Although the turning point usually comes at the end of a large-scale portion, it need not. In *Muppet Treasure Island* (1996), for example, the young hero's expressed goal in the setup is to escape the inn where he does menial work and to have an adventure. Near the end of the setup, a dying man gives him the treasure map that will provide that adventure—clearly the initial turning point. Yet a comic action sequence then ensues in which Muppet pirates attack the inn searching for the map; this sequence simply adds a bit of suspense and delays the boy's departure. After it ends, the lad sets out with the map and his sidekicks, and the film's first fade-out signals the move into the complicating action.

A turning point may also occur just *after* the move from one large-scale segment to another. In *Back to the Future*, for example, the setup ends as Doc prepares to travel into the future. A brief ellipsis marks the transition, and the Libyan attack launches the complicating action. As these examples suggest, the "turning point" is not literally a single moment but an action that may last for some time. When I divide films into large-scale parts, I will do so by the moments at which such actions end or begin. The goal of making such segmentations is not to pinpoint the exact moment of transition but to define the crucial functional change brought about by the turning point.

Usually a turning point serves to change both lines of action in a different direction. Sometimes, however, the plotlines are handled separately, and each has its own turning point. The development section of *The Godfather* ends with two turning points. The development of the romance line between Michael and Kay ends when he predicts that the Corleone family will be "completely legitimate" in ten years and asks her to marry him. The next scene provides the turning point in the criminal line of action, as Michael takes over as head of the family and assigns the various gang members their new positions; the elder Don Corleone's pat on Michael's cheek signals the end of the entire development section.

The Bodyguard goes further, providing double turning points for the two lines of action at every move from one large-scale portion to the next. These two lines involve Frank's attempt to protect Rachel from a stalker and Frank and Rachel's on-again-off-again romance. Although the stalker plot brings the couple together, it develops quite separately from the romance. The romance's first turning point comes when Rachel spies on Frank watching a video of her singing and realizes that he loves her; from here she will drop her rather hostile teasing of him and ask him on a date. The complicating action then begins, with a second turning point quickly following for the stalker plot: Rachel gets a letter from the stalker and learns from her staff that they have concealed earlier threats from her.

The complicating action of *The Bodyguard* ends with another romantic turning point as Frank inexplicably breaks off the affair with Rachel. The midpoint moves us into the development, which again begins with a turning point relating to the stalker: the man who will later be revealed as the stalker attends a party and tries to rape Rachel. The development ends with a single turning point relating to both plotlines: the revelation of Nikki as the villain, the attack on the house, and Nikki's death. The climax is devoted to the defeat of the stalker, and the epilogue resolves the romance plot as Rachel and Frank part.

Probably the most contentious structural claim I am advancing is the existence of a centrally located turning point. This action has the effect of breaking Field's problematic "middle" into two large-scale portions.

Field himself has more recently suggested that there is something in the film's center called a "Mid-Point." His definition makes it clear, however, that he does not consider the mid-point a third plot point that ends an act: "The Mid-Point connects the First Half of Act II with the Second Half of Act II; it is a link in the chain of dramatic action."[46] How that link differs from all the other links that make up the dramatic chain of events remains unclear. In the one film that I have identified as conforming to Field's proportions, *Speed*, the mid-point would be the moment when Howard makes phone contact with Jack, a significant event because a subsequent conversation will tip Jack off to the fact that a video camera is present and in turn allow him to trick the bomber and save the passengers. That moment does seem to be significant, but it is hardly a turning point.

As I have suggested, however, such sustained central "acts" are rare indeed. As my *Witness* example implies, I am instead proposing that the "mid-point" is usually at least as structurally important as the other turning points. A careful analysis of a wide body of films, both classic and modern, strongly supports this case.

Many historians would claim, for example, that *Casablanca* is a model of Hollywood filmmaking. Ilsa's visit to the bar just after Sam sings "As Time Goes By" leads to her attempt to tell the drunken Rick the story of her relationship with Victor. He has to decide whether to accept or reject her story, and he rejects it, slumping down on the table despairingly after she leaves. In the second half of the film, Rick initially treats Ilsa as a tramp during the development. Then, during the climax, Rick finally reverses his earlier decision, accepts her story, renews his love for her, and decides to help her escape with Victor. Rick's crucial rejection of Ilsa ends 51 minutes into a 101-minute film.

Similarly, in *Queen Christina* (1933), the famous love idyll in the country inn between Christina and the Spanish ambassador ends 52 minutes into a 99-minute film; from the point where they part, their troubles gradually escalate until the Spaniard's death in the climactic scene. The first half of the 1954 Warner Bros. epic *The Egyptian* concerns the rise of the orphan Sinuhe to become the physician of the Pharaoh Akhenaten and the former's later obsession with a courtesan who strips him of all his possessions. His disgrace and flight into exile culminate 75 minutes into this 140-minute film. The midway turning point is followed by a montage sequence covering several years of time spent in exile, shortly after which Sinuhe conceives the new goal of returning to Egypt. The second half of the film will concern his gradual acceptance of the new, proto-Christian religion espoused by the Pharaoh.

One could almost set one's watch by the central turning point of *Jurassic Park* (1993). Eliminating the credits, the film's narrative lasts for 120 minutes. The central turning point comes when the treacherous geek Nedry sabotages the park's entire computer-based support system, shutting off the electricity and freeing all the dinosaurs but the velociraptors. The scene ends with the discovery of the problem by Arnold and Hammond, and specifically with the latter's line, "Where did the vehicles stop?" That line, spoken 60 minutes in, forms a dialogue hook into the T-Rex attack scene. After this point the plot centers around the characters' two chief goals: to restore the park's power and to get the children back to the visitors' center. Thus *Jurassic Park*'s narrative falls into halves, the first centering around communion with gentle dinosaurs which do not need to be fenced in, the second around attacks by vicious dinosaurs which should be fenced in but are not.

I am not the only observer to notice central turning points. *Variety*'s reviewers not infrequently comment on crucial, temporally centered events that divide films into halves, as in *Deep Impact* (1998): "The mission, which concludes precisely halfway through the picture, proves a dismal failure. . . . The logistics and repercussions stemming from this announcement take up the film's second half."[47] Thus even an effects-based action film generally does not simply set its plot in motion and let it race ahead for an hour-long central act without decisive new premises.

I am also not the only writer to suggest that films can contain more than three acts. In his 1997 scenario manual, *Story*, Robert McKee posits that three acts are the norm but are not as invariable as Field claims. McKee gives his own optimum proportions, with act one being 30 minutes, act two 70 minutes, and the climax a mere 18 minutes. If the long central act bogs down, "There are two possible solutions. Add subplots or more acts." He prefers the subplot solution but points out that some films, such as *The Fugitive* (1993), are better off without them: "If the writer builds progression to a major reversal at the halfway point, he breaks the story into four movements with no act more than thirty or forty minutes long." This central turning point between two acts he rather confusingly terms the "mid-act climax" (which by his own definition in fact divides the middle into two acts). He explains the advantage of this approach: "a major reversal in the middle of Act Two, expanding the design from three acts to an Ibsen-like rhythm of four acts, accelerating the mid-film pace."[48] McKee offers no indication, however, of how these two middle acts differ from each other or how they might shape the narrative's central portions.[49]

Returning to the definition of turning points, we can see that they need not be moments of high drama. Often a turning point is a small but decisive action that determines the shape that the next large-scale portion must take. *Jaws* provides an excellent example of "quiet" turning points, as well as an opportunity to summarize how the four parts of a narrative typically work.

To the casual observer, *Jaws* undoubtedly seems shaped by its series of shark attacks, and indeed the attacks and the more subdued events that come between them constitute rising and falling action. Yet not one of the plot's turning points comes at a shark attack. The overall trajectory of the action is to destroy the shark—but not to do so before it has provided the requisite thrills for nearly two hours. Quint is the main element that will ultimately permit the destruction of the shark, and all three turning points have to do with him.

During the setup, two lines of action are established. One is Sheriff Brody's desire to solve the shark problem revealed by the opening attack. During the first half of the film he will encounter obstacles that arise from the local business people's resistance to closing the popular tourist beaches; during the second half, the obstacles involve Quint's eccentricities and the elusiveness and menace of the shark. The second line of action involves ex–New York cop

Brody's inability to fit into his new community, symbolized by his fear of the ocean. Although this line of action is clearly subsidiary to the shark threat, the film's last line of dialogue will refer to its resolution.

The setup ends at the town meeting following the second attack, as the locals wrangle over whether to close the beaches. Quint appears and offers to kill the shark for $10,000. His proposal is rejected as too expensive, and the town's hopes are pinned upon the $3000 reward already offered by the second victim's mother. The meeting's end is the first turning point. By now the basic situation is evident, and the main causal element that will eventually solve the problem has been introduced. (In this 123.5-minute film, the setup is relatively short at 22.5 minutes; the reason for this is partly the simplicity of the basic situation and partly the delay in the introduction of the third major character, the shark expert Hooper.)

Early in the complicating action, Brody closes the beaches. The arrival of Hooper serves to confirm that the amateur hunters are dangerous and in fact present obstacles to Brody. Hooper also prevents Brody from abandoning his goal by proving that the shark caught by the fishermen is not the killer. Against Brody and Hooper's advice, however, the Mayor insists that the beaches remain open for the lucrative July fourth holiday. The third attack endangers Brody's son, and in the hospital Brody defiantly insists to the Mayor: "We're gonna hire Quint to kill the shark." This picks up the dangling cause from the first turning point. The central turning point comes as the Mayor signs Quint's contract. (The complicating action, with its introduction of Hooper and the lengthy suspense-and-action beach sequence, lasts nearly 44 minutes.)

The entire second half of the film consists of the shark hunt, but here the narrative risks becoming repetitious through a string of sightings and failed attacks until the final one works. To avoid this, the opening of the development consists of a scene creating animosity between Quint and Hooper. Because all three men will contribute to killing the shark, the climax will not begin until they reconcile. And the series of shark sightings is made more dramatic by the men's bickering over tactics. As is common in development sections, relatively little actual progress is made. The boat sets out and the shark is located, but by the end the fish has resisted all efforts to kill it and has disappeared again. Along the way, significant elements like the compressed-air tanks are introduced, and Brody makes his correct prophecy, "You're gonna need a bigger boat." (True to the rule of three, he twice repeats this in later scenes.)

This section also, by the way, provides an example of a subtle virtuosity that some of the best Hollywood films display. As Hooper mentions his compressed-air tanks, Quint scoffs: "Yes, real fine, expensive gear you've brought out here, Mr. Hooper, but I don't know what that bastard shark's gonna do with it—might eat it, I suppose. Seen one eat a rocking chair one time." Brody ultimately kills the shark by shooting the tank it has indeed tried to eat. This line is not important as motivation; indeed, most viewers would not notice it on first viewing. But it creates a bit of foreshadowing that unifies the plot.

The development ends with the crucial scene in which the three men sit drinking and comparing their scars; Quint then tells his story about being on the USS Indianapolis and spending days in shark-infested waters. The three break into song, confirming that Quint now accepts Hooper as a comrade. This is the turning point that ends the development, since now the men will cooperate to kill the shark. Absolutely no new information needs to be introduced now, and thus we are ready for the climax section. (The development has lasted 28 minutes, right around the norm.)

The climax, as we have seen, begins with the barrel popping up to signal the shark's return. The fish attacks the boat, and the entire climax consists of its repeated assaults, with intervals for the men to make repairs and plans. During this action Quint becomes increasingly irrational, endangering his comrades. And this is one of his main narrative functions: to get the three out in a dangerous situation in a flimsy wooden boat instead of a larger, sturdier one. The climax segment reaches its peak as the shark eats Quint and begins to sink the boat. Brody is able to kill it only through a combination of the specialties of the three men: Quint's ability to locate the shark, Hooper's air tank, and Brody's marksmanship.

During the brief epilogue, Hooper surfaces, and the two survivors swim ashore. Brody's last line, "I used to hate the water," signals that the accomplishment of his first goal has also achieved his second one. Through the cathartic experience of fighting the shark, he is cured of his fear. Presumably he can finally settle into the community. (The climax and epilogue together last 29.5 minutes, with the epilogue occupying about 3 minutes.)

The fact that the turning points of *Jaws* do not come at the moments of high action when the shark attacks is worth examining briefly in light of claims that "post-classical" films favor spectacle over causal logic. The emotional seesaw of the attacks undoubtedly provides the audience's most intense connection to the film. Yet most spectators would undoubtedly be dissatisfied with a string of shark attacks alternating with Brody's ineffectual attempts to destroy the fish, ending arbitrarily with his inexplicably succeeding at about the two-hour mark. A dominant causal logic based on character motivation, new premises, goals, decisions to change tactics, and the like creates the shape within which those affectively potent moments can be embedded. We are a long way from seeing formless series of pure action sequences of the type that appears occasionally on television (such as "America's Scariest Police Chases") become the basis for Hollywood films.

A Matter of Timing

Even more influential than Field's "three-act" strictures have been his requirements about running times: he contends that the script for a properly constructed two-hour film should end its first act about 30 minutes in and begin Act III about 30 minutes from the end. It seems likely that modern screenwriters' problems with the second act arise partly from this requirement that large-scale parts be of unequal lengths. (The notion of a lengthy middle presenting difficulties to the scriptwriter seems not to have cropped up before the 1970s.) The setup is fairly indisputable as a major portion, and Field was right to suggest that this tends to last about one quarter of a two-hour film. Likewise, the ending section can be clearly marked out. Again, Field accurately notes that this section usually occupies approximately the last quarter of the film. Presumably his insistence that "Act II" should last about an hour derives from simple arithmetic: 60 minutes remain when one subtracts these two half-hours from a two-hour film.

There is good reason, however, to hold that plots tend to be composed of roughly *equal* parts. If we study a large number of films, we find that large-scale portions do not significantly expand to fill up longer films and contract to create shorter ones. Rather, throughout the history of the Hollywood feature, large-scale portions have remained roughly constant, averaging between 20 and 30 minutes in length. This has allowed filmmakers to create subtle patterns of balance in the running times of each section.

For a two-hour film, such balance typically means four large-scale segments. Of the ten films I will be analyzing in this book, all illustrate the tendency of parts to run between 20 and 30 minutes. Nine of them break into four roughly balanced parts, and thus we will see how this happens in considerable detail.

In addition, I have analyed the timing of ten more feature films from each decade since the standardization of the feature during the 1910s (the results appear in Appendix A), and the majority of these narratives also reflect this pattern of large-scale parts typically running between 20 and 30 minutes. These films were chosen mainly with the aim of providing a considerable variety of directors, genres, studios, and budgets. I deliberately included several musicals to see how the songs and dances would affect the timings. (Answer: they did not, being tucked neatly into the normal large-scale parts.) To specify where the turning points come in all these films would require a book in itself, and such detail would serve little purpose. Virtually all, however, are available on video, and the reader is free to test my decisions on turning points and segmentations. The crucial point is that actual films are far more flexible and varied in their handling of the length of parts than the stringent three-act paradigm dictates.

The tendency for large-scale parts to average in the 20- to 30-minute range also holds good for films that vary from Field's two-hour standard. (Most films, after all, are not exactly two hours long.) For example, features lasting significantly less than 100 minutes may break into three parts. When they do, those parts tend to be approximately equal thirds. Likewise, very long films of, say, 150 minutes or more frequently fall into five roughly balanced parts.

Given that scenario advice manuals seldom mention anything but films in the 110–120 minute range, it may be interesting to look briefly at some examples of distinctly longer and shorter movies.

The existence of films that have more than four parts does not pose a problem for my scheme of setup, complicating action, development, and climax. In long films, the complicating action or more frequently the development section is simply doubled, with an additional turning point setting off the extra part. *Heat* (1995) displays this approach well. Without credits, it runs 168.5 minutes, yielding an average of 33.5 minutes for each of the five parts. The 37-minute setup establishes the situations of the cop Vincent (Al Pacino) and the professional thief Neil (Robert De Niro) and ends when Nate (Jon Voight) tells Neil that the bond deal has been arranged with the corrupt banker Vansant. The complicating action includes Neil's romance and decision to quit after this job; it lasts 30 minutes and ends when Eady agrees to go to New Zealand, defining Neil's new goal. The first development section lasts for 34 minutes and involves the maneuverings between Vincent and Neil. It ends with the hiring of a new driver for the bank heist, followed by brief, quiet shots of two of the female characters at home. The second development portion then begins with a turning point, the beginning of the failed bank robbery which occupies nearly the entire portion. This second development lasts 33 minutes. Eady realizes that Neil is a thief, and the turning point that ends this section is Neil's renewed request that she go to New Zealand with him, saying that he will not go alone. The climax ends as Vincent shoots Neil, and the epilogue shows Vincent holding Neil's hand as he dies; together these parts last 31 minutes. To accommodate a longer running time, instead of stretching three or four parts, the film provides extra parts. The important point here is that the timings still correspond with remarkable fidelity to the principle of balanced large-scale portions. We shall examine another example, *Amadeus*, in Chapter 7.

Similar principles hold for short features, which often break into three equal parts. This has been true throughout the history of Hollywood. Buster Keaton's *Our Hospitality* (1923) is 72 minutes long and consists of three long segments, each built around a different theme-and-variations gag situation: (1) the train trip and arrival in town (25.5 minutes); (2) Willie wandering around town and inadvertently surviving assassination attempts (22 minutes); and (3) the dodges and chase that follow the title "By the next day Willie had decided to become a permanent guest" (24.5 minutes, with epilogue). *The Producers* (1968), clocking in at 89 minutes, also contains three balanced parts: the setup reveals Max's financial troubles and decision to perpetrate a theatrical fraud, ending with Leo's ecstatic decision to join him (33.5 minutes, including the pre-credits and credits scenes); the central part is the search for script, funding, director, and cast (31.5 minutes); and the climax involves the unexpected success of "Springtime for Hitler" and its results (32 minutes, including the 3-minute epilogue in jail). In the case of three-part short films, the complicating action is usually the portion eliminated. In *The Producers*, the process of gathering the elements for the production adds few new premises and could have been handled in a montage sequence. The scenes are played out for humor, however, simply developing upon the premise established in the setup. Timings for two further examples of three-part short films, *When Harry Met Sally* (1989) and *Assault on Precinct 13* (1976), are included in Appendix A.

It is equally possible for short films to consist of four parts, again usually roughly balanced in length (see Appendix A). As early as the mid-1910s, this structure was an option, as in *The Italian*. Examples from the studio era include *The Mummy* (1932), *The Thin Man* (1934), and *The Lady Eve* (1941). More recently, *Liar Liar* (1997), though a mere 86.5 minutes, surprisingly turns out to have four parts of nearly equal length. The first turning point, 20.5 minutes in, is obviously the son Max's wish "that for only one day Dad couldn't tell a lie." Max's failed attempt to cancel the wish constitutes the second turning point (making the complicating action 21.5 minutes). Fletcher's first display of sincere feeling for Max comes in this scene and initiates his redemption, which will occupy the plot's second half. The development lasts for 20 minutes and centers on Fletcher's seemingly hopeless efforts to win his current case without lying. His unexpected success provides a transition into the climax and epilogue (18.5 minutes), which involve Fletcher's attempts to regain his ex-wife and his son.

Longer films occasionally do break into three large-scale parts as well. As with the shorter films, however, these parts tend to be roughly even in length rather than following Field's ¼ - ½ - ¼ proportions. One elegant example of such a film is *Adam's Rib* (1949), which is 101 minutes long; its three parts all run within two minutes of the 33.5-minute average.

I want to emphasize here that I offer these patterns of balanced parts as observations based on what is commonly used in actual films. I do not in any way mean to imply that films must stick slavishly to this pattern in order to be good. Indeed, segments can be unusually long or short for any number of reasons.

In *The Ghost and Mrs. Muir* (1947), the first three parts of the 104-minute total are 28, 28, and 27 minutes long respectively. The climax, however, is a mere 19 minutes long. This truncated climax results because one of the two original plotlines—Mrs. Muir's money problems and her romance with the Captain—had been settled back in the development portion. The Captain's literally ghost-written memoirs had provided Mrs. Muir with financial security. The climax consists simply of her disillusionment with the caddish publisher Miles and a lengthy montage sequence as she ages, punctuated by a brief scene of her daughter's engagement. The only goal left is the romance, which she achieves by being reunited with the Captain at her death.

The Wrong Man (1957), at 105 minutes, has an unusually long complicating action of 35 minutes, while the other three parts are closer to average at 20.5, 24, and 25.5 minutes. The turning point that ends the setup is Manny's arrest, and his release on bail provides the second turning point, ending the complicating action. Clearly Hitchcock and Maxwell Anderson, the writer, were most interested in the subjective depiction of Manny's frightening ordeal in police custody. Similarly, in *A Night at the Opera* (1935), the complicating-action segment is nearly double the length of the other three segments. It consists of the shipboard sequences, padded out by the parting song between the romantic couple, the famous stateroom sequence, and the obligatory piano and harp solos by Chico and Harpo. *The Pink Panther* (1964) is 114.5 minutes long, yet it has only three parts because its setup is fully 52.5 minutes; despite the opening reference to the "Pink Panther" jewel, absolutely no progress is made toward its theft during this opening. Instead, the nearly hour-long segment centers entirely on the sexual frustrations of the Peter Sellers, David Niven, and Robert Wagner characters. Exactly at the midpoint, however, the forward progression begins, and the two remaining portions are roughly balanced at 31 and 27.5 minutes. All these films are distinctly off-kilter by any formulaic standards, yet in no case is the imbalance necessarily a flaw.

It is apparently even possible for a film to have no turning points at all. I cannot find any point in *It's a Mad Mad Mad Mad World* (1963) that changes the trajectory of the action noticeably. Instead, the premise of the hunt for missing bank-robbery loot is set up in the opening of this 154-minute film and pursued in doggedly episodic fashion until the final revelation.

I have focused on Syd Field's account of structure and timings because his books have exercised an enormous influence during the past two decades. Here, however, I am developing what I take to be a more versatile set of analytical tools. To highlight the comparative advantage of my frame of reference, I turn to one last example.

Field has published a lengthy analysis of *Terminator 2: Judgment Day*,[50] one which makes many excellent observations and eloquently defends the film against those who would dismiss it as a potboiler. I would suggest, however, that Field has not adequately marked out the film's large-scale segments, and this has crucial consequences for understanding the dramatic propulsion of the film.

True to his system, Field treats *Terminator 2* as a three-act film with a lengthy central act punctuated by a "Mid-Point." The film is almost exactly 136 minutes long, including about 6 minutes of credits. As I have suggested, a narrative this long would be very difficult to sustain in three parts, and in fact I believe the film has four, along with a brief epilogue. Field identifies the turning point (or "Plot Point," as he terms it) that ends the first act as "the moment when the Terminator rescues John from the T-1000," involving "the exciting chase sequence that establishes the structural foundation for the entire film" (p. 116). I would argue, however, that the exposition of the initial situation is far from over by this point. The nature of this new Terminator and his relationship with John have not been defined. If the chase really were the film's entire "structural foundation," the remainder would be nothing but a long series of similar chases.

What gives the film much of its shape comes at what I would consider the first turning point, the conversation just after John prevents the Terminator from killing the two men in the parking lot. He discovers that the Terminator has been programmed to obey him and orders two things that essentially focus the two plot lines and their related goals: that the Terminator must do his job of protecting John without killing anyone, and that they must rescue Sarah from the mental hospital. This second goal will govern the complicating action and will determine the nature of the next turning point.

Field also considers this dialogue between John and the Terminator important, though he places it well into Act II. For him, it initiates "the Terminator's transformation of character" through a "learning process." It is that learning process that gives the film its moral and thematic shape, culminating in Sarah's final speech in the brief epilogue: "The unknown future rolls toward us. I face it for the first time with a sense of hope. Because if a machine, a terminator, can learn the value of human life, maybe we can too." At the conclusion of his analysis, Field rightly dwells on the Terminator's transformation, arguing that his character helps raise *Terminator 2* above the ranks of ordinary action films. So it is reasonable to conclude that the beginning of that transformation, rather than a chase scene, is what contributes so much to the film's structure.

Field is rather vague about the "Mid-Point" of the narrative. Initially he identifies it as the driving scene in which John teaches the Terminator some current slang (p. 132). Later he states: "This takes us to the Mid-Point, when they pull into a deserted [*sic*] desert compound near the Mexican border" (p. 134). Apparently Field considers the series of low-key scenes in this portion of the film as an extended Mid-Point, "a rest point, the place where these strange comrades in arms recuperate from their wounds, establish a connection with each other, and make a plan of attack" (p. 133). In fact they do not formulate a plan of attack; Sarah departs from the agreed-upon plan of fleeing south in order to attempt on her own to assassinate Dyson.

Yet there are structural reasons to flag a specific scene in this passage as a turning point, one which ends the complicating action. Here the Terminator presents expository information about the history of the 1997 war and its roots in Miles Dyson's invention of Skynet. This scene is far more than a rest or lull; rather, it presents vital new premises. Up to now the abiding goal has been to allow John to escape from the T-1000 so that in the future he can help win the war against the Machines. The Terminator has been programmed to accomplish this single goal. It is Sarah who realizes that the war itself can be averted by aborting the invention of Skynet; her new goal is signaled quite clearly when she demands: "I want to know everything. What he [Dyson] looks like, where he lives—*everything*." Her critical role explains the fact that the entire complicating action is devoted to getting her out of the hospital and away from the immediate threat of the T-1000. Her realization triggers a major new goal for the rest of the film, with the second parallel goal still being to escape from the T-1000.[51] Surely this radical shift in goals meets Field's own definition of a "Plot Point" as spinning the action into another direction.

The development includes two efforts to accomplish Sarah's new goal, first in her attempt to kill Dyson as the immediate cause of the future war and second in the theft of the chip from the Cyberdine laboratory. I would agree with Field that "the escape from Cyberdine is the Plot Point at the end of Act II" (p. 141), and I accept his characterization of the climax: "The entire act is an action sequence" (p. 143). Only with the destruction of the last chip, the one in the Terminator, is the main goal accomplished and the invention of Skynet foiled. The exact break between the development and the climax can be located at the brief pause interjected by the shot of the T-1000 driving his motorcycle up to the Cyberdine building and assessing the situation.

The timings of these large-scale parts do not fall into the neat ¼ - ½ - ¼ pattern on which Field insists. The exposition is unusually long at 42 minutes, but the narrative certainly demands this length. It results partly from the fact that the setup contains two major action sequences, the bar fight at the beginning and the lengthy chase near the end. Moreover, the four main characters who need to be established are all spatially apart for most of the action, engaged in different activities. In most films some of the newly intro-duced characters engage in conversations, thus giving us exposition about two or more of them simultaneously. Here the narration must move among the four characters to reveal all salient information. The complicating action then occupies 34.5 minutes. The extensive introduction of expository material in the film's first two parts means that no new information needs to be intro-duced thereafter, and the development and climax are shorter, consisting almost entirely of intense action sequences. They are also nearly identical in length, with the development clocking in at 26:40 minutes and the climax (including the brief 35-second epilogue) at 26:55.

Terminator 2 offers a model of classical plotting. As with many films, one large-scale section—the setup—is longer than the others, but the extra length serves important narrative functions. The narrative also offers the double plotline, and although there is no romance, John's friendship with the Termi-nator and that relationship's humanizing effect on the latter provide compara-ble emotional appeal. The film's events are thoroughly motivated, and clarity of time, space, and causality is maintained.

Why Are Large-Scale Parts Balanced?

What are the functions of balancing these large-scale parts? One may be to provide a simple, flexible framework for that rising and falling action which has been discussed by practitioners and commentators since the earliest days of feature filmmaking. The early American cinema quickly became noted for being action-packed. The high points were universally assumed in the scenario manuals to generate those staples of narrative action, suspense and surprise. Why not jam as many in as possible? As has often been pointed out, by placing the high points at intervals, the filmmakers afford the spectator a bit of room to breathe.

In addition, I suspect the use of lulls in the plot may be included in order to provide other staples of classical storytelling: most importantly exposition, motivation, romance, and redundancy, but also humor, motifs, subplots, and the like. These elements need to be interlaced with the strong action.

Large-scale parts also foster clear, gradual character change. We shall see several examples of this, including Michael Dorsey's improving attitude toward women in *Tootsie* and Jack Ryan's gradual shift from armchair strategist to man of action in *The Hunt for Red October*. If characters are to change their initial traits, there must be time allotted to thoroughly motivate their progress.

Balanced large-scale segments provide the "structure" that Ernest Lehman and other veteran screenwriters have so often mentioned as critical. Each part has a shape of its own and guarantees variety. Without this shaping principle, *Jaws* might indeed just be a string of shark attacks, *Tootsie* a series of gags about a man in a dress, *Amadeus* a simple drama of Salieri's escalating schemes against Mozart.[52]

The 20- to 30-minute range might also cater to the attention span of the spectator. The studios need not have pinpointed exact timings consciously, but careful attention to the minute-by-minute reactions of preview audiences (used since the 1920s) may have given practitioners an instinctive sense of when to change the direction of the action. Time and again scriptwriters have described this instinctive feel for structure. Caroline Thompson, who wrote the script for *Edward Scissorhands* (1990; see timings in Appendix A), notes: "One reason Tim [Burton] wanted to work with me is that I wasn't stuck with all these rules, like, 'The first act turns on page blah-blah.' On the other hand, I did have instincts for the form—internalized. A prose writer learns to write by reading books; a screenwriter learns by watching movies."[53] These generalizations about the large-scale parts of narratives do not offer a detailed or definitive explanation as to why they exist. Such an explanation could lie in the realm of cognitive psychology, which might suggest through experimentation what advantages the parts might offer for perception and comprehension of a movie.

Still, we should not be surprised that a film's large-scale parts so often fall within a narrow average time-range. Most classical and popular arts have some sort of balanced parts, whether temporal or spatial. Vivaldi's many concerti tend to have first and third fast movements of similar lengths with a slightly shorter slow second movement.[54] Daily comic strips have generally consisted of four panels, usually of the same size (or more recently, with the shrinkage of newspaper space devoted to comics, three). Medieval altarpieces typically balanced subsidiary hinged side panels designed to swing in and close at the center against a larger central one. (Indeed, such altarpieces are the only type of artwork I can think of that might consistently conform to the Fieldian notion of two small parts framing a middle section twice their size.) The awe-inspiring effect of Khufu's Great Pyramid at Giza results from the simple joining of four triangular sides of virtually identical size (the bases of the sides deviating less than one-fifteenth of one degree from the four cardinal directions). The acts of traditional plays are usually of roughly similar lengths.

One could cite many more examples, but the point is that the evident use of proportions in many narrative films provides one more indication of the enduring classicism of the mainstream Hollywood system. Presumably what practitioners have intuitively assumed to be the optimum range of lengths for each part was discovered early on. It has been passed down the generations of filmmakers as a result of the simple fact that most practitioners gain their basic skills by watching a great number of movies.

TEN EXEMPLARY FILMS

I have chosen to analyze in depth the narratives of ten films in order to demonstrate that classical storytelling techniques are still very much in use in many American films and to reveal how such techniques are woven together in often complex ways. On the assumption that films that are considered models of narrative technique might prove the most revelatory, one criterion I used in making my selection was that the films had to have enjoyed a fair degree of both critical acclaim and popular success. Another criterion was simply that I had to like the films well enough not to get tired of them in the course of the repeated viewings and close scrutiny that such analysis entails.

The ten films are the following: *Tootsie* (1982), *Back to the Future* (1985), *The Silence of the Lambs* (1991), *Groundhog Day* (1993), *Desperately Seeking Susan* (1985), *Amadeus* (1984), *The Hunt for Red October* (1990), *Parenthood* (1989), *Alien* (1979), and *Hannah and Her Sisters* (1986). They range from a prestigious best-picture Oscar winner like *Amadeus* to a low-budget sleeper, *Desperately Seeking Susan*. Two won screenplay Oscars (*The Silence of the Lambs* and *Amadeus*), while three others were nominated for this award (*Tootsie*, *Back to the Future*, and *Hannah and Her Sisters*).

I have grouped the films in a rather unusual way, by the number of protagonists each one contains. It would seem that in achieving a comprehensible chain of cause and effect and keeping spatial and temporal shifts clear to the spectator, a scriptwriter has to use different strategies, depending on whether one goal-oriented protagonist appears in nearly every scene or the narration keeps shifting between two major characters with different goals or even shifts among a whole group of major characters. Thus the analyses are gathered into three clusters: films with single protagonists (Chapters 2–5), those with parallel protagonists (Chapters 6–8), and those with multiple protagonists (Chapters 9–11).

Such a division makes sense, I think, because the Hollywood cinema depends so thoroughly on characters with clearly established traits for both causality and comprehensibility. In discussing his adaptation of *The Silence of the Lambs* from novel to film, Ted Tally emphasizes the centrality of protagonist point-of-view: "So really the most fundamental decision you have to make in an adaptation is the primary point of view. Whose story is it more than anyone else's? Or, in Hollywood terms, who are we rooting for? It seems like such an obvious, simplistic question, but you'd be amazed how often it doesn't get asked or answered. It will determine every other choice you make in the adaptation."[55] The same would presumably be true of original scripts, and the writer would have to make adjustments when balancing two or more point-of-view characters.

Films with single protagonists are far and away the most familiar, and I have already presented several examples in my discussion of character and goal orientation. Such films typically present the fewest challenges to audience comprehension as they move from scene to scene. In *Tootsie, Back to the Future, The Silence of the Lambs*, and *Groundhog Day*, the narration sticks close to the central figure most of the time.

The three films in my second group display an unusual but interesting approach to narrative. Rather than having a single protagonist, such films introduce two parallel protagonists who pursue distinctly different, sometimes conflicting goals and who are often spatially separated during much of the action. I am not referring here to films of the "buddy" genre, such as *Butch Cassidy and the Sundance Kid*, *48 Hours*, *Lethal Weapon*, and *Thelma and Louise*. Such films essentially split the function of the single protagonist between two roles: the characters share a goal and typically work together toward it. I will call these "dual-protagonist" films in order to differentiate them from my parallel-protagonist category. The problems of organizing a narrative based on dual protagonists are not much different from those of building one with a single protagonist. The parallel-protagonist film, however, offers some unique challenges.

Parallel protagonists are usually strikingly different in their traits, and their lives initially have little or no connection. Yet early on in the action, one develops a fascination with the other and often even spies on him or her. Hidden similarities between the two are gradually revealed, and one character may change to become more like the other. If the two main characters are male and female, the parallel plot pattern may develop as an unlikely romance that gradually blossoms. (To the best of my knowledge, mainstream American cinema has yet to produce a parallel-protagonist romance involving a homosexual couple.) A prototypical example would be *Sleepless in Seattle* (1993), where the Meg Ryan character seems successful in her career and satisfied in her engagement to a rich, if allergy-ridden, beau. Yet while listening to a radio talk show she becomes fascinated from afar with a grieving widower and begins investigating him through radio reports, computer searches, and a secret visit. Ultimately the two link up romantically.

If the two protagonists are of the same gender, one character's fascination may develop as a desire to become more like the other. At first glance, *Amadeus*, *Desperately Seeking Susan*, and *The Hunt for Red October* could seemingly not be more unlike in terms of subject matter and tone. Analyzing the underlying patterns of narratives, however, can reveal striking similarities in films of very different types. Both *Amadeus* and *Desperately Seeking Susan* center on two protagonists. One of the pair, prosperous and apparently successful, becomes fascinated by a less successful but eccentric figure. The envious character spies on the other and begins to imitate him or her, and finally seeks in some way to take on the other's identity. In *The Hunt for Red October*, Jack Ryan tracks the activities of Marko Ramius in order to aid the latter's defection to the West. Yet Ryan's attitude is hardly neutral; he admires Ramius and eventually gains him as a friend and father figure. This pattern of one protagonist's fascination with another, often with the latter unaware of this attention for at least a substantial portion of the plot, seems to be common in parallel-protagonist films. Prior to *Amadeus*, Milos Forman had directed a variant of the parallel-protagonist narrative, *Hair*, in which the John Savage and Treat Williams characters are mutually (and consciously) intrigued and in the end inadvertently switch identities.

In many such films, the two protagonists either do not know each other or, as in *Amadeus*, are only slightly acquainted, and hence are seldom together.[56] As a result, the filmmakers face the problem of moving between the two and still maintaining a clear, redundant, linear classical narrative progression.

In the case of *Amadeus*, one might ask whether Antonio Salieri is not simply the antagonist, since he in effect murders Mozart. Yet I would argue that he is in fact a true protagonist. He provides the narrating voice for much of the film, and we are clearly supposed to sympathize with his dilemma as well as deplore his actions. He is a quasi-tragic protagonist in the tradition of classical drama: a man with lofty ambitions and ideals flawed by his overwhelming sense of the irony of his own inferiority.[57] A somewhat similar situation occurs in *Heat*, where one might wonder whether master thief Neil McCauley (Robert De Niro) is an antagonist or a parallel protagonist to Al Pacino's police detective.

Dana Cooper, an American Film Institute scriptwriting instructor, has suggested why such characters are not antagonists. She differentiates four types of heroes: the "Idol" (a lofty, self-confident figure like James Bond), the "Everyman" (Roger Thornhill in *North by Northwest*), the "Underdog" (Forrest Gump), and the "Lost Soul." This last is a doomed figure, such as Jake La Motta in *Raging Bull* or Michael Corleone in *The Godfather*. The audience initially feels some sympathy for this character—though often grudgingly—but ultimately rejects his or her actions.[58] Salieri is such a character, and hence he forms a protagonist parallel to Mozart.

My third group consists of multiple-protagonist films, which are more common than parallel-protagonist plots. We can arrange them along a spectrum. At one pole, the narrative may involve a series of plotlines which are connected by some shared situation but which do not have significant causal impact on each other. In *The Towering Inferno*, for example, the romance subplot between the Fred Astaire and Jennifer Jones characters develops along its own trajectory in the midst of the disaster plot. Altman's *Nashville* takes the approach to an extreme with its famous inclusion of 24 important characters. In such films, as in parallel-protagonist films, the main characters have different goals which they pursue independently. The characters may cross paths, but their narrative lines have only occasional and tangential causal effects on each other.

At the opposite pole lies the multiple-protagonist narrative involving a group of people, several or all of whom are roughly equal in prominence and who work toward a shared goal—however much they may disagree on the means of achieving it. Typical examples would be disaster films and other types of plots in which a team works together to overcome danger. *The Poseidon Adventure* (1972) provides a simple example, with the Gene Hackman and Ernest Borgnine characters frequently clashing over what escape strategy to pursue but with the group generally cooperating.

In the middle of the spectrum we find the multiple-protagonist narrative involving several major characters and plotlines which have independent resolutions, but which crisscross and affect each other. *Grand Hotel* is perhaps the quintessential example, as the hotel itself provides the setting for a group of major characters who have not previously met to come together, form new individual goals, and affect each others' lives crucially. *The Big Chill* (1983) is a more recent instance, with old friends with very different careers and projects coming together briefly and interacting intensely, then parting.

The three films which I will examine in Chapters 9–11 fall into these three regions of the continuum. In *Parenthood*, despite the fact that all the protagonists belong to the same family and gather at intervals, the main plotlines progress with virtually no causal interaction. Instead, the material that binds these lines together is largely conceptual and motivic, functioning to create generalizations about the challenges and rewards of parenthood. *Hannah and Her Sisters* seems in some ways similar to *Parenthood*, with its examination of an extended family which assembles at intervals for parties. Yet in *Hannah* the plotlines cross each other in deliberately untidy ways, not behaving like the neat parallel tracks of *Parenthood;* in *Hannah* this interweaving serves the film's thematic treatment of love as unpredictable. *Alien* exemplifies films with group protagonists dedicated to a shared goal. Here the use of a group keeps us in suspense as to which character will survive the disaster visited upon them all—a common aim of "shooting-gallery" films.

In analyzing a film, it is often desirable to subordinate the plot order of the film's events to the critic's conceptual argument. When the scene-by-scene progression of the action dictates the structure of the analysis, the latter may occasionally give the impression of a glorified plot synopsis. Nonetheless, in each chapter that follows I will track the film scene by scene, since there is really no better way to show how the plot breaks into discrete parts, how dangling causes prepare us for a change of time and space, how motifs create echoes and parallels, how goals are formulated, recast, thwarted, or achieved—and, most basically, to see how classical films achieve their fine-grained, scene-to-scene comprehensibility. One further aim of analyzing the films in chronological order is to facilitate video viewings of each with these analyses in hand.

I will also use each film to formulate an additional generalization that can be applied to contemporary classical cinema—a "final lesson." Some of these will address issues of how storytelling in the New Hollywood might be improved. There is a widespread perception that Hollywood filmmaking entered a period of doldrums during the mid- to late 1990s, with formulaic narratives predominating. Yet there is also evidence that this slump has been a passing phase in a generally stable system. I will develop this theme further in the final chapter.

2

Tootsie

1982. Released by Columbia. Directed by Sydney Pollack. Screenplay by Larry Gelbart and Murray Schisgal, story by Don McGuire and Gelbart. Running time: 115 minutes; setup, 25; complicating action, 31.5; development, 21; climax and epilogue, 34 (epilogue alone, 15 seconds); end credits, 3.

"I guess some people never change, or they quickly change and then quickly change back."

—HOMER SIMPSON

As usual, Homer Simpson is only partly right. In some films the central characters do not change, and their traits introduced in the setup remain constant. Indiana Jones, for example, remains the scholarly but intrepid archaeologist throughout the three feature films of which he is the protagonist. Other characters change slightly, as we have seen with Sheriff Brody in *Jaws;* he loses his fear of the water through winning his battle with the shark. But protagonists in classical Hollywood films seldom change quickly, and when they do change, they usually acquire desirable traits which they retain to the end. There are exceptions, usually films where good characters are temporarily led astray or lose sight of their ideals, as in *Muriel's Wedding* (1994). In such cases, however, we typically assume that the characters' underlying traits are suppressed rather than lost. Still, plots in which central characters gradually reform or mature are common in American films.

Tootsie provides an excellent example of a central character who gradually undergoes a permanent change of some traits. Michael Dorsey is introduced as being hardworking and dedicated to the profession of acting, qualities which he will retain. He is also, however, professionally uncooperative and sexually exploitive of women; both of these traits—particularly the latter— will be tempered during the action. By the end of the film we assume his change will be permanent (as the line "for all of my life" in the song "It Might

Be You" redundantly stresses). Michael's progress can be traced by changes in his goals, which mark off the film's large-scale parts.

Virtually all scenario manuals stress the importance of the goal-oriented protagonist. Yet most advisers seem to envisage the goal as a static desire that does not change across the course of the plot. The goal is conceived early on, and the character struggles to achieve it, encountering obstacles along the way that provide conflict and action for the narrative. Syd Field advises: "First—define the NEED of your character. What does your character want to achieve, to get, during the course of your screenplay? Is it a million dollars? To rob the Chase Manhattan Bank? To break the Water Speed Record?" Once the scriptwriter has defined the need, he or she then, according to Field, should concentrate on creating a "biography" for the character.[1]

Other manuals convey the idea that goals are usually fixed early on and stable throughout. Linda Seger speaks of a "character spine" which "is determined by the relationship of *motivation* and *action* to the *goal*." According to her, the goal must meet three requirements: something important must be at stake, the goal must run counter to that of the antagonist, and it must be difficult to achieve.[2] These requirements are indeed usually met in Hollywood films, but Seger allows for no modifications to the goal. Similarly, Michael Hauge suggests: "Enable a sympathetic character to overcome a series of increasingly difficult, seemingly insurmountable obstacles and achieve a compelling desire." Hauge notes that there are exceptions, but these involve the protagonist failing to achieve a goal (his examples are *One Flew Over the Cuckoo's Nest* and *Out of Africa*) or realizing that the goal was wrong (*Raising Arizona, Wall Street*).[3]

For simple stories of searches, investigations, and so on, the basic goals may indeed remain the same throughout, with the parts defined by changes in tactics to achieve them. There are other possibilities, however, which involve definite changes of goal. Quentin Tarantino describes how the heroine's goal emerges gradually in *Jackie Brown* (1997), which is arguably his first classically constructed film:

"It's always unfolding: it's not a movie about Jackie figuring out in the first ten minutes how to get half a million dollars and then doing it—no! It's like little by little it starts coming to her, as life and situations change and she's being torn in this direction and that. It slowly evolves, and then from that point on, it's straight ahead until she does it. It's very novelistic, in that the first 90 minutes are just about characterization. Then, it's all execution: the last half-hour is just them doing it, the money switches and all that."[4]

Shifting or evolving goals are in fact the norm, at least in well-executed classical films, and *Tootsie* and most of the films I will be discussing will demonstrate how such changes occur.

In treating Michael Dorsey's goals as static, Hauge is led to describe them in a somewhat misleading way: *Tootsie* "is a story about an out-of-work actor who wants to pose as an actress on a soap opera and win the love of one of his costars." These desires "drive the plot" and "determine the story concept."[5] Actually, Michael's initial goals are simply to get an acting job—*any* job—and to make $8000 to produce his roommate Jeff's play. Late in the setup he aims at getting a specific job by pretending to be a woman; his love (as opposed to lust) for Julie provides a goal only relatively late in the development. Thus these two intertwined goals are only part of the overall story concept. Hauge's description misses Michael's character changes.

The fact that screenplay advisers seem to conceive of goals as static may suggest a further reason why they often see the central portion of the film as an hour-long "act" which they find difficult to write, define, or analyze. As I intend to show in greater detail in this and subsequent chapters, the portion of the film that lies between the setup and the climax often follows a trajectory that depends on more than simply throwing obstacles in the protagonist's path. That trajectory includes modifications of existing goals or even the formation of entirely new ones.

Tootsie is also a model of the classical cinema's thoroughgoing motivation. Given the film's absurd main premise, the writers faced a challenge: How do you get a man who is neither gay nor a cross-dresser to pose as a woman? How do you get him to keep on doing this despite the many complications this ruse creates for him? Such problems often provide the genesis of plots, especially in the "high concept" narratives common in recent Hollywood cinema. The great humorist P. G. Wodehouse described how he generated plot ideas in just this way:

I find that the best way to get my type of story is to think of something very bizarre and then make it plausible. I remember in Full Moon I started with a picture in my mind of a man crawling along a ledge outside a house, seeing a man through the window and gesturing to him to let him in, and the man inside giving him a cold look and walking out of the room, leaving him on the ledge. I find that, given time, I can explain the weirdest situation.[6]

Tootsie, too, takes something extraordinary and makes it plausible.[7] Let us examine how this is done.

THE SETUP: "NO ONE WILL HIRE YOU"

Tootsie centers around a single protagonist. Michael appears in every scene, and departures from him consist of brief cutaways. Essentially, we are attached to Michael, and the bulk of the action is presented through him. (Since Michael Dorsey is playing Dorothy Michaels, I will switch between the two names according to which persona Michael is presenting to the other characters.) Thus the narration simply needs to link scenes as they relate to temporal and causal changes in a single character's situation. The process begins with the credits sequence.

Many American films introduce a great deal of expository information as soon as possible. (Again, there are exceptions; action films, such as *Cliffhanger* and *Terminator 2*, often start with action at fever pitch, then fill in backstory.) The credits sequence can present an opportunity for packing the early portion of the setup into a short span of time. The main lines of action may not actually begin, but we usually learn something about the characters' traits, their social situations, their appearances, and so forth. To varying degrees, the same thing happens in every other film I will be analyzing.

It has become a convention of Hollywood films that the credits sequence can be filmed and cut more freely than an orthodox dramatic scene. Stylistic flourishes may call our attention to objects. The action may jump about without sticking as closely to the characters as in other scenes. In *Tootsie*, the credits sequence cuts among several spaces and times, showing Michael at auditions, acting classes, and a rehearsal.

The film begins with closeups of stage makeup. Though we know nothing about the character who is putting the makeup on, we already suspect that the narrative will involve the theater. Michael's donning of a false moustache prepares us for his later claim that he is a character actor (as opposed to a leading man). The theater milieu is strengthened by a cut to an acting class. The woman onscreen, Sandy, is not identified here, but we are likely to recognize Terri Garr. She practices a vocal exercise that makes her seem silly and awkward, and these will be among her stable traits. (In her second big scene, the surprise birthday party, she comments on her toast to Michael,

"This is a really dumb speech," and later she accidentally gets locked in the bathroom.) Sandy is the first student introduced, and she remains prominently in the background of subsequent shots. Thus we are prepared to remember that she is Michael's student, motivating the six-year platonic friendship that they have had.

At this point, the sequence begins to alternate brief scenes of Michael performing in a series of auditions with scenes of him teaching his acting class. The credits consist of a montage sequence just under six minutes long. There is no indication as to when the events occur in relation to each other. Apparently two or three acting classes (judging from costume changes) are intercut with several auditions. Temporal relations are incidental, since the sequence exists mainly to reveal some of Michael's traits rather than to initiate a definite line of action.

During the first audition, Michael is asked to turn to page 23 of the script. Without looking, he recalls which scene that involves. Here we see evidence of Michael's first character trait: he is dedicated and meticulous, having carefully studied the script. He lives by the earnest advice that he gives his students. We *must* understand this in order, first, to care about him despite his flaws, and second, to believe he can change for the better. This tryout includes a comic bit in which a man cues Michael by flatly reading a woman's lines, a moment which anticipates both Sandy's spiritless rehearsal for her own audition and Michael's more successful acting as a woman.

In this first audition, Michael is told he is too old for the part. This declaration acts as an ironic dialogue hook into the next brief scene, in which he unsuccessfully tries out for a role as a child. At the next audition, he is rejected as too tall, despite revealing that he is wearing lifts. These three auditions rapidly and amusingly establish that Michael will try out for *any* part and will go to great lengths to get it.

Still, we gain little sense from these auditions as to whether Michael can really act. In his class, he lectures on intensity in acting. And indeed, this leads to the fourth audition, in which he gives an impassioned reading, only to be ignored by the whispering auditors. Back in the class, he urges the students: "If you can't make the part yourself, then don't play it." Later, when Michael plays Dorothy, her imaginary traits begin to mingle with his own and eventually change him.

The brief scene in which Michael is ordered to cross the stage despite the fact that his character is dying is not an audition. This is a blocking session, so presumably he actually has a part. Now we see his temperamental side for the first time as he abandons this precious job. (His line "Not with me as Tolstoy" further suggests that he is even forsaking a lead role.) The director's order may be arbitrary, but Michael offers no compromise.

It is noteworthy that the director who is telling Michael how to play his part is portrayed in terms that seem to imply he is gay. For a character that appears so briefly, the film must quickly telegraph his traits, and hence it employs stereotypical signals. (The director is prissy and calls Michael "love"—a parallel with Ron's later casual use of terms of endearment when he thinks Michael is a woman.) He is indeed the only real homosexual we see in the film, and he seems stupid and unpleasant. This moment links to a major motif in the film. Repeated references to homosexuality function not only to create comedy but also to make it utterly clear to the audience that Michael is *not* gay, even though he spends much of his time impersonating a woman. Other characters may mistake him for a homosexual or tease him about being a transvestite, but there are many moments that confirm that Michael is neither. This is crucial to the thematic point that he becomes a better (straight) man by coming to understand women's feelings. Yet even though the film plays with gender roles in a purportedly liberal way, it takes a fairly regressive stance on homosexuality as such.

Note also that we see Michael's positive traits of dedication and intensity first, then his uncooperative streak. Once the main action begins, we witness his selfishness and callous attitude toward women. The film thus gives us his positive traits first and negative ones subsequently. If we saw him leave the stage in a snit earlier in the credits sequence, we might be less likely to accept his dedication and intensity as being sufficient to make him a basically positive character.[8] Such early motivation of a later character change is important in classical narratives. By way of contrast, a review of *My Giant* (1998), a comedy in which the cynical Billy Crystal character eventually becomes humanized, elicited this comment from *Variety*: "Seltzer's script waits much too long to provide Crystal's character with the means to change."[9] *Tootsie* provides a model of character change made plausible from early on.

Michael's abandonment of his role as Tolstoy leads into an ironic contrast as he tells his class that "You gotta work . . . You gotta find ways to work." He mentions that the unemployment rate among actors in New York is 90 to 95 percent. This line later helps convince us that he would go so far as to impersonate a woman when he despairs of finding employment *in propria persona*.

The first shot after the credits shows that Michael does have work—as a waiter. He and a fellow waiter, Jeff, then walk home in a brief scene that establishes crucial narrative information. Jeff has written a play which Michael is helping him revise. It is Michael's birthday, and he is depressed, despite professing to be unaffected by age because he is a character actor. This latter fact helps motivate his later ability to play a middle-aged woman, since he is used to performing a great variety of roles. Jeff also makes a remark that becomes a major motif in suggesting Michael's need for change: "Well, instead of trying to be Michael Dorsey, the great actor, or Michael Dorsey, the great waiter, why don't you just try to be Michael Dorsey?" Other characters will make similar remarks, which establish that Michael is good at acting but not at living a fulfilling life. Ultimately his skill at assimilating the role of Dorothy will allow him to progress toward being Michael Dorsey. (As he says in the final scene, "I just gotta learn to do it without the dress.") This notion of "being yourself" is a Hollywood (as well as a social) cliché. When a character is said to be incapable of being himself or herself, this is an immediate cue to the spectator that the character needs a change of traits.

The surprise birthday celebration is the first of three major parties that help structure the action of *Tootsie*. It redundantly confirms what we have learned and adds new traits to Michael's character. A friend toasts him: "To Michael Dorsey, who—like it or not—makes you remember what acting's all about!" Another chimes in, "Being unemployed!" The toast reconfirms that Michael is a consummate professional but not necessarily pleasant to work with. Unemployment also continues as the fundamental motif that will motivate Michael's willingness to pose as a woman. This scene also introduces the more specific goal of Michael and Sandy's needing $8000 to produce Jeff's play. This desire is plausible, given Michael's extreme dedication to the theater.

The project to put on Jeff's play forms a subgoal of Michael's more general goal of wanting employment, and it helps give the film an overall trajectory. After all, wanting employment is rather open-ended. Michael gets one job, and he will presumably always want more and better roles. The line of action concerning Jeff's play achieves closure, however, at the point late in the climax portion where we see the sign announcing the production (Fig. 2.1). Starring in this play is an acting job for which Michael need not compromise his principles.

The party introduces new traits for Michael. We see him trying to pick up various female guests. Later, his manipulative attitude toward women will gradually change as he learns from his experiences as Dorothy and from his resentment of Ron's treatment of Julie. There is also a significant moment at the party when Sandy tries to show Michael a friend's baby. Michael ignores it, and though Sandy assures the friend that "he loves children, he really

2.1

does," she is clearly wrong. Much later the film will use Michael's attitude toward Julie's baby, Amy, to help chart his personality change. When he is at the farm visiting Julie and her father, he cuddles Amy—a complete contrast to his attitude in the party scene. And even though he dislikes babysitting for Amy later on, his willingness to go to such trouble for Julie further indicates his sincere love for her. (He also refers to himself as "Uncle Dorothy" during his time alone with Amy, suggesting that he can imagine himself as having a familial relationship with her.) Eventually, just before his revelation of his identity, he gives Julie a present for Amy. Michael's intuition that Julie would not accept a present for herself reveals how much he has learned about romantic relationships.

As the party winds down, additional interesting information about Michael emerges. We might have gotten the impression that he has many friends from different age groups and walks of life. Jeff's comments reveal a different situation: "I wanted it to be a surprise. I invited ten people, they all invited ten people. You met about forty new people tonight, and I think they all liked you a lot. I heard a lot of nice things about you. You got new friends now." When a man wishes Michael a happy birthday, he remarks, "Thank you, Sam—one of the five people I know tonight." Not only does Michael exploit women, but he has few friends.

Jeff's girlfriend, who appears only in this scene, is worth noting despite her minor role. She is beautiful and stays around with Jeff through all his rambling talk about his plays. At the end, they sit affectionately on the couch as Michael turns to walk Sandy home. Thus Jeff seems to have a happy, stable relationship that contrasts with Michael's incessant pick-up attempts. Despite

Jeff's wackiness, he provides a comic running commentary that traces Michael's increasingly desperate attempts to juggle his deteriorating private life. In this way Jeff parallels Michael's agent, George, whose comic remarks trace Michael's increasingly convoluted professional situation.

After the party, the film moves quickly through the setup, giving us additional information that prepares for Michael's transformation into Dorothy. Michael walks Sandy home—a moment similar to Jeff and Michael's walk home before the party. There Jeff had discovered that Michael was depressed; here Michael learns that Sandy is upset. So far the situation laid out during the setup has been static, involving who the characters are and what they want. Michael's line, "You're worried about your audition tomorrow, aren't you?" introduces the first causal action that will propel the plot forward. There is a role available, and Michael is aware of it.

Sandy's despairing response as to what kind of role she's auditioning for—"A woman!"—acts as a dialogue hook into the scene of Michael coaching her. He goads her to be more aggressive: "Stop being such a doormat." Thus the scene plays out in miniature what Michael will later do with Julie, pushing her to dump Ron. When Michael demonstrates his point by reading Emily Kimberley's lines, he does a much better job than Sandy had, motivating his ability later to get the part. This scene ends with Michael agreeing to accompany Sandy to the audition: "OK, I'll pick you up at 10 A.M. and enrage you"—a combined dialogue hook and appointment.

A cut takes us to an establishing shot of the exterior of the television studio where the audition is to occur. From Michael's final line, we grasp that this scene takes place the next morning. We are introduced to the female producer of the soap, "Southwest General." Miss Marshall is the sort of tough executive that Dorothy plays on the show—but a New York version instead of a southern-belle type. This characterization motivates her appreciation of Dorothy's aggressive approach to her audition. Also during this scene, a tour passing through the lobby quickly introduces some of the show's main characters.

After a fleeting hint at Ron and Julie's romance as they kiss while exiting the elevator, we learn that Sandy has been deemed physically wrong for the part. This is the same reason Michael was repeatedly rejected in the credits sequence. It is also the same reason that Ron later gives for not wanting Dorothy to read—her appearance is too "soft and genteel." Interestingly, Michael himself chose this soft appearance for Dorothy, despite knowing that the producers want a tough woman. No motivation is given for his choice, though perhaps he thinks delicate makeup and clothes will counteract his underlying maleness.

In this scene Michael learns that he has been passed over for a part in a Broadway play, and he rushes off to see George, his agent. This is the first of Michael's many failures in his commitments to Sandy. Here she is confused by his departure, asking, "Will he be back?" This is a dangling cause, since we too wonder if he will return. He will—but in an unexpected way.

Michael and George's conversation summarizes what we already know and also introduces some important information, all in order to motivate Michael's sudden change into Dorothy. George repeatedly reiterates that Michael is a good, dedicated actor, but says that he is too difficult to work with. He belittles Michael's offbeat projects, calling him a "cult failure." Michael again mentions that he needs $8000 for Jeff's play, which is now revealed as one of those offbeat projects, dealing with Love Canal.[10] Recapitulating his initial goal, Michael demands: "I want you to put me up for anything—I don't care what it is. I will do dog commercials on television, I will do radio voice-overs." George reveals that Michael could not even get such minor acting work: "You've got one of the worst reputations in this town, Michael. Nobody will hire you." This exchange is typical of Hollywood's redundancy, in that the film has emphasized over and over that Michael is temperamental and that he desperately needs work. By now there is nothing more that we need to learn about Michael's difficulties as an actor and his and Sandy's desire to stage Jeff's play. The scene ends with yet another statement of Michael's goal: "I'm gonna raise $8000, and I'm gonna do Jeff's play." George reiterates emphatically, "Michael, you're not gonna raise twenty-five cents. *No one* will hire you," and Michael replies, "Oh, yeah?"

Michael's defiant line provides a rather vague but dramatic dialogue hook into the next scene, in which we see him in the street, suddenly dressed as a woman. He has clearly set out to prove George wrong and to achieve his goals, with the jaunty music picking up the "Oh, yeah?" cheekiness. Thus the causal link between the two scenes is clear.

Initially Ron declines to let Dorothy read, rejecting her as too soft and genteel. As he places his arm around Dorothy and calls her "honey," she instantly launches into a tirade, denouncing him for trying to imply through his casting of the character of Emily Kimberley that power makes women masculine; she also denounces Miss Marshall for allowing him to do so. Here Michael is hardly making a bold feminist statement through Dorothy's mouth. His outburst is simply an effective ploy to induce the producer to give him an audition. This scene, however, does set up Dorothy's later denunciation of Ron for calling her "Tootsie," a moment that will lead directly into the part of the development portion where Michael falls genuinely in love with Julie and finally changes his traits for the better.

In the lead-up to the audition as Emily Kimberley, Michael is instantly attracted to Julie. Her first lines reveal one of her major traits, a cynicism about the television show; she remarks that the production staff would not notice if the script were read out of order and calls them "a firing squad." Julie will only gradually become central to the action, but when she does, this cynicism remains prominent. Her unhappiness with her job will motivate her excessive drinking and her eventual willingness to end her relationship with Ron. More positively, it also motivates Julie's eagerness to applaud Dorothy's audacity, to accept her as a friend, and finally to emulate her.

The audition itself fulfills expectations that have been set up earlier: Michael gives a strong performance, as we would expect after seeing him coach Sandy. A cut reveals Miss Marshall reacting positively to him, a moment that motivates Dorothy's later success with TV audiences. The conflict with Ron is confirmed when he says, "There's something about her that bothers me." Marshall responds, "I like it," and then speaks the line that ends the setup: "We'll send the contracts over to George today, Miss Michaels." Later the renewal of the contract will lead into the turning point that leads into the climax portion.

We now know the initial premises of the plot. Michael has achieved part of his goal by getting a job. His tactics, however, will throw his life increasingly into confusion and will considerably delay his putting on Jeff's play.

COMPLICATING ACTION: "ONE OF THE GREAT ACTING CHALLENGES"

As often happens in classical films, the complicating action is triggered by a decisive event that reverses some of the major premises of the setup. From "No one will hire you," we have abruptly seen Michael get the next job for which he tried out. The complicating action will introduce a combination of circumstances that replaces the setup's situation.

The producer's mention of sending the contracts to George acts as a dialogue hook. Michael must meet with George again to get his money, given that the contracts will baffle George when they arrive under Dorothy's name. Moreover, now that Michael has succeeded in passing himself off to strangers as a woman, his problem will be to maintain the deception. Here he tests his ability to fool a friend. His successful hoodwinking of George demonstrates his skill at maintaining his new identity.

This lunch sequence and the two following scenes function partly to reassure us that Michael is not a homosexual or transvestite. George seems foolish for assuming Michael has become a transvestite ("Oh, God, I begged you to get some therapy!"). After Dorothy's shopping spree, she tosses a man out of a cab, a comic bit stressing that Michael is still "manly." When Jeff asks, only half-jokingly, if Michael is really doing this just for the money, Michael replies disdainfully, "It also happens to be one of the great acting challenges an actor could have."

Having redundantly established that Michael is dressing as a woman only to achieve his initial goals, the film develops several other lines of action. Michael mentions that his biggest problem is Sandy. She is unstable ("She gets suicidal at a birthday party") and would be devastated to learn that she has lost a role to a man in drag. Jeff suggests not telling her. Once Michael agrees to that, the pattern is set for most of the action. He will deceive everyone but Jeff and George. Hiding his identity creates problems with Sandy, then Julie, then Julie's infatuated father Les. This pattern will not be broken until the climax, when Michael unmasks himself on live TV.

The deceptions begin as Michael asks Jeff how he can explain to Sandy his sudden acquisition of $8000. The answer creates a dialogue hook. Michael says, "What am I gonna do, tell her somebody died and left it to me?" (Fig. 2.2). A cut creates a false shot/reverse shot with Sandy, who, in a new space and time, looks offscreen at Michael and asks, "Oh, my God! When did she die?" (Fig. 2.3; the apparent shot/reverse shot is reinforced by the fact that both characters have drinks). This new scene initiates an important line of action as Michael unintentionally begins a brief affair with Sandy. (It is not clear why Michael would be so foolish as to undress in Sandy's bedroom; we must assume that he notices Sandy's dress and in his zealous dedication to acting forgets everything else in his desire to see how the dress might enhance his performance as Dorothy.)[11] Up to now we have seen him trying to pick up strangers, but now he deceives one of his closest friends, emphasizing the necessity for him to improve his character. Sandy laments that the end of their affair will leave her waiting by the phone—as it does, sooner than she perhaps expects. Michael reassures her, however, and accepts a dinner invitation for the next evening.

The line "Dinner tomorrow" both creates an appointment and provides a

2.2

2.3

dialogue hook into the next day, as Michael wakes and gets into his Dorothy disguise. At the station he meets his roommate April and receives new pages for that day's script. April remarks, "Aw, they always throw stuff at you at the last minute. You could lose your mind around here." Her disdain echoes what Julie had said about the production staff not noticing if the pages were read out of order. It also prepares for Dorothy's increasingly improvisational approach to her performances—and ultimately for Michael's frantic improvisation as he sheds his Dorothy guise on live television.

The improvisation begins with Dorothy's first performance, as she wallops the lecherous actor John van Horn to avoid his kiss. Apparently van Horn has had the script changed, as is his custom, to allow him to kiss the new actress.

Like the director Ron, he uses his power to gain sexual advantages. For the first time Michael finds himself on the receiving end of male sexual exploitation, beginning a motif that will culminate with van Horn's attempt to rape Dorothy. That event, combined with Sandy's denunciation of Michael, will finally drive him to reveal Dorothy's identity.

Dorothy pretends to have been instinctively inspired in her improvisation by Ron's direction. But Ron delivers an ultimatum: "I'll handle the instincts here. Now it happened to be a very good instinct, Toots, but next time you wanna change something, discuss it with me first, you understand?" Dorothy: "Yes, I was wrong not to." Ron (patting her arm): "Good girl." This dialogue hints at a slight change in Michael. As Dorothy, he uses tact rather than his usual hotheadedness to deal with a director. As a result, he defuses the situation. Ron's ultimatum, and Dorothy's acceptance of it, will govern the rest of the complicating action. Eventually, however, Michael's decision to have Dorothy consistently improvise will form the narrative's middle turning point.

Michael's attraction to Julie provides a sound bridge to the next scene: "She's really a very, very attractive girl [cut to new scene] and she's no dummy." Chatting with Jeff, Michael deplores Ron's treatment of Julie, concluding, "I think Dorothy's smarter than I am." These lines suggest that Michael is changing by gaining insights into sexual relations. But his musings are undercut when he realizes he has stood Sandy up.

After a brief montage showing Dorothy's growing fame, Michael sets up another dinner date with Sandy for Thursday at 8:00: "I will *not* forget." Later, at the studio, several important pieces of motivation are introduced. The producer announces that some takes have been ruined and must be reshot. Julie tells Dorothy this happens occasionally: "You know, we actually had to do it live once," thus preparing for the final live broadcast. On her way to Julie's dressing room, Dorothy spots Ron kissing April, thus providing some motivation for Michael's willingness to try and seduce Julie; she is clearly not in a stable relationship. Julie's overindulgence in wine first appears here as well, as she invites Dorothy to dinner.

The dinner scene at Julie's apartment confirms that her affair with Ron is not a happy one. She is drinking again and remarks with gentle irony: "There are lots of men out there. I'm selective. I look around very carefully, and when I find the one I think can give me the worst possible time, that's when I make my move." Her words suggest that it would not be caddish of Michael to win her away from Ron—assuming that he does not in turn deceive her. Julie describes how she would like to have a man simply declare he wants to make love to her, though she does not say she wants this to occur as soon as they meet—as happens later when Michael uses this tactic in attempting to seduce her.

At the end of this scene Julie mentions that Ron had stood her up for dinner the night before, leading Michael to realize that he has again missed his date with Sandy. His repeated failures to telephone Sandy or to show up for dinner, plus his lying when he makes excuses, all parallel the way Ron behaves toward Julie. Later in the film, just before Michael leaves for the visit to Julie's father's farm, Jeff points out that Michael is still lying to Sandy; Michael replies that he is just trying to avoid hurting her feelings. Later, when Dorothy confronts Ron over the way he lies to Julie, Ron claims, "I know she doesn't want me to see other women, so I lie to her to keep from hurting her." Dorothy is annoyed: "That's very convenient." Yet Michael treats Sandy in the same fashion until near the end, when she finally confronts him and says their friendship is over.

Michael's belated visit to Sandy prepares for the end of the complicating action. She criticizes the actress playing Emily Kimberley: "She's supposed to be so tough, right? You said she's supposed to be tough. She's a wimp!" Distressed by this slur on his acting, Michael replies, "Well, maybe it's the lines. After all, she doesn't make up her own lines." Sandy responds, "I think she should. They couldn't be worse." Her comment provides a dialogue hook into the taping scene where Dorothy improvises extensively as her character deals with a battered wife. Dorothy then adamantly defends the changes. The actress playing opposite Dorothy declares, "I can't act with this," a line that suggests that Michael's difficult temperament is resurfacing. Now, however, his refusal to cooperate is motivated by the way Dorothy is becoming part of his own personality. His budding feminism leads him to change lines that he considers demeaning to women.

This, Dorothy's first unrepentant use of improvisation, ends the complicating action. It occurs about 56.5 minutes into this 112-minute film, a clear-cut central turning point.

DEVELOPMENT: "YOU'RE A COMPLICATED LADY"

The montage sequence of Dorothy's rise to super-stardom provides a transition into the development portion of the film. This sequence, with its lively music, is in effect a reversal of the credits sequence, which had been about the struggle to overcome unemployment. Now there is a celebration of success and celebrity, providing a prelude to the obstacles Michael will encounter in the development. The credits had been followed by a conversation in the street at night, with Michael depressed over his situation and Jeff trying to console him. Now the montage sequence leads into the first scene of the development, with Michael walking in the street during the day with George. He is exuberant, bubbling over with ideas, and George tries to calm him. This creation of parallel scenes provides further evidence that many films have a true middle turning point and not just a mid-point of a lengthy "second act."

The three turning points that separate *Tootsie*'s four major parts all come just before or after conversations between Michael and George. George's "No one will hire you" had precipitated the events that led to Dorothy's hiring, the first turning point. Later their discussion of renewing Dorothy's contract will open the climax portion and motivate the scene where Michael unmasks on camera. Here the pair's conversation in the street also occurs shortly after a turning point and opens the development proper.

The conversation helps to define Michael's new goals and changing character. Earlier he had said that he thought Dorothy was smarter than he. Now he sees no split: "I *am* Dorothy. Dorothy is me. No one's writing that part, it's coming out of *me*." George's reply echoes Jeff's earlier advice that Michael just try to be Michael Dorsey: "You are Michael, you're acting Dorothy." Michael responds: "It's the same thing." Thus Michael has, as he had advised his class, made the part himself. He wants to do other roles—TV specials, Ophelia, Lady Macbeth, "The Eleanor Roosevelt Story"—as Dorothy: "There's a woman in me. I'm experiencing deep feelings." He also says, "I feel I have something to say to women, something meaningful."

Yet his euphoria is tempered by a sense of helplessness: "When I finally get a job, I have no control. Everybody else has the power, and I've got zip." This loss of control results from the deceptions Michael practices. His fruitless search for a way out of the situation dominates the development. His ultimate realization of his powerlessness will come when the studio renews his contract—a turning point that precipitates the climax.

Although this conversation with George seems to suggest that Michael is becoming more sensitive to women, it leads directly into a scene where he calculatedly tries to seduce Julie at a party. Michael's presence there is motivated at the end of the scene with George; trying to get Michael to relax, George invites him to be his guest at a ritzy affair. This is the film's second party, paralleling the earlier birthday celebration, which Jeff had thrown to cheer Michael up. At both parties, Michael knows few of the guests. (At both, too, Sandy stuffs food into her purse.)[12] The parallels serve to underline that

Michael has not yet changed significantly; he tries to pick Julie up much as he had with other women in the earlier scene, repeating nearly word for word the "I'd like to make love with you" speech Julie had spoken to Dorothy during their first dinner.

The party scene emphasizes Julie's untenable relationship with Ron, who flirts with another woman at the bar. At the same time, Julie turns down the overtures of a powerful producer (seen chatting with George and Dorothy in the Russian Tea Room), referring him to her agent. Thus we see that she does not sleep around, even if it might benefit her career, and she remains loyal to a man who frequently cheats on her. Her fidelity suggests that she just needs to find the right man in order to establish a happy, monogamous relationship. Michael's casual pick-up attempt and her contemptuous rejection indicate that he is not yet ready to be that man. Her gesture of tossing champagne in his face establishes that she has some gumption and could develop more.

Indeed, in the very next scene Julie's character on the soap, a nurse, makes a defiant speech telling the van Horn character that she has filed charges (presumably of sexual harassment) against him. Dorothy watches this scene intently. All applaud after the take as Julie raises her fists in triumph. Dorothy mouths "Perfect" at her and further encourages her. Julie refers to Dorothy as her "coach," and thus Sandy's role as Michael's pupil and disciple is here definitively transferred to Julie. In contrast, Ron squelches the kudos and offers Julie no praise or encouragement. This is the point at which Ron calls Dorothy "Tootsie" for the first and only time, causing her to blow up at him: "*Ron*. My name is Dorothy. It's not Tootsie or Toots or Sweetie or Honey or Doll." Now Dorothy is not only improvising in defiance of Ron's ultimatum, but she is also telling him off in front of the cast and crew. The film's development portion centers primarily around the process of Dorothy defying Ron (and providing a model for Julie to do likewise in the climax) and the parallel action of Michael's falling truly in love with Julie.

This confrontation leads to the moment when Julie invites Dorothy to visit her and her father for the holidays. Her words hint at the comic confusion to come as Les falls for Dorothy: "You know, since my dad met you, he's your biggest fan." This line of action had already been subtly planted shortly before the beginning of the "superstar" montage, when Les smiled at Dorothy during personal appearances by the soap's cast (Fig. 2.4).

The brief scene of Michael packing for the trip reminds us that he still has a long way to go in his character improvement. He again lies to Sandy, telling her that he is ill and can't see her. (Sandy mentions rehearsals, introducing the idea that Michael might want to get out of his part on "Southwest General" in

2.4

order to stage Jeff's play.) Jeff's deadpan mocking, "I'm just afraid you're gonna burn in hell for all this," is a comic version of the narration's stance: Michael *is* still behaving badly.

To a considerable extent that bad behavior is forgotten in the scenes at Les's farm. There hazy cinematography and slow, sentimental music imply that Michael is falling in love with Julie. His character traits are changing. He holds Amy affectionately and manages to sleep in the same bed with Julie without doing more than sympathetically stroking her hair—a "feminine" gesture that reminds Julie of her mother. (A similarly celibate sharing of a bed will be one test of the hero's worthiness in *Groundhog Day.*) Most important, in the scene in the yard swing Michael apparently is about to tell Julie that he is a man—though he is interrupted by a phone call. There are similar moments to come, as Michael hovers on the brink of confessing to Julie and Les, motivating his revelation to the whole world on the broadcast.

Paralleling the main romance line in the farm scenes is Les's obvious attraction to Dorothy. This complication seems to be included primarily for comic purposes, but it also provides an example of an old-fashioned, courtly romantic relationship that could serve as a model for Michael in his attempts to woo Julie.

Indeed, the farm scenes underscore the film's ambivalence about sexual relationships. Both Julie and Michael have clearly had multiple lovers. Michael has preyed upon women, while Julie suggests that her unhappy affair with Ron is only the most recent in a string of similar disappointments. The narration fails to suggest that their premarital alliances would rule out a relationship for them. Michael seems mildly upset when he hears that Amy was born out of wedlock, but the issue is quickly dropped, and by the end he presumably will accept her as his daughter. Yet at the same time both are also blamed for their past affairs—Michael's as casual and exploitive, Julie's as sincere but misguided. The narration posits that Michael and Julie can make up for their pasts only by marrying and forming the stable, ideal American family. Thus, as in many Hollywood films, the sexual revolution is exploited for its entertainment value while the ending upholds traditional mores.

Les's views are privileged in other ways as well. He expresses the narration's stance on feminism: "Don't get me wrong. I'm all for this equal business. I think women ought to be entitled to have everything and all, etc. *Except*—sometimes I think what they really want is to be entitled to be men. Like men are all equal in the first place—which we're not." He goes on, "You know, I can remember years ago, there was none of this talk about what a woman was, what a man was. You just were what you were." His speech offers another echo of Jeff's early admonition to Michael about just trying to be Michael Dorsey, as well as George's reminder that "you are Michael, you're acting Dorothy."

After Michael returns to the city, a crucial plot twist occurs. The producer, Miss Marshall, meets with Dorothy and declares, "You're a complicated lady." To say the least, we know this already. She goes on to describe how Dorothy has made Ron "defensive and hostile." In other words, Michael, as Dorothy, has been behaving as his old cantankerous self. Yet as Dorothy he can also be conciliatory, sweetly replying, "Oh, I don't mean to." Marshall then reveals that the show's boosted popularity means that the studio is picking up her option for a year.[13] There is a track-in on Dorothy's fixed smile as she gulps apprehensively.

This scene parallels the one late in the setup where George's "No one will hire you" had accompanied a close view of a defiant Michael. After the latter's successful audition as Dorothy, he had earned a contract offer. The complicating action had then begun with Michael returning ebulliently to George. The development ends with a scene in which Michael phones George—now desperate for Dorothy to escape her contract. Michael seems ready to take the obvious way out—telling the truth: "You get me outa this. I don't care how you do it, or I'm gonna go in right now and tell them." George provides the obstacle that the narrative needs to prolong Michael's reluctant impersonation of Dorothy: "Tell them what? That you deliberately put an entire network on the spot? That you're making a fool out of millions of American women every day? They'll *kill* you. Look, I got a secretary out there wants to be like Dorothy Michaels. I'm ready to fire her. Michael, we're talking *major fraud* here. *Major* fraud." He tells Michael to make it work.

Michael now has a new goal: he must get out of playing Dorothy without being charged with fraud. This is the end of the development. No new complications or delays will be introduced—only variants of old ones that push Michael over the edge.

CLIMAX AND EPILOGUE: "THE WOMAN THAT WAS THE BEST PART OF MY MANHOOD"

This portion of the film begins with Jeff administering Valium to the distraught Michael. He makes a comic suggestion that proves prophetic: "You know, maybe there's a morals clause in your contract. Perhaps if Dorothy did something really filthy or disgusting they'd have to let you go. But I really can't think of anything filthy and disgusting that you haven't already done on your show." This speech contains a hint of how Michael will get out of the contract. Of course, Dorothy does not do anything filthy or disgusting, although the scene of van Horn's attempted seduction will parody that idea. Rather, Michael will eventually conceive of a way to make not Dorothy but Emily Kimberley do something so outrageous that it will presumably lead the producer to void the contract voluntarily (or possibly, though this is never specified, to Michael's continuing to play Edward Kimberley on the soap).

Here Jeff confuses Dorothy's behavior with the show's moral tone. The plots of "Southwest General" are so "filthy and disgusting" that nothing in Dorothy's private life could top them. But Michael will solve his problem precisely by incorporating his own real-life deception into the plot of the soap—and hence, paradoxically, becoming honest with the people he has deceived.

From this point on, the plot lines begin to be resolved. A phone call from Julie summons Dorothy to her apartment. Julie has decided to break off her relationship with Ron: "You have influenced me, though, Dorothy. I've been seeing Ron through your eyes lately." Dorothy's reply, "Julie, I don't want that responsibility," indicates Michael's changed character. The old Michael might have embraced this chance to rid himself of his romantic rival; now he thinks of the consequences for Julie.

Julie asserts that Dorothy "wouldn't compromise your feelings like I have. You wouldn't live this kind of lie, would you?" Dorothy has difficulty replying, finally saying, "Julie, you mustn't idealize me. Honesty in many ways is a relative term." By now Dorothy has pushed Julie to the point where she is ready to become honest and end her compromised life. Despite being "a doormat" and requiring a man (though she does not realize it) to solve her problem, she does make her move toward honesty by dumping Ron at a time when Michael is still embroiled in deception. He pushes her to do the right thing, and then by doing it, she pushes him to tell the truth as well.

Thus the "feminine" and "masculine" values mutually influence each other for the better in *Tootsie*. Why, then, does the narrative come across as portraying Michael as the positive force and Julie as just a flighty woman who needs a man's help to define how she should live? This happens in part, I think, because she is a heavy drinker and hence not in control of her life. The effect results also from the fact that this film is told almost entirely from Michael's point of view. Moreover, Michael is allowed to be funny but Julie is not. (Sandy takes over the role of the comic female character.) Julie remains the beautiful damsel waiting to be awakened from the spell, while Michael is the modern, hip hero—however misguided.

While Julie is putting Amy to bed, Ron and Dorothy have a conversation that further emphasizes and motivates Michael's character change. Dorothy finally criticizes Ron's treatment of Julie: "I don't like the way you patronize her. I don't like the way you deceive her. I don't like the way you *lie* to her." We, of course, recognize these as problems Michael himself still has.

After the comic montage of Dorothy trying to cope with Amy's sleeplessness, Julie returns, depressed. She attributes her new problem to Dorothy: "I'm so grateful to have you as a friend and at the same time, I've never felt lonelier in my whole life." Here we have the classic convention of cross-dressing plots, in that Julie is drawn, though unaware of it, to someone who she thinks is of her own gender (as Orsino is drawn to Viola in *Twelfth Night*, for example). Her loneliness signals an instinctive longing for Michael. Indeed, her line, "It's as though I want something that I just can't have," makes no sense unless we assume that she somehow "really" senses that Dorothy is a man. As always, the film adamantly rejects any implication that Julie's attraction to Dorothy could result from homosexual impulses.

At this point Michael forgets himself and, still as Dorothy, tries to kiss Julie. She reacts badly, and his attempts to explain his actions are cut off by the comic business that follows. Dorothy falls awkwardly and clumsily regains her feet as "she" pursues Julie around the room. This is Michael's renewed attempt to tell the truth, and again it is derailed. Julie assumes that Dorothy is a lesbian and will not listen to any explanation. Michael is now hovering halfway between roles. He tries to confess to Julie, yet he still uses his "Dorothy" voice. In the scene at the Russian Tea Room Michael had revealed his identity to George by briefly dropping from his "female" voice to his normal tones. He has the option of doing the same here and so ending the deception, and perhaps we are to suspect that he might eventually have done so.

Once again, however, his confession is interrupted, this time by a phone call from Les. An appointment and dialogue hook lead to a date between Dorothy and Les at a nightclub. Michael again attempts to reveal his identity, and once again he is interrupted by Les's proposal of marriage. By this point we are primed to believe that Michael is ready to tell the truth, at least to Julie and Les. He tried at the farm, he tried in Julie's apartment, and now he tries again. By Hollywood's rule of three, his dramatic revelation on television has been sufficiently motivated. He simply needs a final push.

Returning to her apartment, Dorothy encounters van Horn. He is a comic version of Les, the aged seducer rather than the honorable wooer. At the same time, he is the old failure and lecher that Michael could easily have become. (As Dorothy asks when van Horn calls himself a "has-been," "Were you ever famous?" van Horn: "No." Dorothy: "Then how can you be a has-been?") Michael has come to a point where he must in effect decide between Les and van Horn as models. By playing a middle-aged woman who attracts both of these older men, he see the consequences of his own actions. Indeed, as Dorothy, Michael has suffered an escalating series of indignities at the hands of Ron and van Horn, ending in this near-rape. Though handled in a comic way (despite Michael's statement to Jeff that "Rape is not a laughing matter"), van Horn's aggressive seduction attempt helps motivate Michael's decision to reveal his identity.

Sandy's final visit brings Michael's deceptions full circle. He had begun by deciding not to tell her that he had gotten the soap role in drag. Now he gives her Les's candy, pretending that he bought it for her. When Sandy finds Les's card and asks why he would thank Michael for "a lovely night in front of the fire," Michael gives up: "My mind's a blank." For once he fails to improvise a line; in actors' terms, he has dried up. Sandy demands to know what is going on: "No matter how bad the truth is, it doesn't tear you apart inside like dishonesty—*dishonesty*. At least it leaves you with some self-respect and dignity." Again Sandy is right. Her advice at the end of the complicating action had been for Dorothy to make up her own lines, and that had worked. Now she tells Michael to be truthful, and soon he will be. Despite the film's comic treatment of Sandy, she is the source of causes that precipitate major shifts in the action.

Michael finally gives in: "OK, OK, I'm not gonna lie to you anymore. I'm gonna tell you the truth. Sandy, I'm in love with another woman." She reacts badly, launching into a virtuosic comic tirade against him. This gets her out of the romantic line of action and back into the plotline concerning Jeff's play: "I think I should tell you to shove your play—but I won't, because I never allow personal despair to interfere with my professional commitments. I am a professional actress." Here we see that Sandy, like Michael, has matured. She no longer becomes suicidal over depressing news, and she thinks of herself as the professional actress Michael had exhorted his students to be in the opening sequence. The point is not emphasized, but she gets her reward in the shape of a lead role in Jeff's play (see Fig. 2.1).

The final scene between Michael and George takes place late at night in the latter's apartment. It summarizes Michael's impossibly convoluted situation in relation to his professional and private lives. As he says at the scene's end, "I'm in *trouble*, man!" Michael's main goal remains to find a legal way to get out of Dorothy's contract. Presumably after that his goal will continue as he mops up the personal problems that Dorothy's existence has created—primarily relating to Les and Julie. As a result, the climax portion of the film is quite long. In particular, Julie's forgiveness of Michael comes very late indeed.

In the next scene, the producer reveals that part of that day's show has been ruined and must be done live. (This is coincidental, but the notion of mistakes, retakes, and live broadcasts had been planted, as we have seen.) In the dressing room, Dorothy tries to reconcile with Julie, but she breaks off their friendship, not wanting to lead Dorothy to believe that a lesbian relationship is possible. She repeats the motif of being yourself: "You taught me to stop hiding and just be myself, because you're always yourself." Michael then tries one last time to tell her the truth privately—"Julie, I don't know how to say this . . ."—but she cuts him off once more.

Julie's final line, "I can't love you," leads into an announcement: "Places, everybody. Immediately!" The live broadcast constitutes the plot's third major party, with the soap opera's hospital staff gathering to toast Emily Kimberley. All three parties are linked to the "just be Michael Dorsey" motif. Jeff had given Michael that advice just before the surprise birthday party, and George had reminded him that he is Michael Dorsey, not Dorothy, before inviting him to the posh central party. Finally, before this televised party, Julie had told Dorothy that she was always herself. Here Michael does reveal himself—within the fiction as Edward Kimberley but in real life as a man. He launches into his elaborate speech, a parody of soap opera plots, with their frequent shifts of locale and situation and their lurid events. His honesty is certainly not immediately recompensed. Julie punches him, and van Horn ends the scene with a comic sting by asking confusedly, "Does Jeff know?" His tag-line recaps the motif of people being in love with each other without knowing the other's gender.

The climax moves into a series of wrap-up scenes. Michael pushes a street mime over—an unexplained but satisfying moment.[14] We learn that Jeff's play is in production, so Michael's initial goal is being realized. Thus the main professional plotline has been resolved, but the romance line remains open. We see Les encounter Michael in a bar, where the latter cajoles him into a reconciliation. In the final scene, we learn that Michael had gone to the bar hoping to see Les, so an apparent coincidence is motivated retrospectively. At that point, Michael also tells Julie that he and Les had played pool. So that plot complication ends pleasantly. Les is not the type to hold grudges, let alone beat Michael up. Indeed, he says he is now dating "a real nice woman," so his infatuation with Dorothy has apparently benefited him by renewing his interest in romance, missing since the death of Julie's mother.

The main romantic plotline is resolved in the final scene when Michael meets Julie in the street. She hints that Michael's revelation of his gender has helped his career: "So, you're pretty hot after the unveiling, Michael. What's your next triumph?" He mentions the Syracuse production. It is hardly a triumph but rather one of his offbeat projects, suggesting that despite his success he retains his original ideals. As he says: "I just did it for the work. I didn't mean to hurt anybody. Especially you." When Julie says that she misses Dorothy, he insists that he is, in effect, Dorothy. She accepts his claim that they are already "good friends," and they go off together.

Since the climax of the romance line of action comes so late, there is only the briefest epilogue, consisting of Michael and Julie walking away down the street under the final credits.

Throughout *Tootsie*, the fact that we are almost continually with a single central character makes the progression from scene to scene linear and easy to follow. Most scenes end with a dialogue hook and/or a dangling cause that is picked up early in the next one. As we saw, Michael's response to his agent that he will get a job leads straight to our seeing him in disguise as Dorothy, heading for an audition. When Julie invites Dorothy to visit her in the country, the scene ends with her saying, "I'd just like you to come." The scene ends before Michael responds, but the invitation is a dangling cause. As the next scene opens, Michael is packing, so we know he has accepted. Throughout the film, Michael's goals consistently provide the action with a forward impetus from scene to scene.

As befits the source of so much narrative causality and clarity, Michael remains consistent and understandable as a character. Those traits that change do so gradually, with clear motivations provided to explain the transformation.

Tootsie's four major portions depart slightly from the ideal 20- to 30-minute average for classical films. Not counting the final credits, the film runs about 112 minutes. The first half lasts approximately 58 minutes, the second approximately 54. Thus the midway turning point, Michael's decision to have Dorothy improvise many of her lines, comes about two minutes from the dead center of the film. At slightly over 34 minutes, the climax portion is a bit long. As I have suggested, however, it needs that length in order to clear up the many entanglements caused by Michael's impersonation of Dorothy. Moreover, although the two main lines of action are bound up together, the means for resolving each are different; hence the professional and private lines of action require separate sets of events for resolution. In contrast, the development can be short because it mainly involves Michael's falling in love with Julie—something which can happen relatively quickly since we have been prepared for it by the earlier friendship between Dorothy and Julie.

Although the subject matter of *Tootsie* is very different from the second film I will analyze, *Back to the Future*, the principles underlying the narrative structure of the two films are similar in many ways. Each of the protagonists must struggle to make a change. In *Tootsie*, Michael changes his character traits without intending to do so. In *Back to the Future*, Marty must change the course of history in order to preserve (and unintentionally to improve) his own life. As we shall see in the next chapter, Marty also has consistent character traits and provides most of the means for stitching one scene into the next with causal, spatial, and temporal clarity.

A FINAL LESSON: MULTIPLE WRITERS

Given all the unity, clarity, and even subtlety that I am claiming the best Hollywood films achieve, one might be puzzled by the fact that often such films are the product of a whole series of writers, rewriters, and script doctors. How can such a group, often not even working in coordination, achieve tight-knit narratives? When *Eraser* went through multiple rewrites and tinkerings, color coding was used to flag each generation of changes.[15] Presumably this was in part to provide evidence of authorship, since fully one-fifth of Hollywood theatrical films require Writers Guild arbitration to determine which names are included in the credits, and hence which authors are entitled to residuals.[16] Such a system almost guarantees acrimony within at least some teams of writers.

Tootsie was the product of a notoriously convoluted writing process. In 1978 producer Charles Evans acquired a play, *Would I Lie to You?*, written by Don McGuire. During 1979 the script was written and rewritten by Bob Kaufman, Dick Richards (originally to direct George Hamilton in the lead role), and Evans. When Richards showed it to Dustin Hoffman, the latter brought Murray Schisgal in for another rewrite, and when Pollack became the project's director in late 1981, he assigned Larry Gelbart to it. Pollack rewrote the result yet again, assisted by Elaine May and Robert Garland. Even after shooting finally began, serious disagreements between Hoffman and Pollack led to frequent tinkering: "'We always have our big fights on Monday,' Sydney commented. That was because all weekend, each man had been working on the script."[17] (Ultimately, after Writers Guild arbitration, Gelbart and Schisgal shared screenplay credit, and Gelbart and McGuire split the story credit.) Despite all this, here is *Tootsie*, leading off my series of ten models of good narrative structure. And, as we have just seen, only a few minor causal lapses might be attributable to the many rewrites.

The historian Michael Sragow has pointed out that the use of multiple scriptwriters goes back to the classic studio era:

> *Casablanca* had a screenplay history almost as complicated as *Tootsie*'s: Julius J. and Philip G. Epstein took the first swipe at the Murray-Burnett-Joan Alison play, *Everybody Comes to Rick's*; Howard Koch then brought it close to final form; and Casey Robinson and Lenore Coffee helped director Michael Curtiz slap it to life.[18]

Indeed, rewriting scripts was a common chore of contract writers, as an interview with Julius J. Epstein suggests:

> *How is it that you and your brother acquired such a reputation in Hollywood as script doctors?*
>
> We don't have a big reputation as script doctors. Everybody at the studio was a script doctor—"Who isn't doing anything at the moment? Here, see what you can do with these scripts."[19]

Sragow suggests how *Tootsie* could be so unified despite its labyrinthine authorship:

> In *Tootsie*, all scripts led to Pollack, who pieced together the characters, gag lines, and bits.
>
> Pollack: "Even when there are ten names on a script, the reason is that you couldn't get what you wanted from the first screenwriter so you went to the second one, got a little bit more, incorporated what you wanted, left out what you didn't."[20]

Indeed, it is quite common for a director to do the final rewrite of a script, or at least to collaborate on it. The result presumably would be that the product of several successive scriptwriters would be unified in the process. The point is that multiple authors do not necessarily lead to a violation of classical narrative principles. On the contrary, such a method of scriptwriting can exist precisely because all those involved in the production share the same set of assumptions about such elements as goals, motifs, and dialogue hooks. Rather than adding disunity and unclarity, the successive rewrites ideally strive to clear them up.

3

Back to the Future

1985. Released by Universal. Directed by Robert Zemeckis. Screenplay by Zemeckis and Bob Gale. Running time: 116 minutes; setup, 27; complicating action, 32; development, 18; climax and epilogue, 34.5 (epilogue alone, 6.5); end credits, 4.

The mechanics of the plot are as complex and pleasing as those of the novelty clocks that tick and whir under the credits.

—DAVID SKERRIT, *Christian Science Monitor*

A CLOCKWORK PLOT

Back to the Future was the top box-office hit of 1985, but its genre and tone hardly made it Oscar bait. The Academy of Motion Picture Arts and Sciences has been notoriously reluctant to honor comedies, science fiction tales, and youth-oriented movies. As with so many successful films perceived as lacking prestige, Robert Zemeckis's film figured in some minor categories, Sound and Best Song, and it won in the category of Sound Effects Editing. It also, however, received a nomination in the category of Best Screenplay Written Directly for the Screen. Competing with more respectable films—*Brazil, The Official Story, The Purple Rose of Cairo,* and *Witness* (the inevitable winner)—Zemeckis and fellow writer Bob Gale stood virtually no chance of carrying home statuettes.

Yet the very nomination of this breezy film in the writing category reflected a recognition on the part of industry professionals that here was an extraordinarily intricate, unified, and well-motivated narrative. Undoubtedly part of the sense of unity and complexity the film conveys results from its many motifs. Almost everything that happens in the early parts of the film returns: apparently minor details of the mise-en-scene are repeated in comic ways when the hero returns to the past, and the important early scene of Marty's family at the dinner table is systematically reversed after his return to the present, near the end of the film. If any film in this book supports my claim

3.1

that an "ordinary" mainstream entertainment movie can be as complexly constructed as a prestigious art film, *Back to the Future* is it.

SETUP: "HISTORY IS GONNA CHANGE"

As in *Tootsie*, the action under the credits gives us a great many hints about the characters' traits and situations. In addition, bits of causal material are quickly presented, and motifs are introduced. Over the opening logo and production credits, we hear the sound of clocks ticking, and the first image shows us clocks of various types. One of them (Fig. 3.1) refers to the famous sequence in *Safety Last* (1924) in which Harold Lloyd dangles from a clock on the side of a skyscraper. Later, in the climactic scene of *Back to the Future*, Doc will hang from a clock tower; moreover, that character is played by Christopher Lloyd (whose name in the credits fades out about ten seconds before the Harold Lloyd clock becomes recognizable). As I suggested in the discussion of *Jaws* in Chapter 1, some recent Hollywood films contain motifs of a surprising subtlety.

During the credits, the camera moves about the room, revealing details of the mise-en-scene—always catching the action at exactly the right moment. The clocks themselves hint at an eccentric collector, and their varied styles suggest accumulated decades of pop culture—a motif that will be extensively exploited in the contrasts between 1985 and 1955. The first bit of causal material relating to the story comes in the form of two old framed newspaper clippings, one of which announces "Brown Estate Sold to Developers." This event is never mentioned in the film itself. At one point, however, Doc (whose

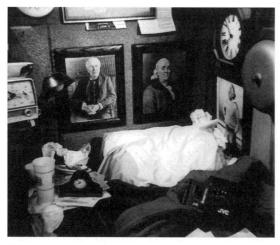

3.2

real name is Dr. Emmett Brown) remarks that he has spent his entire family fortune to create the time machine. These clippings specify that he sold a large family estate (apparently after the house burned down in an unexplained blaze). Presumably he used the money for his research. As we shall see, Doc's sale of his land fits in with a carefully developed motif of the changing geography of the town over three decades: the decline of the town square, the rise of suburbs like the one in which Marty's family lives, and the construction of the mall on former farmland.

The camera pulls back to reveal an empty, unmade bed surrounded by pictures (Fig. 3.2): Thomas Edison, Benjamin Franklin, Albert Einstein. These are important scientists and inventors, of course, but more specifically, each is associated with a motif important to the plot: Edison with electricity, Franklin with lightning, Einstein with relative time. Later, in one of the 1955 scenes, Doc speculates on how to generate the enormous quantity of electricity needed to run the time machine; taking down the same picture of Edison, he asks "Tom" how it can be done. During the credits sequence, the moving camera pauses briefly on both the clippings and the inventors' portraits, making these elements more significant than the jumble of clocks. The framing furthest to the right also allows us to glimpse a video camera on the rumpled bed (at the lower right in Fig. 3.2); seemingly a mere detail, it will be crucial to the action when Marty records the time machine with it and thus can show the tape to Doc in 1955.

The film has barely begun, and already ideas are being linked in a way that suggests its central concerns. The motifs build up associations: current time (the clocks), past time (the newspaper stories), inventors and scientists (the portraits). We might already infer that the occupant of this room is associated with all of these. At this point the first action occurs. A radio switches on, advertising a sale on 1985 Toyotas: "October is inventory time," giving the month and year of the film's action. We will soon learn that Marty covets a Toyota pickup, and his possession of it by the end of the film helps signal his family's transformation. Such a casual and rapid presentation of information and motifs packs a great deal of material into a short scene.

The camera now moves back toward the left, revealing elements that suggest that all is not well. A coffee-maker, activated automatically, squirts water onto an empty hot-plate. This and the other malfunctioning appliances on timers (burnt toast, spoiled dog food) seem to confirm that we are dealing with some sort of inventor—but one who is unexpectedly absent. (The name on the dog dish, Einstein, reemphasizes the temporal side of the absent inventor's concerns.) A mystery is beginning to form. The television switches on, providing us with information that will be crucial in solving that mystery: a case of plutonium is missing from a local nuclear power plant. The announcer also mentions a Libyan terrorist group, and these terrorists later kill Doc and chase Marty in the time machine. Such information motivates otherwise inexplicable events later in the story. A group of Libyan terrorists would ordinarily not appear in a small town's shopping mall; yet, long before they do, we know that they have come to steal plutonium from the nearby nuclear power plant. Doc would normally have no access to plutonium, but because the Libyans have already stolen it, he can obtain it from them.

The film has thus presented us with a great deal of information before a character actually appears. Now Marty enters, calling out the name of the absent inventor, Doc. Marty's knowledge that the house key is under the mat and his replacement of it in its hiding place identify him as a regular and trusted visitor. The camera glides rightward once more, following as Marty's skateboard rolls across the floor and bumps into the plutonium case under the bed. By now we have had a string of associated ideas, in this order: current time, past time, an inventor, missing plutonium, the inventor is missing, the inventor has a hip young friend, the missing plutonium is in the inventor's home. Without specifying what is actually going on, the film thoroughly prepares us for the moment when Doc summons Marty to meet him; it also motivates the revelation that his invention is a time machine.

Not noticing the plutonium, Marty sets up the equipment for his electric guitar practice. Why Doc has all this expensive audio equipment is never specified, though we might infer that he uses it and the other gadgets scattered around his home in his experiments, allowing Marty to use it as well. Marty turns all the controls to their maximum level, introducing the motif of his preference for extremely loud music. When the circuit overload triggers an explosion, Marty seems less disconcerted than awed, muttering "Wo-ho. Rock and roll." (The director credit disappears at the cut to a closeup of Marty's hand holding a guitar pick, but the last credits have come at such wide intervals that we are unlikely to notice this as a break in the sequence.)[1]

The scene ends as Doc calls and makes an appointment to meet Marty that night at 1:15 A.M. at Twin Pines Mall, providing a dangling cause that carries over to the last scene of the setup. As the multitudinous clocks chime 8:00, Doc triumphantly declares his experiment a success, since they are all 25 minutes slow.[2]

All the information and suggestions in this opening scene relate to the time-machine line of action. There are two other plotlines as well, and most of the rest of the setup focuses on them. First there is Marty's romance with Jennifer, the conventional romantic subplot, which is in this case largely supplanted by the romantic triangle established among George, Lorraine, and Marty in 1955. Second, and more important, Marty belongs to an unsuccessful family headed by a weakling father. Throughout these scenes, actions and motifs pile up that will be paralleled and contrasted once Marty travels to 1955. For example, as Marty races for school, we glimpse a van with campaign posters for the reelection of Mayor Goldie Wilson, a middle-aged black man; this background detail returns as a motif in the past. Similarly, he flirtatiously waves to women performing aerobics in a glass-fronted gym—a building later revealed to have been a malt shop in the past. (Upon arriving in 1955, an ironic touch has Marty trying unsuccessfully to purchase a diet cola there.)

A crucial moment in preparing for Marty's overall goals comes when Marty arrives late to school and is confronted by an official, Strickland. This sequence takes place in a corridor of the high school, and at the left there is a poster advertising an upcoming dance. In a parallel scene in 1955, Doc and Marty will stroll through this same corridor, festooned with posters for the "Enchantment Under the Sea" dance. In this scene, Strickland discourages Marty from auditioning his band for the upcoming dance, thus setting up a dangling cause that leads into the next scene, the audition itself. He also calls Marty a "slacker" and compares him to his father: "You're too much like your old man. No McFly ever amounted to anything in the history of Hill Valley." Marty defiantly replies, "Yeah? Well, history is gonna change." And of course it will. The overall shape of the narrative aims at changing Marty's family's situation, though at this point Marty has no specific goal or notion of how to effect that change. Indeed, he will never really attempt to change history for the better. Once he gets to 1955, he apparently changes it very much for the worse, wiping out himself and his siblings. His efforts to restore history as he had known it inadvertently result in improving it.

The reasons why Marty wants history to change arise from the traits of several of the characters first seen in this expository section. As in *Tootsie* and other typical classical films, we learn the main traits of each character when he or she is introduced, and those traits will be accurate, consistent indicators of how that character will act. When we first encounter Marty, he seems to be a pleasant teenager, interested in rock-and-roll music, concerned for his friend Doc, a bit flirtatious, trying to get to school on time. His girlfriend, Jennifer, also seems nice: she risks getting caught herself in order to warn Marty that Strickland is looking for him, and later she encourages him concerning his musical ambitions. The initial impression that they are both nice kids will be confirmed by the rest of the film's action, yet Strickland dislikes Marty and predicts he will be a failure. Events seem at first to prove Strickland right: Marty has been late for school in the past, and he is quickly eliminated during the musical audition. Yet when he tells Strickland that "history is gonna change," we assume that he is right. This assumption is based partly on the fact that Marty is played by Michael J. Fox. Jennifer's confidence in Marty also helps to confirm that he is a talented musician and that he is simply misunderstood by everyone except her and Doc.

Jennifer forms the center of the secondary romance line of action, but she also functions to help motivate our belief in the idea that Marty *can* change. In the scene where the two stand talking in the town square after the audition, Marty is ready to abandon his band. Jennifer urges him to pursue his music; she reminds him: "It's like Doc's always saying—" He interrupts, "Yeah, I know, I know, if you put your mind to it, you can accomplish anything." This line will become an important motif, returning twice to signal the ways in which history does change. As Marty tells the young George McFly about the planned rescue of Lorraine at the school dance, he concludes: "You know, if you put your mind to it, you can accomplish anything." At the end, when George is a success, his new novel arrives and he announces to his family: "Like I've always told you, you put your mind to it, you can accomplish anything." This cliché originates with Doc and is then passed to Marty, who says it to George, who in turn has instilled this attitude in his whole family by the end. In effect, at the beginning Doc has been acting as a substitute father for Marty, whose real father is a failure. By the end, Marty has helped to make George into a strong father, and hence Doc can depart into the future.[3]

The setting for Jennifer and Marty's conversation fairly bristles with motifs. As the couple walk through the town square, the van with the "Re-elect Goldie Wilson" sign passes behind them. They move to a bench with an advertisement for a jewelry store in the "Twin Pines Mall," the place where Marty is to meet Doc that night. During this scene, a woman campaigning to preserve the clock tower asks them for a donation. Her enthusiastic garrulousness motivates an expository speech describing how the clock tower— prominent in the background of the shots of Marty and Jennifer—had been struck by lightning at a specific time. The woman also presses a flyer on Marty, who will in turn give it to Doc, allowing them to predict when the lightning bolt will break the clock.

After Jennifer's father summons her away from Marty, he casts one look up at the offscreen clock tower, momentarily underscoring its importance. A brief transition then shows him skateboarding to his suburban home, with a long shot establishing the aging stone entrance to the "Lyon Estates" (whose streets are lined with medium-sized trees just about tall enough to have been planted in the mid-1950s). The scene at Marty's home reveals the true sources of his problems. George's inability to stand up to the offensively overbearing Biff and his abject "I'm sorry" to Marty concerning the wrecked car apparently confirm Strickland's characterization of George as a slacker.

A short ellipsis moves to the end of dinner, with George offering Marty a dish of packaged peanut brittle. Marty's faint frown of distaste as he refuses suggests what we already suspect and will later see confirmed: that Marty at least has a chance of escaping the sorry adulthood that seems to be his father's lot. The other members of the family, however, are also marked as failures, with the brother working in a fast-food restaurant and the sister unable to find a boyfriend. Their low status becomes especially apparent when Marty's mother, Lorraine, brings out a cake purchased to celebrate her brother's unsuccessful bid for parole. This scene reveals the family's problem: they are not goal-oriented in the way that traditonal Hollywood characters are. They accept their dreary fate, whereas Marty dimly has a sense that he wants to escape it. Doc's time machine will provide him the means to do so.

Eventually Lorraine recounts how she fell in love with George. At first she seems to be happily remembering her youth, assuring her daughter sagely that "it was meant to be." Her line, suggesting that she was fated to marry George, echoes Strickland's dictum that Marty is doomed to be a slacker. It also reflects a typical 1950s notion of girls waiting for Mr. Right to come along and find them. Indeed, the basic movement of the three *Back to the Future* films will tend to scotch ideas of fate by showing that tiny actions can deflect causality into a completely unexpected direction. Doc's speech to Jennifer and Marty at the end of Part III summarizes this idea in clichéd terms: "It means your future hasn't been written yet. No one's has. Your future is whatever you make it."

By the time Lorraine ends the tale of her romance with George, she looks sad: "It was then that I realized that I was going to spend the rest of my life with him." She has apparently become an alcoholic as a result of her life with George. Again the element of time comes forward as we are invited to contemplate this grim life stretching into the future. Her story also sets up the single most important premise in the family line of action: "If Grandpa hadn't hit him, then none of you would have been born." That is, if Marty's grandfather had not hit George with his car, then the initial cause that led to the family's existence would not have occurred. The moment when Marty saves his father from that accident will be the main complicating action in the film and will begin to change history.

Lorraine obviously recognizes her pathetic family's problems but is powerless to solve them. Of the three offspring, only Marty seems disturbed by the situation. We might wonder why Marty has escaped the resigned attitude of the others. Presumably the motivation is in his relationship with Doc, who has given him the support and fatherly advice ("If you put your mind to it . . .") that set him apart.

Like characters in earlier scenes, those who first appear in the scenes at Marty's home live up to our initial impressions of them. Strickland says George McFly is a failure, and George subsequently allows Biff to bully him, both in the present and in the past. Biff's initial behavior is also consistent with his actions in the 1955 scenes. The one exception to my generalization about characters remaining true to their initial traits would seem to be Lorraine. Marty's mother is puritanical, criticizing girls who are so bold as to telephone boys or park with them. When Marty encounters her in 1955, however, she flirtatiously pursues him, sneaks liquor without her mother's knowledge, and is quite willing to park. Yet there is no real inconsistency, since this is presumably the real Lorraine, needing only the right kind of husband to retain her youthful vim. Marriage to the "old" George has beaten her down, so that she disapproves of Jennifer. Marriage to the "new," transformed George has allowed Lorraine's original traits to endure, so that she sees nothing wrong in Marty's big date to go camping with Jennifer (the pickup truck with its sleeping bags in the back being an up-to-date version of parking). The scene ends with Lorraine drinking vodka as she watches George laugh inanely at a rerun of a "Honeymooners" spaceman sketch. This apparently trivial touch, which seems aimed mainly at driving home the negative characterization of George, will return in the scenes in 1955 and become part of a motif of visitors from outer space.

The final scene of the setup begins with a shot of a clock reading 12:27 and pulls back to reveal Marty asleep in bed. Given that the locale is still his house, the spectator can easily infer that this new scene takes place later the same night. The basic significance of this shot is simply that Marty has gone to sleep and thus has forgotten his appointment with Doc. It also paves the way, however, for a motif of Marty believing at several points that his experiences are part of a dream which, if real, would have begun at this point. Doc's phone call reminds him of the appointment and thus reactivates the mysterious dangling causes introduced in the opening sequence.

As Marty arrives at the shopping mall, the sign "Twin Pines Mall" is clearly visible, along with a digital clock that reads 1:16, redundantly recalling the appointment made in the first scene. The scene provides exposition at a great rate, as Doc describes his experiments and clears up the mystery of the missing plutonium. The dog Einstein's brief trip one minute into the future confirms that Doc is a genuine inventor and not merely an eccentric dabbler. Despite his plan to go into the future, Doc initially demonstrates how to set the time machine's controls by setting them at November 5, 1955, the day he invented the "flux capacitor." His brief recollection of that day will allow Marty to convince the Doc of 1955 that he has come from the future. Doc also mentions that it has taken "my entire family fortune to realize the vision of that day," picking up on the opening scene's clipping announcing the sale of the Brown estate. Even Doc's passing reference to the mall's having been built on farmland where the farmer Peabody was breeding pines will become a motif. Doc's final explanation concerning how he stole the plutonium from the Libyan terrorists creates a dangling cause that will soon return.

At this point we have all the information relevant to the narrative's initial situations regarding Marty's family and Doc's invention. The end of the setup provides a clear-cut case where the turning-point action—the attack by the Libyans—comes after the new large-scale segment has begun. The switch between the setup and the complicating action is marked simply by the end of Doc's explanations and a brief ellipsis. After the turning point does occur, the action continues uninterrupted for some time. The complicating action will then follow Marty's probe into the exact nature of his new circumstances and what he must do to get back to 1985.

COMPLICATING ACTION: "SERIOUS REPERCUSSIONS ON FUTURE EVENTS"

During the brief ellipsis between the large-scale parts, Marty and Doc have donned radiation suits. The outfits make them more parallel visually, and indeed both are fired upon within the next few minutes: Doc fatally by the Libyans, Marty harmlessly by the farmer Peabody. The suits will also be crucial in saving both characters' lives: Marty when he uses his to frighten George into agreeing to attend the dance, Doc when he hides a bulletproof vest under his in order to foil the Libyan attack the second time around. Such parallels are another tribute to the film's skillful manipulation of details.

As the pair load one vial of plutonium into the flux capacitor, Doc remembers that he needs to put the rest of the case into the car. "How do I ever expect to get back? One pellet, one trip! I must be out of my mind!" When he tries to load the plutonium, he is interrupted by the Libyan attack. Doc's forgetfulness was established in the first scene, when he had neglected to turn off his automatic gadgets. Now his failure to load the plutonium leads to his own death and Marty's accidental entrapment in the past.

Marty's arrival in 1955 leads to a dense series of comic incidents that contrast motifs established in the setup with the settings and characters of 1955. Marty's fright at a harmless old-fashioned scarecrow is immediately set against the Peabody family's terror at the strange apparition in their barn. The radiation suit is linked to space travel when Peabody's son, carrying a "Tales from Space" comic book, urges his father, "It's already mutated into human form—*shoot* it!" The reference is to the spate of science fiction films in the 1950s, including *Invasion of the Body Snatchers* (1956), in which giant pods mutate into artificial humans. The boy's comic book prepares the way for George's interest in not only reading but also writing such tales. As Marty flees from the farm, he knocks over one of two small pines in its yard, prompting invective and further shots from Peabody: "You space bastard—you killed a pine!" At this moment, Marty drives past a sign reading "Twin Pines Ranch." Doc had mentioned Peabody's ranch as having stood on this site before the "Twin Pines Mall." The destruction of the pine sets up a neat little surprise for the climax.

Driving along, Marty tries to reassure himself: "Get a grip on yourself. It's all a dream. Just a very intense dream." Given that we had seen him asleep before Doc's summons, we may keep this possibility in abeyance. Having turned toward town, he now encounters Lyon Estates in the early stages of being built. We can infer that the town is expanding outward, since the Estates will be an aging suburb by 1985, with the newer mall still further out. As Marty fails to start the car, he watches the November 5, 1955 readout switch off, giving us one more redundant reminder of what has happened. A close shot also shows him putting his personal stereo and the video recorder down on the seat, preparing dangling causes for the moments when each will resurface as a key plot element.

The scene of Marty's arrival in town lingers once more over comic contrasts between the two decades. The self-service "Gas War" price of $1.09 in 1985 has become a full-service "Price War" at 19½ cents. The movie playing in the local theater is *Cattle Queen of Montana*—which actually came out in 1954 but would plausibly be in a late run in such a small town. It also plants the idea that Ronald Reagan is still an actor at this point, preparing the way for Doc's later comic exchange with Marty about who is president in 1985. In general, the brief tour of the square gives a sense of a prosperous downtown. Whereas in 1985 the area establishments include porn theaters and a pawnshop, the 1955 square boasts a family theater, a paint store, a stationer's, and the like.

Apparently at this point Marty is still too dazed to realize that he has really gone back in time, since he checks a newspaper heading to confirm the date as November 5, 1955. Though he again insists to himself, "This has gotta be a dream," he sets out to do something about it. His actions quickly instigate two patterns that will determine the shape of the rest of the narrative. First, he conceives what will develop into one of his main goals: he sets out to find Doc and get help. Initially this plan is vague, but once he locates his friend, the two concoct the specific long-range goals that they will pursue throughout the rest of the plot's 1955 portion. Finding Doc's name and address in a phone book in the malt shop, Marty tries unsuccessfully to call him.

This delay deflects his actions into the second major pattern: Marty begins to change history. Sitting in the malt shop, he encounters his father, whose humiliation at Biff's hands confirms that his traits are no different than in 1985. At the same time Marty sees Goldie Wilson, who is working as a janitor. Goldie urges George to stick up for himself, adding that he himself attends night school and will eventually become somebody important. Marty interjects, "Yeah, he's going to be mayor," and Goldie is delighted with the idea. Possibly Goldie would have decided to run for mayor without Marty's suggestion, but more likely Marty's trip into the past has now changed history. Goldie's assertiveness also jibes with Doc's typical advice ("If you put your mind to it . . ."). Much later George's unpredictable ability to stand up to Biff will not only save but also improve his future family. The scene ends as Marty runs after the departed George, yelling, "Hey, you on the bike!"

This line acts as a dialogue hook into the next scene, which takes place a short time later in a residential area. Spotting the bike, Marty pushes George out of the path of a car and is struck by it himself. Now Marty has demonstrably changed history, though he does not immediately realize the implications of his action. George's smarmy action of spying on Lorraine undressing plus his cowardly departure after Marty saves him reinforce the negative character traits already established for him. Indeed, the more we see of George in the past, the more plausible it is that his traits have caused Lorraine to become the embittered frump introduced during the setup.

As Marty wakes up in a darkened bedroom, he again assumes that he has been dreaming, the third mention of this motif since the trip back in time. The scene with Lorraine quickly reestablishes that he is actually in 1955. Her aggressive flirtatiousness is redundantly emphasized, since the implication is that she was the one who undressed him and read the "Calvin Klein" label on his underwear. When Lorraine's mother calls near the end of the scene, she reacts in a panic, "Quick! Put your pants back on!" and flees. The fact that she is so different from her 1985 self, while George seems much the same, again confirms that his failings have led to her decline after their marriage.

The subsequent lengthy comic scene over dinner serves primarily to establish that Lorraine has become romantically interested in Marty, which blocks her becoming attached to George. It also creates another dangling cause, however, when Marty gets directions to Doc's house. (His failure to know its location is motivated in this scene, since Riverside Drive has subsequently been changed to John F. Kennedy Drive.) The science fiction motif returns as the new TV plays the same "Honeymooners" episode that Marty's family had watched, and Marty identifies it as one in which the Jackie Gleason character dresses as a spaceman.

Disconcerted by Lorraine's suggestive invitation that he stay the night in her room, Marty flees to Doc's home. This turns out to be a large house and lawn, with an expensive car parked outside—recalling again that Doc spent his entire "family fortune" on the time machine (and motivating his whimsical decision to make it from a Delorean). As Doc tries his absurd mind-reading machine, Marty describes his plight and states his main goal: "Now I need your help to get back to the year 1985." Doc dismisses this at first, but as he removes the mind-reading helmet, a small bandage on his forehead becomes visible. He emphasizes the bandage by putting his hand to his head as he ponders: "Time machine. I haven't invented any time machine." We know from his lines late in the setup that he got the idea for the flux capacitor when he fell in the bathroom. Still trying to convince Doc of his origins in the future, Marty shows a photo of himself and his siblings, with his sister wearing a 1985 high school shirt. Doc assumes it is faked, pointing out that his brother's hair is missing. This minor flaw becomes another dangling cause, later serving as a gauge of Marty's family's increasingly uncertain future.

Finally Marty describes the scene of Doc falling and getting the idea for the flux capacitor, "which is what makes time travel possible." His line creates a dialogue hook into the next scene, as Doc and Marty visit the time machine and Doc finally is convinced: "It works! I finally invent something that works!" This is the third time that Marty has changed history. Doc does not seem to know what use the flux capacitor that he has just drawn could have, so it is not clear that he would have invented the time machine without Marty's visit. (The other inventions we have seen are either crackpot failures, such as the "mind-reading" machine, or mere gadgets, like the dog food dispenser in the opening.) Yet of course Marty could not be in 1955 had Doc not invented a successful time machine after 1955. Marty's provision of the information Doc needs to invent the time machine creates a contradictory causality.[4]

Once he accepts that Marty has come from the future, Doc adopts his goal: "We've gotta get you home." Back at Doc's house, the tape reveals to him the necessity for 1.2 gigawatts of electricity, and the pair realize that the trip back to 1985 can occur only when the bolt of lightning strikes the clock tower. (As Marty holds the flyer up so that Doc can read Jennifer's scrawled message, "I love you," the "Save the Clock Tower" slogan is visible to the audience.) This sets up a critically precise deadline as Doc declares: "Next Saturday night we're sending you back to the future!" Here Doc introduces the idea that Marty must stay in the house and avoid making any contacts that would have "serious repercussions on future events." Later on, Doc will raise the stakes, claiming that such changes could have cosmic effects on the "space-time continuum." (In practice, he and others seem perfectly willing to play fast and loose with the space-time continuum when it suits their purposes, and the very phrase comes to be a comic motif in the other two films.)

In the meantime, however, Doc realizes that the photograph of Marty and his brother and sister is beginning to fade, indicating that Marty's action of saving George has changed history in the wrong way: eliminating the three children by preventing their parents' marriage. The photograph serves as a link into the scene at the high school, since that scene begins as Doc explains to Marty that his brother, his sister, and he will disappear in turn unless George and Lorraine can be successfully brought together. Logically there is no reason why the three figures should gradually disappear from the photo, literally limb by limb. They might more plausibly vanish immediately or fade overall, like superimposed ghosts (as Marty's own body begins to do when George and Lorraine nearly fail to kiss at the dance). The photo device, however, generates suspense by letting us easily gauge the looming deadline of the dance.

In the scene at the high school, Doc further realizes that Lorraine has no interest in George but is all too fascinated with Marty. Doc tells Marty to get Lorraine and George together for a date and suggests the upcoming "Enchantment under the Sea" dance prominently advertised in the hallway. Marty's realization that that event was where his parents had originally fallen in love specifies his goal in the romantic line of action, and the scene ends with Doc ordering Marty: "You stick to your father like glue and make sure he takes her to the dance." This acts as a dialogue hook into the next scene, when Marty talks with his father in the school cafeteria.

By the end of this scene, which closes the complicating action, Marty and Doc have formulated specific goals for the two major lines of action: to bring Marty's parents together and to return him to 1985. The second portion of *Back to the Future* perfectly exemplifies one common pattern in classical complicating-action segments, in that it has thoroughly reversed the situation as it existed at the end of the setup. There Doc intended to depart into the future, but instead Marty travels into the past. Marty had declared to Strickland that history would change—implicitly for the better and in the future. Instead he has changed past events in such a way as to wipe out his family's existence. Now his goal is simply to restore things as they were when the narrative began.

DEVELOPMENT: "I'M YOUR DENSITY"

In the next scene, Marty is amazed to find George in the school cafeteria writing science fiction stories: "I didn't know you did anything creative." Their dialogue functions in part to make the motif of space travel far more central to the narrative's action. This motif had begun rather inconspicuously when Marty's family watched the "Honeymooners" episode on TV, one which is later revealed to involve Ralph Kramden dressing as a spaceman. It intensified when Marty, dressed in his radiation suit, was mistaken for a spaceman by farmer Peabody's family upon his arrival in 1955. It had come up again when Marty watched the "Honeymooners" episode with Lorraine's family. The motif will become bound up with George's change of character between 1955 and 1985.

What is just as important, this scene in the cafeteria establishes that writing science fiction is to George what performing rock-and-roll music is to Marty. Both Marty and George are creative, but both are also afraid to risk rejection by showing their work to others. Earlier Jennifer had urged Marty to send in a tape to a record company, and Marty's response was: "What if I send in the tape and they don't like it? I mean, what if they say I'm no good. What if they say, 'Get outta here, kid, you've got no future.' I mean, I just don't think I could take that kind of rejection. Jesus! I'm starting to sound like my old man." Thus Marty's earlier reluctance to pursue his dreams had been linked to his father's reputation as a slacker. George's speech refusing to let people read his stories is similar: "Well, what if they didn't like them? What if they told me I was no good?" Marty reluctantly recognizes the parallel between himself and his father in this scene. This moment sets up the possibility that George has the potential to be something other than a failure. That is the real change in history that Marty wants to accomplish, though he does so by accident.

There is one central difference between the two speeches, however. It is not until Marty urges his father to ask Lorraine to the dance that George, though visibly tempted, echoes Marty's earlier line: "What if she said 'no'? I don't know if I could take that kind of a rejection." George's fear of rejection comes in the romantic line of action, and that fear will jeopardize the existence of Marty and the rest of the family. Marty seemingly has no such temerity when it comes to his romance with Jennifer, but his lack of gumption in his other interests threatens to turn him into the traditional McFly slacker. His realization in this scene that his father shares his own problems makes it possible for him to devise ways to force George to change. Indeed, the moment when George kisses Lorraine will happen at the same time that Marty has his own big success playing with a professional 1950s band.

The scene continues as the two witness Biff manhandling Lorraine and making crude sexual suggestions. Marty's challenge in getting George to shape up becomes clear as the latter disappears and Marty is left to confront Biff. Eventually Marty will attempt to stage-manage a similar scene in which he parks with Lorraine at the dance and allows George to rescue her from his presumably unwelcome advances. At that point Biff will step in to carry through the threats he made in this scene, and George will finally come to Lorraine's defense.

That final triumph will not take place, however, until the climax. The development section of *Back to the Future* follows a classic pattern of postponement, as Marty encounters greater obstacles that delay him in achieving the goal of bringing his parents together at the dance. George resists asking Lorraine to the dance, and Lorraine becomes less likely to accept as her infatuation with Marty grows. During this portion of the film, his chances of getting back to the future also look dim as Doc's arrangements for the time machine's trip falter.

George's disappearance provides a simple dangling cause that is picked up immediately in the next scene as Marty confronts George in front of his house. Again he urges his father to ask Lorraine to the dance. Up to now the signs of George's interest in Lorraine have been dubious at best. When rescued by Marty from being hit by Lorraine's father's car, he had been spying on her undressing in her bedroom. Although he had tentatively tried to talk to Lorraine when Marty introduced them in the high school corridor at the end of the complicating action and had eyed her in the school cafeteria in the following scene, George had shown little serious interest in her. Now George refuses to ask Lorraine to the dance, saying he does not want to miss "Science Fiction Theater." He stymies Marty's goal by declaring firmly, "Look, I'm just not ready to ask Lorraine out to the dance, and not you nor anyone else on this planet is gonna make me change my mind." The science fiction motif coalesces here as Marty pulls out the photo, now showing his brother invisible down to his knees, and mutters, "Science Fiction Theater."

This dialogue hook leads into Marty's nocturnal appearance in George's bedroom. He claims to be Darth Vader, "an extraterrestrial from the planet Vulcan." The scene breaks off before Marty actually threatens George, thus combining with the following scene to emphasize this action's central role in the plot. This is the moment which Marty hopes will counterbalance his inadvertent interference in history when he rescued his father in the car accident. Here he combines his own interest in hard rock with his father's fascination with science fiction to motivate George to ask Lorraine to the dance.

Marty's night visit acts as a dangling cause picked up immediately in the next scene in the town square, where he meets George. As the scene begins, two children on soap-box scooters are seen in the background, setting them up for Marty's epic "skateboard" escape from Biff's gang. George joins Marty and says he wants to take Lorraine to the dance. During this scene Marty buys a bottle of Pepsi from a machine and tries to twist the top off manually. George's gesture of showing him how to use the dispenser's opener is a small gag, but it marks the first time that George is more competent than Marty. He reveals, "Last night Darth Vader came down from planet Vulcan and told me that if I didn't take Lorraine out that he'd melt my brain." Thus his motivation is not love for Lorraine but the same kind of submission that makes him a slacker. Marty cannot make George attractive to Lorraine. He will try to fake such attraction with the staged "rescue" scene, but George must actually change his traits in order to change history for the better.

The scene in the malt shop does provide some sparse motivation for George and Lorraine's eventual love. Prompted by Marty, George awkwardly tells Lorraine, "I'm your density." When he manages to correct this with, "I mean—destiny," he seems to relax and smile sincerely at her. Lorraine returns his smile briefly. This moment of attraction is interrupted by Biff's threats, Marty's defense of George, and his spectacular escape via the lengthy chase around the square. The chase delays any actual progress in the causal action, and thus it is typical of the way development sections often function in classical films. The chase ends with Biff's car under a load of manure, providing him with a goal that threatens Marty: "I'm gonna get that son of a bitch!" Similarly, Lorraine is thrilled by Marty's antics and, when asked where Marty lives, declares, "I don't know . . . but I'm gonna find out." Her renewed fascination with Marty and consequent indifference to George form a major obstacle to the romance plotline.

The next scene returns to the time-machine plot, as Marty goes back to Doc's place to find his friend watching the footage of the Libyan attack. Doc refuses to hear Marty's explanation, declaring: "No man should know too much about his own destiny." Knowing about his own future could cause Doc to endanger his "own existence." Marty initially agrees, but the moment remains as a dangling cause that will motivate Marty's third goal of trying to save Doc by warning him about the Libyan attack.

The scene continues as Doc demonstrates his plan to send Marty and the time machine to 1985. His three-dimensional model previews how the operation will work, reiterating when and where the lightning will strike and introducing the new hook-and-wire system running into the flux capacitor. The scene also sets up some suspense concerning whether Doc is capable of accomplishing such an elaborate affair, since his toy car catches fire while enacting the planned maneuver. (The fire also suggests how Doc's house may eventually have been destroyed, presumably in another experiment gone awry.)

Lorraine's unexpected appearance at Doc's house provides the final premise needed to resolve the romantic plotline. Nervously she admits to having followed Marty to Doc's house, thus picking up the dangling cause of her statement that she would find out where he lives. She pressures him to ask her to the dance (the reverse of the prudishness about girls phoning boys that the middle-aged Lorraine had expressed in the setup). Marty mentions George, and she describes both her attraction to and rejection of her future husband: "George McFly? Oh, he's kind of cute and all, but not, well, I think a man should be strong, so he can stand up for himself and protect the woman he loves. Don't you?" Having stood up to Biff in the malt shop, Marty placed himself firmly in the position of Lorraine's defender. Despite Doc's shocked disapproval, he ends by agreeing with her and hence implicitly commits himself to taking her to the dance.

This dangling cause is picked up instantly in a scene between Marty and George as the latter hangs up laundry in his back yard: "How am I supposed to go to the dance with her if she's already going to the dance with you?" Marty replies, "She *wants* to go with you—she just doesn't know it yet. That's why we've gotta show her that you're a fighter." Marty sets up an appointment with George for 9:00 on the same Saturday night when he has his 10:04 deadline to travel back to the future. That tight schedule will generate suspense during the climax portion of the film as Marty waits around until the big kiss takes place and thus nearly misses the crucial bolt of lightning. The scene also provides another small clue that George may be genuinely attracted to Lorraine, since he reacts jealously to the idea that Marty will paw Lorraine as part of the lead-up to the "rescue."

The final scene of the development reveals that Marty has conceived a new goal. Picking up on the dangling cause from the scene of Doc watching the Libyan attack on videotape, Marty writes him a letter warning of the attack. Despite Doc's wish not to know his future, Marty's affection for his friend has clearly made him decide to risk the consequences of telling him. He slips the letter into Doc's pocket, thus creating another dangling cause that will eventually save Doc's life. This is the last causally important premise introduced into the film. (Other new premises relate solely to the comic by-play concerning Marty's performance with the Marvin Berry band.) From this point on, Doc and Marty will work swiftly toward accomplishing their goals in the climax portion. The development is distinctly shorter than the other three large-scale portions (which are well balanced against each other), primarily because of the fact that it is unnecessary for us to see many of Doc's preparations for Marty's return trip in the time machine.

CLIMAX AND EPILOGUE: "A MATCH MADE IN SPACE"

Up to this point, the film has been able to maintain a strong temporal, spatial, and causal comprehensibility from scene to scene partly because Marty is almost continually present. Now, with both of the main goals being achieved simultaneously, the film begins to move back and forth between Doc preparing the equipment for Marty's trip to 1985 and Marty trying to get his parents to kiss at the dance. Given that the entire action up to Marty's successful trip into the future takes place on the Saturday night of the redundantly established deadline, the temporal relations are transparent. We are already very familiar with the high school and town square settings, so these provide spatial coherence. Finally, the entire development section has been devoted to explaining Doc and Marty's schemes for accomplishing their goals. Hence occasional departures from our lengthy attachment to Marty have no effect on the action's clarity.

The climax begins with a track-back from a drum labeled "Marvin Berry and the Starlighters," then a pan across the dance floor. Thus the time is established as Saturday night, with the 9:00 appointment and the 10:04 deadline looming large. Marty arrives with Lorraine, having borrowed Doc's car in order to stage the "rescue" scene. (This creates yet another neat parallel, since the solutions of both of Marty's problems involve expensive cars owned by Doc.) Lorraine further confirms her somewhat wild traits by readily agreeing to park with Marty, then pulling out liquor and cigarettes. The film skirts the issue of incest, however, as Lorraine kisses Marty and declares: "This is all wrong. I don't know what it is—but when I kiss you, it's like I'm kissing . . . my brother." Marty says this makes sense, but it does not on the literal level. The scene is rather like the one I have already examined in *Tootsie* where Julie says that paradoxically her friendship with Dorothy has made her feel lonely; somehow she senses that Dorothy is really a man, and she longs for him without realizing it. This notion of characters having some sort of sixth sense about things like gender is a common Hollywood convention and hence needs no additional motivation within the plot.

Biff's surprise appearance in place of George was motivated at the end of the chase scene when he declared that he would "get" Marty. Coming to carry out his threat, he discovers Lorraine and leaves Marty to his gang in order to carry through his earlier taunts about forcing himself upon Lorraine. George's successful rescue of Lorraine implies that some long-suppressed strength of character surfaces when he sees her being pushed to the ground by Biff. Lorraine's dazzled expression suggests that she has found the protector she thought she had in Marty. A neat parallel underlines how Marty has actually managed to change George's character. Initially George was a passive sexual victimizer, peeping from a tree through a window as Lorraine undressed. Marty had caused him to fall into the street in front of a car and then pushed him out of the way and was hit himself. Later, George looks through the car window and sees what he assumes are Marty and Lorraine tussling. Once the door is opened, he is confronted with Biff trying to rape Lorraine, and he saves her from this far worse sexual victimization. George's character growth and Lorraine's acceptance of him as her new date seem to draw that line of action to a close.

Marty, however, now finds that his sister has half-disappeared from the photo and realizes that his problem remains unsolved. A cut to Doc waiting impatiently near the clock tower reveals that the time is now 9:36, ratcheting up the suspense. The action returns to Marty, who is urging the band to play. The rescue *and* the kiss are the key to George and Lorraine's falling in love, and Marty has budgeted too little time. (Once the epilogue reveals Marty's improved family, we can realize that in a complex way the kiss restores history and the rescue changes it.) One band member declares, "Hey, man, the dance is over unless you know somebody else that can play the guitar."

This dialogue hook covers an ellipsis to a new scene of Marty onstage with the band. The guitarist announces a song that continues the space travel theme, "Earth Angel," which in turn prefigures George's science fiction novel, *A Match Made in Space*. The dance injects a bit of additional suspense, as George seems to back down when a rowdy boy attempts to cut in. Marty notices that his image is nearly gone from the photo, and he himself even begins to fade. After faltering, however, George pushes the bully away and proves that his character change is complete. The kiss resolves the parental-romance line of action.

Marty's exultation apparently makes him forget his big deadline, now less than half an hour away, and he agrees to stay on for another song. His singing of "Johnny Be Good" primarily functions to delay the action and create a few comic contrasts between the musical tastes of 1955 and 1985. Marvin Berry's call to his cousin Chuck constitutes the film's sole suggestion that Marty's actions could change real, extradiegetic history. The result is the same paradoxical causality introduced earlier with the invention of the time machine.

Marty knows the song from 1985 because Chuck Berry had written it; now Berry presumably writes the song because he hears Marty sing it. The result is to reinforce the idea that in this particular narrative world, such circular causality can exist. Indeed, a third instance soon occurs, as Lorraine comments on what a nice name "Marty" is, implying that she later calls her son that as a result. The "Johnny Be Good" number also helps to indicate that Lorraine's infatuation with Marty is over—as was already strongly suggested by her reaction to kissing him. Despite the fact that the students admire Marty's rendition of "Earth Angel" (and hence Lorraine might once again consider him a "dreamboat"), they find his punkish cadenzas at the end of the second number too loud and strange. Lorraine's hesitant compliment, "Marty, that was very interesting music," confirms her transfer of affection to George.

Marty's departure links to the next scene as he arrives at the town square at 9:55. Describing George's great punch, Marty adds, "I didn't know he had it in him. He's never stood up to Biff in his life." Doc responds, "Never?" and Marty replies, "No, why, what's the matter?" Doc abstractedly dismisses the subject with a wave of his arms, but the implications of this brief exchange can be teased out. Marty assumes that when he returns to 1985, he will be in the old situation of Biff bullying George, who will be incapable of standing up to him. Yet Doc realizes that from the vantage point of 1985, George has stood up to Biff once, and hence he may suspect that the future Marty is about to return to will be different. Thus history has changed, motivating the epilogue's surprise revelation of the new, improved McFly family. The moment slides by, however, since Doc is too distracted to speculate on the implications of his question. Instead, the emphasis is solely on the restoration of history to its original status, with Doc staring at the photo of the three siblings throughout this dialogue.

Doc reiterates and specifies the deadline, now seven minutes and 22 seconds away. At this point he tears up the note about the Libyans' attack, and a broken branch that detaches the cable draws Doc away from hearing Marty's attempt to warn him verbally. Marty determines to make another attempt to achieve his third goal of saving Doc, and he sets his arrival time in 1985 for ten minutes before the Libyan attack. This is logical, in that Marty has changed his own family's history in the relatively distant past in 1955, and thus he should be able to do the same kind of thing in the recent past of 1985. The problem turns out to be that his arrival in 1985 occurs at the town square, not the shopping mall—redundantly established as far out on the edge of town.

Once Marty arrives in 1985 at 1:24, he cannot start the time machine again to drive out to the mall—a failure motivated in the first 1955 segment when the car also would not start. Rather implausibly, he manages to run after the Libyans' van all the way to the edge of town by 1:33, just in time to witness Doc's death and his own original departure to 1955. (Oddly, the narrative does not include him taking his skateboard into the past, in which case he could have it with him now.) Doc's revelation that he taped Marty's warning letter back together and thus knew to wear a bulletproof vest leads Marty to ask, "What about all that talk about screwing up future events—the space-time continuum?" Doc's casual reply, "Well, I figure, what the hell?" brings the climax portion to a close. All three of Marty's goals are accomplished: his own existence and that of his siblings have been restored, he has returned to the future, and he has prevented Doc's death.

The unusually long epilogue[5] begins with a close view of the clock that shows it reading 10:28, then tilts down to reveal Marty asleep. He lies in the same position as he had near the end of the setup, before Doc had originally called to remind him of their appointment. Now, upon waking, he comments, "What a nightmare!" At this point there does seem to be a serious possibility that all the events beginning with that phone call have been a dream; the film is close enough to being over that some such trick of narration might reasonably occur. Moreover, the decor in Marty's room has not changed, and he is wearing the same clothes as on the night he went back in time. Only as he discovers his family's transformation do we receive confirmation that the time-travel action was no dream.

Despite the fact that the rest of the house and the family have been transformed, Marty remains the same as before his trip—except for his new ownership of the Toyota pickup he had so desired. This seems to confirm that Marty was basically a nice kid to begin with, rescued from his family's general slackerdom by his relationships with Doc and Jennifer. Indeed, with the sister now working at a boutique and juggling several boyfriends and the brother dressing for success at his office job, Marty has become less respectable than they—a typical teenage kid brother. ("What, did you sleep in your clothes again last night?")

Our natural assumption that this transformation dates back to the events of the school dance is corroborated when a servile Biff, reduced to running a small car-maintenance business, lies to George about how many coats of wax he has applied. George reprimands him and comments that Biff is "always trying to get away with something" and has been that way since high school.

Given that one thing he had tried to get away with was raping Lorraine, the couple's amusedly indulgent attitude is a bit strange. Still, the reversal in George's and Biff's positions is so extreme as to suggest that they can afford to be magnanimous.

After this surprise epilogue, the film provides another twist as Doc returns to fetch Marty and Jennifer into the future. When Marty inquires, "What happens to us in the future? Do we become assholes or something?" Doc answers, "No, no, no, no, Marty! Both you and Jennifer turn out fine. It's your kids, Marty, something's gotta be done about your kids!" This line makes for a cute ending and might have been fine had there been no sequel. The scriptwriters probably were not sure that there would be one, given that the film's enormous success was unexpected. (The title "To be continued . . ." did not appear on prints at the film's initial release.) One might be tempted to wonder why, if Marty and Jennifer turn out so well, Doc does not simply enlist their adult selves' help in the future—unless perhaps the problem is so awful that the 17-year-old Marty and Jennifer must work alongside their 47-year-old selves to solve it. In practice, the script for the sequel opted for contradicting Doc's words, making Jennifer and Marty turn out badly and thus creating a new family of McFly slackers in 2015.

A FINAL LESSON: EXPOSITION IS OUR FRIEND

Back to the Future contradicts a myth which has grown up in recent years and which may actually have contributed to the decline in quality of Hollywood films of the mid-1990s. With today's stress on fast-moving action, some practitioners seem to have decided that exposition is innately bad and should be minimized.

An older script manual, Eugene Vale's *The Technique of Screenplay Writing*, written in 1944 and revised in 1972, takes a fairly neutral view of exposition early in the film: "It is no easy task to supply all the primary information without becoming slow or boring. By the successful solution of this problem one can recognize the experienced writer."[6] More recently, however, the approach seems to be not to solve the "problem" but to sidestep it by not including much exposition. Lew Hunter's manual revises the Fieldian model of a half-hour setup, insisting instead that the first large-scale portion of the film should end on page 17: "A frequent problem with new writers is their jamming much of their information up front in screenplays. Then the Act One ends at page 35 rather than 17. The audience reading your script will be asleep by then. They want to know the situation much earlier." He adds this remarkable piece of advice: "The story starts at the point where nothing before is needed. Don't 'set up' the action. Start with the story in motion."[7]

Starting *in medias res* is certainly appropriate for some films, as *Terminator 2: Judgment Day* amply demonstrates. There are many films, however, that manage to utilize straightforward exposition for long stretches of their openings and to do so in an entertaining way. One need only watch some of the classic studio-era films, such as *The Little Foxes* (1941) or *The Shop Around the Corner* (1940), to see how sophisticated and fascinating good exposition can be. The setup of *The Shop Around the Corner* runs a mere 17.5 minutes of a 98-minute film (Hunter's ideal!), not because little information is given, but rather because Ernst Lubitsch and Samson Raphaelson are so virtuosic at rapidly introducing us to the characters and their traits.

In *Back to the Future*, the entire setup, which lasts nearly 28 minutes, is essentially exposition. By the time Marty arrives for his appointment with Doc at the mall, he has not conceived either of the major goals that will shape the rest of the narrative, and hence of course he has not made one jot of progress toward achieving them. His vague goal that "history is gonna change" has so far not led to anything. Yet that first half hour hardly bores the audience. Screenwriting adviser Linda Seger rightly points out that the same thing is true of *Tootsie*:

> *Tootsie* also has a situational beginning. We know that Michael is an out-of-work actor. We know he is difficult to work with. We know he's a good actor. We know that no one will hire him because of his attitude. And we know that there is a job available on a soap opera—for a woman. It takes almost the entire first act to build this information, but by the end of the action we're oriented, and the story is ready to unfold.[8]

Again, I think few would be bored during *Tootsie*'s setup.

The screenwriter William Goldman's classic memoirs contain a telling anecdote about a revision he made for *Harper* (1966). The original script began with a car pulling up to an old mansion, presumably a standard *in medias res* opening. The studio asked him to add a sequence to run under the credits. He reluctantly devised a montage of expository bits revealing something of Harper's personality. A little gag about him making bad coffee from yesterday's grounds provoked laughter from audiences. Goldman concludes, "The audience certainly knew a lot more about him than the way the movie originally opened." He realized in retrospect that the gag set them up to like both the character and the movie.[9]

More recently, an expository credits sequence had to be added to *To Die For* (1995):

> After test audiences drew a blank about *To Die For*'s plot, Pablo Ferro whipped up a witty montage of fictional tabloid headlines and stories that quickly established Nicole Kidman's character. "They needed to find out who she was before they met her," he says. . . . "I'm able to tell a 10-minute story in a minute," he says, explaining why directors entrust him with valuable screen time. "It would take them weeks and years to do that."[10]

Given the lack of exposition in many recent films, it is no wonder that such doctoring proves necessary. After viewing *Men in Black* (1997), I left wondering if its makers had filmed from the treatment and skipped fleshing it out into a full script. The film gets by on the witty repartee between the Tommy Lee Jones and Will Smith characters, but there is virtually no backstory provided on them that could give the narrative more substance. We get no sense of why Will Smith would be willing to cut himself off from his current life to take the alien-hunting job. Similarly, the last scenes of *Liar Liar* (1997) ring so untrue because the film basically exists only to exploit its one clever premise; it does not bother with filling out the characters. The clever premise of *The Truman Show* (1998) is considerably vitiated by a lack of exposition. We have not learned about any of the hero's eccentric, engaging traits that might lead a vast audience to watch his entire life on television. In a much later scene, technicians spying as he fantasizes by drawing a "spaceman helmet" in soap on his mirror comment that he is back to his usual self, yet we never got a sense of that Walter Mittyish side of his nature to begin with. Rather, the foul-ups that lead to Truman's discovery of the broadcast of his life begin almost immediately, with the lamp falling from the sky (leading in turn to questions as to why such mistakes suddenly multiply, when apparently they have not happened for the thirty years of "The Truman Show" already aired). A run-through of a typical day in Truman's life (comparable to the first February 2 in *Groundhog Day*) would have provided a far firmer foundation for the film.

Skillful Hollywood filmmaking does not sacrifice complexity and clarity in order to get the plot's action rolling faster. Subtle exposition is still valued, as Todd McCarthy's review of *The Horse Whisperer* (1998) suggests: "Redford displays great intensity and concentration in his direction, abetted by an agile shorthand in the service of character revelation that deftly skirts any obvious exposition."[11] We will return to this issue in Chapter 8, when looking at the recent phenomenon of stacked-up climaxes. Good exposition, hard though it may be to write, is not boring.

4

The Silence of the Lambs

1990. Released by Orion. Directed by Jonathan Demme. Screenplay by Ted Tally from Thomas Harris's novel. Running time: 118 minutes; setup, 26.5; complicating action, 32.5; development, 27.5; climax and epilogue, 31 (epilogue alone, 8).

TRANSFORMATIONS: PROTAGONIST STARLING AND HER TWO ANTAGONISTS

The Silence of the Lambs may at first glance present a challenge to the classification I am using to group my analyses. Clarice Starling is clearly the protagonist, and Jame Gumb (a.k.a. Buffalo Bill) is the most obvious antagonist—the horrific killer whom Clarice must track down. But what of Hannibal Lecter? Is he the real, more menacing antagonist? Or might he, perversely, be a dual or parallel protagonist alongside Clarice? After all, one of the conventions of the cop/detective genre is an emphasis on the similarities between the hero and the villain, as in the Clint Eastwood film *Tightrope* (1984) and the first Hannibal Lecter film, *Manhunter* (1986), from Thomas Harris's novel *Red Dragon*. Does *Silence* simply represent one further step in that direction? Lecter is certainly important enough that one could imagine a sequel with him as the main character and with Clarice entirely absent.

It is particularly tempting to see Lecter as a sort of parallel protagonist. After all, he pursues a separate, major goal that is not opposed to Clarice's. Having spent eight years in his windowless cell, he declares: "What I want is a view." And he achieves his goal by escaping. As I mentioned in the opening chapter, in cases of parallel protagonists, one character may harbor a fascination with the other, spying on and pursuing the counterpart. We quickly realize that Lecter takes a prurient interest in both Clarice and Buffalo Bill and is getting vicarious thrills from exploiting both sides of the case. He questions Clarice about the most traumatic experiences of her past: the murder of her father and her attempt to rescue one of the spring lambs that were being slaughtered on the ranch where she lived. Thus during their brief exchanges of information, Lecter skillfully elicits from Clarice the stories of two deaths that affected her mightily.

The power of the scenes between Lecter and Clarice, with the intense acting by Anthony Hopkins and Jodie Foster and the subtle variations of the shot/reverse shots nearly or directly into the lens, suggests a rapport between the two. That rapport might seem to imply that they are in some strange way alike. Yet this, I think, is not the case.

Lecter, after all, has another, equally perverse, fascination. He also uses Clarice to obtain Buffalo Bill's case files so that he can view the grisly details of the serial killings. Such files presumably include the same graphic photos of partially skinned women that we see on Crawford's office walls. The narration de-emphasizes this grim aspect of Lecter's activities by only showing Lecter poring over some official-looking forms and giving Clarice her vital clue via a note on a map—rather than, say, scrawling the information on a photo of a butchered body. Playing down Lecter's fascination with the most awful aspects of the case has at least two effects. It makes him a more ambiguous and compelling character, one to whom Clarice can plausibly relate,[1] and it renders the one big scene of his violence all the more shocking.

Ultimately, however, Lecter is not parallel to Clarice. She understands him not because she is in any way like him but because she is smart and desperate and inquiring. She uses his fascination with her to elicit clues concerning Bill. In the end, Lecter essentially takes Buffalo Bill's place. Viewers, of course, assumed that the ending is a setup for a sequel (almost an inevitability since the surprise 1999 publication of *Hannibal*—which conveniently sets its action years after that of *Silence*). Ideally the second film would pit Clarice against Lecter, and hence he would become the true and main antagonist.

In effect, what we have in *Silence* is a rare case of a film with parallel *antagonists*. There is one clear-cut protagonist, Clarice Starling, but she faces two opponents. Jame Gumb is the obvious villain, the subject of Clarice's search. Through much of the film Lecter simply leads a vicarious existence as a serial killer, studying Gumb from a distance. As happens in many parallel-protagonist films, Lecter in a sense aspires to become the character he spies upon—and he succeeds. This parallel-antagonist notion was the contribution of novelist Harris. By making Hannibal Lecter an incarcerated serial killer who manipulates ongoing investigations of other such killers, Harris created a distinctive twist on the usual cop/crook parallels.

The parallelism between Lecter and Gumb is worked out in a set of contrasts that are difficult to appreciate fully on first viewing the film. Again we have an example of a Hollywood film providing redundant narrative threads in a virtuosic fashion, creating both large-scale and fine-grained levels of unity. In *Silence*, the overall trajectory of Lecter's fortunes is a remarkably precise reversal of the trajectory of Gumb's.

Gumb has progressively isolated himself from the world. There is a hint that he has at some point been in the Far East. True, the fact that he is obsessed with a rare breed of moth from Suriname would not necessarily imply that he had been there. But when he kidnaps Catherine Martin, he is wearing a tacky Japanese souvenir jacket that might suggest that he had traveled in Asia. (As a soldier in Vietnam? The right-wing patriotic paraphernalia in his cellar may evoke Hollywood's stereotype of the crazed veteran.) Later Gumb has apparently lived, at least briefly, in two cities. Gumb's single indirect brush with Lecter came when he was in Baltimore, where Lecter had practiced psychiatry. Gumb murdered his lover, Benjamin Raspel, a patient of Lecter's; Lecter put the body in the Your Self Storage garage. Perhaps Gumb was in Baltimore in part in the hope of getting a sex-change operation at Johns Hopkins, the medical center that provides the FBI with Jame Gumb's real name. Gumb later apparently moved (though this is not made entirely clear in the film) to a suburb of Chicago. Crawford gets the address in Calumet City from the customs bureau, which had stopped a shipment of the death's-head moths headed to Gumb. That address turns out to be out of date. Gumb had moved two years earlier to Belvedere, Ohio, and bought a house, isolating himself in the cellar. He has blocked off the windows and adorned the rooms with pictures and other material. He goes about his business to blaring rock music. Thus Gumb apparently has moved from an exotic setting to various American cities and further to a hermetic small-town existence in a cellar.

Gumb's lair bears a distinct resemblance to Lecter's cell, with the latter's stone walls, decorative pictures, and lack of windows. Lecter also occasionally endures loud TV soundtracks piped in when Dr. Chilton wants to punish him. The picture upon which Clarice remarks is "the Duomo as seen from the Belvedere." Lecter's Belvedere is in Florence, not Ohio, and we may infer that he too used to travel to exotic, distant places.

This motif, used to compare and contrast Lecter and Gumb, is an example of the virtuosic, almost throwaway motifs that some Hollywood films contain.

The two mentions of "Belvedere" are in Harris's novel, but clearly the filmmakers have noticed, retained, and enhanced the motif by making Lecter's cell and Gumb's cellar visually similar. "Belvedere" is Italian for "beautiful view," the very thing that Lecter desires.[2]

Even though their current circumstances may be somewhat similar, the two men's goals diverge considerably. Gumb seems to have withdrawn into his fantasy world permanently. Lecter, on the other hand, wants the opposite—to get out of his cell at the very least, and ideally to travel once more to exotic places. In the end we see him on a Caribbean island, about to revenge himself on Dr. Chilton.

Thus the film's major parallel is between Lecter and Gumb. Clarice can exploit Lecter to catch her quarry, but she is not in any significant way like either man.[3] Even at the level of motifs, Clarice is associated with open spaces from the initial jogging sequence onward, and a bullet she fires in the cellar at the end breaks one of Gumb's blacked-out windows, letting sunlight into the room.

Lecter's escape and his move into the role of sole antagonist do contrast with the single most important structuring device in the narrative: Clarice's maturation into Special Agent Clarice M. Starling. We surely could not believe that the Clarice of the opening scenes could go up against Lecter and have any hope of winning. Yet by the end, we can imagine a sequel in which she would track Lecter down. And she might well win—or at least foil his plans, leaving him free for another sequel.

After all, Clarice almost does defeat Lecter in *Silence*, and quite early on at that. Just before the central turning point, she presents him with the supposed FBI offer of a transfer to a prison in New York State, with yearly vacations on Plum Island—which, he quickly notices, houses an animal-disease research site. It is clear in this scene that Lecter believes her—or at least, as Hopkins makes clear, that Lecter desperately wants to believe her—and he falls for the scheme. He reveals more information to her here than in any other scene: that Bill preys upon large women, that the moths signify transformation, and that Bill thinks he is a transsexual but really is not. These are not necessarily essential clues, but in general Lecter is quite communicative here, following through on his bargain.

The clue about transsexuality leads to the search at the main centers for sex-change operations: Johns Hopkins, the University of Minnesota, and Columbia Medical Center. That search ultimately provides a red herring, in that hospital records divert Crawford to the out-of-date address in Calumet City. Still, it also yields a name, Jame Gumb, the killer's real name (verifiable only in the end credits). All of Buffalo Bill's mentioned aliases use the initials J. G. (a clue that echoes Lecter's habitual anagrams). This may be one of the factors that help Clarice recognize that the man she meets as Jack Gordon is her quarry.

It is quite possible that if, in the next scene, Chilton had not told Lecter that the FBI's offer was a ruse, Lecter would have been completely taken in. Indeed, in his final meeting with Clarice, he mockingly compliments her on her part in the trick:

> *Lecter:* Anthrax Island. That was an especially nice touch, Clarice. Yours?
> *Clarice:* Yes.
> *Lecter:* Yes, that was *good.* Pity about poor Catherine, though. Tick tock, tick tock, tick tock, tick tock.

His line implies that Clarice's deception has destroyed their bargain and that he will not help her save Catherine. Yet later in the scene it turns out that all along he has at least provisionally decided to go on helping her. Even as he is mocking her, he has his final, vital clue written on the map, ready to turn over if she cooperates by telling him more about her past.

Clarice's maturation process takes place over a remarkably short time, but its speed is motivated by her intense determination to do whatever it takes to save Catherine. The brief scenes of her continuing her training give a sense of her dedication and, although she could not plausibly learn much about FBI procedure in just a few days, we assume she has been this conscientious all along. But the main sign of her growing competence is her increasing ability to deal with Lecter. During their first conversation, she is tense and nervous with him, awkwardly challenging him to turn his "high-powered vision" on himself. This does not work—but it is not really about Lecter's crimes that we need to learn.

Once his real purpose becomes apparent, however, Clarice learns to play his little games, as when she automatically assumes the name that Lecter gives Senator Martin is an anagram and works out the puzzle. During their final face-to-face conversation, Clarice is confident enough to mock him in turn: "Your anagrams are showing, Doctor. Louis Friend—iron sulfide, also known as fool's gold." Lecter proves to be a good teacher for Clarice—better perhaps even than Crawford, who follows Lecter's clues to the wrong house. The ultimate sign of her understanding of Lecter comes when, after his escape, she predicts that he will not try to kill her ("He'd consider that rude"). And sure enough, in their final phone conversation, Lecter gallantly confirms that "I have no plans to call on you, Clarice. The world's more interesting with you in it."

We have seen that Clarice is not parallel to Lecter in any significant way. She does, however, have other parallels within the film: the victims of the serial killer. Not that Clarice herself is a victim. I distinctly remember my reaction to the opening scene upon first seeing the film (knowing very little about it beyond its stars and director). Watching Jodie Foster jogging alone in a wood, accompanied by melancholy music, I assumed that this was the old "woman-in-danger" cliché. Fortunately, the film raises that expectation only to reverse it.[4]

Yet Clarice is from a background similar to that of the first victim, Frederica Bimmel—motherless from a young age (all of Frederica's photos show her with her father or friends), lower-middle-class, raised in a small, declining industrial town (West Virginia vs. Ohio). Clarice's ambition to escape this background has led her to try to shed her backwoods accent and to dress for success. That experience in turn allows her to realize that the corpse she examines, with its pierced ears and glitter nail polish, is not from the rural area where it was found: "Looks like town to me."

Such parallels do not, as I have emphasized, suggest that Clarice is a victim, despite her unpleasant encounters with Miggs, Lecter, and others. She is nervous with Lecter at first but soon gains confidence, and ultimately she manipulates him as much as he does her. Instead, her similarities to the two victims help motivate her ability to understand the circumstances of the case and thus to solve it. She accomplishes a breakthrough by chatting with Frederica's friend Stacey (dissatisfied, as Clarice had been, with small-town life); there she learns the address of the house Gumb now owns.

Moreover, the similarities between Clarice's background and those of the victims (and of Stacey) serve to emphasize once more Clarice's trajectory of maturation and achievement. The scene with Stacey begins with the girl asking Clarice, "Is that a good job, FBI agent? You get to travel around and stuff? I mean, better places than this?" Clarice's reaction is a little smile and a moment of thought before she replies simply, "Yeah, sometimes you do." The smile might be an ironic reflection on how much traveling she has done lately, but she also kindly tries not to flaunt the glamour of her own situation in comparison to Stacey's. Yet the little scene with Stacey gives us a succinct look at what life could be like for a Clarice Starling with less ambition and brains—thus emphasizing the enormity of what she is about to achieve. The course of her maturation helps structure the large-scale parts of the film itself.

The film's setup begins in a forest, with a title superimposed briefly in the lower right corner: "Woods near Quantico, Va." Graphically the letters look as if they could have come from a typewritten report. The narration presents expositional information succinctly and coolly; the suggestion is of objectivity and aloofness—a tone that contrasts sharply with the strong attachment we will soon develop to the heroine. Clarice appears, jogging through a training course.

Abruptly, an offscreen male voice hails her: "Starling! Starling!" A man who we later learn is her FBI instructor has come to summon her to the office of Jack Crawford, head of the Behavioral Science Services. The instructor's shout initiates a major motif of the film: variations of names that reflect Clarice's status. As she goes into the FBI building, she passes her roommate, Ardelia, who affectionately greets her as "Clarice." This exactly reverses the instructor's shout. Both the instructor and Ardelia are first heard speaking offscreen, and both immediately enter from foreground offscreen right. The man is gruff and impersonal (as he remains in his few subsequent scenes), the woman warm and supportive. This contrast sets up a mildly feminist motif that ultimately helps motivate Clarice and Ardelia's cooperation in solving Lecter's final puzzle. Indeed, Clarice will soon be established as liberal in her politics when Crawford remarks that she had grilled him on the FBI's "civil-rights record in the Hoover years." (In keeping with this trait, Clarice later successfully admonishes Crawford on being a role model to other law enforcement officers in gender matters.)[5]

The variants on naming continue when Crawford enters his office, saying "Starling, Clarice M." It sounds as if he is reciting the name from a file folder or an enrollment list—and indeed, we learn that she has taken his seminar. But he does not speak as abruptly as the instructor had. He smiles, apologizes to her ("Sorry to pull you off the course at such short notice"), shows that he remembers her, and praises her academic work. Thus Crawford is established as a compromise between the authoritative instructor and the warm-hearted Ardelia. This exchange motivates our later understanding of why he sends Clarice to interview Lecter. On the one hand, Crawford is simply using an attractive woman to try and intrigue Lecter into helping on the Buffalo Bill case. On the other, he recognizes Clarice's abilities, fostering and appreciating her efforts to solve the case.

Thus the beginning of the setup presents the protagonist as "Starling," then "Clarice," then "Starling, Clarice M." In contrast, the epilogue begins with a man at a podium, announcing: "Clarice M. Starling." Clarice steps up to receive her badge as a special agent at the graduation ceremony. By now she has achieved her two goals, to catch the serial killer and to become an FBI agent. The motif of names thus traces the progress of her growth. The epilogue begins with her full name, in correct order, being given for the only time in the film.

More is done with names. When Crawford first mentions Lecter to Clarice in the opening scene, she replies "Hannibal the Cannibal." In all her dealings with him, she calls him "Dr. Lecter" (and "Lecter" to others). The last significant line of dialogue comes in the epilogue, when Lecter telephones Clarice at her graduation. She stands in shock, repeating "Dr. Lecter, Dr. Lecter, Dr. Lecter, Dr. Lecter," into the dead phone line.

Lecter reverses the overall pattern by initially calling Clarice "Agent Starling"—a title he soon realizes she has not yet earned. Though he dismisses her at their first meeting as "little Starling," he later consistently calls her "Clarice" to her face. The only time Lecter calls Clarice anything other than that is when he refers to her as "Clarice Starling" in the conversation with Senator Martin at the Memphis airport. There he says, "Clarice Starling and that awful Jack Crawford have wasted far too much time already. I only pray they haven't doomed the poor girl." It is significant that he mentions Clarice first, whereas it would be more logical to place the main blame on Crawford, saying something like "that awful Jack Crawford and his minion Clarice Starling . . ." Here he mentions her first partly because he has begun to think of her as more important than Crawford, whom he hates, and partly because this phrase separates her from the "awful" epithet. Hence we get a clue that Lecter may plan to go on playing his quid pro quo game with her on the same terms, despite her attempt to trick him. The naming motif is emphasized by the fact that both of Lecter's anagrams are based on names.

Returning to the film's opening scene, we can see that the setup establishes Clarice's initial goal: to become an FBI agent. This goal is emphasized when Crawford mentions that Clarice wants to work in his own unit and she replies, "*Very* much. *Very* much." Her desire to become an agent will persist unchanged until it is achieved in the epilogue. The scene also establishes character traits that will be consistent and decisive. As she walks through the hallways of the FBI building toward Crawford's office, Clarice keeps looking from side to side, scanning everything that she passes. Thus one of our first impressions of her is that she is active, inquisitive, and attuned to her surroundings. Foster uses the same kinds of glances in Crawford's office and in every new environment Clarice encounters, thus motivating her final ability to pick up on small clues missed by other FBI agents.

During the scene in Crawford's office, we learn about the Buffalo Bill case briefly from clippings on Crawford's wall. These go by too quickly to give us much information, but we might catch the headline "FBI Links Skinning Murders But Finds No Pattern: Murder Across Three States." Clarice's discovery of a pattern in the killings (with considerable help from her unsung roommate Ardelia) will be what allows her to break the case. This early placement of newspaper clippings within the mise-en-scene (rather than in a separate montage sequence) in order to establish major motifs is quite similar to what we saw in the opening of *Back to the Future*.

The setup is also very redundant in introducing the idea that Clarice should not get close to Lecter, either physically or psychologically. This is necessary in order to suggest how dangerous Lecter is, since we will not actually see him commit any violent acts until much later. Moreover, the opening scene introduces the idea that Lecter could somehow harm Clarice despite being securely locked up. Crawford says she must not tell Lecter anything personal: "Believe me, you don't want Hannibal Lecter inside your head." He also mentions that Dr. Chilton will tell her the physical procedure, preparing us for the next scene. There Chilton gives her a set of additional rules, including an insistence that she not accept anything Lecter offers her. Later, of course, she violates all these rules.

The end of the opening scene provides a good example of an easily comprehensible transition to a new scene. Clarice now has an appointment (she is to interview Lecter "today") and a deadline ("Have your memo on my desk by oh-eight hundred Wednesday"—presumably the next day). That deadline is never met, since the discovery of Raspel's head sets off a more important line of action, but Clarice will soon face a new, more urgent deadline.

As Clarice is about to leave Crawford's office, he advises her ominously, "Never forget what he [Lecter] is." Clarice asks, "And what is that?" Her question forms a dialogue hook into the next scene, which begins with a long shot of a building and a sign, "Baltimore State Forensic Hospital." Chilton's voice off seems to reply to Clarice's question: "Oh, he's a monster. A pure psychopath." Thus the two scenes flow effortlessly together, since we have been thoroughly primed for what is coming.

The brief scene with Chilton establishes his salient character traits with the usual speed and clarity of the classical cinema. His big grin as he describes his famous patient—"From a research point of view, Lecter is our most prized

4.1

asset"—reveals him as ambitious and smug. His leering flirtation with Clarice and subsequent pique when she rejects him prepare the way for his later attempts to thwart her investigation.

Chilton's blatant pass at Clarice and then his comments about how Crawford has sent "a pretty young woman to turn him [Lecter] on" establish another important motif in the film. Almost every time sexual matters come up in relation to Clarice, the implication is sleazy, prurient, weird, or downright perverse. Lecter's neighbor Miggs masturbates and tosses semen at her; Lecter tries to get her to speculate on Crawford's possible fantasies concerning her or to reveal sexual abuse by her mother's cousin's husband when she was a child; Crawford pretends to want to spare her the details of the "sex crime" when he deals with local Kentucky police—leaving Clarice alone to cope with the stares of several hostile troopers; even the two entomologists she visits at the Smithsonian, one of whom flirts with her, are seen as owlish and eccentric—isolated, like Buffalo Bill, with their insects in a spooky environment.

Clarice manages to cope with most of this, as she must in such a job as she aspires to. But the effect of this erotic motif is, oddly enough, largely to de-emphasize Clarice's sexuality. This is a relatively rare case of a Hollywood film with a female protagonist in which neither of the two major lines of action is a romance. (Lecter's snide remark, "People will say we're in love," and his brief caress of her finger in their final meeting create a grim parody of the usual romance line.) Both of Clarice's goals, becoming an agent and solving the case, are professional—another instance of the film's quasi-feminist bent. This is not to say that Clarice is seen as completely asexual, but even the slightest hint of romance is deferred until the two goals have been met. In the epilogue, our initial impression concerning the two entomologists is reversed when they attend the FBI graduation ceremony (Fig. 4.1) and are possibly romantically interested in Clarice and Ardelia. Even the fact that this possibility is so little explored emphasizes the film's downplaying of traditional sexual matters in relation to Clarice.[6]

The scene with Chilton ends as he escorts Clarice down to the high-security cells. A guard, Barney, tells her yet again not to get near the glass, giving us an additional reminder about the rules. By now we have been cued again and again to expect Lecter to be a "monster," and hence we are startled by our first view of him, standing smiling amid his sketches and greeting Clarice politely. But quickly his voice takes on a dangerous edge as he asks Clarice to bring her identification card closer to the glass. She hesitatingly obeys, though even as she searches in her purse for the card, her eyes scan the cell as is her habit and as Crawford had ordered her to do when interviewing Lecter. After finding her ID card, she holds it very close indeed to the glass. In effect, Clarice has already violated the rule about not approaching the glass. It may seem odd that this should happen so soon, but the script must begin establishing the relationship between the two so that Lecter will provide the first clue and set the action in motion.

Lecter is annoyed to discover that Clarice is a mere student, but she regains contact by deciding to answer his question about what Miggs had hissed at her: "He said, I can smell your cunt." She soon follows up by asking if his drawing of the Duomo was done from memory, and he replies, "Memory, Agent Starling, is what I have instead of a view," setting us up for the later revelation of Lecter's goal. Clarice's clumsy pun emphasizes the moment, "Well, perhaps you'd care to lend us your 'view' on this questionnaire, Sir." This annoys Lecter: "No, no. You were doing *fine*. You had been courteous and receptive to courtesy, you had established trust with the embarrassing truth about Miggs, and now this ham-handed segue into your questionnaire." (Lecter proves capable of ham-handed puns too, as in the later scene when Clarice mentions the terns on Plum Island; Lecter replies, "Terns? If I help you, Clarice, it will be turns with us too.") Thus his rules for their relationship are revealed. She must be courteous, able to deal with even the most intimate questions, and adept at matching him in cleverness.

It is at this point in the scene that Lecter asks how Buffalo Bill got that nickname. Clarice again unflinchingly provides the answer: some police remarked that he "likes to skin his humps." At this point, we know of no causal connection between Lecter and Bill. (Indeed, Crawford had specifically denied any such connection.) Lecter seems just to be seeking to gratify his curiosity. But his next question to Clarice, "Why do you think he removes their skins? *Thrill* me with your acumen," begins the Socratic questioning that he will use throughout the film to provide her with clues. And although she fails to answer his question correctly now, a breakthrough moment in the case will come early in the climax section, when she does finally answer it by searching Frederica Bimmel's sewing closet.

Clarice's attempt to give Lecter the questionnaire backfires. It annoys him, and he drops into a mock–West Virginia accent in giving her a devastatingly accurate account of her background and aspirations—with unpleasant images of sexuality associated with the things Clarice wanted to escape ("And oh how quickly the boys found you. All those tedious, sticky fumblings in the back seats of cars while you could only dream of getting out, getting all the way to the F.-B.-I."). And when she tries to push him to answer the questionnaire, he implicitly threatens her with his now-famous speech about eating a census taker's liver accompanied by fava beans and a nice Chianti.

Thus Clarice is rejected and forced to leave—until Miggs flings his semen into her face. Lecter is very upset. "I would never have had that happen to you. Discourtesy is unspeakably ugly to me." He then makes the critical offer:

> *Lecter:* I will make you happy—I'll give you a chance at what you love most.
> *Clarice:* And what is that?
> *Lecter:* Advancement, of course. Listen carefully, look deep within *yourself*, Clarice Starling. Go seek out Miss Mofet, an old patient of mine.

Thus Clarice receives Lecter's first clue (as he calls her something closer to her full name), including what will prove to be an anagram.

Lecter's instructions provide an exemplary case of a dangling cause, since Clarice does not follow up on them right away. Instead, we get some brief scenes where the "Miss Mofet" reference is not mentioned. Outside, Clarice pauses in tears, and we see the first of two flashbacks to her childhood (looking "deep within herself," as Lecter had suggested). This brief scene confirms the small-town background deduced by Lecter. There then follows a brief montage of scenes of her training at the FBI headquarters. Since Clarice has still not followed up on Lecter's clue and since we already know she is training as an FBI agent, no dialogue hooks or appointments are necessary to cover the transitions. The cut from her sobbing by her car to the frontal closeup of her firing during target practice, however, creates an abrupt contrast. Here we see her sensitive and tough sides juxtaposed—the mix that will allow her to crack the case where Crawford and others have failed.

These training vignettes contain one significant action that has implications for what will come. During an exercise involving a simulated invasion of a room, Clarice is "killed" by a gunman behind her. The instructor grills her:

Instructor: Starling, where's your danger area?
Clarice: In the corner, sir.
Instructor: Did you check the corner?
Clarice: No, sir.
Instructor: That's the reason you're dead.

The suspense of the climactic cat-and-mouse game with Jame Gumb in the labyrinthine cellar is thus heightened: Will Clarice make the same mistake, especially in the dark? But there Clarice will check many corners, having learned from this one slip-up.

She also soon follows up on her interview with Lecter, doing microfilm research on his background. A phone call from Crawford neatly reminds us of this dangling cause and the name involved: "He mentioned a name at the end. Mofet. Any follow-up on her?" Already Clarice is learning to analyze Lecter's mind: "The 'your-self' reference was too hokey for Lecter," she says. She describes discovering a "Your Self" warehouse in Baltimore, and this line provides a dialogue hook, with sound bridge, to the scene of her discovery of the head of Bill's early victim.

That discovery ends the film's setup, because it establishes indispensable premises for the entire plot. Lecter really is willing to aid Clarice. He is not fully cooperative, however, insisting that she provide him with mental stimulation by playing psychological games. Her search of the warehouse also shows that Clarice is capable of understanding at least some of his clues. Thus a careful balance of progress and delay is created. Clarice can move forward on the case, but only slowly, as Lecter makes further demands before he will provide more hints.

COMPLICATING ACTION: "QUID PRO QUO"

The complicating action of *The Silence of the Lambs* begins with Clarice's second visit to Lecter. In effect she has passed a test, as she reveals with her first line to him: "Hester Mofet—it's an anagram, isn't it, Doctor? Hester Mofet—the rest of me. Miss The-Rest-of-Me." She also violates another

Chilton rule by taking the towel Lecter offers her (again proving herself "receptive to courtesy"). Here Lecter reveals the link between Raspel and Buffalo Bill, focusing and defining Clarice's second goal. Initially she simply wanted to be an agent; now she has a crime to solve. Lecter also states his own goal: a transfer away from the hated Dr. Chilton to a cell with a view. Then he makes explicit what he will give in exchange for that transfer: "I'm offering you a psychological profile of Buffalo Bill, based on the case evidence. I'll help you catch him, Clarice." But that help will not come quickly, and he will use a new time pressure on Clarice and Crawford to get what he wants: "All good things to those who wait. *I've* waited, Clarice, but how long can you and old Jackie-boy wait? Our little Billy must already be searching for that next special lady." Lecter's offer will remain a dangling cause for several scenes before being taken up.

His final line also serves as a dialogue hook into the next scene, the abduction of Catherine. This is the only other major event in this part of the film that could be a candidate for a crucial plot point ending the setup. Yet it actually changes none of the main premises of the narrative. It only puts much more pressure on Clarice and her colleagues to act quickly and hence pumps up the suspense considerably.

This scene also provides a neat example of how the clear motivation of narrative material can take precedence over considerations of realism in a classical film. The action takes place in a well-lit parking lot, and we are able to see Catherine quite clearly. Yet Gumb uses a pair of night-vision goggles to watch her. (The point-of-view shots through the goggles actually make her *less* easy to see.) This gesture sets up the fact that he owns such goggles, since they will be vital when he stalks Clarice in the dark cellar. Most audience members, nervously anticipating a violent attack, would overlook the implausible use of the goggles in a lighted area. They also serve to introduce the villain as fearsome-looking. Thus they help to dramatize our first switch in point-of-view, away from Clarice, briefly to Catherine, and then to Gumb. Even the seemingly insignificant detail of Catherine's waiting cat (with which the scene ends) helps motivate her later ability to manipulate Gumb's dog in her desperate efforts to save herself.

Most of the rest of the complicating action involves Clarice's participation in the examination of a newly discovered body. On the way to the funeral parlor, Crawford reveals that, for an unknown reason, Buffalo Bill keeps his victims alive for three days. Thus Clarice is working against a deadline, and although the decreasing time approaching that deadline is not mentioned again, the passing days and nights create increasing suspense.

During this scene Crawford also shows Clarice a photo of the first girl killed, Frederica Bimmel, and remarks: "Her body was the only one he took the trouble to weight down, so actually she was the third girl found." Our knowledge of this fact is carefully established here, since it will later be crucial to our understanding of Ardelia and Clarice's solution of Lecter's final puzzle. The photo of Frederica alive also distinguishes her from the other victims so that we will remember her.

While Clarice is waiting to begin the examination, she looks through a door at a funeral in progress, and this triggers the second flashback to her childhood. Shots of her as an adult walking down the aisle toward the coffin (a fantasy, since we learn at the end that she never actually entered the chapel) are cut together with shots of her as a child approaching her father's coffin and looking at his body. This flashback (or more strictly speaking, these mini-flashbacks) proves to us that Clarice tells the truth to Lecter in most cases, since she will soon tell him that her father's death was her worst childhood memory. Perhaps more important, however, the intercutting of past and present is a slightly "arty" touch. The only other moment of this sort comes in the climax, when intercutting tricks us into thinking that the FBI SWAT team is closing in on Gumb in Calumet City, when actually Clarice is ringing his doorbell in Belvedere. The flashback helps justify the presence of that later sequence as another artistic flourish rather than merely a cheating trick.

The examination itself gives us a chance to see Clarice's competence and resolve, qualities that motivate her ability to solve this difficult case. She also picks up a clue that will be important in that solution: the moth in the girl's throat. It contradicts Crawford's claim that the fact that the bodies were in the water "leaves us no trace evidence of any kind." (Presumably the FBI has overlooked cocoons in the throats of the previous five bodies and Raspel's head—the latter being found subsequently.)

The cocoon becomes the dangling cause that lingers into the next scene. Again there is no dialogue hook or setup of an appointment, but clearly Clarice has one. We see her entering the Smithsonian to consult the two entomologists about the cocoon. Their identification of the death's-head moth provides another dangling cause, the crucial clue that will allow Clarice to recognize Gumb when she sees an adult moth in his house.

Once again, however, the film goes beyond scene-by-scene mechanics, setting up a virtuosic set of linked motifs. The two slits cut in the cocoon casing by the scientist to reveal the skull pattern on the back of the developing moth within (Fig. 4.2) recall the two long diamond-shaped patches of skin

4.2

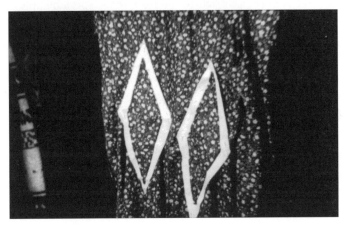

4.3

flayed from the back of the girl just examined. These diamond shapes return in the dressmaker's marks that Clarice finds on a garment in Frederica's closet (Fig. 4.3), leading her to realize that Buffalo Bill is making a "woman's suit" of skin and must be skilled at sewing. Shortly thereafter, in Gumb's house, Clarice spots a death's-head moth landing on one of several professional-size spools of thread (Fig. 4.4). The combination of the moth motif and the sewing motif—not the moth motif alone—is what causes her to realize that she is face to face with the killer.[7]

The Smithsonian scene ends with a dialogue hook. One scientist remarks of the moth, "Somebody loved him." There follows a brief scene in Gumb's lair, with moths flying about and pictures of insects on the walls redundantly confirming his link to the body Clarice had examined. The scene ends as the

4.4

poodle "Precious" stands at the edge of the deep well in which Catherine is imprisoned, setting up her later use of the dog as a hostage.

No dialogue hook or other link is necessary for the next transition, which returns us to the by now familiar FBI training center for the scene of Senator Martin broadcasting an appeal to the killer. This scene functions primarily to introduce the senator so that her part in Chilton's scheme will be apparent.

In the next scene, Clarice revisits Lecter to make him the fake offer of a transfer. His offer in their previous encounter has dangled for quite some time, but we were hardly likely to forget it. Here Lecter spells out what he wants in addition to the move to a new prison: "*Quid pro quo. I tell you things, you tell me things. Not about this case, though. About yourself. Quid pro quo.*" From the start, Lecter has been trading clues for information from Clarice—especially embarrassing revelations—but this line makes the bargain redundantly clear to the audience. In addition, their exchanges become much more formalized, as each in turn demands some information from the other. And now for the first time Lecter asks Clarice about her childhood. This change recalls Crawford's line in the first scene: "Believe me, you don't want Hannibal Lecter inside your head." Clarice thoroughly disobeys that rule as well, to her advantage.

After Clarice tells Lecter the story of her father's death, he appears to have tears in his eyes: "You're very frank, Clarice. I think it would be quite something to know you in private life." This is a key line for the action of the entire narrative. For one thing, it signals that Lecter finally accepts Clarice, so completely that even her false offer of a transfer does not make him back out of their bargain. For another, it sets up the fact that he will not try to kill her when he escapes ("The world's more interesting with you in it").

It is ironic that this is the one time when Clarice is *not* being frank with Lecter; she has just tried to trick him. But she does so only because of her dedication to her job and her goal. In their "private" relationship she is always sincere.[8] That relationship in effect takes the place of a conventional romance. Clarice must get Lecter to trust her, then betray him (as she does here), then win him back in order to achieve her real goal of finding Buffalo Bill. (The whole Clarice-Lecter plot is close to girl gets boy, girl loses boy, girl gets boy.) But she never responds to his flirtatious or sexual comments, always deflecting the conversation. Here, for example, when Lecter says, "I think it would be quite something to know you in private life," she responds insistently, "*Quid pro quo*, Doctor," leading him to point out that Buffalo Bill's victims are all large women. (As Clarice realizes later, this is so their skins will fit Gumb.)

Lecter's obsession with the grim aspects of Clarice's childhood may seem simply prurient curiosity, a way of his experiencing her most vulnerable emotions. But it also connects to Lecter's explanation of Bill's background. "Look for severe childhood disturbances associated with violence. Our Billy wasn't born a criminal, Clarice. He was made one through years of systematic abuse." Lecter himself is a serial killer and presumably speaks from personal knowledge; we can infer that he was also abused as a child. Now he seems eager to think that Clarice was the victim of such abuse as well; in this scene he asks of her mother's cousin's husband, "Did the rancher make you perform fellatio? Did he sodomize you?" Clarice replies simply, "No, he was a very decent man," and again turns the conversation back to Buffalo Bill: "*Quid pro quo*, Doctor." Lecter perhaps seeks parallels between himself and Clarice, but he finds none. Hers was a sad childhood but not one which damaged her irredeemably. Her trauma, which Lecter later symbolizes as the screaming of the lambs, can, the film suggests, be healed by her ability to save Catherine and others. Thus "the silence of the lambs" emerges as another implicit goal for Clarice; her success as an FBI agent will help lay to rest her tragic memories. Lecter and Gumb, however, are far beyond such redemption.

In return for Clarice's anecdote, Lecter gives her more information about the reasons behind Buffalo Bill's murders. "Billy is not a real transsexual, but he thinks he is. He tries to be. He's tried a lot of things, I expect." This dialogue is important for the fundamental motivation of the action, as well as for the ideological import of the film as a whole.

I have suggested that *The Silence of the Lambs* has a mildly feminist ideology (women can be good FBI agents). To some, it may suggest a stronger feminist meaning (women can be especially good FBI agents because of their sensitivity to aspects of cases overlooked by their male counterparts). Yet at the same time, the film created a storm of controversy when it first appeared because it was perceived by some as homophobic.[9] In the dialogue I have just quoted, the filmmakers seem to have tried to forestall this objection. Despite his past affair with Raspel, there is no suggestion that Bill is committed to homosexuality. Furthermore, Lecter declares that Buffalo Bill is not a transsexual but only thinks he is.

What exactly that might mean the film never explains. Bill has been turned down by at least one reputable hospital that does sex-change operations, yet he still believes that he is a transsexual to the point where he is driven to kill and flay women. Perhaps we are to believe he is simply insane and there is no explanation for his behavior, apart from his assumed abuse as a child. Ultimately, however, the filmmakers seem to dodge the issues of homosexuality and transsexualism, opting to leave the question of fundamental motivation vague in order to sidestep the volatile issue of gender altogether.[10] Such ideological ambiguity has been common in Hollywood films from early on, through fear of censorship or other stigmas that might lower box-office appeal.

And as often happens in such situations, the result is an uncharacteristic refusal to provide clear motivations for fundamental actions in the plot. In the end, we cannot fully understand why Gumb kills women if he is not really someone driven to extreme means to change his sex. In a later scene in Memphis, Clarice says to a police officer who asks her about Lecter, "They don't have a name for what he is." The same is certainly true of Gumb. The filmmakers cannot offer any real explanation of why he does what he does without offending some group, and hence they have opted for obscurity. Still, many viewers probably want such an explanation and assume Gumb is some sort of homosexual and/or transvestite and/or transsexual (categories that may not be distinguishable to some audience members). While the filmmakers probably wanted to avoid any suggestion of homophobia, they have failed to provide an explanation that would forestall such a reaction.

Returning to the scene of the false offer of a transfer, we again get a good example of classical cinema's motivic unity. Clarice gives Lecter a map of "Plum Island," his supposed vacation venue. At the end of their final encounter, Lecter returns the case file, including another map upon which he has written the final clue. As in other examples we have examined, there is no causal necessity for both of these actions to depend on maps, but the film gains a certain symmetry from this flourish.

In this scene, Clarice seems to be making rapid progress on the case. Apparently believing the transfer offer is real, Lecter gives Clarice another clue, suggesting that the FBI check the records of three hospitals that perform sex-change operations. We assume that his suggestion will take Clarice another step closer to solving the crime. In fact, it never does and remains a dangling cause for quite some time. In the climax portion, Crawford indeed finds the killer's name by following Lecter's lead. But the address given is outdated, and the clue's main result is that Crawford and his SWAT team go to the wrong house, leaving Clarice to confront Gumb alone.

The complicating action ends with a brief scene of Gumb and Catherine, in which the latter realizes she is going to be killed and starts screaming. This moment builds suspense by emphasizing the need for haste in the investigation.

DEVELOPMENT: "NOT RANDOM AT ALL"

As we have seen, a film's development often involves some major new obstacles that delay the protagonist in the rush toward the goals. We have also seen that the turning point may come after the break between large-scale parts. Both strategies operate quite clearly in *The Silence of the Lambs*. The development section begins as Chilton reveals to Lecter that the FBI's offer of a transfer was false.[11] He then makes a real offer to send Lecter to another prison in Tennessee (using the same deadline under which Clarice is working—"in time" to save Catherine). Thus Clarice cannot revisit him as soon as she might have, and she very nearly is thrown out before he can give her the case file. The offer thus creates considerable suspense and delay, in that we strongly anticipate that Lecter will henceforth refuse to help Clarice. That seemingly insuperable obstacle creates delay until near the end of the development. Another dangling cause is introduced, as we realize that Lecter will eventually turn to his own advantage the ballpoint pen left behind by Chilton.

Most of the rest of the development is taken up with Lecter's move to a cell in Tennessee, Clarice's visit to him, and his escape. A few brief scenes stress the threat that the transfer poses to the FBI case. The head of the FBI castigates Crawford for making the false offer. His statement that Senator Martin is upset leads to the introduction of a new character, Paul Krendler, from the Justice Department, who is supposed to take over the case. Although a fast track-in introduces him as a menacing figure, in fact Krendler will turn out to be only a minor character. At this point in the plot, however, Crawford and Clarice have been caught in a mistake, so Krendler looks like a major threat. The notion that the case could be taken away from the FBI (Crawford and Clarice) by "Justice" (Krendler) is set up. Eventually, Lecter will take all this conflict into his own hands by sending Krendler off on a false lead and giving the indispensable clue to Clarice. Nonetheless, the apparent reversal puts more pressure on her to solve the case fast, as well as generating suspense by casting considerable doubt on her ability to do so.

The scene at the Memphis airport is a parody of the initial scene between Lecter and Clarice. Lecter banters with Senator Martin, alternately polite and insulting. She does not cope with him as well as Clarice had:

> *Lecter:* Tell me, Senator, did you nurse Catherine yourself?
> *Senator:* Yes.
> *Lecter:* Toughened your nipples, didn't it?

At this point, Senator Martin is ready to send Lecter back to his viewless cell. Yet this is much the same way he has dealt with Clarice, testing her with shocking questions. This airport scene demonstrates how well Clarice deals with him. Senator Martin and her entourage treat Lecter as if he were a normal person, then get upset when he suddenly switches to his psychopathic side. Even Chilton, though familiar with Lecter in a superficial way, becomes ruffled when his prize offering turns nasty. Clarice, on the other hand, had quickly steeled herself to treating Lecter's worst comments as matter-of-fact events to be turned aside or to her advantage.

The scene at the airport ends with Lecter's coy compliment to Senator Martin: "Love your suit!" This contrasts with his cruel remarks during his first meeting with Clarice about her trying to dress well—a contrast underlined by the similarity of Senator Martin's hair style to Clarice's. Criticizing Clarice's cheap shoes and purse had provided a way for Lecter to test her—a test that she had barely passed by admitting the truth of his insights and trying to direct them against him ("Are you strong enough to point that high-powered perception at yourself?"). With Senator Martin, a compliment becomes Lecter's means of cutting off communication. And Lecter will not cooperate in any *quid pro quo* games here. His proffered clue proves false. Lecter's "Love your suit" line also provides a "sting" to end the scene. We do not need a strong causal transition to the next scene, since a title reveals that the action will take place at the "Shelby County Courthouse"; that action is also essentially a continuation of the transfer.

When Clarice meets Lecter, she offers him his old sketches. "I thought you might like your drawings back, Doctor. Just until you get your view." This line suggests that she is clinging to the faint hope of renewing their bargain by offering the only thing she has left related to his goal, however inadequate it may seem. (How she got the drawings is not explained, but we might suspect that the helpful guard, Barney, was involved.) Lecter, however, is back to his mocking manner and replies in a voice dripping with sarcasm, "*How* thoughtful." Our fears that he will not cooperate seem to be confirmed, especially when he taunts Clarice by referring to the deadline that hangs over her: "Pity about poor Catherine, though. Tick tock, tick tock, tick tock . . ."

After a bit more banter, however, he assures her that everything she needs to solve the case is in the file, thus affirming that he is willing to help her despite her trickery. He questions her as to why Buffalo Bill kills: "What *needs* does he serve by killing?" Here he alludes to the antagonist's goal—the one that provides a counterweight to Clarice's own. When she can answer this question—as she cannot here—she will be close to catching her quarry.

There follows a bit of Socratic questioning in which Lecter leads Clarice through the notion of coveting, which will be pivotal in her interpretation of the clue written on the map. He is clearly quite determined to help her, despite her distracted, incorrect answers to his questions. Then he asks her, "Don't you feel eyes moving over your body every day, Clarice?" Lecter seems to be taunting Clarice, using her sexually. But that is, as he would say, incidental. For he continues, "And don't your eyes seek out the things you want?"—pushing her to guess the right answer to the puzzle.

In fact, we have no sense of Clarice as covetous. She does not want "things," except in a tangential way. We have been told that her cheap shoes and other accessories reflect her ambition, but the film has not made this concrete for us. Her desire to become an FBI agent is never suggested to be a means to material ends, and her dedication to saving Catherine has temporarily placed her beyond any notion of personal ambition.

That dedication prompts Clarice's reply, blithely taking upon herself any amount of covetousness if it will help to solve the case: "All right, and please tell me how!" At this point Lecter demands his final bit of gratification, the story of Clarice's attempt to save the doomed lamb. She resists at first, with a reference to the deadline hanging over her: "Doctor, we don't have any more time for any of this now." He replies, "But we don't reckon time in the same way, do we, Clarice? This is all the time you'll ever have." She then tells him her story.

Why does Lecter continue to help Clarice? It might seem at first unlikely, since she has tried to trick him concerning his dearest goal. Yet in retrospect his actions are carefully motivated. As we have seen, when Clarice arrives for

4.5

her final visit, he taunts her about the offer of a transfer to "Anthrax Island." Despite his sarcasm, however, it becomes apparent that Lecter admires Clarice's cleverness in coming up with an offer that fooled him. Rather than making the island sound impossibly wonderful, she had admitted that it had drawbacks (drawbacks which she invented); hence it was more plausible as the sort of place where the FBI might really send a dangerous criminal.

Moreover, Lecter already has planned his escape and knows he will be getting out soon anyway. He has presumably experienced his prurient thrills looking at Buffalo Bill's files and has no more need of such stimulation. Now he is primarily interested in hearing one final story about Clarice's childhood. By the time she finishes telling about the death of the lamb she had tried to save, he again has tears in his eyes. Clearly by this point he has fallen a bit in love with her or at least admires her very much. He deliberately brushes his finger against hers as he hands back the case file, making this idea explicit. (Their sole physical contact also provides Clarice's last and most extreme violation of the rule not to get close to Lecter.) Moreover, between Clarice's departure and his escape, he draws a picture of her, not as a child but as an adult, holding her lamb (Fig. 4.5).

Clarice's story of her failed attempt to rescue a single lamb from slaughter, skinning, and consumption creates an important image that subtly but thoroughly contrasts her with the two serial killers. They both butcher people: Gumb to flay the corpses and Lecter to cannibalize them. Lecter recognizes in Clarice's increasingly desperate pleas for his assistance that she is not simply the ambitious student he had initially suspected of trying to use him for her own advancement. Catherine implicitly becomes the one lamb that Clarice hopes to rescue amid the bloodshed of Gumb's killings. Despite their being so much the opposites of each other, Lecter's respect for Clarice's dedication clearly also plays an important role in his decision to give her the final clue. He expresses this respect humorously by ordering a new meal of lamb chops, a meat he now associates with Clarice but pointedly does not intend to eat. Thus the film provides plenty of motivation to suggest why Lecter would continue to help Clarice rather than shifting his aid to Krendler and Senator Martin.

There follows the violent scene of Lecter's murder of his guards and his escape. This has little impact upon the main plotline, since Clarice already has the final clue. As often happens in the development sections of films, a major sequence functions primarily to generate action, suspense, and delay. Ultimately, the escape scene serves to remind us (and indeed to show us quite literally and viscerally for the first time) that Lecter is a savage criminal. Thus at the end Clarice's triumph is marred by the fact of Lecter's freedom, and the possibility is raised that the narrative will continue into a second film.

The development ends with a scene between Ardelia and Clarice. There is a strong hook from the previous scene, which ends with Lecter in an ambulance, tearing off his mask and preparing to kill the ambulance attendant. Cut to Ardelia racing away from a telephone, to inform Clarice of Lecter's escape. They soon sit down to work out the final clue that Lecter has written on the map, realizing that the pattern of killings was "not random at all." Buffalo Bill coveted what he saw every day: "He knew her." This conclusion provides the turning point into the climax, since the correct interpretation of Lecter's final clue allows Clarice to begin the investigation in Belvedere that will solve the case. The development ends on a POV closeup of the photo of Frederica Bimmel. This photograph acts as a hook into the climax section of the film.

CLIMAX AND EPILOGUE: "SPECIAL AGENT STARLING"

The climax portion of the film begins with an extreme-long establishing shot of Belvedere, Ohio, with a superimposed identifying title. We might infer that the car crossing the bridge into the town is Clarice's—presumably after she has driven all night from Virginia.

The course of the action in the climax is fairly straightforward. More motivic parallelisms are introduced. Mr. Bimmel, the first victim's father, raises pigeons (similar to Gumb's moths); he is a hunter and skins small animals, the hides of which we see hanging on his house. Frederica is revealed to have been killed during the course of a trip for a job interview in Chicago. This suggests that her aspirations to move away from her childhood environment may have paralleled Clarice's own. It also provides a bit of apparent support for the FBI's identification of Calumet City as Gumb's current home, since we may wrongly infer that Frederica met her killer during her trip.

Clarice carefully searches the victim's room, finding small indications of Frederica's mundane life. The point of the scene is not so much to reveal clues as to suggest the close links between Clarice's background and that of the victim. Yet the scene presents one of the few false notes in the film. Clarice intuits that the lining of Frederica's musical jewelry box might hide secret treasures, and she finds some Polaroid cheesecake photos of Frederica, presumably taken by an unknown lover. These contribute no causal information to the narrative, and Clarice drops them casually as she is distracted by the cat and moves into the sewing room. Given Clarice's character traits as they have been set up, we would not expect her to drop the photos for Mr. Bimmel to find; she would have tucked them back into the secret compartment and sealed the lining over them. Given that they are causally irrelevant, the flaw seems all the more apparent.[12]

In another throwaway bit of virtuosity, Frederica's sewing room is decorated with butterfly-patterned wallpaper, paralleling the pictures of butterflies that hang in Gumb's house. Once Clarice realizes that the killer is sewing together bits of women's skins to make a body suit for himself, she calls Crawford and is told that the killer has been located in Chicago. He praises her efforts: "Starling! We wouldn't have found him without you. No one's gonna forget that—least of all me." Remarkably, Foster manages simultaneously to convey Clarice's pleasure at his words, her frustration at not participating in the capture, and her disappointment at her apparently faulty interpretation of Lecter's clue. We might therefore anticipate that her guard will be down when she actually encounters Gumb. She goes to his house thinking that she is now on a routine mission and expecting to find Mrs. Lipman, the woman for whom Frederica had done alterations.

A lengthy scene of intercutting between the preparations for the raid on the house in Calumet City and Gumb and Catherine's activities in the cellar seems to confirm that the FBI is closing in. Finally Gumb opens the door (in response to a ringing bell that we are led to think is in the Calumet City house) to confront Clarice. This is followed by a brief continuation of the intercutting, based in part on the name motif:

(Belvedere) medium closeup (MCU) Clarice seen past Gumb in the foreground:
    "Well, I'm investigating the death of Frederica Bimmel."
(Calumet City) MCU FBI officer to Crawford:

"There's no one here, Jack."
Reverse shot, track in to tight CU of Crawford: "Clarice!"
(Belvedere) MCU Clarice, as before: "Your name is . . .?"
Gumb, in foreground: "Oh, uh, Jack Gordon."

The name Frederica Bimmel has alerted Gumb, and he now knows more than Clarice does. He lures her inside by claiming to have Mrs. Lipman's son's card. As he pretends to search for it, Clarice slowly comes forward to the door of the dining room, scanning her surroundings as usual. The camera pans slightly to the right to bring a print on the wall into the frame; it depicts a large butterfly. Thus the narration overtly reminds us one more time of the importance of this motif, just before Clarice sees the death's-head moth land.

Clarice's search through the cellar provides an indication of the advantages the film derives from having a female protagonist in a genre role previously usually played by men. Foster can make Clarice's terror quite palpable for the audience. It is hard to imagine Clint Eastwood or Sylvester Stallone playing the situation with anything but aggressive confidence, tinged with caution.[13] Clarice's bravery in going into the cellar despite her fear is thus emphasized, and the film exploits the situation by keeping Gumb's location a mystery until well into the scene.

When Gumb does reappear, there is an abrupt shift to his point of view through the night-vision goggles. In a sense, this is the old cliché of the killer's viewpoint on the female victim. Yet here it primarily functions to allow us to see Clarice in the dark. We are so tied to her at this point that we are hardly likely to switch to identifying with Gumb.

Why does Gumb reach out and nearly caress Clarice's hair during this scene? This is a puzzling moment, since it seems to be unmotivated by the rest of the narrative. There are at least three possible explanations, two of which are highly unlikely. The most obvious, in terms of the usual stalker-versus-woman genre conventions, is that he is attracted to her, and we might expect him to try to rape her. We know, however, that Gumb has not raped any of his victims and that he believes himself to be a transsexual, so there is no motivation for that idea. We can also quickly dismiss the idea that he "covets" her skin and wants to add her to his series of victims, since she is a far cry from the "roomy" size-14 women upon whom he preys. Yet perhaps this fact hints at the reason for his gesture. Gumb wants to touch her because she embodies what he can never plausibly become: beautiful, female, small. (This interpretation, which strikes me as the most reasonable explanation for

Gumb's gesture, is not really successfully cued by the film. The moment apparently appeals to banal thriller conventions; I suspect that only in retrospect could a viewer come up with this interpretation.)[14]

Another point that puzzles some viewers is how Clarice is able to shoot Buffalo Bill in the dark, when he has night-vision goggles and she does not. She hears a click as he switches off his gun's safety mechanism, and she spins around and shoots at the sound. This moment has been motivated, since we had seen her take the safety off her own gun upstairs upon realizing that Gumb is the killer. Thus she has a chance to replay the FBI exercise at which she had failed, and this time she succeeds.

The epilogue begins with a brief scene of Crawford comforting Clarice as Catherine (and Precious) are led away to an ambulance. Thus Clarice has achieved her more pressing goal of saving Gumb's intended victim. Since Crawford appreciates her feat, she also appears well on her way to reaching her initial, long-term goal by graduating as a special agent and beginning a career under his supervision. She also, however, receives a telephone call from Lecter.

As I have suggested, this is a film with parallel antagonists, and the narrative cannot end until we learn something more about Lecter's circumstances. The epilogue is unusually long, around 8 minutes, since the final shot of Lecter following Chilton goes on under the entire credit sequence. Even though Lecter soon disappears into the crowd, I think the whole shot is part of the story. We are left to speculate on what must be happening as Lecter stalks Chilton, so our involvement in the action does not really end until the final fade-out. Overall the film preserves a careful balance, with none of its large-scale sections departing by more than three minutes from the 29.5-minute average.

Despite the complexity and unity of the narrative structure of *Silence*, there are a few unmotivated or problematic loose ends, some of which I have already mentioned. The fact that Gumb, an expert sewer, has moved into the house of Mrs. Lipman, for whom Frederica did alterations, is a considerable coincidence; one would have expected at least some connection to be made between Gumb and Lipman (she was, say, an elderly relative who died and left him the house). Moreover, why does the photo that is faxed to Crawford aboard the plane en route to Calumet City clearly show a different man from the one we know as the killer? At the time, this discrepancy might lead us to assume that Crawford is mistaken in his identification of Gumb and that the killer never lived in Calumet City. Yet the credits (though nothing else in the film) confirm that our villain is indeed Jame Gumb. How does Crawford get the right name and a correct, though out-of-date, address, but the wrong photo? Such quibbles aside, however, *Silence* presents an excellent example of the strengths of modern classical narrative construction.

A FINAL LESSON: VIRTUOSIC MOTIFS

The "Belvedere" references in *Silence* resemble other such subtle motifs we have already seen at work: Quint's scoffing reference to the shark "eating" the compressed-air tanks in *Jaws* (Chapter 1), the Harold Lloyd/Christopher Lloyd joke in *Back to the Future* (Chapter 3), and the switch of the mall's name from "Twin Pines" to "Lone Pine" in the same film. Such touches are nearly impossible for first-time viewers to catch. Why bother to include them?

Interestingly, such extremely subtle touches seem to have been used only very rarely in the studio era. One example would be the references to Ralph Bellamy and Archie Leach (Cary Grant's real name) in *His Girl Friday*. Yet such motifs are not so rare in films of recent decades. My hunch is that they have crept in because of the hugely increased amount of time most screenwriters spend laboring over their scripts in the preproduction phase. Whereas studio contract writers wrote on a regular and relatively short schedule, freelance authors may rework their creations for years, making extensive changes if the prospective star is replaced or a new production executive takes over the project. As of 1997, "spec" scripts (written without an advance contract) were the single largest source of Hollywood narratives, accounting for 43 percent of all that year's features.[15] The process of working up a spec script into a package deal and seeing it into the shooting phase can take years.

I suspect that as a result, some authors may revivify their own interest in their projects by adding clever touches as they hone and polish. They may also assume that at least the best of their fellow scriptwriters will notice and enjoy these touches—a common function of virtuosity in any art. Here we have one case where the contemporary cinema has apparently devised an improvement on the studio-era approach, albeit a minor one. Thus we see again that the modern classical cinema has the potential for a complexity that pervades the most incidental details.

5

Groundhog Day

1993. Released by Columbia. Directed by Harold Ramis. Screenplay by Ramis and Danny Rubin, from Rubin's original story. Running time: 101 minutes; setup, 30.5 (including credits); complicating action, 36.5; development, 16; climax and epilogue, 16.5 (epilogue alone, 1); end credits, 3.

These points that stand out beyond the others give us at once our big scenes to play up to. All those stories so popular, for instance, that represent a change of heart in a leading character fall naturally into two big scenes. The first of these two scenes represents the character's complete surrender to evil ways, either through some great dramatic clash in his life or through natural propensities, and the second big scene represents the elements of the story so come together that the character goes through an upheaval equal to, or greater than, the first, which sets him again into harmony with the world.

—MARGUERITE BERTSCH, *How to Write for Moving Pictures* (1917)

LAST YEAR IN PUNXSUTAWNEY

My final example of a film built around a single protagonist is *Groundhog Day*. I chose it in part because at first glance it might seem not to be a classical film and hence might support the notion of a "post-Hollywood" or "post-classical" era in the American commercial cinema. The idea of a character's repeating the same day so many times is certainly original and a bit daring for a Hollywood feature. I will argue here, however, that the film is almost completely classical (as the quotation at the beginning of this chapter, written by Marguerite Bertsch in 1917—just as the classical formula was being developed—hints). Certainly, as we shall see, *Groundhog Day* compensates for the complexity of its plot by being extremely redundant, even for a Hollywood film and especially for one otherwise so complex and subtle.

The only real departure from tradition—admittedly a striking one—is the failure to motivate or explain the plot's sudden move into an impossible situation. Hollywood films do occasionally place their characters in fantastic time schemes; two obvious comparisons would be *Back to the Future* and Frank Capra's *It's a Wonderful Life*, each of which offers a very clear motivation for its shifts in time. *Back to the Future* contains a time-travel machine. In *It's a Wonderful Life* an angel takes the hero into an alternative time, one that would have existed if he never had been born.

Groundhog Day gives no explanation as to what force causes the same day to repeat for the protagonist and for no other character. By the end, however, there is some suggestion that a supernatural agency of some sort has intervened in Phil's life in order to force him to become a better person. Once he changes his character traits and becomes worthy of Rita's love, time begins to proceed normally. In this way, the film is like *It's a Wonderful Life* with the angel not present, only implied. As Danny Rubin said of his original script, "It's still Hollywood, it isn't a Luis Buñuel film."[1]

The result is an interesting case of a classical film with no antagonist. The force that opposes Phil's initial selfish goal of self-advancement is never embodied or identified, but it nevertheless sets up considerable obstacles for him and thus creates the necessary narrative conflict. In effect, for the purposes of the narrative causality, Phil is literally his own worst enemy—protagonist and antagonist rolled into one. The entire plot is structured around changing his character from the cynical, nasty, exploitive man we first see to someone who is vastly different—kind, considerate, and lovable.

The film's trajectory is a bit like that of *Tootsie*, where the actor Michael had to learn how to be decent to women. At the start of *Groundhog Day*, however, Phil is much worse than Michael ever was, insulting everyone around him. It is almost as if *Tootsie* had been made with the goal of reforming not Michael but Ron, the TV director. Michael had to learn his lesson by fairly extreme means—posing as a woman—but Phil's transformation will require even more. Indeed, such a drastic character change is unusual for a classical narrative. Still, as I will show, a great deal of motivating material is provided.

THE SETUP: "WHAT IF THERE IS NO TOMORROW?"

The setup as a whole consists of four days: the opening day, which is February 1; the first, "real" Groundhog Day; and the first two repetitions of that day.

A brief credits sequence opens the setup. Its fast-motion clouds introduce the notions of weather and of time passing unnaturally. Through a dissolve, the blue sky is matched graphically with the blue screen Phil is using for his weather forecast in the opening scene.

For the first few moments of that scene, he seems like a nice fellow, amiably telling jokes in comic weatherman fashion. This action motivates the fact that he is able to manipulate people so skillfully when his days start repeating; in particular, he can easily slip into a nice-guy role to seduce women. His slick surface also makes plausible the idea that he would have a chance at a network job, as he will claim he does. The broadcast also clearly establishes that the action is taking place on February 1 and that Phil will be covering the emergence of the groundhog the next morning at Punxsutawney, a dangling cause that we later see picked up over and over. Thus television news acts as an expositional device comparable to the newspaper clippings that appear in the opening scenes of *Back to the Future* (which also includes a brief TV news broadcast) and *The Silence of the Lambs*.

As soon as the camera is off Phil, he reveals his real character, a mixture of egotism and contempt for everyone around him. He already has a goal, which he condescendingly reveals to the female anchor of the news program: "For your information, Hairdo, there is a major network interested in me." So Phil wants to leave his job as a local weather forecaster in Pittsburgh and move to a big city and a network. By the end, his goal will have turned upside down, as he suggests to Rita that they live in the little town of Punxsutawney which he had so despised.

When Phil mentions the "major network," the camera operator Larry quips, "Yeah, that would be the Home Shopping Network." In another instance of Hollywood's virtuosic use of unifying motifs, the climax of the romantic line of action comes when Phil and Larry are "sold" at a charity auction of bachelors during the Groundhog Day party in the film's final repetition of February 2.

The bickering relationship between Phil and Larry is quickly established, and Phil's dismissal of Larry by telling him to wait in the van reinforces the transition to the next scene, the journey to Punxsutawney. The back-up weather forecaster then points out Rita to Phil, saying that she wants to stay in the small town longer in order to gather local color items. Phil responds, "Oh, come on. I wanna stay an extra *second* in Punxsutawney?"—a pun (on February 2nd) which provides another example of virtuosic motivic play. Rita delightedly plays with the blue-screen effects, and the forecaster praises her, predicting, "You guys are gonna have *fun*" covering the Groundhog Day festivities. The closeup of Phil as he watches Rita suggests that he might find her attractive; he stares with a relatively blank expression (Fig. 5.1). But he then quickly recovers his cynical look and comments, "Mmm, mmm, she's fun. But not my kinda fun." This brief moment sets up the much later revelation that he had been attracted to her the first time he saw her. To some extent, it also motivates the possibility that his unpleasant behavior is a defensive pose and that he would be able to change as radically as he does. (His

5.1

charming presentation of the opening weather forecast also suggests this suppressed decency.) There will be other subtle suggestions that deep down Phil is really a pleasant person, thus further preparing for his character change.

In addition, Bill Murray's star persona helps motivate Phil's change. Usually he plays charming but odd, often vulgar, characters. He had played engaging rogues in such films as *Caddyshack* (1980) and *Stripes* (1981). He had also played characters who reform, undergoing a considerable character change in *Scrooged* (1988) and a slight one in *Ghostbusters* (1984), where he also begins as a womanizer but then falls in love with the heroine. In many classical Hollywood films of all eras, a central character's traits will be determined by the star's public persona. In some cases a character must "grow into" his or her star persona, as when the protagonist of *Meet John Doe* becomes worthy of being played by Gary Cooper. Murray's talent for broad, even low humor was balanced in the early 1990s by the perception of him as a virtuosic, multi-talented actor. Such a persona stretches to encompass both the obnoxious and the transformed Phil. Moreover, the casting of Andie MacDowell suggested at once that the film would evolve into a truly romantic situation.

The second scene is a montage of the drive to Punxsutawney in the van, while the main credits roll. The conversation initiates the film's pattern of presenting narrative information with considerable redundancy, since it largely reiterates and elaborates on material from the opening. Phil refers back to his goal: "Can you keep a secret, Larry? I'm probably leaving PBH, so this will be the *last* time we do the groundhog together" (an ironic comment, of course, given the coming cycle of repetitions). He also bickers with Rita, again scoffing at her naiveté and at the world in general:

Phil: People like blood sausage, too. People are morons.
Rita: Nice attitude.

It turns out Rita is one of the "morons" who like blood sausage. Thus she is established as a straightforward, nice, unpretentious person, and these traits will remain consistent. Indeed, she will be the measure by which Phil's change is judged. When he becomes nice enough to deserve her love, the mysterious time warp disappears.

The arrival in Punxsutawney involves an exchange in which Phil actually tries to be nice. He complains that he cannot abide the hotel on the town square where Rita will be staying. When Rita informs him that she has booked him into a bed-and-breakfast place, he praises her work as a producer, then ruins the effort with sexual innuendo by asking her to help him with his "pelvic tilt." She passes this off with a noncommittal smile, saying, "Within reason." It becomes apparent that Phil simply cannot be a decent fellow even if he tries. The scene ends as Phil says, "I'll see you in the morning" and Rita responds, "Don't be late," setting up the morning appointment that keeps coming back. (As in other comedies, *Groundhog Day* adds a brief joke as a tag to the scene, as Larry remarks, "Did he actually call himself 'the talent'?" Thus, as in several later instances, the dialogue hook is separated from the very end of the scene by an additional line, but it functions in the same way, leading smoothly into the shots of the bed-and-breakfast place the next morning.)

The first Groundhog Day serves primarily to lay out the sequence of events that will be repeated, always with variations, until the end of the climax portion of the film. Motifs and traits that have already been introduced are reinforced here. Phil keeps his appointment at the groundhog celebration, greeting Rita with another sexual remark: "So, you sleep OK without me? You tossed and turned, didn't you?" Up to now, Rita has simply laughed off Phil's rude remarks, but now she replies disgustedly, "You're incredible." Even the most generous and tolerant person cannot put up with Phil, which provides a measure of his need for a thorough change of character traits.

During his first taping of the Groundhog Day events, Phil refers to his namesake, Punxsutawney Phil, as "the world's most famous weatherman." Given his own national-network ambitions, that is presumably what Phil longs to become. This brings up the question of why our protagonist and the groundhog share the name Phil. Perhaps this scene suggests one reason—Phil resents the attention given to a creature he contemptuously describes at various points as a rat and a squirrel, while he himself is stuck in a local news show. As we shall see, Phil's increasing despair over being trapped in time will lead him to try and kill not only himself but also the groundhog, and eventually his redemption will be signaled by his decision to live in the town famous for its Groundhog Day celebration. The double use of the name Phil underlines this trajectory.

In the first Groundhog Day scene, the groundhog officials declare that Punxsutawney Phil has seen his shadow and predicted six additional weeks of winter. The human Phil has optimistically claimed that the impending blizzard will bypass the region around Pittsburgh, but he proves to be wrong when snow strands him and his crew in Punxsutawney. The long winter that the groundhog supposedly predicts turns into Phil's inexplicably repeated February 2.

Indeed, the number of days specifically represented or mentioned in the film after this prediction may well be 42, thus filling out the six weeks of additional winter.[2] Of course, there are many more repeated days not shown or mentioned but merely implied; it is across these periods that Phil becomes an expert piano player, ice carver, and general good-deed-doer. But given that the number of days shown or mentioned seems to be 42, one must suspect that the filmmakers at least intended to associate Phil's ordeal with the additional six weeks of winter predicted by his furry namesake.

Not that the end of the film brings spring with it. Conventionally, positive character traits are linked to images of warmth. Yet in *Groundhog Day*, the weather imagery relates Phil's makeover to coldness and winter. The very first line of the film is his declaration that the place he would most like to be that day is Elkhorn, Nevada, predicted to be the nation's hot spot. Later he recalls an idyllic day spent in the Virgin Islands. For much of the film he is plagued by cold weather. In the opening he wrongly predicts that the storm will not come and advises people to leave their galoshes at home, yet one of his recurring annoyances is stepping into a deep, slushy puddle in the street near the groundhog celebration. Eventually, he will take up ice carving and decide to live in the town that symbolizes the possibility of prolonged winter. His final taping of the Groundhog Day festivities speaks of winter in glowing terms. As we shall see, this switch to a love of cold weather is linked to his transformation into a feminine ideal of masculinity.

The scene that traps Phil and his colleagues in Punxsutawney occurs on the highway leading back to Pittsburgh. For the fourth time in the film—extra redundancy again—Larry tauntingly refers to Phil's inaccurate prediction: "Perhaps it's that giant blizzard we're *not* supposed to get."[3] When a traffic cop tells Phil the road is closed, Phil seems to go a bit crazy. In a strange, singsong voice, he again repeats some of his earlier predictions, declaring: "I make the weather. All of this moisture coming up out of the Gulf is gonna push off to the East and hit Altoona." The cop replies, "Pal, you got that moisture on your head." This exchange raises the possibility that Phil is starting to lose his mind and that he could be pushed over the edge by being forced to stay in the detested Punxsutawney. We might thus expect that when the repeated days begin, they are Phil's hallucinations. This motivation seems quite weak, and I do not think that most spectators would take the repetitions as anything but fantastic in their origins.[4] Still, this exchange does motivate Phil's later visits to a neurologist and a psychiatrist, which are designed to assure us that the repeated days are not mental phenomena.

A brief scene in a gas station simply reconfirms that Phil and the others are unable to get out of Punxsutawney and that Phil considers himself a celebrity. The next shot is an establishing view of the hotel, revealing that the group is back in Punxsutawney for the night. Inside the hotel, Rita asks Phil if he will join her and Larry at the Groundhog Dinner. He declines, saying that he will return to his room for a hot shower, after which he will read *Hustler*. This is his third tawdry reference to sex. It also ironically sets up the ending of this first Groundhog Day, when he gets an unexpected cold shower. Most important, however, the conversation at the hotel establishes the party on the evening of Groundhog Day. Phil does not attend the party on this or any of the other repeated days until the climax, when we see it for the first and only time. At that point, he will demonstrate his reformed character to Rita, win her heart, and escape the perpetually repeated Groundhog Days.

The first Groundhog Day ends as Phil meets his hostess in the hall and points out that there is no hot water. She cheerily responds: "Oh, no, of course not. There wouldn't be *today*." This line sets up a major motif for the rest of the film. Phil has gotten *this* day of all days for apparently eternal repetition. As he complains later, it is not a particularly good one. At various points, he will redefine the ideal day that he would want to be repeated, and he will try to transform his own cyclical February seconds into that day. When he finally hits upon the right ideal day, he inadvertently breaks the spell.

On the first repeated day, Phil simply reacts in confusion to each literal recurrence of what he had already done the day before. Indeed, he again seems somewhat demented in his responses, slamming the man he encounters in the hall up against the wall, then going a bit catatonic in his dialogue with the hostess of the bed-and-breakfast. Perhaps the best sign of his disorientation is the fact that, after that first hallway encounter, he is not snide or nasty to the people he encounters. As he goes outside the bed-and-breakfast, he speaks to a woman on her way to Gobbler's Knob for the celebration; she will be his piano teacher much later in the film.

Arriving for the first of his repeated tapings of the festivities, Phil asks Rita to slap him to make sure he is not dreaming. Since all of Phil's colleagues are established as disliking him, Rita's obliging slap seems natural. (Larry offers to administer a second.) This moment sets up the later intensive local motif of her slapping Phil after his numerous seduction attempts. It also raises again the possibility that Phil's repeated days could be the result of mental problems. He declares: "I feel really *weird*."

After another cold shower signals that we have reached the end of the second Groundhog Day, Phil tries to make a phone call but is told it is impossible until tomorrow. He responds, "Well, what if there *is* no tomorrow? There wasn't one today." This line prepares us for a similar line that Phil utters a few scenes later—one that will be crucial for the formation of his next goal. After the abortive phone call, Phil makes his first rational attempt to figure out what is happening to him. He breaks a pencil and puts the two halves by his bed. In the morning, he finds the pencil whole. At this point he pushes into completely irrational behavior, avoiding contact with everyone he meets. He refuses to speak to the man in the hall, his hostess, his old classmate Ned Ryerson, or anyone else. (His future piano teacher, recognizable by her bright red bag, is again passing outside, but this time he does not hail her.)

Finally Phil sits in the café and tells Rita about the repetitions of Groundhog Day, asking for help. Her response is predictable: "You want my advice? I think you should get your head examined if you expect me to believe a stupid story like that, Phil." Later, in the development section, Phil will tell Rita a similar story. This scene also sets up the two men with whom Phil will later go driving. They are seated at a nearby table and tease him about having the same name as the groundhog—another moment that stresses that motif. As the scene ends, Rita reiterates, "Phil, I think you need help." Phil responds, "That's what I've been saying, Rita. *I - need - help*," providing a dialogue hook into the next two brief scenes.

What kind of help Phil needs is the real question. These two scenes basically exist to establish that the help is not medical or psychiatric. The comic doctor who myopically examines X-rays of Phil's brain finds no problem, and his suggestion that Phil needs "a psychiatrist" provides a dialogue hook into a scene with a psychiatrist who is equally ludicrous. This recent graduate cannot cope with even simple problems; he suggests that Phil should come again: "How's tomorrow for you?" Since we cannot take the two doctors seriously, from this point on we will have to assume that Phil's days are really repeating and that this does not result from his mental instability. In fact, as I have suggested, most spectators probably never ascribe the repetitions to a mental source. Still, the realistic reaction of a character to such repetitions would be to assume insanity, so these scenes help to banish that notion.

The two doctor scenes end the setup, since they preclude any possibility of Phil's getting professional help to escape his situation. His initial goal of going to a major television network has been rendered impossible. He has no goal. Figuring out what his real goals should be will occupy the next two major parts of the film, and, as usual, their accomplishment will form the climax.

COMPLICATING ACTION: "NO CONSEQUENCES, NO HANGOVERS"

The complicating action begins with the scene of Phil talking with two drunken men in a bowling alley. (The bowling alley is nearly empty, suggesting that most of the town's residents are off at the Groundhog Day dinner and that only the losers are hanging around here.) Phil describes what he considers the best day in his life so far—meeting a woman in the Virgin Islands, eating and drinking with her, and making love at sunset. (At the end of the film, Phil will make love with Rita at dawn.) Phil asks: "Why couldn't I get *that* day, over and over and over?" As we have seen, the notion of an ideal day reverberates through the film. At first Phil will attempt to recreate that same day through sex, casually seducing women. Later he will try to improve the day by substituting Rita for the fantasy object of seduction. During one of those seduction attempts, Rita will refer to "the perfect day," and eventually he will make a perfect day by acknowledging his love for Rita and inducing her to fall in love with him.

The conversation in the bowling alley introduces a new premise that will govern this section of the film. Phil asks the two men what if "nothing you did mattered," and again asks after they go out driving, "What if there were no tomorrow?" One of his pals remarks, "No tomorrow. That would mean there would be no consequences, no hangovers. We could do whatever we wanted." In effect, the conventional laws of cause and effect that operate in the Hollywood cinema would be suspended. Phil accepts this logic at first, and his belief rules the complicating-action section.

Acting on this assumption, Phil drives the car onto the railroad tracks, nearly getting hit by a train. He laughs and says, "I'm not gonna live by their rules any more!" Here he gains his first new goal by deciding to exploit the fantastic situation to indulge himself utterly. He acts quite consistently with his character traits as we saw them at the beginning of the film, but now those unpleasant traits go unchecked and become exaggerated.

At the end of the scene with the two drunken men, we see Phil cheekily asking the police, "Too early for flapjacks?" and one shot of him in jail. The next shot shows him, as usual, jerking awake to the strains of "I Got You, Babe." Thus we know that the consequences of Phil's crimes have been wiped out, and we are presented with what seems to be a profoundly anomalous situation in a Hollywood film: a character has performed major actions which seemingly have no consequences, no effects.

Yet classical logic and coherence have not actually been suspended, and eventually they will triumph. Phil's actions do in fact have important effects— on him. He remembers each day (even though the characters around him do not), and he discovers that the nasty things he does have a cumulative impact, driving him to despair and eventual suicide. The result will be his turnaround, to the point where he tries to cram as many effects-producing actions as he can into a single day. A film that is seemingly free of effects thus becomes a panegyric to linear causality. The final consequence will be Phil's escape from repeated time.

The accumulating days progress in a clear fashion through the continued use of dangling causes and further setups for upcoming events. (There are relatively few dialogue hooks once the repetitions begin, but this is because the plot can move through a repertory of already-familiar events.) In the scene in which Phil lingers over a grotesquely huge breakfast, obviously in no hurry to return to Pittsburgh, Rita remarks, "I thought you hated this town," and he replies, "Well, it's beginning to grow on me." He likes it for the wrong reasons at this point, but the line prepares us for his eventual decision to live in Punxsutawney. Similarly, the initial conversation with Nancy in the diner establishes a dangling cause that returns early in the next scene as Phil uses the information he had gained to pick Nancy up at the Groundhog Day festivities. This in turn establishes how Phil will go about trying to approximate the ideal day he had reminisced about in the bowling alley scene.

Most of his day with Nancy is elided, and we next see them making love in his room. His inadvertent mention of Rita's name creates another dangling cause—one which will not be picked up for some time but which is crucial. He wishes that the object of his seduction were Rita rather than Nancy, and his hedonistic goal will eventually focus on her.

From a shot of Phil and Nancy kissing, there is a straight cut to him sitting outdoors and predicting upcoming events. We soon learn that he is doing so in order to time his robbery of an armored car. No dialogue hook or dangling cause connects the two scenes, and this is the film's first move into a new repeated day that has not been accomplished via a closeup of the digital alarm radio. (It is also the first transition that implies that an indefinite number of days have passed without any part of them being shown to us.) Yet even here we quickly grasp what is going on. The temporal shift is reasonably clear, since a night scene is followed by a daytime one. The basic premise of this section of the film—that there are no consequences—still holds. The events of these scenes are conventional notions of what a selfish man would do under such circumstances—indulge himself with sex and money. Moreover, we have learned in the case of Nancy that Phil is now using memorized information to carry out hedonistic projects, so his actions are motivated. Thus we need no additional information to grasp the robbery scene or the subsequent brief scene outside the movie theater with Phil dressed in a cowboy costume.

A straight cut leads from that scene to a close view of two monitors in the news van as Rita checks Phil's latest groundhog coverage. This is the only time in the film when we see any of Phil's tapings played back. The technical fact of videotape's ability to repeat action provides another motif that stresses the cyclical days in which Phil is trapped. The repeated Groundhog Days also call the audience's attention to the common practice of making multiple takes during the shooting of a film. In *Groundhog Day*, no shots are actually repeated, but several are so close that some spectators might initially wonder if the same take is being reused. As a result, the film calls attention to its own editing and cinematography to a degree unusual for a classical film. Still, this little meta-cinematic touch is heavily motivated and adds to the comic tone of the film. In my experience, audiences tend to laugh in surprise and delight the first time that the narrative jumps "backward" within the same scene—that is, in the scene where Phil joins Rita in the bar and learns what her favorite drink is, then immediately is seen entering again and ordering the same drink for them both. Thus the realization of the paradoxical temporal possibilities of editing adds to the film's entertainment value.

The scene in which Rita runs through a video playback of the Groundhog Day tape marks the point at which Phil begins to concentrate on seducing Rita. She had been presented in the setup as having an almost excessively sweet nature. Now her list of the traits of her ideal man reconfirms that. The image she paints is essentially the popular 1980s feminist notion of the caring, sharing male: unashamed to cry; sharing housework and child rearing; artistic, sensitive, and kind. Phil ludicrously claims to fit this image, and he manages to learn how to pretend he has these traits well enough to lure Rita into a series of romantic days with him. He never quite manages to seduce her, but she does admit angrily that she had been tricked into caring about him.

On the first day, he is very awkward with her, making her suspicious immediately: "Is this for real, Phil, or are you just trying to make me look like a fool?" Phil responds, "I'm just trying to talk like normal people talk. Isn't this how they talk?" She replies dubiously, "Close" (a line echoed later in the scene when Phil declares that he is "close" to conforming to Rita's ideal). Given how perfect Rita is, however, it comes as no surprise that she sees through Phil's seduction attempts, no matter how he hones his tactics.

Just in case any viewer might miss the point and assume that Phil has "really" turned nice when he starts trying to seduce Rita, there is a shot of him yanking a part out of the van in order to strand her in Punxsutawney with him. We are thus made aware that he is acting only through self-interest. In the climax section, this moment will be contrasted with his good deed of helping some old ladies by changing their flat tire—one of those "errands" that presumably prevent Larry and Rita from setting out for Pittsburgh.

The attempted seductions involve the most concentrated set of brief repeated days, beginning with the series of drinks Phil and Rita have in the hotel bar. This scene reveals the subtle care the filmmakers have taken to make each day repeat in a literal fashion. For example, when Rita first orders a "sweet vermouth on the rocks with a twist," a waitress with a tray passes in the background, out of focus. In the next repetition, Phil orders a vermouth, and just as Rita says, "The same" (a joke in itself), the waitress passes by again—as she does on the next go-through when Rita repeats, "The same." Similar care has been taken with the background elements in most other scenes.

Each of the scenes in the bar and restaurant stops when Phil makes a mistake and then goes back far enough to allow him to correct it. The repetitions substitute for dialogue hooks, and the pattern is very easy to follow.

The point at which Phil finally gets it "right" is when he quotes French poetry to Rita, allowing their relationship to develop for a while without repetition. After the snowball fight they nearly kiss; then they share a romantic dance in the town square. As they walk through the wintry evening, Rita remarks on how her expectations about Phil have changed; it is, she says, "The perfect day. You couldn't have planned a day like this." Phil replies, "Well, you *can*. It just takes an awful lot of work." But the day is not perfect. Once Rita goes to Phil's room, she realizes that she has been set up: "I could never love someone like you, Phil, because you'll never love any one but yourself." Phil's reply is crucial: "That's not true. I don't even *like* myself. Give me another chance." After Rita indignantly slaps him and leaves, he does get several more chances, summarized in a montage of slaps.

The series of seduction attempts will be important for the resolution of the romance. Later we must believe that Rita can really fall in love with Phil very quickly during the final repetition of Groundhog Day. There she will not even spend more than a few minutes with him, since he will be occupied all day with his good deeds. Yet because we see them getting along so well during portions of these days of failed seduction, we are cued to believe that Phil really does love Rita underneath but simply is not worthy of her. In a sense we are getting here the action that should come later, in the climax portion. (That portion is in fact relatively short, while this complicating action is proportionately very long.) The moment in the climax when Rita finally reaches up to accept Phil after having "bought" him depends on our sense that they have had a romantic courtship—even though during that final day she presumably remembers nothing of these earlier scenes. But Phil does, and we do, and by the end that is enough to give us a sense that they are ready to marry.

Phil's line about not even liking himself gives us our second clue that he is aware of how obnoxious he is. (The first was his remark to Rita about trying to talk as normal people do.) His dissatisfaction with himself hints once more at an underlying, suppressed decency that he can perhaps regain. This self-awareness will motivate most of the rest of the film. After his repeated failures to seduce Rita, he sinks into despair, guzzling whiskey as he impresses the elderly bed-and-breakfast guests by anticipating all the right answers on

"Jeopardy," smashing the alarm clock/radio repeatedly in his attempts to silence the "I Got You, Babe" song, and finally deciding to commit suicide.

The suicide attempt follows logically from the series of clock smashings. Having failed to destroy the object that signals his daily repetitions, Phil apparently decides to break the spell by trying to stop the groundhog from seeing its shadow. His incoherent recording of his annual Groundhog Day coverage suggests this: "There is *no way* this winter is *ever* going to end as long as this groundhog keeps seeing his shadow. I don't see any other way out. He's gotta be stopped. And I have to stop him." He then steals the truck in which the groundhog's cage had been placed and races away, pursued by the police and by Rita and Larry in the van. The chase parallels the earlier one with the two drunks and the police at the beginning of the complicating action. There he had declared "I'm not gonna live by their rules any more!" and had ended by using the car to knock down a giant sign representing a groundhog. By now he cannot live without rules and kills himself and the groundhog by driving off a cliff with it. After waking up alive the next morning, he futilely tries to commit suicide using various other methods. The complicating action ends with the final suicide, as the sheet is pulled up over his face in the morgue.

By the end of the complicating action, Phil has learned that, no matter how many times he tries to commit suicide, there is a tomorrow to be dealt with. He has learned that there are consequences, despite the fact that only he can remember what happens from one repeated day to another. As a result, he has also learned that the only way he can cope with his situation is to change his personality.

DEVELOPMENT: RITA'S IDEAL MAN

The development section of the film begins back in the café, with Phil telling Rita that he's a god. He tries to prove this by giving intimate details about the people around them, as well as by predicting events just before they happen. His description of his repeated days ends, ". . . and there's nothing I can do about it." Yet he can do something about it by making the day perfect in a way that he had not previously anticipated. That goal, once he conceives it, will govern the rest of the film.

Phil's claim that he's a god seems to fit in with his old egotism. Indeed, it follows a motif of imagery relating to gods. In the opening scene Phil had pretended to blow on his television weather chart to make the fronts and other features move across the country. Later Phil will read the line from Joyce Kilmer's "Trees," "Only God can make a tree." Yet this imagery is comic, and Phil's assertion that he is a god hardly fits in with his earlier mean-spirited braggadocio.

Indeed, a change is already apparent in him. As he introduces Rita to the people in the café, he seems much friendlier than he had been in previous scenes. He also has lost his earlier frantic desperation. He does not eat an enormous breakfast; he will not try to seduce Rita. Instead, he calmly tells her the literal truth about what has happened to him and finds convincing ways to demonstrate that he knows more about both past and future events than he possibly could under normal circumstances. In keeping with the religious imagery, he tells Rita that she looks like an angel in the snow.

The development section focuses on Phil's transformation. Because he has already changed so much, Rita half believes his story. She agrees to stay with him all day and test his claim. As they sit in his room and flip cards into a hat, they discuss his situation. This conversation contains one of the narrative's few hints as to how much time has passed in repeated days. Rita's shots go wildly astray, and she complains, "It would take me a year to get good at this." Phil responds, "No—*six* months, four to five hours a day, and you'd be an expert." To some extent, Phil is still in despair at this point. Soon he remarks, "It doesn't make any difference. I've killed myself so many times I don't even exist any more." We are perhaps supposed to take literally the idea that Phil at one point spent four or five hours a day for six months flipping cards into a hat—presumably during his period of despair and eventual suicide. One other clue had come during the brief scene in front of the movie theater, when Phil had remarked to his date, "I love this film—I've seen it over a hundred times." Thus the repetitions apparently add up to years, since after pulling out of despair Phil has time to develop such positive traits as studying the piano.[5]

Rita remarks: "Well, sometimes I wish I had a thousand lifetimes. I don't *know*, Phil, maybe it's *not* a curse. It just depends on how you look at it." This line echoes the scene at the beginning of the complicating action, when the drunk had opined that Phil is "a glass-is-half-empty kind of guy." Rita helps him find a goal with her suggestion that he could take advantage of the repetitions. As a result, he essentially makes himself over into the ideal man that Rita had described.

As Rita falls asleep, she tells Phil, "I want you to know it's been a really nice day for me." He responds, "Me, too"—not his ideal day, but getting there. Once Rita is asleep, Phil declares his love for her, concluding: "I don't deserve someone like you, but if I ever could, I swear I would love you for the rest of my life." This makes explicit his new goal in the romance line of action. (Beyond the two goals is a third, to escape the time repetitions, but in effect, achieving his two immediate objectives leads to success there as well.) His declaration serves at least three major purposes. First, it shows that he is not just getting really good at pretending to be sincere in order to seduce Rita. Even though she is in his bed, he has not tried to make love to her. (And she is now asleep and cannot hear him anyway.) His love for her is clearly genuine. Second, the speech supplies substantial motivation for Phil's later hard work to become worthy of her. Third, it reveals that he has been in love with her from the first time he saw her. We would not have guessed this from the way he scoffed at her naiveté in the early scenes, and perhaps he himself only now realizes that he has loved her all along. The fact that he fell in love with her provides further motivation that he has possessed worthy traits all along, however much they might have been hidden by his cynical behavior.

By the end of this scene, Phil has his two new goals. First, he has realized that his earlier premise, that nothing you do matters, has failed him. His repeated attempts to exploit everyone around him had eventually led him to suicide. He is still stuck in an endlessly repeating day, yet he must find some way of making his actions matter. The only way will be to reverse himself and become a nice guy by doing constructive things. That becomes his first goal. Second, he is in love with Rita and must make himself worthy of her—so worthy, in fact, that she will fall in love with him in a single day. Here again we see how the two goals of the Hollywood protagonist typically are bound up together.

After this speech, Phil wakes up the next morning, alone. For once, he jumps out of bed quickly, as if his new goal of bettering himself and doing good deeds has spurred him on. The development section continues with short scenes of Phil's improvement. He gives money to the beggar; he takes piano lessons. Here the time scheme becomes a bit shaky. Phil seems already to be an expert ice carver just after he starts the piano lessons. Still, the action passes so quickly that we are hardly likely to notice the disparities. In fact, the development section of the film is quite short—only about 16 minutes. This is because the complicating action portion had to be unusually long in order to motivate sufficiently Phil's decision to change his traits.

The development ends with an important series of scenes, as Phil tries day after day to save the beggar's life. Initially he finds the old man in an alley and takes him to a hospital, where he dies. A nurse assures Phil that the man just died of old age, that it was his time to go. But Phil continues to try and save him over an unknown number of subsequent days. The development ends with a scene in the alley, where Phil gives the beggar mouth-to-mouth resuscitation. The old man dies anyway. At the very end, Phil looks up sadly at the sky.

By this point, Phil has become a much better person. He is kind to a point unimaginable at the start. The Phil we saw at the beginning of the film would never have given first aid to an old drunkard. Indeed, he has become as nice as he possibly can. Nothing is made explicit in the dialogue, but these scenes with the old beggar are clearly parallel to the suicide attempts that had ended the complicating action. During that second part of the film, Phil had thought that nothing mattered and that he could do anything. The failed suicides finally convinced him of the contrary. During the development he has taken the opposite approach, struggling to make his actions matter. Now he has reached the limit. He is not, as he had said at the beginning of this section of the film, "a god." He cannot make himself kind and concerned and diligent enough to save the beggar. Apparently the nurse was right—it was just the old man's time to die. (To make this acceptable, we must assume that he is simply the victim of too much exposure, privation, and drinking for one day's worth of kindness to make a difference.) The beggar's death leads Phil to another realization. He must give up trying to be utterly perfect and settle for being Rita's ideal man.

The fact that a male protagonist would conceive and achieve a goal of becoming the ideal of a modern, liberated woman is certainly an unusual one for a Hollywood film. In *Tootsie*, Michael becomes a better man in his relations to women through having to pretend to be one, yet it is also he who dictates how Julie should change herself to fit his newfound model of femininity. Thus, as was widely remarked at the time *Tootsie* came out, it was another case of it taking a man to allow a woman to become liberated. In *Groundhog Day*, for a change, the opposite occurs.

As I have suggested, Phil's transformation has been associated with a growing love for winter, as when he had played and danced in the snow with Rita. His weather forecasts mention the "high altitudes" at which snow is formed, and he uses this same phrase in the restaurant during one of the seduction attempts, telling Rita he would like to live at "high altitudes," an idea with which she concurs. Finally, at the end, he wants to live with her in Punxsutawney, a snowy Allegheny Plateau town which was established during the initial van ride as being in a hilly area. The last action we see him perform on the final repetition of Groundhog Day is sculpting Rita's face in ice, an additional motivation for her sudden love for him. Thus Phil's transformation has been traced by the film's winter imagery.

CLIMAX AND EPILOGUE: "THE BEST DAY OF MY LIFE"

The climax section of the film consists mainly of the last repetition of Groundhog Day. It begins with Phil taping a touching speech about the people of the town: "When Chekhov saw the long winter, he saw a winter bleak and dark and bereft of hope. Yet we know that winter is just another step in the cycle of life. But standing here among the people of Punxsutawney and basking in the warmth of their hearths and hearts, I couldn't imagine a better fate than a long and lustrous winter." All those listening are moved by his words. Now the initial situation of the film has been reversed. Phil, who had hated cold weather, embraces it. Larry, who had been at loggerheads with Phil, thanks him for his speech. Rita, who had disliked him, now offers to buy him coffee. He refuses because he has "errands" to do. These consist of all the good deeds he has worked into his schedule over the repeated days.[6]

In effect, once Phil realizes that he cannot save the old beggar—that he is not a god—he becomes content with the range of good deeds that he can actually accomplish. That includes everything from changing a spare tire to saving Buster from choking in a restaurant. Thus he acquires the sort of kindness and decency that Rita has represented throughout.[7] The climax portion reaches its high point that night, when we see the party mentioned during the setup. Presumably Phil has never attended this party on previous repeated days. Throughout the earlier scenes, we have seen him doing other things at night—most recently, trying to save the beggar.[8] His attendance at the party allows Rita to see evidence of how nice he has become. As a result, she finally falls in love with him and buys him in the comic auction.

This auction carries through the Groundhog Day imagery from early in the film. Buster, the same man who had stepped up to the microphone and acted as Punxsutawney Phil's voice (Fig. 5.2) now uses a similar platform to auction off Phil to Rita (Fig. 5.3). Thus his earlier prediction of ongoing winter is compared to this moment when the romantic line of action is re-solved, suggesting that the relationship between Phil and Rita will extend through the winter into spring and through years of repeated winters and springs—and real, ordinary Groundhog Days.

As I have suggested, Rita becomes captivated by Phil very quickly here, given that she presumably has not been in contact with him since offering to

5.2

5.3

buy him coffee early that morning. But her sudden love has been motivated. First, she, like the others, had been touched by Phil's morning speech. Second, she presumably sees his musical ability and the many testimonials to his kindness as evidence that he possesses the qualities of her ideal man. Most important, the time she spent with Phil, during both his attempted seductions and the day she devoted to testing his story about the repeated days, have given *us* a sense of them as a romantic couple. We cannot but believe that she—despite not remembering those days—has sensed them and feels their resonance romantically. Indeed, in the candy shop that Phil and Rita had visited during one of the days of attempted seduction, Rita had remarked, "There is something *so* familiar about this. Do you ever have *déjà vu?*" This of course created humor and called attention to the film's main premise, but it

5.4

5.5

may also help to suggest that the repeated days with Phil have had an effect on her. (Given that Phil's escape from his time warp hinges on his relationship with Rita, it would make sense that whatever force has caused the repetitions has affected her as well, albeit without her knowledge.)

Rita's gesture of raising her hand to help Phil down off the stage negates her many earlier slaps (Fig. 5.4). He is now worthy of her. As if to signal this, outside the auditorium Phil pauses in front of a quilt on the wall, showing four groundhogs; three of them create a sort of comic halo around his head (Fig. 5.5). Here Ned Ryerson reveals that one of Phil's good deeds has been to sign up for every imaginable insurance policy, implicitly still on the assumption that there is no tomorrow. Ned declares, "This is the best day of my life!" Phil responds, "Mine too," and Rita chimes in, "Mine too." Thus the perfect day that Phil has tried to create is finally achieved.

The last scene of the climax section begins with the clock flipping down to 6:00 for the last time. In what surely must be one of the subtlest cues in recent Hollywood cinema, the change in causality is signaled by the fact that a slightly different passage from "I Got You, Babe" starts on the radio.[9] Phil does not notice this, but upon seeing Rita still in his bed, he realizes that this really is a new day, February 3.

Phil pinches Rita's arm and declares, "Something is different." She asks, "Good or bad?" and he replies, "Anything different is good." This line makes it clear that Phil's acceptance of his peculiar situation and his decision to become a better person have unexpectedly allowed him to accomplish his original goal of escaping the cyclically repeated days. He gets up and looks out the window, confirming that a new day really has started. Then he rejoins Rita in bed and asks, "Do you know what today is?" She replies, "No, what?" He says, "Today is tomorrow. It happened. You're here." This line reiterates and specifies the now-achieved goal: for Rita to be there in bed with Phil at 6:00. It must also be said that Bill Murray's delivery of this line is quite touching and helps motivate the fact of Phil's complete character change.[10]

The dialogue in this scene makes it redundantly clear that Phil's motive during the Groundhog Day party was not simply to seduce Rita. She remarks that she had wanted to make love the night before, but he had not. They make love now, as the camera moves discreetly away to the window. Phil is definitely a transformed character, able to escape from the endlessly repeated days. Thus all goals have been achieved.

There is an ellipsis and a short epilogue. Phil and Rita run out into the snow, and he says he wants them to live in Punxsutawney. This statement caps the change in his character, marking his rejection of his goal of moving to a big city. (His decision that they will begin by renting is a sensible one, since he is now going to owe Ned Ryerson a good deal of money. After all, we know that in Hollywood films, there are always consequences.) The cloud motif of the opening credits reappears under the closing ones, but now the clouds move at a normal, almost imperceptible pace.

Groundhog Day clearly has four major portions and an epilogue, but the timings of these sections are quite disproportionate in terms of the scheme outlined in the opening chapter. The setup lasts for just under 29 minutes, the complicating action for about 36 and a half, the development for about 16, and the climax and one-minute epilogue together total 16 minutes. It seems likely that the scriptwriters were aiming at a three-act structure, since adding the development and climax together makes for three portions that are all around half an hour long. (This still does not conform to the traditional three-act timing as dictated by Syd Field and others, in which the middle act is supposed to be twice as long as both the first and third acts.) Yet the short series of scenes concerning the beggar's death which ends the development is surely a critical turning point, since they lead Phil to the major realization that he is not godlike.[11] Hence he modifies his goal, and everything that has stood in the way of a movement into the climax portion is now past. These traits, as we have seen, are typical of the turning point that leads into the climax portion.

The disproportionate lengths of the sections probably result from the fact that the complicating action is so convoluted. The script needs to squeeze in plenty of incidents that will finally drive Phil to despair and motivate his radical character change. (And no doubt the filmmakers were also catering to the audience's desire to see Bill Murray in his mischievous persona as long as possible before he reforms.) The climax involves Rita falling in love with Phil very rapidly, but the earlier parts of the film are so crammed with incident that the whirlwind climax does not strike the viewer as thin; rather, the delight comes in seeing how the pieces of Phil's elaborately planned day fall neatly into place.

A FINAL LESSON: HIGH CONCEPT

One might argue that *Groundhog Day* is a "high-concept" film. As I noted in Chapter 1, the notion of high concept has been cited as evidence that current filmmaking is "post-classical." For many, a high-concept film is distinguished by its ease of summary. As Steven Spielberg puts it, "If a person can tell me the idea in 25 words or less, it's going to make a pretty good movie. I like ideas, especially movie ideas, that you can hold in your hand."[12]

Given Spielberg's mastery of classical film technique, it may seem odd to quote him as evidence for contemporary departures from that approach. Moreover, one could probably summarize the core idea of *any* movie in a brief statement. For *Groundhog Day*, one could say, "An obnoxious weatherman finds himself living the same unpleasant Groundhog Day repeatedly until he improves enough to be worthy of the sexy woman he idolizes" (25 words exactly). The same could be done for venerated classics ("Diligent investigative reporter seeking the meaning of the enigmatic final utterance of a controversial tycoon uncovers conflicting, ambiguous, even sleazy accounts from the man's associates") and even for art films ("Tantalizing 'he said, she said' tale of couple disputing whether they had consensual or forced sex at a fashionable resort, a year or so ago"). Indeed, during the studio era there already existed a term for the briefly summarizable kernel of a film's story: the "wienie."

For Justin Wyatt, high concept is the defining feature of post-classical cinema, and he suggests that this approach arose in the wake of the decline of 1970s auteurist cinema:

> To gauge the importance of high concept, consider how a film historian might chart the death of the rich period of experimentation in American film of the '70s. As indicated in the chapter on industrial and aesthetic history, this period is frequently described in auteurist terms. And examination of the fate of these auteurs illuminates just how powerful high concept became within the industry and how high concept, in many ways, irrevocably altered the career paths of these auteurs.[13]

As we saw in the first chapter, however, the auteurist directors never dominated Hollywood; they gained a high profile through attracting considerable critical attention and making several commercially successful films. Thus they enhanced the general development of Hollywood but did not initiate a new phase.

High concept, to the degree that it describes an actual phenomenon, seems to me to have little to do with the decline of the auteurists. Rather, it is an intensification of certain elements of the old system resulting from the exponentially rising production costs of films and the unpredictability of the exhibition market. This unpredictability has resulted in the boom-and-bust cycles of recent years, the sequel mania, synergy, and other aspects of modern filmmaking.

Most important, the simplicity and clarity offered by high-concept plots *conform* to classical principles rather than offering an alternative to them. Such plots can be condensed to a simple summary precisely because anyone reading or hearing that summary presupposes that it will be developed using the traditional principles of linear causality, double plotlines, unifying motifs, and all the rest of the classical system. Wyatt summarizes the producer Peter Guber's view of high concept: "Guber states that high concept can be understood as a narrative that is very straightforward, easily communicated, and easily comprehended."[14] Ease of comprehension was the basis of classical

Hollywood narrative from the beginning, and that value is at the center of industry practice today.

If we can actually characterize how "high concept" is different from the approach of the studio era, it might be as an intensification of the formulaic and the simplistic (as opposed to the simple). The "pitch" idea becomes more and more a recombination of proven elements. *Speed* was widely referred to as "*Die Hard* on a bus," and there have been several "*Die Hard* on a plane" concoctions, such as *Air Force One* (1997). This notion of recombination is most memorably portrayed in the lengthy opening take of *The Player*, which moves among offices where increasingly absurd combinations of existing films are pitched by scriptwriters ("*Out of Africa* meets *Pretty Woman*"). Indeed, high concept would seem to be not so much a departure from studio-era practice as an elevation of the sorts of formulas earlier used in B movies to the high-budget "event" film of today. It is ironic that this elevation of B-movie genres to the high-budget level has also been one of the legacies of the auteurist generation.

Groundhog Day reminds us that "high concept," if we want to use the term at all, need not be pejorative. A strikingly original idea might be easily summarized, result in a complex but intelligible film, and even against expectations find favor with a popular audience. In 1998, shortly before the release of *Pleasantville*, with its central premise of two modern teenagers trapped in a 1950s sit-com, *Entertainment Weekly* commented: "Good thing *The Truman Show* has primed audiences for high concepts."[15] Given the widespread critical acclaim for *The Truman Show*, the implication is clearly that some high-concept films can challenge audiences' expectations.

Indeed, *Groundhog Day* seems to fit into a small but growing sub-genre of fantasy films that are both witty and arguably high-concept. *Pleasantville*'s release prompted two reviewers for popular magazines to offer new terms for this sub-genre. Citing two other films in which the writer-director, Gary Ross, had been involved, *Big* (1988) and *Dave* (1993), Richard Corliss called them "fantasies of displacement."[16] In the *Entertainment Weekly* review of *Pleasantville*, Lisa Schwartzbaum also cited *Big* and *Dave* as "magical comedies."[17] Other examples would perhaps include *Splash* (1984), *Peggy Sue Got Married* (1986), and *Sliding Doors* (1998). Such efforts to define a novel trend in filmmaking by appealing to genre offer further evidence that "high concept" may simply be a modern term for ways of spinning new variants on old formulas. Those variants may be quite unusual and yet remain comprehensible to a broad audience. In short, such films show us that a skillful application of the classical system can motivate just about any loony narrative premise.

6

Desperately Seeking Susan

1985. Released by Orion. Directed by Susan Seidelman. Screenplay by Leora Barish. Running time: 104 minutes; setup, 25.5; complicating action, 24.5; development, 24; climax and epilogue, 28 (epilogue alone, 2); closing credits, 3.

WHAT A PAIR!

Certain films supply phrases that pass into the English language. How many variants of "The Good, the Bad, and the Ugly" have there been? How many deals have people been offered that they cannot refuse? How many groups have been dubbed "the usual suspects"? Since 1985, "Desperately seeking . . ." has, rather remarkably, moved from the personal pages into everyday discourse.

It is a phrase that well describes the strong goal orientation of most classical Hollywood plots. But it seems particularly apt for parallel-protagonist films. Typically one character is—usually unwittingly at first—desperate for something that the other can supply or aid in gaining. The something may be an exciting and happy life (as in *Desperately Seeking Susan*), immortal artistic fame *(Amadeus)*, the averting of a military crisis *(The Hunt for Red October)*, or any number of other goals. Most such films end in either intense friendship or love between the two characters (or, as in *Amadeus*, the ironic failure to achieve such a relationship). They differ from single-protagonist films in their elevation of the desired or envied person to equal or nearly equal status. As *Desperately Seeking Susan* shows, the redundantly clear techniques of classical Hollywood narrative can help weave together the plotlines in such films.

The American posters for *Susan* featured a picture of its two stars with a slogan: "It's a life so outrageous, it takes two women to live it" (Fig. 6.1). This

ROSANNA ARQUETTE AIDAN QUINN AND MADONNA AS SUSAN

DESPERATELY SEEKING SUSAN

It's a life so outrageous
it takes two women to live it.

6.1

emphasis on the similarity of the two characters represents the situation at the film's end. Indeed, the ads exaggerate the film's parallelism in that both women wear identical "pyramid" jackets, even though there is only one such jacket in the film. Certainly during *Susan*'s theatrical release, it would have been nearly impossible to see it without having been exposed to this image and hence cued to see the protagonists as similar.

Yet as the film begins, the narration stresses the extreme contrasts between Susan's and Roberta's life-styles. Indeed, it is easy to imagine publicity material that would play on this early disparity. An equally catchy poster might, say, show Roberta in her original housewife persona juxtaposed with Susan in the pyramid jacket, with the two women staring at each other in bafflement. The narrative's gradual movement toward greater similarity between the two clearly reflects *Susan*'s dependence on the pattern discussed in Chapter 1, the parallel-protagonist plot. Roberta, bored with her comfortable upper-middle-class existence, becomes fascinated with Susan and Jim's romantic relationship. Once she decides to begin spying on them rather than just reading their personal ads, she initiates the process of becoming more like Susan and, later, the pattern of Susan becoming more like Roberta. The danger introduced by the plotline of the stolen Egyptian earrings and the gangster's attempt to recover them from Susan and Roberta make it vital for the two women to come together and fight their mutual threat.

Roberta's change may seem more obvious and central because it starts so early. But once Susan finds out who Roberta is, she begins to change, living in Roberta's house, wearing her clothes, reading her diary (paralleling Roberta's perusing the personals), and perhaps sleeping with her husband. By the end, Susan seems ready to settle down with Jim, just as Roberta has found her romantic ideal with Dez. The point is that Roberta's life is far too staid at the beginning, while Susan has become so wild that she consorts with gangsters and risks being murdered. The film seeks a happy medium for both of its protagonists.

The final solutions—settling down into relationships with a struggling projectionist and a player in a minor band—are hardly the glamorous happy endings of Hollywood romance. And of all the films I am analyzing in detail in this book, *Susan* lies the furthest from the mainstream. Upon its release, it was praised for its offbeat qualities. Yet its difference lies almost wholly on the level of its tone. It conforms quite closely to classical narrative usage, with two major plotlines, character traits established quickly and clearly, considerable motivic unity, and a redundant, linear causal progression. Certainly its large-scale parts show the conventional balance of a classical film, as the timings

6.2

given above show. One reviewer noted *Susan*'s polish in comparing it to Seidelman's first feature. *Smithereens* (1982), she says, "dealt with the adventures of a street-wise punkette in the East Side jungle, and can in some ways be seen as a dry run for *Desperately Seeking Susan*, which shares some of the previous film's themes and quirky humour but none of its rough edges. But the success of *Desperately Seeking Susan* is due largely to a clever script confidently handled by a director with a fine visual sense and a talent for screwball comedy."[1] Indeed, *Susan* takes one clichéd technique of the classical cinema and emphasizes it to the point of parody: the use of newspaper or television stories and advertisements to disseminate plot information. Personal ads, television news broadcasts, TV ads, and newspaper headlines (not to mention police mug shots, Polaroid photos, and postcards) draw the characters together and provide them with information about each other. In short, the sort of analysis that applies to the other classical films examined in this book works equally well here.

Consider, for example, two unifying pieces of imagery that trace the two women's character changes. The film's MacGuffin is the pair of stolen ancient Egyptian earrings that Susan nonchalantly takes from her gangster lover's pocket, unwittingly putting herself and later Roberta at risk of being rubbed out by the blond thug Nolan. Susan puts on one earring before she leaves her bag in a locker, and Roberta dons the other after finding the bag. The inevitable reunion of the earrings and their restoration to the museum lead to the epilogue's images of the two protagonists feted by public officials and pictured in a newspaper under the headline "What a Pair!"—a reference to both the jewelry and the women's newfound similarity (Fig. 6.2).

Moreover, the newspaper image reverses the opening scene's closeup of Roberta circling Jim's "Desperately seeking Susan" ad. The homeless Susan started in the faintly tawdry world of the back-of-the-paper personals and has moved to the front page. Similarly, Roberta has gone from experiencing romance vicariously through the personals to living out a real adventure with her idol. The two women's new life-styles were funky enough to make the film appeal to college and art-house audiences. After all, they and their boyfriends end up at the Bleeker Street Cinema in Greenwich Village. But their heroism in thwarting a crime and their new monogamous relationships testify to their essential respectability. Roberta is fulfilled, Susan somewhat tamed. By the end they are, as the poster claimed, living the same life.

SETUP: "SOMETHING DIFFERENT — NOTHING WEIRD"

The first portion of the setup moves back and forth between Roberta and Susan, but there is no apparent causal connection between them. Roberta's interest in the personal ad, however, becomes a dangling cause that will later drive her to get involved in Susan's doings. Initially the film uses a variety of contrasts between the two women's life-styles to link their alternating scenes. As is typical in classical narratives, each character's traits are rapidly and clearly established, motivating the subsequent events of the narrative.

In the initial scene in the beauty parlor, we learn that Roberta is naive and romantic. She reads a personal ad from a man named Blackie who is trying to contact a woman he saw walking her dogs in Washington Square: "Give love a chance." Roberta remarks, "I hope she gives him a chance." Her companion (who we later learn is her sister-in-law Leslie) replies cynically that the man is probably a pervert. The ad's mention of Washington Square hints that romance is associated with Greenwich Village, where the film's two pairs of lovers will end up.

Leslie mentions that today is Roberta's birthday, and her present is a new hair style (though the still-mousy Roberta wants only a trim). Leslie instructs the stylist: "Adrienne, give her something different—nothing weird, you know." This is an explicit description of what Roberta needs—a change, but not to something as extreme as the life Susan is leading. By the end, both protagonists will wear their blonde hair loose and wavy.

Indeed, this scene introduces a motif of makeup, hair styles, clothes, and accessories that will run through the film and chart the character shifts of the two protagonists. The early shot of toenails being painted is echoed in a later scene where Susan's friend paints her own. The pyramid jacket causes both Dez and Nolan to mistake Roberta for Susan. Gary finds Susan by tracing the shopping bag from the store where Roberta had bought the jacket. The Egyptian earrings are associated with the women's merging personalities. Oddly enough, in an avowedly feminist film, this motif does not come across as demeaning to the protagonists. Rather, the pursuit of fashion is presented as pleasurable in itself. The times when women dress up to appeal to men mainly occur at the Magic Club, when Susan's friend and later Roberta don clownishly "sexy" wigs and dresses; this is presented as a sleazy means to earn a living. (After Susan's friend loses her job, she considers whether she should have slept with the manager.)

It emerges during the opening scene that Roberta is reading the ads because she is looking for a job. Leslie advises her not to settle for a salary under $50,000. This line, uttered in the luxurious beauty parlor, redundantly establishes that Roberta is quite well off. Her desire to take a job despite not really needing to do so suggests that her boring life as a housewife has driven her to romantic fantasies.

Late in the scene, Roberta also reads the message from Jim to Susan, setting a date to meet in Battery Park, again in lower Manhattan. Roberta comments that the meeting is for "tomorrow," setting up an appointment that she, Susan, and Jim will all keep. Susan is linked to Roberta's romantic fantasies by the phrase in the ad, "Desperately seeking Susan." Roberta says, "Desperate, I love that word. It's so romantic." Leslie scoffs: "Everyone I know is desperate, except you." Roberta protests feebly: "I'm desperate . . . sort of." She circles the ad in red, and it remains a dangling cause picked up shortly into the next scene. Indeed, the alternation between the two protagonists creates relatively few dialogue hooks but many dangling causes that keep the progression clear. (As we shall see, *Amadeus* takes a different approach to stitching together the scenes of a parallel-protagonist film, using Salieri's narration to supply many dialogue hooks.)

From the closeup of the ad, we move to the main title credit over a shot of a city street. The phrase from the ad, "Desperately seeking Susan," thus carries over nondiegetically and promises us that a link will be established between the two women. The next shot shows Susan, photographing herself in a hotel room. Her action immediately suggests her self-indulgence, and the lyrics of the song playing in the room establish further traits: "You're not shy, you get around / You wanna fly, don't want your feet on the ground." Her theft of money, the earrings, and some trifles from the hotel room establishes her unscrupulousness. This stealing and her casual sex with a man who turns out to be a gangster hint that she is only one step up from prostitution. Yet she is genuinely delighted to find Jim's personal ad—"Jimmy! It's about time!"—drawing a heart around it that echoes Roberta's red circle. This delight and the fact that she keeps returning to Jim motivate her eventual apparent decision to settle down with him.

Susan is already wearing the pyramid jacket that will figure so largely in the narrative. She takes the Egyptian earrings, remarking simply "Nice!" but they turn out to be the stolen jewelry of the famous Nefertiti. This slender motif of "Egyptian" items links to the name of Roberta's husband's spa store, "Gary's Oasis." The Egyptian/Arabian element is not developed extensively, but it is firmly associated with fantasy and romance. Shortly into the next scene, Gary's ad will emphasize that at his store, "All your fantasies can come true." Indeed, the Egypt depicted is a fantasy as well. The jacket's pyramid is not a real one, but the Masonic symbol with the surmounting eye that adorns the Great Seal of the United States.[2] The Egyptian jacket and earrings create a vaguely New Age motif. Susan takes the earrings simply to be a piece of attractive retro-chic. Subsequently, when she learns that they were Nefertiti's, she thinks this is neat. Only later will the earrings provide the means for the two protagonists to gain public acclaim and respectability.

As Susan leaves the hotel room, we see the ominous number 1313, initiating a minor motif of Susan's bad luck. Later Susan's friend will remark, "Bad luck really seems to be following you around." Possibly we are also to associate her misfortunes with the old cliché of mummies' curses, but this is never really cued strongly.

After Susan leaves the hotel room, she is spotted by Nolan, who views her from the back and hence sees mainly the pyramid jacket and her blonde hair. At this point, the narrative shifts without a transitional device back to Roberta. She and Gary are giving a party, during which the ad for Gary's Oasis airs. As he turns on the television, however, the news is just ending, with the announcer mentioning a recent robbery of ancient Egyptian artifacts. We might suspect that the earrings we just saw Susan steal were part of that robbery, and what had seemed a casual theft becomes a more important dangling cause.

During the TV spot, Roberta moves to the window and looks out longingly. Offscreen, we hear Gary's television voice say, "Gary's Oasis—all your fantasies can come true." Gary's fantasies are of the most banal and un-Egyptian sort—blonde babes in hot tubs. Roberta seems upset by the ad, and we suspect that she is not entirely happy with her husband. (Later we discover that he is in fact carrying on an affair.) Roberta's fantasies will lead to her

6.3

6.4

involvement with real Egyptian artifacts (though we do not know this yet). She moves out onto the balcony, and we see her point-of-view of the skyline of southern Manhattan (Fig. 6.3) with the George Washington bridge prominently in the foreground. This shot is followed by another one of her wistful face. These shots reinforce the idea that southern Manhattan will be the place where her romantic fantasies are acted out. Presumably Roberta is here pondering whether to attempt to witness Jim and Susan's appointment at Battery Park the next day. (That appointment is still a dangling cause, set up twice now.) A cut then leads to another view of the same bridge, but from the opposite end (Fig. 6.4); a bus drives up and Susan gets off, walking past an ad for Atlantic City.

This transition stresses both parallels and contrasts between the women. Just after the credits they are both in New Jersey: Susan has been having an affair in Atlantic City and Roberta, as we learn from her point-of-view of Manhattan, lives in New Jersey (where Gary's Oasis is also located, as the TV ad reveals). Yet Susan returns to Manhattan immediately, and Roberta's romantic fantasies are focused on New York as well. Thus the cultural cliché of sophisticated and exciting Manhattan juxtaposed with mundane New Jersey across the river is used to characterize the two protagonists: Roberta's boring life as a Fort Lee housewife drives her to act out her fantasies, while Susan's Greenwich Village life is full of excitement and glamour. Moreover, the cultural association of Atlantic City with organized crime motivates the fact that Susan and Roberta accidentally get mixed up with gangsters. The film emphasizes over and over that Susan has been in Atlantic City. Her suitcase is full of cheap souvenirs from that town. Later, when she goes to the Magic Club, the cigarette girl says to her, "Susan! My God, we all thought you were dead." Susan replies, "No, just in New Jersey." Apart from reinforcing the hopeless boredom of life in New Jersey, the line also suggests that as a result of Susan's fling there, either she or Roberta could end up literally dead.

The scene in which Susan stashes her suitcase in the locker sets up later causal links between her and Roberta. The postcard for the Magic Club will provide a clue that brings the two together. Susan puts on only one of the earrings, leaving the other, so that at the end each woman is wearing one when Nolan goes after them. At this point, however, the significance of these objects remains mysterious, and the transition from Susan back to Roberta is again based on a contrast between their traits: from the unscrupulous Susan using a nail file to avoid paying for a locker to the romantic Roberta watching a scene from *Rebecca* on television. Max (Laurence Olivier) says, "It's gone forever. That funny, young, lost look I loved." This line stresses Roberta's naiveté by comparing her with the Joan Fontaine character. The latter is a mousy type who compares herself unfavorably with her image of the glamorous dead Rebecca—only to learn at the end that she is herself more desirable than her imagined rival. The two plots are certainly not similar in other ways, since Rebecca turns out to have been evil, and Susan is merely wild. In *Susan*, Roberta's romantic naiveté leads her to become friends with the object of her fantasy. More immediately, Roberta's watching of *Rebecca* also serves to reinforce our impression that Roberta is disenchanted with her husband. Gary suggests that she come to bed with him and watch the film on TV with earphones, but she chooses to sit alone and watch it. (She has also just washed her hair to rid herself of the elaborate hair-do provided as Leslie's birthday present.) At the end of the scene she picks up a newspaper, looks at it, smiles, and sighs. Again we can infer that she is fantasizing about Jim and Susan's rendezvous.

The next scene, in which Susan goes to the Magic Club, is linked by the postcard not to the previous scene, but to the second scene back. The use of dangling causes to span intervening scenes is common in classical films in general, but especially in those using parallelism to contrast two protagonists. The progression through the plot is still linear, with two or more lines of action simply interrupting each other. This use of dangling causes to skip over scenes functions well in *Susan* partly because most of the scenes are quite short and we are likely to remember the causes easily once they return. The dangling causes also succeed partly because we have been redundantly cued to expect that the two women will be connected ever more closely.

Once Susan gets permission to stay in her friend's apartment, a fade-out signals a major break in the film. The second half of the setup begins with a shot of Roberta driving across the same bridge we had seen earlier, on her way to witness the meeting between Jim and Susan. A panning camera movement reveals a view exactly opposite to the one seen when Susan arrived by bus. Again the film emphasizes that New York City equals glamour and romance. At this point intercutting between Roberta and Susan briefly replaces the alternation of short but complete scenes involving each. We see Susan accept a man's offer of a free newspaper from a vending machine; she tosses the whole stack on the sidewalk for anyone to take. Her action reinforces the sense of her freewheeling attitude (which puzzles even a presumably blasé Manhattanite) but also provides more exposition: a lead story in the newspaper reveals that Susan's gangster lover has been killed. A return to Roberta shows her walking into Battery Park, where a pedestrian map placed prominently in the foreground portrays the section of lower Manhattan in which much of the film's action occurs. While the Gary's Oasis ad played on fake exoticism, evoking a Middle Eastern setting, Roberta now mingles with real members of various ethnic groups, as when she passes a black drummer wearing an African-style outfit.

The brief exchange between Jim and Susan hardly lives up to Roberta's romantic expectations. Their conversation (inaudible to her) serves in part to bring the gangster plot into more prominence, as Susan reveals to Jim that she had been with the murdered man shortly before his death and Jim expresses his apprehension about her safety. It also establishes that Jim is more eager to stabilize their relationship than Susan is. As part of his attempt to protect her, he scrawls Dez's phone number on a scrap of paper, a dangling cause picked up much later when Roberta finds it in the jacket pocket. Jim's

6.5

parting words to Susan are, "Be here the next time I get back." And she will be there, though their reunion at the climax of the film will be convoluted. It will apparently also, however, signal her final acceptance of his desire for a stable relationship.

Up to now the film has stressed the differences between the two protagonists, but once Roberta sees Susan in Battery Park, the similarities between them become more obvious. As this scene ends, Roberta is framed in the foreground and Susan in depth, with the two women walking in synchronization (Fig. 6.5). Roberta has progressed from reading the personal ads to spying on Susan, and now to following and perhaps imitating her. Her first goal is now clear, if somewhat amorphous: she wants to become more adventurous, more like Susan. (The gangster threat will later become the basis for her second goal.) The increasing emphasis on parallelism prepares for the moment when Roberta buys Susan's jacket.

Indeed, as the setup draws toward its end, the film begins to use a series of objects and messages to link the many scenes in which Susan and Roberta appear separately. Eventually all the characters become involved in searches: Susan looking for her bag, Gary looking for Roberta, Jim looking for Susan, Nolan trying to recover the earrings, and Roberta and Dez trying to solve the mystery of why Nolan keeps following her. These searches gradually define the various characters' goals.

The objects and messages act simply as clues, with one turning up whenever the plot needs to move one step further. The jacket becomes the first direct link between Susan and Roberta, as Susan sells it in a used-clothing store and Roberta buys it. The store's name, "Love Saves the Day," relates to the motif of romantic fantasy. (Susan's claim to the clerk that the jacket

DESPERATELY SEEKING SUSAN   165

belonged to Jimi Hendrix sets up a further contrast between her traits and Roberta's; the clerk quickly sizes Roberta up and assures her that the jacket belonged to Elvis.) Here the progression from scene to scene comes to depend less on parallelism and more on repeated references to these objects, and especially to the key that is in the jacket pocket.

After Roberta tries on the jacket, the scene shifts to her kitchen, and she enters wearing it. The jacket becomes a way of confirming that her marriage to Gary is disappointing. When she explains that she bought the jacket because it belonged to Jimi Hendrix, Gary replies uncomprehendingly, "You— you bought a used jacket? What, are we *poor?* What's goin' on here?" When Gary is unable to stay and eat the elaborate Julia Childs meal that Roberta had set out to fix, the narration stresses that even her domestic efforts go unappreciated.

Soon the key falls out of the jacket pocket. This crucial moment establishes the means by which Roberta will temporarily assume the identity of her fantasy figure. Immediately after this we see her in the bathtub, on the edge of which are a picture of Susan (one of the polaroids taken in the Atlantic City hotel room), a newspaper clipping about her, and the key. The clipping states: "Mystery woman sought for questioning." Roberta apparently knows that Susan is in some trouble, yet she still chooses to pursue her. The moment at which she slips down under the water apparently signals her decision to try and meet Susan by placing an ad. It also suggests her desertion of her old life and her hope to assume a new, more daring personality. That new goal ends the setup.

COMPLICATING ACTION: "YOU CAN'T MISS HER"

The key provides a dangling cause picked up immediately in the next scene. Susan is in the clothing shop, inquiring about the jacket: "You sold it! I had a key—it was really important." She then leaves her name and address, setting up another dangling cause that will resurface much later when Gary tracks Susan down and they become allies in the search for Roberta. Finally, the act of writing provides a transition: Susan writes her phone number, and we cut to Roberta writing her advertisement. She heads it with the same phrase that she had found so romantic, "Desperately seeking Susan." She then instructs Susan to meet her in Battery Park the next day "regarding key," signing the ad "A Stranger." Thus a new appointment is established. (Once again Roberta has her hair up in a towel, as if washing it signifies a change of character; when she had read the first personal ad, she had been under a dryer in the beauty salon.) Immediately there is a cut to the published ad with Susan reading it and saying, "Good going, Stranger." The key serves to tie these various scenes together and move the action swiftly along to the point where Roberta will develop amnesia and think that she is Susan. Her designation of herself as a stranger hints at her change into someone more venturesome and mysterious. When Susan calls her "Stranger," the narration prepares us for her own eventual acceptance of Roberta (using the same phrase) as a friend. A brief scene shows Jim reading the same ad and getting upset: "Well, what fuckin' stranger?" He assumes that the "stranger" is linked to the gangster threat hovering over Susan, motivating the transition to the next scene where he calls his friend Dez to solicit protection for Susan.

This phone call introduces Roberta's future romantic partner, Dez, a projectionist at the Bleeker Street Cinema. The disruption in Dez's life that will be caused by Roberta/Susan is suggested by the fact that Dez inadvertently lets a reel run out before the next one is prepared. This gaffe will be echoed in the final scene as he lets the film jam and burn as he kisses Roberta in the projection booth. The phone conversation between Dez and Jim reveals that Dez's girlfriend Victoria has just left him, thus announcing his availability for a new liaison. The phone call also helps to make an explicit comparison linking Roberta to Susan, as the sound of the conversation bridges over a single shot of Roberta dressing to keep her rendezvous. She has put on the jacket and done her hair in a more casual style, imitating Susan, whose picture is attached to the mirror. Jim's voice is heard on the track, describing Susan: "You can't miss her. Uh, she's incredibly pretty: blonde hair, medium height, oh, and she's got this green and gold jacket with a pyramid with an eye on top like a dollar bill." This description now also fits Roberta, redundantly motivating the moment when Dez mistakes her for Susan. Up to now Roberta has just been a voyeur, spying on Susan and Jim in a vague attempt to escape her boring life. Now she is changing her life, though it is still not clear exactly what she hopes to accomplish by imitating her idol.

The scene of the second rendezvous at Battery Park begins with Susan in a cab, looking annoyed as she listens to the driver complaining at length about sushi. This minor moment connects to the motif of cultural exoticism associated with lower Manhattan, echoing the theme of characters not being open to new experiences. It also prepares for Susan's removal from the scene of the appointment, as she is arrested for trying to stiff the cabbie.

During the scene at Battery Park, Nolan mistakes the transformed Roberta for Susan, approaching and pursuing her.[3] Seeing this, Dez follows and also mistakes Roberta's identity, calling out "Susan!" Roberta reacts, hitting her head, and her purse rolls into the water—a moment emphasized by the film's sole use of slow motion. The round purse is parallel to Susan's round bag, which contains all her belongings and sits in a Port Authority locker, inaccessible to her as long as Roberta has the key. Now Roberta loses her memory and is cut off from her bag and any belongings that could link her to her New Jersey life.[4]

Here, for the first time, the narrative becomes concerned primarily with Roberta: her search for her identity and her flight from Nolan. Susan temporarily becomes a secondary character. Instead Roberta's future romance with Dez is set up as he reluctantly helps her to find "her" bag in the Port Authority locker. The presence of Dez's phone number and the key in the pocket of the pyramid jacket seem to prove that Roberta is Susan. Yet the fact that Dez mistakes Roberta for Susan also delays their romance. Jim has convinced Dez that Susan is wild and unpredictable, and Dez warns Roberta, "I mean I know a little bit about you, OK? So don't even consider jerking me around, because I'm not in a great mood today" (a redundant reminder of his breakup with Victoria). Roberta's baffled reply reflects her naive personality, despite her loss of memory: "Sure, I mean, I wouldn't . . . jerk you around. I don't even know you." She is not and never will be the exploitive character that Susan is at the beginning of the film.

Dez and Roberta's visit to the Port Authority bus terminal leads to the acquisition of the bag and motivates Roberta's attempts to discover her identity by following the clues it contains. Dez offers to let her stay at his place for one night, thus setting up a deadline for Roberta to find out who she is and where she belongs. For a long stretch of the following action, Roberta and Susan again appear in separate scenes, but now Susan is less important. The film continues, however, to use parallelisms in order to cut occasionally to Susan. For example, when Roberta finds cigarettes in the suitcase, she tries to smoke, even though she is obviously a novice. A cut moves the scene to Susan in jail, getting a light for her cigarette from a guard. (Another parallelism is set up in that Roberta will later be in this same cell, charged with prostitution.) This scene serves to show that Susan gets out of jail and discovers that the suitcase is missing from the locker, but we quickly return to Roberta.

During this section the characters gain new goals that will drive the narrative forward for much of the film. Susan wants her suitcase and possessions back; Roberta must recover her memory. Gary, Roberta's husband, also becomes a more important character here, as he tries to find her. Nolan's goal is also at work: he wants Nefertiti's earrings back, though we only learn the complete story of the theft of the ancient artifacts late in the film.

The oscillations among the characters and plotlines become more elaborate here. In many cases, one scene will end with some sort of action that will be echoed in the new scene, even though there is no causal connection between the two. This kind of connection by analogy is common in Hollywood cinema, since it gives an impression of an actual hook between the two scenes. (As we shall see in the next chapter, *Amadeus* often links Mozart and Salieri via graphic matches.) Thus when Dez discovers that his previous girlfriend has taken most of his belongings, the scene ends with a shot of the empty space where his refrigerator had been; a graphic match moves us to Leslie's kitchen, showing her refrigerator as she talks to Gary. This scene establishes that they have no clue as to why Roberta has gone missing. Leslie reveals that Gary has had at least one affair and questions Gary about whether Roberta has orgasms when they have sex. His equivocation suggests that perhaps Roberta's sex life has been bland. (Later Susan finds a sex manual in Roberta's drawer, perhaps confirming this notion.) Most important, Leslie's reference to Roberta's wedding ring abandoned by the bathtub seems to imply that when Roberta had slipped down into the water, she had also forsaken her marriage. At the end of this scene, Gary, Leslie, and her boyfriend Larry discuss Roberta's disappearance as the two men eat delicatessen food.

A cut then shifts the scene to Roberta and Dez, eating Chinese food on the roof of his apartment building. There is no dangling cause from the first scene that connects it with the second, but the link involving takeout meals creates a transition. And indeed, there is a connection between the two scenes, though it is not immediately apparent. We have been prepared to expect that Roberta may be romantically linked with Dez. In the scene where Dez and Roberta had come to his apartment for the first time, his former girlfriend, Victoria, had been moving her furniture out; at that point she had assumed that Roberta was Dez's new girlfriend and had remarked, "He's a really nice guy. You'll be happy together." Now Dez and Roberta seem attracted to each other, and she even kisses him. More important, Dez resembles Susan's boyfriend Jim. In this scene Roberta asks what Jim looks like, and Dez replies, "Sort of my build." Yet Dez is less wild than Jim. He has a steady job as a projectionist rather than roaming the country with an aspiring band. Similarly, the basic movement of the film is to turn Roberta into Susan minus the promiscuity amd irresponsibility.

In the short run, however, this rooftop scene serves two purposes. First, the couple agree that Roberta is in danger from the gangsters and should "lay low for a while." Thus the gangster line of action is more firmly transferred to Roberta. Second, the scene also establishes the attraction between Roberta and Dez, which in turn motivates his willingness to continue helping her despite the dangers involved. He remarks, "You know, you are not at all what I expected," emphasizing that Roberta has not become as wild as Susan and thus is a desirable partner for Dez.[5] Slightly drunk, Roberta kisses Dez, then apologizes. The following scene of them sleeping restlessly in adjoining rooms of his apartment suggests their sexual attraction and repeats this motivation for Dez's willingness to continue helping Roberta.

That willingness is important, as shown by a cut to Nolan outside in his car. He has tracked Roberta to Dez's apartment. From this point on, Roberta must regain her memory, get out of her marriage to Gary, and achieve her romance with Dez. Moreover, since the gangster plot has caught up with her again, she must find a way to thwart Nolan. This threat will intensify in the film's second half. Here we reach the convergence of Roberta's two goals. Hence the complicating action ends, and we move into the obstacles and delays of the development.

DEVELOPMENT: "SHE OWES ME A COAT"

The development begins as Dez wakes up and watches Roberta dressing, then pretends to have been asleep. She comes to him in a dress covered with spangles, wearing for the first time the single Egyptian earring. He asks, "What've you got on, some sort of disguise?" She is indeed wearing a costume put together from Susan's bag and is in a way masquerading as Susan. She reacts badly to his question, and he responds, "No . . . it's sort of charming." Thus Roberta has turned Susan's wildness into something more subdued and acceptable. But the adventure must also go forward. Roberta has explored Susan's bag and found a $100 bill and a matchbook from a coffee shop. She offers to treat Dez to breakfast there, hoping to find a clue to her identity; this provides a dialogue hook into the scene at the coffee shop.

Indeed, after this point the film continues to be structured around searches, with most of the dangling causes consisting of clues that various characters find. None of the transitions depends upon parallels between the characters involved, as many in the earlier portions of the narrative had. After Roberta and Dez are thrown out of the coffee shop, Nolan finds the Magic Club postcard on the floor, providing a hook into the next scene, which takes place at the club. This scene shows that Susan's friend has lost her job there and that they are going to a double feature—thus getting Susan out of the way for a while. The scene ends with yet another dangling cause, a hand putting out a "help wanted" sign. Immediately after this Dez drops Roberta at the Magic Club, picking up the dangling cause of her decision to visit it. When the manager asks if she is looking for a job, she replies, "Yeah, yeah, I think I am." At the beginning of the film Roberta had spotted Jim's personal ad when she was looking for a job. Now she finally gets one—though it is a far cry from the high-paying work that Leslie had urged her to find, since Roberta's salary turns out to be $20 a night. Since she became an amnesiac, Roberta has been trying to imitate Susan, struggling to smoke and putting on outlandish clothes. Now she seems to be redefining herself, but not as either Susan or the old Roberta.

By this point the film is cutting increasingly freely among the characters, using fewer hooks. Even so, the progression is clear because long-dangling causes are revived. Next a straight cut leads to Gary eating a TV dinner and spotting the shopping bag from the store where Roberta had bought Susan's jacket. It enables him to track down Susan's name and phone number. In other cases, scene changes are accomplished using trick transitions to make the actions seem related. These tricks are often entirely based on visual or auditory techniques. At the end of the scene where Gary calls Susan, there is a closeup of her friend's feet waving back and forth to dry the nail polish. A drum roll is heard over this shot, and then there is a cut to a drummer playing. This new scene, which shows Roberta's first performance at the Magic Club, has no direct causal connection to the previous scene. Yet the movement of the feet, vaguely matching the movement of the drumsticks, links the two scenes. (We have already seen a similar device used with the graphic match of the refrigerator that moved from Dez's apartment to Leslie's kitchen.)

Straight cuts between spaces contrast Gary's meeting with Susan in a dance club with Roberta's inept debut at the Magic Club. As Roberta walks along a dark street afterward, she hears Nolan following her and ducks into the office of a night watchman. There the same ad for Gary's Oasis is on the TV, dubbed into Spanish except for the last line, repeated in English: "At Gary's Oasis, all your fantasies can come true." This ironically leads into the moment when Roberta goes out again and is grabbed by Nolan. She is only saved by the police because they mistake her for a prostitute and want to arrest her. Roberta's fantasy of imitating Susan and leading a more exciting life has come all too true. This moment confirms that Susan's life-style is too extreme. Had Nolan not misidentified Roberta, he would have tried to grab the real Susan, perhaps with even worse results. The development section functions in part to demonstrate vividly that both women need to change, and it will draw to an end when Roberta takes steps to create a less dangerous but still interesting new life.

Nolan's attack on Roberta results in her bumping her head and recovering her memory, echoing the fact that his attempt to manhandle her during their first meeting at Battery Park had led to her losing her memory. Her recovery from amnesia puts Roberta in a position where she can begin to build her new life.

A straight cut leads from the arrest to Susan exploring Gary and Roberta's home. She takes a jacket from Roberta's closet, and when Gary objects, replies, "She owes me a coat." The pyramid jacket has been the main symbol of the two women's swapped or merging identities. The fashion motif resurfaces: the jacket Susan chooses is covered with spangles and is somewhat similar to the spangled boots for which Susan had traded the pyramid jacket. Thus Roberta has at least one item in her wardrobe that fits in with Susan's style, hinting that all along Roberta had the potential for a more Susan-like, adventurous existence.

During the scenes between Susan and Gary, we realize that he is somewhat dissatisfied with his marriage, considering Roberta too uptight. Surprisingly, he and Susan get on quite well, smoking marijuana together. Susan enjoys the luxurious suburban life-style far more than Roberta did; upon arriving, she lies in the empty bathtub and tells Gary, "You know, I could get used to a place like this." This framing recalls the earlier scene in which Roberta slid down into the water as she decided to contact Susan. We have known that Roberta wants to be like Susan; now it becomes clear that Susan might aspire to the sort of comfortable bourgeois existence that Roberta has been leading. This suggests that Susan might be ready to settle down, as Jim later claims. There is even a hint that Susan and Gary might form a romantic couple, but it is never developed. These scenes also emphasize that Susan has jumped to the conclusion that Roberta is allied with the gangsters and is trying to pin the murder on Susan. Thus she is not yet willing to help Roberta. Such delaying tactics, as we have seen, are typical of the development portions of classical films.

During the pot-smoking episode, Roberta calls from jail and discovers that Gary is with another woman. Quickly she hangs up and asks the matron, "Could I call someone else?" This quiet moment is the turning point that ends the development and leads into the climax portion of the film. Here Roberta has attempted to return to her old life, only to assume that Gary is cheating on her. (And indeed he may be, though there is no explicit indication that Susan and Gary sleep together.) Her decision to call Dez marks her definitive abandonment of her old New Jersey existence and her decision to seize the chance for romance. But we do not learn all this right away. The scene ends before we find out whom she is calling, though we may strongly suspect it is Dez. (She gets the number from a slip of paper that looks like the one Jim gave Susan and that has been in the jacket pocket ever since.) So far the film has progressed in a linear fashion. Now there is a key omission, and we do not definitively learn for a few more scenes that Dez bailed Roberta out. This arousal of curiosity helps emphasize the transition into a new phase of the action.

CLIMAX AND EPILOGUE: "NOBODY'S LIFE COULD BE THIS BORING"

The simple intercutting of brief scenes continues as the climax begins with Leslie and Gary at the police station, learning that someone has bailed Roberta out. Switch to Dez's apartment as he and Roberta enter. He tells her, "Consider it my final favor, Susan. I must say, you are really livin' up to your reputation." As has been the case since Roberta and Dez met, he keeps assuming she is the wild Susan that Jim had warned him about. Thus we continually see Roberta's potential for change, yet there is an ironic gap between Dez's perception of Roberta's supposed wildness and her actual character. Whereas Susan behaves in a deliberately provocative way (as when she takes the newspapers from the vending machine and tosses them on the sidewalk), Roberta is "wild" only by mischance.

The pair find the apartment ransacked, and Roberta realizes that the culprit was Nolan. Dez is upset, and Roberta begins to leave. Again Susan's bag flops open, as it had when Susan left the Atlantic City hotel room and Nolan first spotted her. The pause allows Dez to relent and kiss Roberta, carrying her off to his bed. Answering the "Desperately seeking Susan" ad has brought Roberta a new romance at last.

A straight cut returns us to Susan in Gary's swimming pool. A news show on a poolside TV reveals that Richard Nolan (the thug) and Bruce Meeker (Susan's dead lover from the Atlantic City hotel) are smugglers and that they stole Nefertiti's earrings. Susan is impressed to discover what it was she took from Bruce's coat—"Nefertiti. No shit!" Susan formulates no new goal here, but this scene dispels the mystery surrounding the gangsters and prepares the way for the defeat of Nolan and the recovery of the earrings.

Another straight cut leads to a scene of Leslie and Gary returning to the Fort Lee house. Susan tells them she has found Roberta's diary, and that it records her everyday life: "It's gotta be a cover. Nobody's life could be this boring." Roberta's life *was* that boring—though it has definitely changed. The diary also reveals that Roberta reads the personals, especially the ads that Jim uses to contact Susan. Here we have a moment in which one protagonist finally realizes that the other is fascinated with her and has been spying on her. Susan also realizes that her earlier suspicions that Roberta is in cahoots with Nolan are unfounded. It is a moment of revelation for Susan, comparable to Roberta's revelation when she called Gary from jail and found him partying with another woman. As a result, Susan gains a new goal: to contact Roberta and help her escape from the murderous intentions of Nolan.

To further this new goal, Susan places the third and final personal ad in the film, asking "Stranger" to meet her at the Magic Club at 9:30 the next night. The advertisement sets up the film's final appointment, to be kept by all the characters.

Even very well constructed classical narratives contain occasional causal flaws. The only major one in *Susan* occurs in the next scene, where Roberta and Dez wake up the morning after having made love. Roberta tries again to explain that she is not Susan, but Dez dismisses this as part of her supposed eccentricity. Jim arrives at the apartment and Dez, wary of an attack by Nolan, accidentally knocks him out. Then Dez admits to Jim that he has fallen in love with Susan and apologizes for having stolen her affection away from Jim. Roberta has by now regained her memory and realized that she is not Susan. She overhears this conversation between Dez and Jim and knows that the two men are really in love with two different women. Indeed, she also knows that Jim could back up her story and convince Dez that she is not Susan. Yet she does not tell them this; instead she sneaks out of the apartment, leaving them to think that they are both in love with Susan. The film provides no motivation for her silence and her departure.

Two brief scenes follow. Roberta reads Susan's ad by noticing it in a newspaper covering a homeless man's head. Then Jim finds it and shows it to Dez. The two men still assume that "Stranger" is the gangster or some other man, thus ensuring that they will keep the appointment in order to protect Susan.

The big scene of the climax takes place at the Magic Club. All the characters meet here, and this scene resolves most of their goals. All of them have been desperately seeking either Susan or Roberta, and all of them—for good or ill—find what they have been looking for. The scene progresses through a series of realizations as each character strives to sort out who Susan and Roberta are. Gary is baffled to find his wife performing as the female assistant in a cheap magic act. Dez realizes that he and Jim do not think of the same woman as "Susan." Most important, Nolan still assumes that Roberta is Susan. He picks Susan as a hostage purely randomly, without any realization that she has the second Nefertiti earring.

Indeed, the idea of "desperately seeking Susan" loses the romantic flavor that Roberta had initially lent it; it becomes threatening as Nolan drags Susan through the backstage area of the theater. During this chase sequence, the film could have taken the conventional approach by having all the characters pursue and capture the villain. Instead, it continues to keep the male characters in the background. Jim responds to the gangster's kidnapping of Susan by simply looking around in confusion; Gary passes a window and fails to see the gangster outside with Susan. In the end, Roberta saves Susan, and the film concentrates on the two female protagonists, despite the presence of all the other characters. Susan's greeting to Roberta, "Good goin', Stranger," both seals their newfound friendship and affirms the fact that Roberta's initial staid personality has loosened up.

The epilogue in the Bleeker Street Cinema begins with a science fiction film on the screen, then cuts to the projection booth. Roberta arrives and tells Dez her real name. She looks very pretty here, with loose hair but no heavy makeup. Physically she is the ideal cross between her earlier self and Susan. They kiss and accidentally cause the projector to burn a frame of film, recalling Dez's failure to switch reels on time when we were first introduced to him. Now Susan and Jim are in the audience, and their smiling reaction to the burning frame indicates that they are somehow aware of the romantic cause of the mistake. Susan has gone from consorting with gangsters in Atlantic City hotels to cuddling with Jim in an art cinema, and we must assume that these two romantic couples are both destined for happy endings.

The epilogue does not end here, however. The final brief scene shows Roberta and Susan receiving a slip of paper from a man at a podium (a reward?). They join hands and hold it up, like prizefighters. A freeze-frame pulls out to show the image as a headline, "What a Pair!" A smaller image of the earrings has a separate headline, "Stolen Earrings Returned" (see Fig. 6.2). Presumably Roberta and Susan are now friends, having struck a happy medium between dangerous romance and respectability.

I suspect that most people who have seen *Susan* have assumed that it was made independently. In fact the project originated with Orion, where it was produced by two women, Midge Sanford and Sarah Pillsbury, and greenlighted by Barbara Boyle, then the company's vice-president. Susan Seidelman, the director, has described the good timing that worked in her favor as she sought a producer:

> [*Susan*] was the kind of project which a lot of women who were vice-presidents of development had responded to—women tended to like the script. And then they would show it to their male bosses who didn't like it enough to give it the go-ahead. For a brief period of time, there was a little window in which Barbara Boyle at Orion was given the opportunity to develop and give the go-ahead to movies which could be made for $5 million or under, and *Susan* was one of the projects which fell into that category. Luck and good timing play a huge part in so many people's lives. It was chance at this one studio, this one woman was given the power.[6]

Seidelman found the actual production to be unintimidating: "In some ways, it was more of a New York independent movie than a Hollywood film."[7] The difference presumably was in terms of subject matter, the relatively low budget, and the relaxed New York shoot.

The notion of a Hollywood studio producing "a New York independent movie" indicates the blurring of the distinction between studio and independent projects that has occurred in recent years. Hopes are frequently voiced in the popular and specialist press that the virtues of independent films will rub off and help to improve Hollywood cinema. Yet in many cases, Hollywood simply skims off the more commercially promising filmmakers and absorbs them into more mainstream projects. Seidelman's own move to more conventional theatrical fare after *Susan* ultimately proved to be a happy alliance for neither side, and as of mid-1998 she was working in television, having directed the pilot of HBO's "Sex in the City."[8] I will return to this issue of the slippery status of independent film production in discussing Hollywood's continuing stability in the final chapter.

7

Amadeus

1984. Released by Orion. Directed by Milos Forman. Screenplay by Peter Shaffer from his play. Running time: 160 minutes; setup, 37; complicating action, 21.5; first development, 39; second development, 29; climax and epilogue, 27.5 (epilogue alone, 5.5); end credits, 5.5.

Let's generously allow factual license to Shaffer as we do to Schiller for *Mary Stuart* and Brecht for *Galileo* and see what we get in return for our generosity.

—STANLEY KAUFFMAN, *The New Republic*

THE MUSIC OF TRUE FORGIVENESS AND PERFECT ABSOLUTION

Over shots of snowy streets, Antonio Salieri's voice shouts, "Mozart! Mozart! I confess I killed you! . . . Forgive me, Mozart!" When we next see him recovering from his suicide attempt, however, his remorse has vanished, never to return. Instead he refuses to make another sort of confession to a young priest and sets out to convince him that not all men are, as the priest claims, equal in God's eyes. He launches into the story of his rise to fame as court composer and his later obsession with harming his rival Mozart, whom he feels God has favored far above himself. Throughout, Salieri relives his defeats and triumphs, finally declaring himself the "patron saint" of mediocrities and "absolving" the other patients as the dejected priest sits speechless in his hospital room.

Salieri's narrational voice and his delight in what he thinks of as his defeat of God through the murder of Mozart help determine the overall shape of the narrative of *Amadeus*. Salieri's initial gratitude to God for helping make him a successful composer, his subsequent disillusionment and determination to defeat God, and his plotting to damage Mozart's career and finally bring about his death are all laid out in a causally motivated, redundant fashion typical of classical filmmaking. Salieri's shifting relationship with God marks the development of his various goals through the course of the narrative. His narrational voice also creates a profoundly ironic tone that persists through much of the film.

Yet there is another narrational voice above and beyond Salieri's. This impersonal, overarching force presents another set of themes and motifs that shape the film's narrative in counterpoint to Salieri's concerns. While Salieri is obsessed with revenge, the more comprehensive narrational voice suggests the potential for forgiveness. At the beginning, Salieri asks, too late, for the long-dead Mozart's forgiveness. Much later, in the climactic deathbed scene, Mozart apologizes to Salieri: "I was foolish. I . . . I thought you did not care for my work or me . . . Forgive me? Forgive me." Mozart never grasps what Salieri is doing to him, but he has been doubly mistaken—initially in doubting that Salieri respected his music and now in believing that Salieri is his friend. This moment represents the last chance for Salieri to back away from his murderous scheme.

Roughly halfway between the two protagonists' pleas for forgiveness comes the central and longest section of *Amadeus*'s narrative, dealing with Mozart's struggles to produce *Le Nozze di Figaro*. The presentation of the opera itself (as opposed to the rehearsals) concentrates on the final act, in which Count Almaviva finally begs his wife's forgiveness for his infidelities, and she complies. All the opera's plotlines come to happy conclusions in the finale. Salieri describes his experience of listening to it: "I heard the music of true forgiveness *filling* the theatre, conferring on all who sat there *perfect* absolution." In *Figaro*, the Count behaves swinishly throughout virtually the entire opera, suddenly apologizing near the end. One of the historical Mozart's triumphs in this opera is that the music renders this radical change of heart plausible and satisfying.

Like Almaviva, Salieri has one last chance to reveal his hypocrisy, to beg forgiveness from the dying Mozart, and perhaps to save his rival's life. But while Mozart is capable of living out the precepts of his opera, Salieri is not—despite having understood the nature of *Figaro*'s finale. Thus the theme of forgiveness and absolution shapes the narrative as much as does Salieri's obsession with revenge on God, and indeed, the forgiveness theme comments on that obsession. Yet this second theme, far from being treated redundantly, is played out subtly through infrequent references. (Despite Salieri's helpful gloss on the *Figaro* finale, I cannot imagine a spectator grasping the full implications of this motif without knowing Mozart's opera.) This overarching narration works at an even higher level of irony than Salieri's reminiscences. It suggests that Salieri could have begged forgiveness from Mozart and become his friend, to the advantage of both—but that his bitter envy and sensitivity to his own inferiority rendered that impossible.

By comparing Salieri and Mozart, *Amadeus* creates parallels between them. Salieri considers himself vastly different from the vulgar "creature." Yet, in a manner common in parallel-protagonist films, he also envies his rival and longs to become like him. The primary source of parallelism is the overarching narration. As a result, rather than becoming a story primarily about Salieri, the film balances its two protagonists.

Amadeus mixes classical and art-cinema narrational strategies. Salieri's telling of his story is clear and redundant, while the narrational level which comments upon Salieri's recounting is elusive, drawing more upon the art-cinema tradition in which Forman worked during his early career. Films in that tradition use narrative devices such as ambiguity and lack of closure, as well as eschewing the considerable redundancy typical of classical films. Whereas classical films use motifs primarily to provide exposition and unity, art-cinema narration typically cues the spectator to interpret motifs thematically, and thereby to discern a level of commentary beyond the straightforward action. As I will show, these two levels of narration are woven together and create a film that is more subtle then it might at first appear. Because *Amadeus* does cue the spectator to construe its thematic material, I will be depending more heavily upon interpretation in this analysis than elsewhere in the book. Thematic material and narrative causality are inextricably intertwined here. In many cases ironic or symbolic meanings are used to form transitions between scenes, and much of the narrative unity derives from motivic connotations.

This is not to suggest that *Amadeus* is an art film as such, only that it draws upon some conventions of that tradition. Clearly the conspicuous, redundant level of Salieri's story helped make the film surprisingly popular.[1] It probably also accounts for its being given the industry's imprimatur in the form of eight Oscars, including one for the screenplay. After all, the irony of Salieri's ambitions is as apparent as his growing villainy, even if one does not follow the thematic line concerning Salieri's failure to seek forgiveness.

That thematic line and the objective narration that presents it, however, connect the film's narrative and Mozart's own music. Salieri presents Mozart's music as literally the voice of God, but he separates the music from the person of its composer and thus comes to hate Mozart as morally unworthy of his own genius. The objective narration hints more generally that there is something miraculous about Mozart's music but refuses to assign a divine cause to it. It also recognizes that beneath Mozart's vanity and vulgarity lie a sincerity and unpretentiousness that Salieri can never achieve. To fail to realize this, as Pauline Kael did in her review ("Many of the scenes appear to support Salieri in his belief that Mozart's prankish obscenities and his boastfulness are proof that he's unworthy of his artistic gift")[2] is to miss much of the narrative's denotative meaning, let alone its connotations.

As we saw in Chapter 1, some unusually long Hollywood films, in order to retain the traditional timing of their large-scale parts, add a fifth. That section is usually constructed by approximately doubling the length of one of the film's sections and then dividing it into two with a central turning point. In *Amadeus*, there are in effect two development sections, split off from each other by the death of Leopold Mozart. The setup establishes the contrast between the two composers' boyhoods and ends after Mozart's humiliation of Salieri at court by rewriting his march; here Salieri outlines the religious doubts that have arisen from envy of his rival, speaking to his crucifix. The complicating action centers on Mozart's success with *The Abduction from the Seraglio*, which prompts his permanent move to Vienna and his marriage to Constanze. Her visit to Salieri allows him to examine some of Mozart's scores and fully grasp his genius. The turning point that ends this section comes when Salieri burns his crucifix and vows to harm Mozart.

In the first development, Mozart struggles to stage *Le Nozze di Figaro*, only to see it fail. He also gains the mistaken impression that Salieri is aiding his career. Leopold's death forms the turning point that ends this section, inspiring Salieri to consider how he might kill Mozart. This first development section is distinctly longer than the second, and it is indeed the longest large-scale segment of the film. That is partly because it deals with *Figaro* and the attendant, overarching theme of forgiveness.

The second development portion concerns *Don Giovanni* and Mozart's declining health and finances. He is torn between writing *The Magic Flute* and finishing the Requiem commissioned secretly by Salieri. This section ends with Constanze's departure, the final action needed for the murderous Salieri to gain access to Mozart. The climax moves from the premiere of *The Magic Flute* to the death scene, and the epilogue includes the funeral and Salieri's ironic "absolution" of the asylum inmates.

Despite its long central section, the film maintains a remarkably symmetrical balance. At the center is the first development, at 39 minutes long. Taken together the setup and complicating action last for about 58.5 minutes, while the second development, climax, and epilogue total 57 minutes.

Amadeus contains a great many short scenes, and it jumps about in time and space so frequently that abundant transitional devices are required to stitch the whole into a clear and unified narrative. Forman himself has hinted at this problem: "I'd never worked with flashbacks before and never really cared for them, but I didn't mind using this narrative strategy in *Amadeus*, since we had Mozart's music to whisk us through the transitions."[3] In addition to being a long film, *Amadeus* covers a lengthy stretch of story time—far longer than those of the other films analyzed here. Aside from the brief scenes of the two protagonists as boys, the flashback events stretch over about a decade, since initially Mozart gives his age as 26, and he presumably dies when the real Mozart did, at 35. Covering so many events, as well as returning at frequent intervals to the frame story, requires many short scenes sandwiched between a few extended ones. Mozart's music does cover some of the transitions, but the film also contains an enormous number of dialogue hooks and dangling causes. Similarly, the interaction of Salieri's narration and the objective narration necessitates close analysis of a fairly detailed sort.

Such analysis is worthwhile because the film's subtleties went largely unremarked upon its initial release. Most viewers doubtless grasped some implications of the overarching narration; it would be hard to miss the numerous local parallels and ironic juxtapositions. Still, many critics took the film as a middlebrow costume movie along the lines of "Masterpiece Theatre."[4] This judgment seems wide of the mark, if only because it is difficult to imagine Tom Hulce's giggling portrayal of Mozart as being acceptable on PBS. His performance injects a dose of the historical Mozart's vulgarity into the costume-picture genre.

Forman risked critical opprobrium by deciding to have the actors use diction and gestures that seem quite contemporary. One reason why big-budget historical films typically earn critical scorn is that actors almost inevitably freeze up within their never-lived-in settings and costumes. In Michael Curtiz's *The Egyptian*, most of the actors move like puppets in their kilts and armor. By contrast, in *Amadeus* the actors seem uninhibited by period costume and decor. Here a character wears a costume self-consciously only when showing off the latest fashion. What may seem an effort to update behavior for a contemporary popular audience actually enriches the film in a plausible way. Likewise, even Constanze's "Wolfi," so grating to an Anglophone ear, is a reasonable formulation of a German nickname for Wolfgang.[5]

Amadeus mixes strategies of the Hollywood costume film and the art cinema in a way that mildly challenges normal viewing conventions. Ordinarily when a filmmaker sets out to make an art-cinema costume film, he or she signals this clearly. The strategy could be, say, an austerity of style and narration, as in two other period art-cinema pieces based around classical music, Jean-Marie Straub and Danièlle Huillet's *The Chronicle of Anna Magdalena Bach* (1968) and Alain Corneau's *Tous les matins du monde* (1991; this film's first spoken word is *"Austérité"*). Likewise, having Mozart share the spotlight with Salieri can be seen as an acquiescence to conventional reverence for a creative genius. Yet this approach also allows the film to create an ongoing thematic commentary more typical of art-cinema narration. This dynamic is hardly typical of Hollywood costume pictures, but it helps turn a play originally centered on Salieri into a parallel-protagonist movie.

Amadeus demonstrates the enormous flexibility which I have claimed is characteristic of Hollywood narrative techniques and which has allowed this tradition to endure so long. Potentially challenging devices associated with art-cinema storytelling are combined with more classical techniques in a unified way. These art-cinema devices can then help create a somewhat innovative film like *Amadeus*, which still proved acceptable to spectators unused to watching films from outside the Hollywood tradition.

SETUP: "TOO MANY NOTES"

Unlike most of the other films I have analyzed so far, *Amadeus* does not begin by laying out a great deal of information in a short time. Here missing data seem designed to intrigue us. As Salieri shouts out his confession that he killed Mozart and his request for forgiveness, his primary trait seems to be remorse, although he will quickly lose that emotion and reveal new traits: envy, bitterness, and glee over his perceived triumph. The opening follows a well-established classical pattern in which a film sets up a mystery, then investigates it via flashbacks (as in *Mildred Pierce* and *Citizen Kane*).

The opening also introduces several motifs that will become central to the film. Most of the rich motivic play of *Amadeus* issues from the objective narration and provides subtle commentary on the action. An extensive use of motifs is, as we have seen, typical of the classical cinema. In this case, the overarching narration seems to be teasing spectators to notice more and more of these motifs, down to the most subtle underlying ones, such as the forgiveness motif associated with *Figaro*. Perhaps one might say that the film strives to teach the audience to interpret imagery in a way usually associated with European art films—in much the way that Salieri's speeches about Mozart's music aim to educate the spectator about composition.

The second motif (the first being the forgiveness motif itself) appears when Salieri's servant tempts him with a rich pastry and threatens, "Signore, if you don't open this door, we're going to eat everything, and we're going to leave nothing for you." Later we will learn that Salieri has asked God for musical talent, promising "my chastity, my industry, my deepest humility" in exchange. Salieri will consistently resent Mozart for being less virtuous than he is. Yet his own predilection for food, especially sweets, will return repeatedly, hinting that he indulges in the sin of gluttony. One amusing aspect of this motif is that it suggests that, like his music, even Salieri's vice is petty and slightly absurd. But when Mozart appears on the scene, the sin of gluttony is paralleled by a more powerful and dangerous one—envy.

The trip to the hospital indirectly introduces another motif, here originating with Salieri himself, as he hears the first movement of Mozart's 25th Symphony being played in a ballroom. This sets up the idea that Mozart's music is still popular, while Salieri's has faded into oblivion. (Again, the viewer would have to be somewhat familiar with Mozart's music to make anything of this moment.) These budding motifs of gluttony and of Mozart's continued popularity pass quickly, however, and by the credits' end the enigma of Salieri's "confession" and the shock of his bleeding throat are the predominant impressions.

As the director's credit comes up, there is a dissolve from a view of the hospital at night (Fig. 7.1) to the same view during the day (Fig. 7.2). This dissolve conspicuously introduces a device that will become important in *Amadeus:* the graphic match, that is, the juxtaposition of two shots with similar compositions. We will encounter graphic matches repeatedly functioning as a stylistic motif to create parallels between Salieri and Mozart. Such visual comparisons will also shift us between scenes that have no apparent causal link. In other cases where the similarity at the cut links the young and old Salieri, it is usually motivated because the old man is emotionally reliving his past, acting out many of the same gestures.

The priest's first words are "Herr Salieri?" The servants had addressed their master as "Signore." An opposition between the use of the Italian and German languages will later become a motif in Mozart's struggle with the court officials who control opera productions: the German-speaking Mozart versus the Italian Salieri and his allies; progressive versus traditional opera.

A more important aspect of this scene is that Salieri's antagonism to religion is introduced when he tells the priest to leave him alone. A central theme of the film will be a previously pious man's ironic perception of himself as slighted by God in favor of an earthy "creature." When the priest remarks

7.1

7.2

that "all men are equal in God's eyes," Salieri responds, "*Are* they?" This exchange draws Salieri into conversation with the priest, as he begins to demonstrate God's injustice by telling his story. Salieri shifts his wheelchair toward the priest and speaks with a glitter in his eye and almost a smile. Thus his goal in the frame story will be not to atone for murdering Mozart but to justify rejecting God.

Salieri remains obsessed by God and religion throughout the film. Indeed, his main aim within the flashbacks will eventually be to defeat God, with the goal of killing Mozart being the means to that end. Mozart, on the other hand, is not associated with religion, expressing no gratitude to God for his talent. To achieve this contrast between the two men, the film concentrates almost entirely on Mozart's secular works, downplaying the fact that he wrote an enormous amount of church music. Even when his father dies, his "tribute" is an opera, *Don Giovanni*, and he undertakes a requiem mass only because he desperately needs money. Thus the ironic contrast between the two is played out in part through religious imagery.

As Salieri is explaining that he was a successful composer, the first brief flashbacks occur. The young Salieri conducts an opera starring a voluptuous soprano whom we later discover he secretly loves. Twice the gestures of the young and old Salieri making conducting motions link the scenes of past and present in a way that other gestures and graphic similarities will frequently do in the film.

After failing to recognize two of Salieri's successful tunes of the past, the priest delightedly hums along when Salieri plays a passage from "Eine kleine Nachtmusik." Salieri identifies the composer: "Wolfgang [glance upward] *Amadeus* Mozart." This is the film's sole reference to its title and is meaningful only to those who realize that the name means, roughly, "beloved of God." Salieri's glance upward as he says it reveals that he finds the name ironic. Mozart, in keeping with his lack of religious associations, neither uses nor comments on this name.

Having introduced several motifs, the exposition speeds up with a series of flashbacks that rapidly establish the two composers' contrasting childhoods. Salieri's voice-over links these fleeting scenes into a lucid causal chain. He comments that he was jealous of Mozart, "not of the child prodigy, but of his father, who had taught him everything." We see Leopold hovering anxiously as his young son performs for the Pope. Though a relatively minor character, Leopold will be crucial both thematically and causally. While Salieri delights at his own father's death, Mozart becomes racked with guilt after Leopold dies. Though he owes Leopold a great deal, he has flouted his father's wishes in his marriage and career. There is also a suggestion here, however, that Leopold has exploited his son—as Salieri's father's references to little Mozart as a "trained monkey" and a "circus freak" hint. Salieri will seize upon Mozart's mental anguish and weaken him to the point of death by pretending, in effect, to be Leopold's ghost. Thus, in order to defeat the man he envies, Salieri will assume the identity of the father for whom he had so envied Mozart when a boy, exploiting the unspecified psychological scars that Leopold had caused his son.

Initially the two boys seen in the flashbacks are both wearing blindfolds, though for very different reasons. Salieri makes the parallel between the two explicit with his mention of playing—Mozart playing music, Salieri blind-man's buff. Creating visual, motivic, and other similarities between two extremely different characters is a common strategy in films with parallel protagonists, and *Amadeus* will consistently compare the two using such techniques.

When the boy Salieri prays for musical talent, his basic hypocrisy is suggested: "Lord, make me a great composer. Let me celebrate your glory through music . . . and be celebrated myself. Make me famous throughout the world, dear God. *Make me immortal.*" This hardly squares with his offer of "my deepest humility." Throughout, Salieri aspires more to celebrity than to genuine artistry, at the end luring Mozart to write a Requiem that he can pass off as his own. The flashback ends with another cut on a gesture, an attitude of prayer, linking the young and old Salieri.

He goes on to explain that, to some extent, his prayer was answered with "a miracle!"—the unexpected death of his father. The boy Salieri attributed this to God: "Of course I knew God had arranged it all." Salieri's delight in this sudden switch sets up his smug pride in his role as court composer ("Isn't that incredible?") and motivates his later overreaction when he discovers that another composer has been far more favored by God than he. This set of flashbacks then introduces Joseph II, "the musical king." Salieri adds: "Actually, the man had no ear at all. But what did it matter? He adored my music." Here we have our second indication that Salieri, who misses the irony in his own statement, is more concerned with prestige and popularity than with offering truly excellent music to God. Indeed, the few pieces by Salieri that we hear in the course of the film are all designed to impress the emperor. Like Mozart, he seems to compose only secular music. We never hear him fulfill his promise to "sing to God."

The scene of Joseph's music lesson confirms his major traits, a combination of musical enthusiasm and lack of talent. These qualities will be reiterated later on, when he stumbles through a playing of the simple march that Salieri writes to welcome Mozart to court. They also exemplify his role in the narrative, which is to serve as a pivot between the forces aligned with and against Mozart. Joseph has enough musical knowledge to urge Mozart to stay in Vienna, to allow him to put on *Le Nozze di Figaro* despite the ban on its libretto, to let him restore the ballet to *Figaro*, to commission a piano concerto from him, and so on. In the long run, however, he offers insufficient support to prevent Mozart's enemies from carrying the day. His inadvertent yawn dooms *Figaro* to a short run, tipping the balance of the narrative and marking the beginning of Mozart's declining fortunes. Later he dubs Salieri "the brightest star in the musical firmament," confirming his lack of an "ear for music."

By this point we realize that Salieri's prayer has not been fully answered. He has received fame, but not of an "immortal" sort. Even the priest of the frame story, who received some musical training in Vienna, has never heard of his music. Now Salieri explains why: "Everybody liked me. I liked myself—until he came." This line provides a dialogue hook into the most extended flashback thus far, Mozart's concert at the residence of his employer, the Archbishop of Salzburg. Salieri attends, eager to meet Mozart, "and that night changed my life." In describing his father's death, Salieri had declared, "My life changed forever." For him, a death leads to good fortune and the achievement of his early goal, while meeting a supremely talented composer spells disaster and ultimately will provide him with a new goal. By killing Mozart he will try to recreate the "miracle" of his father's death—clearing the way a second time for his own immortal fame.

Soon Salieri's voice-over disappears, and we get the longest stretch of action so far given without his commentary. The gluttony motif set up in the opening scene returns as Salieri spots servants transporting lavish dishes of food, including an arrangement studded with chocolate balls. With a little "Ahhh," he sneaks into the vacant buffet room to pilfer some of the sweets. Thus his private gluttony is paralleled by Mozart's public display of lechery as the latter chases Constanze through the crowd and corners her in the same room. Salieri ducks down behind the table of food to spy for the first time upon the man whom he will consider his rival in God's favors.

Mozart's entry introduces two of his most salient traits: his vulgarity and his sincerity (not to mention his annoying laugh). As he wrestles with Constanze on the floor, he proposes to her by speaking backwards. His four sentences balance vulgarity and sincerity exactly: "Kiss my ass"; "Marry me"; "But I love you"; and finally, to top the tender moment when they become engaged, "Eat my shit." Constanze, though somewhat annoyed by his behavior, obviously also finds it amusing and appears for much of the narrative to accept his vulgarity. Later she will emerge as his staunch defender, finally thwarting Salieri's goal by locking away the unfinished Requiem. Despite an inadequate performance by Elizabeth Berridge (drafted to replace Meg Tilley a week before shooting began), Constanze is clearly supposed to suggest what Salieri should have been to Mozart: someone who realizes his talents despite every-thing and fosters his work.

Hearing his serenade being played, Mozart rushes out, and Salieri realizes that he has been watching his former idol. The camera moves with Mozart as he dashes to conduct the musicians, and for a little while Salieri is left behind. Gradually, across the first half of the film, the narration will shift to a balance

7.3

7.4

between its two protagonists, with the objective narration increasingly taking over and Salieri's narration becoming sporadic. After about the halfway point the scenes will stick closer to Mozart, with less frequent returns to Salieri (both young and old). Here the emphasis on similarities between the two continues, with a graphic match cutting from Mozart conducting (Fig. 7.3) to a shot with the old Salieri's face in the same position and his hand gesturing in a similar pointing way (Fig. 7.4).

After the concert there is a more extended scene without Salieri. Mozart declares, "I think that went off very well, don't you? These Viennese certainly know good music when they hear it." So in addition to being vulgar, Mozart is self-confident and boastful. In that he seems to parallel Salieri, yet he is utterly open and brash about his conceit—and he is more justified in touting his own work. In the scene that follows, the Archbishop urges Mozart to return to Salzburg and to his father. Thus Leopold's goal is revealed: he wishes to continue controlling his son's life. Mozart's own goal is also forming, however: he wants fame and fortune in Vienna, as well as marriage to Constanze. All of these run counter to Leopold's wishes. It turns out that Mozart's professional goals are similar to Salieri's, but he is not secretive, vindictive, or envious. It never occurs to him that anyone else's music could rival his own, so he envies no one and makes no attempt to harm the careers of other musicians (though he unthinkingly humiliates Salieri in front of the emperor and court officials and hence damages the possibility of friendship between the two).

After Mozart's confrontation with the Archbishop, there is a graphic match, cutting from a long shot of Mozart walking among the adoring crowd to Salieri moving in a similar way as he sneaks away to have a look at his rival's conducting score. Here we get the first of Salieri's several brief analyses of Mozart's music. Simple though these are, they are quite effective in conveying to a nonmusical spectator a rough sense of Mozart's technique.[6] They also prove that Salieri recognizes his genius and has a choice: he can accept Mozart as his superior, or he can strive to suppress his rival and preserve his own reputation.

After Mozart rudely snatches the score away, a direct cut places us at Joseph's court. This is the first transition between scenes that has not involved a return to the frame-story situation, confirming that the film will depend less and less upon Salieri's narrating voice. Here the court factions are established, with the Baron Van Swieten, Mozart's most enthusiastic supporter, praising *Idomeneo* and Count Orsini-Rosenberg, the head of the opera, dismissing it as having "too many notes." This notion that Mozart's music is too long and/or complex for the courtiers to understand becomes a motif. Operas of this era were in fact often lengthy, but this idea of "too many notes" offers a simple way to convey the philistinism of the Italian faction to an audience largely unschooled in classical music.

Joseph is impressed with Van Swieten's description and shocks the Italian partisans by deciding to woo Mozart: "We could use a good *German* composer in Vienna, surely." Salieri pretends to be neutral, though secretly he will conspire with his fellow Italians. Joseph can side with either faction, and, as I have suggested, this is what makes him a pivotal figure. He is unpredictable, seemingly under the thumb of the Italians but also capable of defying them. Here his goal seems to be promoting German-language opera, thus motivating Mozart's initial success in Vienna. Yet in the long run Joseph retains no particular devotion to this goal, and his support will evaporate.

During this scene, the Italian faction tries to discourage Joseph from commissioning an opera from Mozart. Unexpectedly, Salieri chimes in: "I think it's an interesting notion to keep Mozart in Vienna, Majesty. It should really infuriate the Archbishop beyond measure—if that is your Majesty's intention." The two men exchange sly smiles. This idea of Joseph having something against the Archbishop is never followed up, but here it helps to establish the atmosphere of intrigue and petty jealousies that exists in the court.

Aside from wanting to curry favor by playing along with what he perceives Joseph's wishes to be, why does Salieri encourage his employer to hire Mozart, whom he already recognizes as the superior composer? Henceforth Salieri will do nothing but attempt to control and thwart him, for fear of being overshadowed. Why not strive to condemn him to relative obscurity in Salzburg? Salieri's words, I think, reflect the tension in his relationship with Mozart. On the one hand, his envy will eventually intensify into obsessive hatred. On the other, he genuinely loves Mozart's music and tries to hear as much of it as possible. Here the pattern common in parallel-protagonist films, of one character being enthralled by the other, begins to jell. Salieri is so fascinated by Mozart that he draws him into his orbit despite fearing that his own work will be cast into obscurity.

The scene of a wigless Salieri composing his march of welcome is followed by one of Mozart trying on three wigs and joking that he wishes he had three heads so he could wear them all. The causal connection between these scenes is unclear, since we only later learn that both are preparing for Mozart's initial meeting with Joseph. Rather, the motif of the wigs links the two scenes. Mozart's indecision concerning which one to buy provides a dangling cause leading to the next scene, where he enters wearing the most dire of the three. This wig purchase is the first action of which Salieri could never have gained any knowledge. Again we inch closer to the objective narration, briefly freed from Salieri's reminiscences.

As the next scene begins, Joseph enters and asks what Salieri and the others have for him, forgetting that they are there to meet Mozart. Thus we are cued to view Joseph as capricious, a trait which later makes him capable of affecting Mozart's fate for good or ill without regard to justice. He is also, however, unfazed by Mozart's social maladroitness. After Joseph tells an anecdote about the six-year-old Mozart's having proposed to his sister, he does not seem bothered by Mozart's loud cackle. Thus he appears to be a potential ally, especially when he delights in Mozart's impromptu revision of Salieri's welcoming march.

Joseph and his court argue about whether Mozart should compose an opera in German. The latter argues for German but concludes: "Majesty, you choose the language. It will be my task to set it to the finest music ever offered a monarch." His boastfulness comes forward again, and Joseph's reply—"Oh, there it is. Let it be German"—seems to confirm that he will support Mozart.

The basic conflict between Mozart and Salieri takes concrete shape during this scene. Mozart unwittingly humiliates Salieri, revealing that he once composed some variations on a melody of his: "A funny little tune, but it yielded some good things." He also plays Salieri's march from memory and partway through begins to improve upon it, remarking: "The rest is just the same, isn't it?" This line turns the "too many notes" motif on its head, implying that Mozart's outpouring of musical genius is the opposite of Salieri's attempts to stretch his own meager inspirations into full-scale pieces. Salieri's enduring resentment becomes focused as a result of this public humiliation—which ends with Mozart's offending laugh.

It is worth noting that as Mozart revises Salieri's dull march into the tune of "Non più andrai, farfallone amoroso" from *Le Nozze di Figaro*, several people in the next room crane to catch a glimpse of him. They are all clerics, echoing the moment in the frame story when the priest had delightedly recognized the main theme of "Eine kleine Nachtmusik." Just as Salieri identifies Mozart's gift as "the very voice of God," men of the cloth seem spontaneously to react to it as well.

Salieri's humiliation provides a dangling cause taken up in the next scene as he growls, "Grazie, Signore," to his crucifix. He had said the same thing, with sincerity, as he composed the welcoming march for Mozart. This crucial scene is the turning point that ends the setup, outlining Salieri's religious disillusionment and marking the reversal of his goal: "All I ever wanted was to sing to God. He gave me that longing and then made me mute. Why? Tell me that. If He didn't want me to praise him with music, why implant the desire, like a lust in my body. Why deny me the talent?" Here Mozart seems to be moving speedily toward his goal of fame and fortune, while Salieri's goal of immortal fame is challenged. The complicating action ends with a parallel moment in which Salieri's rebellion against God becomes absolute and he burns his crucifix.

During this section of the film, the two protagonists begin at last to form the specific goals that will guide them through the narrative. (Salieri of course had his early goal of becoming an immortally famous composer, but until the previous scene, he seemed to think that he had achieved that.)

A brief return to the frame story, followed by a sort of false shot/reverse shot between the old Salieri and the young Salieri, both leaning forward with hunched shoulders, takes us into the next major portion of the narrative. Salieri's reference to "a lust in my body" in his previous speech links motivically into this scene, which depicts a visit by his beautiful, talented, dim student, Madame Cavalieri. She is dressed in the newest "Turkish" fashion and asks what Mozart looks like, suggesting her susceptibility to seduction by him.[7] When Salieri tries to discourage her from starring in *The Abduction from the Seraglio* by hinting that Mozart is ugly, she responds coyly, "Looks don't concern me, Maestro. Only *talent* interests a woman of taste." Salieri admits to the priest that he was in love, or at least "in lust," with this woman. Yet he treats her as a confidante, and she seems not to consider him a potential lover. This scene exists in part to demonstrate that Salieri has kept his vow of chastity. It also, however, sets up his later sexual jealousy when Cavalieri has an affair with Mozart.

The lesson begins, and Cavalieri's high note provides a sound bridge into her showcase aria during *The Abduction*'s premiere in Vienna. Salieri describes it: "*Ten* minutes of ghastly scales." Though the Italian faction seems baffled, Van Swieten is pleased, as are Constanze and her *petit bourgeois* family. Back in the frame story, Salieri reaffirms to the priest his vow of celibacy and reveals his jealousy over Cavalieri: "But I swear to you, I never laid a finger on her. All the same, I couldn't bear to think of any one else touching her . . . least of all, the *creature*." Envy of Mozart that is specifically sexual will not be a major motif, but here this idea is planted as one reason for Salieri's dogged persistence in his plotting. (Cavalieri appears with Salieri in the epilogue during Mozart's funeral, once again his platonic mistress, as it were.)

Joseph's reaction to *The Abduction* brings back the motif of the German-versus-Italian factions in the court. He greets Cavalieri with a mixture of Italian and French, "Brava, madame," and salutes the composer as "Herr Mozart." More crucially, he introduces the idea of Mozart as innovator: "You have shown us something *quite* new tonight." Mozart replies eagerly, "It *is* new, it is, isn't it, sir?" Joseph equivocates a bit here, and Orsini-Rosenberg suggests that *The Abduction* has "too many notes, your Majesty." Mozart objects: "I don't understand. There are just as many notes, Majesty, as I required." By this point we should be inclined to sympathize with Mozart, since we are strongly cued to realize that the Italian faction in the court are philistines. Yet that identification is immediately undercut by the following grotesque scene with Constanze's mother coming forward and fainting upon meeting the emperor; this action is immediately trumped by Cavalieri's outraged reaction when she learns that Mozart, with whom she has plainly had an affair, is engaged to Constanze. Mozart's genius and his vulgarity are carefully balanced here—yet we are progressively being distanced from Salieri's viewpoint. His uncomprehending shrug to his fellow Italians during the performance of the "ghastly scales" makes him look obtuse.[8]

Joseph urges Mozart to stay in Vienna and marry Constanze, pushing the young composer to follow his own goal and disobey his father's wishes. Yet we may recall that Joseph apparently wants to annoy the Archbishop of Salzburg by luring Mozart to Vienna, and although he likes the young composer's music, he will not provide much support. The revelation that Mozart's fiancée is his landlady's daughter also sets up the notion that he is a man of the people—"vulgar" in the oldest sense of the word. The scene leads to a return to the frame-story situation, as Salieri relives his rage over Mozart's affair with Cavalieri: "It was incomprehensible. *What* was God up to? My heart was filling up with, oh, such hatred for that little man. For the first time in my life I began to know really . . . *violent* thoughts." Thus Salieri's later plot to kill Mozart is motivated, though considerably postponed, via this dangling cause.

Joseph's invitation to Mozart to stay in Vienna implicitly contradicts Leopold's desire to have his son return to Salzburg. Thus this issue, brought up late in the scene of *The Abduction*'s premiere, provides a dangling cause that is taken up in the following exchange between Leopold and the Archbishop. This is the first scene in which neither of the two protagonists appears, and hence it signals a still greater departure from Salieri's narrating viewpoint. The irate Archbishop grants Leopold a final chance to convince his son to return. Leopold's letter urging Mozart to obey his wishes provides a negative dialogue hook into the next scene—"Do as I bid, and await my coming" contrasts with the scene of Mozart marrying Constanze against Leopold's wishes—but it also provides a further dangling cause by establishing that Leopold will journey to Vienna.

The wedding scene itself is fairly straightforward in terms of the action it depicts. Yet it also provides a model of Salieri's eventual fantasy of Mozart's funeral, where he imagines himself presenting the Requiem as his own creation. Here the music is the Kyrie of the Mass in C minor, a majestic passage which could equally function in the context of a funeral,[9] and the church interior suggests how we might later visualize the hypothetical scene of Salieri's triumph.

Now Mozart specifies his new goals in a letter to his father: "Remember how you've always told me that Vienna was the city of musicians, to conquer here is to conquer Europe? With my wife I can do it, and one day soon, when I am a wealthy man, you will come and live with us, and we will be *so* happy." Throughout the rest of the film, Mozart's goals will be simple and unwavering: to convince the court and populace that his music is brilliant, to make enough money to support his family, and to be happy. Leopold's goal will be to control his son, though he fails in this early on. His removal will clear the way for Salieri to exert a more thoroughgoing paternal control.

Salieri has already had "violent" thoughts, but his first move against Mozart is a small one: he prevents him from becoming music teacher to the emperor's niece. This action is important, however, because it leads to the revelation that Mozart desperately needs money. In a key scene, Constanze visits Salieri and pleads for aid: "Sir, we're desperate. We . . . we really need this job. My husband spends far more than he can ever earn. I don't mean that he's lazy, 'cause he's not at all," and so on. From here on, financial pressure will provide the main impetus for the Mozart plotline. Constanze's description of their situation presumably makes Salieri realize that the couple would welcome his anonymous donation of the maid, Lorl, whom he sends to spy on their household. We should remember that, aside from spying on Mozart's odd proposal to Constanze at the Archbishop's party, Salieri has encountered Mozart only in public. Constanze provides his first glimpse into their everyday life. Eventually the family's impecuniousness will enable Salieri to exploit Mozart's self-destructiveness in order to kill him.

The motifs of Salieri's gluttony and his sexual rivalry with Mozart return here as he charms Constanze by serving a luxurious candy called "Nipples of Venus." Examining Mozart's manuscripts, he discovers that his rival writes his perfect music without revision, "as if he were taking dictation" from God. Yet Salieri resents rather than reveres that dictation. Ultimately he will try to make one bit of it—the Requiem—his own. The fact that the Requiem is a choral piece links back to Salieri's childhood desire to "sing to God." This scene intensifies Salieri's envy while characterizing Mozart's genius by means of another of Salieri's short musical analyses.

Constanze's question, "So you will help us?" sets in place the basic premise for the rest of the film. Salieri now realizes the true extent of Mozart's genius.

From now on, whatever his opinion of Mozart as a person, he should foster his career. Yet instead the old Salieri declares, "From now on, we are enemies." The young Salieri puts his crucifix into the fire, declaring his new and final goal: "Unfair, unkind—I will block You, I swear it. I will hinder and harm Your creature on earth, as far as I am able. I will ruin Your incarnation." The complicating action ends on a medium closeup of the old Salieri, glaring vindictively, then lapsing into a smile—signaling his lack of remorse. From here on the film will move away from his narrational stance, and our sympathies will lie increasingly with Mozart.

FIRST DEVELOPMENT: "THE BEST OPERA YET WRITTEN"

This section of *Amadeus* begins with Mozart walking through the street, drinking from a bottle of wine. We have not seen him drinking up to now, and this is our first hint that success in Vienna is corrupting him. He finds his father waiting outside the apartment, and a loud chord from *Don Giovanni* suggests the close links between Leopold and that particular opera. Yet although Mozart initially reacts in fright to the dark apparition, he seems genuinely delighted to see his father. The slovenly life that the couple lead dismays Leopold, and he asks why they do not have a maid. The fact that Salieri soon provides the family with a maid creates another parallel between him and Leopold. Mozart assures Leopold that his new project *(Figaro)* will make money: "You are going to be so proud of me, Papa." He is still striving toward his goal of fame and fortune, along with this newly revealed desire to win his father's respect.

The next scene, showing the family going out to a party, serves mainly to point up Mozart's uneasy relationship with his censorious father. The arrival of Salieri motivates his later ability to select the mask he should use in imitating Leopold. The party also reveals the decadent Viennese life that Mozart has adopted, suggesting that perhaps Leopold is right and he should return to prosperous obscurity in Salzburg. When Mozart loses at a game of musical chairs, he demands a penalty from his father. Leopold says he should go back to Salzburg, but Mozart demands "a *real* penalty." Of course the real penalty would be to fulfill Leopold's goal and hence avoid this dissolute life and Salieri's revenge. Yet the film also hints that such a retreat might make Mozart a lesser composer: he thrives in Vienna. Perhaps if he had gone back with Leopold he would have reverted to the "performing monkey." Incidently, here we first see Schikaneder, the vaudeville producer and performer who continues as Mozart's drinking partner and persuades him to write *The Magic Flute*, thus allowing him to escape court snobbery and write a popular masterpiece.

As Mozart performs the "penalty" inflicted upon him by the partygoers— playing a harpsichord in the style of various composers—Leopold and Salieri, both wearing black masks, look on disapprovingly. Again the parallel between them is emphasized, preparing the way for Salieri's eventual adoption of the costume that Leopold now wears.

Salieri anonymously brings on his own humiliation by demanding that Mozart "play Salieri." Mozart plays stiffly and stupidly and ends with a fart. A cut to the elderly Salieri has him declaring, "Go on, mock me, laugh," and a return to the flashback has Mozart obliging him with his cackle. In the frame situation, Salieri declares: "That was not Mozart laughing, Father. That was God. That was God laughing at me, through that, through that obscene giggle. Go on, Signore, laugh, *laugh*. Show my mediocrity for all to see. One day I will laugh at You. Before I leave this earth, I will laugh at You." We have not seen the priest for some time, and his return comes as Salieri declares his own mediocrity, the quality that he will ultimately claim elevates him above the Church. He aims to laugh at the Church, but Mozart will laugh at him one last time.

Salieri blows out candles as the music of *Le Nozze di Figaro* comes up. This opera will be the pivot of the narrative. It allows Mozart to triumph briefly over the Italian officials, in that he gets it produced against their wishes. Yet it also provides the occasion for Mozart to jump to the conclusion that Salieri is his friend and ally, thus setting up the final, fatal collaboration between the two.

The scene after Salieri blows out the candles does not lead directly into a scene of composition, but rather into an argument between Leopold and Constanze over the mysterious arrival of the anonymously donated maidservant, Lorl. Mozart retreats into the next room, composing on his billiard table. The implication is that his longing for domestic peace leads him to compose the great reconciliatory finale of *Figaro*. For each of the operas depicted in detail in the remainder of the film (*Don Giovanni* and *The Magic Flute*), there will be an assumption that Mozart's personal life directly inspires his composition. The billiard ball which he rolls across the table as he writes suggests that his music's perfection equals that of the ball's precise angles as it ricochets, despite his inability to control his private life. Indeed, the second half of the film strongly implies that Mozart's brilliant inspirations come from his personal experience rather than through a divine cause. It is ironic that, in trying to make his rival (and thus God) suffer, Salieri drives him to new heights of genius.

The mysterious appearance of Lorl provides a dangling cause that is soon taken up after a cut to Salieri's home. As during the earlier visit from Constanze, Salieri offers Lorl a plate of sweets. Here they are cheap cookies, light-colored dough with a spot of chocolate in the center, but they resemble the more sumptuous "Nipples of Venus" that Salieri had served to Constanze. This treat recalls the gluttony motif, but the parallel also underscores Salieri's use of both women to spy on Mozart's private life. Like Constanze, Lorl assures Salieri that Mozart works hard, "all day long," confirming that he is, despite his faults, dedicated to music. Salieri's request that she inform him when the Mozart apartment is vacant sets up a dialogue hook into the next scene.

As Mozart's piano is taken away and the family leaves for a concert at the palace, Lorl runs to fetch Salieri. His tour of the apartment reveals that the couple is nearly destitute; they have been forced to sell valuable snuff boxes to keep going. He reads a bit of the manuscript for *Figaro*. Again the objective narration stresses its finale: although Salieri's point-of-view shows the first page of the overture, on the sound track we hear the beginning of the "forgiveness" theme from the opera's climax. *Figaro*'s music, which Salieri so much admires, is what he uses against Mozart in his first major attempt to damage his rival's career.

The film's lengthy change toward a more sympathetic view of Mozart becomes definitive once Salieri passes his information about the composition of *Figaro* to the emperor. A long scene follows in which Mozart is summoned to court and must persuade Joseph to allow him to stage the opera—the problem being that the play on which the libretto is based has been banned as politically inflammatory. By this point the objective narration has gained the upper hand, as it were, over Salieri's storytelling. We increasingly recognize not only his villainy but also the irony lurking behind everything that Salieri tells us. Yet Mozart never becomes a narrating figure, since the objective narration almost constantly suggests implications of his unselfconscious behavior. Instead he becomes a figure of sympathy.

Whatever doubts we may have had about Mozart up to this point must now disappear. For the first time, Salieri (inexplicably) is absent from a court scene, so our attention is focused on Mozart's arguments for producing *Figaro*. This is the first time (apart from briefly during the "too many notes" exchange after *The Abduction*) that Mozart is seen as a victim—a common way for Hollywood films to create sympathy for protagonists. Moreover, traits of his that had been established earlier come across differently at this point, when they are not filtered through Salieri's viewpoint. When he makes a crude remark, he immediately apologizes: "Forgive me, Majesty. I'm a vulgar man. But I assure you, my music is not." This distinction is one which we and the objective narration can make but which Salieri cannot. This is also the first moment when Mozart shows himself capable of begging forgiveness, something Salieri never does after his uncharacteristic outburst in the opening scene.

The elitist courtiers oppose Mozart, and even the usually supportive Van Swieten comments that he should choose a more "elevated" subject than *Figaro*. Mozart replies: "Elevated! Elevated! What does that mean, elevated? I am fed to the teeth with all of these elevated things! Old dead legends! Why must we go on forever writing only about gods and legends?" This lack of snobbery later motivates Mozart's willingness to write *The Magic Flute* for a vaudeville theater rather than the royal opera house. And to a modern spectator, *Figaro* is as elevating an opera as one could imagine. (Again, the film conveniently ignores the fact that Mozart also composed Italian-language operas based on elevated historical subjects—including his last, *La Clemenza di Tito*, written after *The Magic Flute*.)

In contrast, the one opera of Salieri's that we glimpse is manifestly of the "elevated" sort. In earlier scenes, Salieri has been gradually revealed as snobbish. Though he had told Constanze when she visited him that he was from a small town and had insisted that she be less formal with him, throughout that scene he had spoken very condescendingly to her. His horror at Mozart's vulgarity (as opposed to Joseph's apparent indifference to it) is the most obvious sign of his disdain.

By the end of this scene, Joseph is still skeptical, but Mozart begins to describe to him the simple opening scene of *Figaro*. His speech (a dialogue hook) proves convincing, since we next see Mozart rehearsing the opera's first scene. This primarily establishes that the opera has been permitted to go forward—that Mozart has charmed Joseph once again, as he did in persuading him to allow *The Abduction* to be written in German. Mozart is nearing his goal, while Salieri is floundering. The plottings of the Italian faction against *Figaro* then proceed through three short scenes linked by dangling causes and dialogue hooks, from Salieri suggesting to his allies that they "help" Mozart avoid Joseph's ban against ballets in operas, to the scene of Orsini-Rosenberg ripping the Act III ballet out of Mozart's score, to the one of Mozart desperately seeking Salieri's aid in restoring the scene.

This third scene is crucial. For the first time, Mozart and Salieri are alone together, and Mozart is in an inferior position. He is still openly egotistical—

"They say I have to rewrite the opera, but it's perfect as it is"—yet Salieri knows that he is right. Salieri's hypocritical "Thank God" upon hearing that Constanze had rescued the score when Mozart despairingly tried to burn it echoes his two earlier "Grazie, Signore" declarations to his crucifix, initially sincere, then spiteful. Indeed, Mozart's placement of the score in the fire, though not seen, parallels the turning point when Salieri did the same with his crucifix. Mozart, too, had reached a state of despair, nearly rejecting his life's goal—only to be saved by Constanze.

Here Salieri has one of his few chances to become Mozart's friend and supporter, but he only pretends to do so. A brief return to the narrating situation provides a dialogue hook into the next scene: "I don't need to tell you I said nothing whatever to the emperor. I went to the theater ready to tell Mozart something, anything." During the following scene in the theater, Joseph, who never attends rehearsals, unexpectedly arrives. This exceptional act may suggest that he will support Mozart more vigorously. In fact he does not really do so, but his annoyed restoration of the ballet provides a critical motivation. Mozart believes that Salieri has influenced this decision and hence is his friend, and he will act on that belief until his death. Salieri's murder of Mozart and near theft of the Requiem are foreshadowed here, since in the death scene Mozart will still trust him and will accept his "help" with the composition. The transition to the next scene is provided by a frontal shot of Mozart conducting the rehearsal to one of him conducting the premiere.

The premiere of *Figaro* shows once again that Salieri understands Mozart's genius, despite his continuing refusal to support it. As we have seen, the finale of the opera links the general themes of forgiveness and absolution to Mozart's music. Salieri can only take the piece as harmful to himself. "God was singing through this little man to all the world. Unstoppable, making my defeat more bitter with every passing bar." Then: "A miracle!" Joseph inadvertently yawns, which leads to a short run for *Figaro*. This line, "A miracle!" echoes Salieri's description of his father's death. In both cases, someone else's misfortune redounds to his advantage. Here, however, he attributes the miracle not to God but to Joseph, the man whom his own music has been written to impress. The scene ends with a dialogue hook divided between Salieri and Mozart. Salieri begins: "With one yawn, the composer could still get—" Cut to Mozart in Salieri's chambers, irate: "Nine performances! That's all it's had!"

Again Mozart has come to Salieri as a friend, and Salieri patronizes him: "I can speak for the emperor. You make too many demands on the royal ear. The poor man can't concentrate for more than an hour—you gave him four."[10] Mozart is drinking here, as he had not during his previous visit. Salieri, sincere for once, says that *Figaro* was "marvelous." Mozart boasts again: "Of *course*, the best opera yet written." Salieri teases him as being too highbrow: "Do you know, you didn't even give them a good *bang* at the end of songs, to let them know when to clap." Mozart inadvertently insults him again: "I know, I know. Maybe you should give me some lessons in that." Salieri's smile fades, but he invites Mozart to his new opera, concluding, "It would be a tremendous honor for me." Mozart replies, politely if not eagerly, "Oh, no, the honor would be all mine."

In a poignant moment, the film hints at what an actual friendship between the two men might have been like. Mozart now feels a genuine obligation to the man he thinks has interceded on his behalf (and we later learn that, as a result, he can tactfully hide his distaste for Salieri's music). Salieri is also as sincere here as he ever has been with Mozart, tense and worried about asking him to hear his new opera and distinctly relieved at his acquiescence. As with the moment when Salieri had urged Joseph to bring Mozart to Vienna, it is not entirely clear why he would place himself in a disadvantageous position with his rival. But again, he admires Mozart as much as he envies him, and he clearly cannot resist asking Mozart to judge his work. As the scene ends, Mozart toasts him as "Signor Antonio," having in the past addressed him as "Excellency" or "Herr Salieri." He thus shows himself willing to drop the German/Italian feuding, but his rare display of tact and friendship gains him nothing. Salieri once more passes up a chance to abandon his grudge.

The dangling cause concerning Salieri's opera links into the next scene, the finale of the premiere. As it ends, Joseph declares, "I believe it is the best opera yet written, my friends." At this point Mozart and his companions leave their box with somber faces. We might expect that he is stalking out, offended—especially in light of the fact that Joseph's words exactly echo his own more plausible description of *Figaro* in the previous scene ("the best opera yet written"). Yet as Joseph compounds his slight of Mozart by declaring, "Salieri, you are the brightest star in the musical firmament. You do honor to Vienna and to me," Mozart makes his way down to the orchestra pit. Diplomatically he manages both to avoid lying and to convince the skeptical Salieri that he liked his opera: "I never knew that music like that was possible. . . . One hears such sounds, and what can one say but, 'Salieri'?"

A straight cut to Constanze at home with their baby makes the mocking laughter of the group offscreen seem as if it is directed at Salieri. In fact it is Mozart, returning drunk with Schikaneder and two female singers. This scene is interesting in relation to the film's sympathetic portrayal of Mozart. He is clearly an alcoholic, but there is no definite suggestion that he has been unfaithful to Constanze since their marriage (despite his dalliance with Cavalieri during their engagement). Later, on the night of Mozart's death, he will again be seen drinking with similar women and Schikaneder in a way that suggests rowdiness, not debauchery. Indeed, here he unashamedly brings the group back to party with Constanze. Thus it is not clear that Salieri's view of Mozart as lecherous is particularly justified.

The mood shifts with Constanze's announcement that Leopold has died in Salzburg. The narrative has not hinted that Leopold had returned to Salzburg (except in a negative way through his absence since his quarrel with Constanze). This is odd, given that it appeared he had moved in permanently with the couple. A scene of his departure, say, after a stormy scene with Constanze would have helped to motivate Mozart's guilt after his father's death. At any rate, this scene is clearly a turning point. The death does not radically change either protagonist's goal, but it introduces a major premise that alters the development of both goals. Leopold's death later provides Salieri with his means of revenge, and it accelerates Mozart's slide into the drunkenness and poor health that leave him open to Salieri's manipulation.

SECOND DEVELOPMENT: "A MAN SPLITTING IN HALF"

The second development portion begins with Salieri describing his new, more specific goal of murdering Mozart, and the rest of it will deal with Salieri's actualizing his plan to wear down his rival. This section's dominant musical piece is *Don Giovanni*, and chords from that opera provide a musical bridge that links Leopold's portrait to the finale of the premiere. Salieri drives the point home by explaining that the Commendatore's ghost is "Leopold, raised from the dead. Wolfgang had actually summoned up his own father, to accuse his son before all the world" (of what is unclear). The black mask and cloak worn by the Commendatore recall the costume that Leopold had worn to the party. Salieri will use a similar costume to suggest that the mysterious figure who commissions the Requiem is Leopold's ghost.

Now that we are into a new phase of the plot, both characters change distinctly. Mozart is looking much more haggard, but he struggles to carry forward his goal of fame and money. Salieri soon defines his own narrower goal: "And now . . . the madness began in me . . . the madness of a man splitting in half. Through my influence, I saw to it that *Don Giovanni* was played only five times in Vienna, but in secret I went to every one of those five, worshipping the sound I alone seemed to hear." Here we have a remark-ably explicit description of one type of parallel-protagonist plot: one character "splitting in half," "worshipping" another whom in some sense he wishes to become. Salieri continues: "And as I stood there, understanding how that bitter old man was still possessing his poor son, even from beyond the grave, I began to see a way, a terrible way, I could finally triumph over God." Even though Salieri now pities Mozart, he persists in his scheming.

After only polite applause greets the end of *Don Giovanni*, there follows a scene with no apparent causal link with the previous one. An unknown man buys a mask and carries it through the streets. Only in retrospect can one realize that Salieri is working out his plan by purchasing a "Leopold" two-faced black mask. This scene reverts to the tactics of the film's opening, creating a mystery without providing any explanation.

The dangling causal purpose of this scene is quickly picked up, however, when we see Mozart drinking and composing, then receiving a visit from a threatening figure in the frowning black mask. In a voice recognizably Salieri's, he commissions a requiem, "For a man who deserved a requiem mass and never got one." (By implication he castigates Mozart for instead writing *Don Giovanni* in response to his father's death.) Though the masked figure claims to be "only a messenger," he clearly wants the dazed Mozart to confuse him with Leopold. As he turns to leave, the smiling face on the back of his head faces Mozart, a motif recalling Salieri's vow to laugh at God by harming Mozart.

As Mozart fearfully peers through the window at the departing figure, Constanze emerges from the bedroom. Her crucial protectiveness is empha-sized, albeit rather belatedly. From this point on she will badger Mozart about earning money and about squandering his talent. Earlier, Salieri could sneak into the apartment only when the couple were both away. He will be unable to gain total control of Mozart while Constanze hovers about, guarding him. Thus the turning point that will lead into the climax will come when she departs, leaving him alone in the apartment.

To guarantee causal clarity, the film now reiterates and specifies Salieri's goal. We see the priest after an absence of many scenes, enthralled by the old Salieri's description: "My plan was so simple that it terrified me. First I must get the death mass, and then . . . I must achieve his death. [The priest: 'What?!'] His *funeral*. Imagine it, the cathedral, all Vienna sitting there, his coffin—Mozart's *little* coffin in the middle, and then, in that silence, *music*. [Here Mozart's Requiem begins over the words.] A *divine* music bursts out over them all—a great mass of death—requiem mass for Wolfgang Mozart, composed by his *devoted* friend, Antonio Salieri. Ah, what sublimity, what depth, what *passion* in the music. Salieri has been touched by God at last. [Very intense.] And God forced to listen, powerless, *powerless* to stop it. I, for once, in the end laughing at Him." This speech ensures that the scene of Salieri taking dictation from the dying Mozart will be clear to the audience despite the fact that during the scene itself, Salieri's behavior never betrays his true intent. It also makes quite clear Salieri's relationship to Mozart as a parallel protagonist, wishing to pass himself off as the composer of the Requiem.

After this speech Salieri essentially becomes irrelevant until that climactic scene, and his plan remains a dangling cause across two unrelated scenes. Now we switch back, with no transition, to the Mozart plot, via an abrupt and briefly disorienting cut to the vaudeville pastiche of his operas. During the performance Constanze is polite but not particularly amused. She drinks wine sedately from a glass while Mozart delights in the performance and guzzles from the bottle. The scene reminds us that Mozart is no snob. He writes music that the crowd can enjoy, and he appreciates their enthusiasm. These people cannot afford to attend the operas, but they appreciate these recycled tunes, now popular hits. When the famous duettino "La ci darem la mano" from *Don Giovanni* begins, the audience spontaneously sways in time to it—in marked contrast to the reaction of the decorous audience for *Figaro*, eying the emperor to know how to respond. The parody ends with a chorus based on the finale of *Figaro*, reprising the vital forgiveness motif. The audience recognizes the music and applauds enthusiastically. Something of the same air of tranquillity that had attended the finale of *Figaro* returns here, implicitly harking back to the motif of reconciliation.

Schikaneder visits the box and makes the point about Mozart's lack of snobbishness redundantly clear: "I tell you, if you had played *Don Giovanni* here, you would have had a wonderful success. *You belong here!* Not at the snobby court." Mozart's delight in the audience's response motivates his interest in Schikaneder's offer for a vaudeville opera *(The Magic Flute)*. Thus the possibility is raised that Mozart may get one more chance to achieve his goals of fame and money, though not the respect of the court. This offer also further foregrounds Constanze's suddenly vital role as her husband's protector, harping on immediate money. As Schikaneder remarks, "I see you brought your manager with you."

This scene points up the narrative's most problematic element, its portrayal of Constanze. We never get a coherent sense of how to react to her or her actions. Objectively, most of what she does involves trying her best to protect her husband, if sometimes misguidedly (as here). Certainly at the end she is the one who thwarts Salieri's achievement of his full goal by locking the Requiem out of his reach. Yet in the second half of the film she usually comes across as bitchy, snobbish, and moneygrubbing. Here she is annoyed with her husband's companions, who have encouraged his drinking and who have, in her eyes, belittled his serious work. Instead Constanze insists on advance payment and urges Mozart to work on the lucrative Requiem. Later, however, after the opera's premiere, Schikaneder comes to their apartment with a bag of money similar to the one the disguised Salieri had given Mozart. (The parallel is stressed by Salieri's pretense that the bag comes from the mysterious commissioner of the Requiem.) Thus Constanze is wrong in thinking that *The Magic Flute* will not help support them. Still, she is also clearly right in believing that Schikaneder encourages Mozart in the drinking bouts that presumably hasten his death.

In general, too little of Constanze's role in Mozart's life, both positive and negative, has been set up earlier. For example, does her bickering with Leopold help drive Mozart to drink? In that case she would be hypocritical to blame Schikaneder. Berridge's performance is certainly problematic, but the script has made Constanze a contradictory character, and the ambiguities are not the subtle psychological touches typically associated with art cinema. Constanze represents the sort of thankless roles that Hollywood has often provided women. Despite her central place in the narrative structure, the authors seem not to have been interested enough in Constanze to craft her into a consistent character.

The following few brief scenes function mainly to show Mozart's continuing decline and to prepare us for his death from overwork and drunkenness. We are still completely separated from Salieri's narration. Indeed, we make a brief foray into Mozart's mind, hearing the music he is composing—a fact that we realize when the Requiem cuts out abruptly when Constanze calls his attention to a pounding at the door. By showing that Mozart is continuing to deteriorate, the scene hints at madness.

Lorl's brief appearance late in this scene recalls Salieri, who has been absent since before the lengthy sequence at Schikaneder's theater. Her frightened reaction to Mozart's odd behavior and to Constanze's quarrel with Schikaneder provides a hook into the next scene, where she tells Salieri of her fears. She also reveals that Mozart is at work on an opera. Salieri, who presumably assumes that Mozart is slaving away on the Requiem, responds, "Are you sure it's an opera?" providing a dialogue hook into the next scene. There Mozart is shown composing, with the overture of *The Magic Flute* cuing us that he is instead focusing on Schikaneder's assignment. Salieri's realization that Mozart has a new project under way motivates his visit to goad him into returning to the emotionally draining Requiem.

The scene of the visit begins with Mozart writing his score, then pausing to check on his sleeping son. This entire scene presents one of the few positive depictions of Constanze in the second portion of the film. Here she tenderly watches her husband's display of paternal affection. Once outside the bedroom, however, Mozart begins capering wildly, thumbing his nose at the portrait of Leopold. Again his behavior suggests his decline, and Salieri's visit, again as the sinister masked messenger, promises to accelerate it. As when Schikaneder had visited at night, Constanze quickly appears at Mozart's side, but this time she is cordial. She is constantly protective but has chosen the wrong patron. Still, her presence prevents Salieri from gaining full access to Mozart. (Indeed, Salieri does not actually set foot in the apartment on either of his disguised visits.)

Once Salieri leaves, Constanze begs Mozart to work on the more remunerative Requiem. He replies, "It's killing me," confirming explicitly that his decline results partly from that project's pressures. She replies: "It's not fair. I worry about you all the time. I do everything I can to help you, and all you can do is drink and talk nonsense and frighten me." True, and yet so little of Constanze's support has been established earlier in the film that she again comes across as a nag (though here a more adequate performance might carry more conviction). She begs to stay with him as he works on the Requiem, but he sneaks out and joins Schikaneder for a night of drunken revelry.

Mozart's return home the next morning creates a parallel between him and Salieri, as he appears as a silhouette at the end of an arcade, just where the disguised Salieri had earlier been seen. Inside, he discovers that Constanze has left. This dangling cause motivates a cut to his mother-in-law, revealing that she has sent Constanze to a spa to recuperate from her wretched life with Mozart. Thus the final circumstance that will allow Salieri access to Mozart falls into place, and the film's climax portion commences. Again the narration suggests that Mozart's family life inspires his operas, as the mother-in-law's shrill scolding merges into the Queen of the Night's main aria from *The Magic Flute*, providing a transition into the climax.

CLIMAX AND EPILOGUE: "JUST A VAUDEVILLE"

The premiere of *The Magic Flute* reveals that Mozart has returned to his original language, German (represented in the operas by English). He is now near collapse, but the audience applauds enthusiastically, contrasting with the upper-class patrons' tepid response to *Don Giovanni*. Salieri, attending Mozart's performances as always, sees him faint and takes him home. Upon arrival at the apartment, Salieri asks, "Where is your wife?" When Mozart replies that she has gone to the spa, Salieri realizes that he has complete control over his rival.

The next exchange hints again that Salieri still has the possibility to give up his scheme and beg Mozart's forgiveness, repenting at the last like Count Almaviva in *Figaro*. Mozart thanks him: "You are so good to me. Truly. Thank you." Salieri assumes Mozart refers to his bringing Mozart home. Mozart: "No, I mean, to come to my opera. You were the only colleague of mine who came." He also refers to *The Magic Flute* as "just a vaudeville." Such humility is new; earlier he would have complained about the court's neglect and boasted about his great work. The change removes one of Salieri's reasons for resenting his foe, but he does not relent. He does, however, sincerely declare, "I tell you, you are the greatest composer known to me," thus making his determination to go on with his scheme all the more perverse. His pretense that Schikaneder's money comes from the messenger who commissioned the Requiem confirms his villainy—especially since Mozart wants the money in order to support his wife and son. This scene ends as Mozart asks for Salieri's help with the Requiem, a dangling cause that bridges over the next brief scene.

At the end of the second development portion, Constanze's mother had chastised Mozart, with her mention of the spa setting up a dangling cause picked up when we see Constanze dancing there. She in turn sets up another dangling cause, declaring that she wants to return to Vienna. Finally, it seems, we should realize that she is devoted to her husband, even though she has so often come across as a shrew.

The rest of the climax forms an odd variant on the traditional rescue, with long scenes of Mozart dictating his Requiem to Salieri intercut with a few shots of Constanze's coach speeding to Vienna. Yet she does not realize that she needs to rescue her husband, and Mozart does not realize that he needs rescuing. Instead the focus of the climax, remarkably for a Hollywood film, is on the structure of the "Confutatis maledictus" of Mozart's Requiem. The choice of this particular movement fits into the art-cinema thematic import of the scene, since the text is a prayer begging for the soul to be spared the tortures of hell and accepted into heaven. Mozart points up the contrast between himself and Salieri by asking the latter if he believes in the eternal flames of hell, and Salieri answers, "Oh, yes," very sincerely—clearly referring to the suffering that he thinks God has visited upon him in life.

Of course, even assuming that Mozart has already conceived a substantial amount of his unfinished piece, the notion of his dictating so much so quickly to Salieri is quite absurd. Nevertheless, for a general audience, the scene provides a neat breakdown of the various voices and instrumentation and shows how they are combined in the finished piece. Undoubtedly as a result of the film, the public's interest in Mozart and especially in the Requiem increased; recordings of that particular mass proliferated.

One irony of this scene, missed by Salieri, is that he is now taking musical dictation from the man who he thinks is taking musical dictation from God— and thus he participates in a small way in the genius of his idol. Finally, despite his fiendish plot, Salieri becomes so absorbed in Mozart's compositional methods and unorthodox style that the music's form briefly becomes more central to the action than does Mozart's impending death. Indeed, the absurdity of Salieri's continued hatred of Mozart becomes more conspicuous than ever. He has always recognized the genius of his rival's music, but now Mozart even teaches him to understand dimly his compositional methods. After being baffled, Salieri responds eagerly, "Yes, yes, I understand, yes, yes!" Perhaps, had Salieri not been so vindictive and had he become Mozart's friend, he could have learned more from him.

For the only time in the film, the narrational point of view is split in this scene. We are closely allied with Mozart, hearing bits of music sounding in his imagination. We are also with Salieri, because we know what he knows and what Mozart does not—that he is racing to get the Requiem finished and to kill its composer in the process. Yet as Salieri begins to grasp Mozart's methods, he seems also to "hear" the "Confutatis." After Mozart declares, "Now for the real fire. Strings in unison, *ostinato*, on A, like this," they both "listen" to the string portion, and Salieri hums along, declaring, "It's *wonderful!*" Again we see the parallels between them and the missed chance for friendship.

As the intercutting with Constanze's coach heralds her arrival, Mozart says he wants to sleep, then asks forgiveness for having doubted Salieri. We never learn Salieri's response, as there is a cut to Constanze and her son in the street, but clearly Salieri avoids this last chance to apologize in turn to Mozart. Constanze enters and demands of Salieri, "What are *you* doing here?" No explanation for her distrust has been explicitly given, but presumably she has harbored a grudge for his failure to help her husband become music teacher to the emperor's niece.

Constanze's conversation with the dying Mozart belatedly tries to convince us of her concern for him. "I missed you so much. If you'd just show me that you need me. And I'll try to do better, too." Notably, she ignores the coins her son has scattered on the bed, anxious only for her husband. When she finds the Requiem, she declares, "No, Wolfi, not this, not this. You're not to work on this ever again. I've decided." Given the fuzziness of her earlier characterization, the motivation for her rather considerable change of heart is vague. Nevertheless, she saves the Requiem and ejects Salieri, thwarting his desire to assume in a small way the identity of the man he has so admired. Upon Constanze's discovery of Mozart's death, the climax ends.

The epilogue of *Amadeus* is fairly long, since it has to wrap up action in both the central story and the framing situation. Mozart's burial ends the former. We do not see his funeral but can assume that it did not include a composition by Salieri. The Requiem plays nondiegetically as the mourners see the hearse off at the city gate. Salieri is accompanied by Madame Cavalieri, so their platonic relationship has presumably resumed, and Salieri triumphs in his sexual rivalry with Mozart.

A cut from a view of Mozart's wrapped body in a communal paupers' grave smoking with lime powder leads us back to the frame story. The priest clutches a crucifix as if led to the point of despair by what he has heard—harking back to Salieri's burning of his own crucifix. Salieri drives the point home, blaming God for Mozart's death: "He destroyed his own beloved, rather than let a mediocrity share in the smallest part of his glory. *He* killed Mozart . . . and kept me alive to torture." An attendant interrupts this speech, declaring that Salieri's favorite breakfast, sugar rolls, is about to be served. Thus his sweet tooth and gluttony are reprised one final time. He is wheeled out, declaring: "I will speak for you, father. I speak for *all* mediocrities in the world. I am their champion. I am their patron saint." As Salieri moves through the chaotic corridor of insane patients, he ineffectually "absolves" them.

Salieri's words seem to be deliberate mockery, turned against the Church, God, and Mozart. He has taken upon himself a blasphemous version of a holy figure. Thus his portion of the film ends in bitter irony rather than in the true forgiveness that Mozart's music had offered Salieri. The narrative continues a bit longer, however, as the overarching narration inserts a final comment in the form of Mozart's "obscene giggle" on the sound track. I fear that this is a literalized, heavy-handed suggestion that Mozart has, despite Salieri's murderous plot, had the last laugh. His music will go on conferring "absolute absolution" on its auditors indefinitely, while Salieri can only pretend to absolve madmen. Each protagonist has achieved only half his goal. Salieri seems to feel that he has foiled God by killing Mozart, but he has not been able to snatch at part of his idol's glory by claiming the Requiem as his own. Mozart has failed to achieve fame and fortune during his lifetime, but posthumously the immortality which Salieri had craved has instead settled upon him.

VERSION 4 OF AMADEUS

The fact that *Amadeus* was adapted from a widely successful stage piece offers us an instructive opportunity to compare plot construction in the play and the film. Despite the adaptation process, might we expect the large-scale parts of the film to conform to those of the original play? And since the film's sophisticated interplay of narrational levels and thematic implication is unusual for a Hollywood genre piece, might we also trace them to the play's script? In fact, the relationships are somewhat more complicated.[11]

Shaffer's play was repeatedly and extensively revised in the years following its premiere. Version 1 of *Amadeus* was presented in London in 1979. Dissatisfied, Shaffer rewrote it for the New York production in 1980; this is Version 2, the standard text for subsequent performances. I take this as the basic text. A third version was published in 1984. The film might be considered Version 4, and it again transforms Shaffer's conception.[12]

In structure, Version 2 displays some striking parallels with the principles of script composition I have been considering in this book. In particular, the play's large-scale parts are carefully proportioned, as in a four-part Hollywood film. Version 2 runs 75 pages as published (with an average of 17 pages in a four-part breakdown). It contains two acts of nearly equal length, with Act I consisting of 37 pages. Each act in turn breaks into two nearly equal segments separated by turning points, yielding a balanced four-part structure. In the first act, the midway turning point occurs when Mozart improves Salieri's march and Salieri's thoughts first turn to murder. This is essentially the same as the turning point that ends the setup section of the film, though by that point, Salieri is confused and resentful rather than murderous. Similarly, the play's turning point that ends Act I consists of the same action that closes the film's complicating action: Salieri's promise to wage war with God and destroy his creature. Thus the film develops Salieri's character in a more nuanced fashion than does the play.

In the play's second act, the development occupies 18 pages and ends when Salieri decides to starve Mozart to death. The concluding section consists of a climax showing Schikaneder cheating Mozart (17 pages) and an epilogue in which Salieri poisons his rival (4 pages). Thus the action in the second half of the film departs more radically from that of the play.

Nevertheless, the play's relatively short script breaks down into four parts of almost equal length. The film, unusually long in its running time, has five parts, but as we have seen, the extra section is devoted to the expanded role of *Figaro* as a centerpiece underlining the importance of the forgiveness theme—an element not present in the play. Thus, despite the considerable differences between the play and the film, both contain large-scale portions that are carefully balanced against one another. Do modern playwrights, like scriptwriters, sense a need to maintain audience interest by presenting significant developments at intervals roughly equal in length (and containing turning points even where there is no act or scene break)? Students of theater might find this a question worth investigating.

We have seen as well that the film combines a quite traditional classical level of narration with another narrational level, one using such art-cinema strategies as symbolism and authorial commentary. The interplay of levels generates an unusual subtlety in characterization and a complex weave of motifs through the plot. These qualities depend crucially upon the forgiveness theme. To what extent is this rich (if not fully realized) dramatic device derived from the stage piece?

Surprisingly, not at all. The play is designed to be staged in a modern mode, within an all-purpose set which can indicate a variety of locales. The narration proceeds chiefly from Salieri, who addresses the audience directly. There are also two *venticelli* narrational figures, but these are simply gossips who reiterate Salieri's own sour views of the Viennese musical scene. As a result, the play focuses almost entirely upon the bitterly ironic contrast between the vulgar Mozart's God-given powers and the devout Salieri's mediocrity. Shaffer concentrates on a traditional element of the Mozart/Salieri legend: sympathy for the mildly talented artist thrown into the shade by intolerable genius.[13]

Strikingly, Shaffer's play contains no hint of the forgiveness theme so central to the film. As a result, the film's Mozart becomes distinctly more sympathetic than the play's. While this tactic might seem to be a concession to Hollywood values—catering to a mass audience by softening a harsh portrayal of a revered artist—it actually enriches the film. Because of the forgiveness theme and a wide-ranging narrational point of view, the screen version of *Amadeus* balances our sympathies between the two protagonists, asking us to grasp the irony of both their downfalls.[14] The drama critic Richard Adams, commenting on Version 3 of the play, has claimed that it "does not stand or fall according to whether or not we find the finale of *Figaro* unbearably moving." What matters is that "we should be capable of understanding what it is to be Salieri."[15] Yet the film goes much further and asks that we do both. Indeed, it suggests, as the play does not, that one cannot know what it is to be Salieri unless one is unbearably moved, along with him, by the finale of *Figaro*—and then watches him reject its message of forgiveness.

When the film of *Amadeus* first appeared, the forgiveness theme went essentially unnoticed. Perhaps some critics overlooked this theme because they knew the play and re-imagined the film to conform to it. In addition, Shaffer's remarks in essays and interviews at the time suggested that the film would be based solely upon the play's thematic contrast of pious hack and "obscene" genius. Yet despite its flaws, *Amadeus* is a more complex film than critics have generally allowed. More important, by incorporating elements of art-cinema narration, it enables us to understand film narrative, and especially the enormous adaptability of the classical cinema, a bit better.

A FINAL LESSON: THE LONG AND THE SHORT OF IT

No one seems to talk about how lengthy Hollywood films are structured. Screenwriting manuals and interviews with screenwriters usually assume that the ideal length for a script (at one minute per page) is 120 pages or less. Professional script reader Doug Michael identifies ideal lengths thus: "One hundred twenty pages, generally, but it can be as short as 90, even 80."[16] Scriptwriter William Goldman describes producers tackling the first in a stack of scripts: "He may—I know I would—peek at the last page, because if that page reads 180, he knows it's probably not a properly constructed piece of work, just as if it read 90–135 is about right [*sic*]."[17] Asked by William Froug about the typical length for a shooting script, scenarist Jeffrey Boam (*Lethal Weapon 2* [1989] and *Lethal Weapon 3* [1992]) responded: "They'd like to see it about a hundred and twenty or even less. The director always says, 'I'd love to have a script that's about one hundred and fifteen pages.' But if you write a hundred and fifteen page script, it always seems rushed and underdeveloped. So I think you have to write long, so the reader gets what you're trying to tell them."[18] Many manuals are largely aimed at aspiring scriptwriters who would not have the power to get a very long film made. Yet long films do get made in Hollywood.

Michael Mann, who was soon to direct the 176-minute *Heat*, was interviewed by Joel Engel in 1992, when *The Last of the Mohicans* had recently been released. In the course of the interview, the three-act structure had been invoked, but at one point Mann suggested that the model should be flexible:

> *JE:* Does something that goes bump in act one have to crash in act three?
> *MM:* Not necessarily. There are no rules. That's rule one. It's context. Because the whole of a screenplay, the whole of a motion picture, if it works, is a consensual dream. It's a relativistic universe that you create. It's a good idea, when you're creating that universe, to invent some consistent laws by which it operates; and to be cognizant of the fact that this motion picture is going to move through time, approximately two hours of it. There are certain rhythms by which we perceive a flow of events and a story. So it's a fairly good idea to have four acts or three acts.[19]

Mann is, by the way, one of the rare Hollywood practitioners I have run across who has suggested that a film might have four "acts."

If we stretch Syd Field's proportions of ¼ - ½ - ¼ to apply across a very long film, the problem of the unwieldy, lengthy middle becomes exaggerated. *Heat* runs 168 minutes, exclusive of its nearly 8 minutes of credits. This would make for a 44-minute setup, an approximately equal climax, and fully 88 minutes in the middle. To put this in context, this behemoth of a central act would be longer than the entirety of *Liar Liar* (which clocks in at 87 minutes including credits). Thus it seems more reasonable to divide *Heat* into five roughly equal parts, with additional turning points providing structure.

Similarly, in Fieldian terms, the approximately 155 minutes of action (sans credits) in *Amadeus* would yield a 39-minute setup, a similar climax, and a 78-minute central "act." As I have demonstrated, an analysis that divides the film into five large-scale segments better reveals its major narrative twists and turns. The large portions of *Heat*, as I have posited them, average around 33 minutes, those of *Amadeus* around 30.5. Such figures bolster my claim that classical Hollywood narratives are built of large-scale portions that average in a range near 20–30 minutes, and that the total length of the film usually determines how many parts are included. As I argued in the opening chapter, making such divisions is not an idle exercise but highlights patterns of character change, theme, and plot trajectories.

8

The Hunt for Red October

1990. Released by Paramount. Directed by John McTiernan. Screenplay by Larry Ferguson and Donald Stewart, from the novel by Tom Clancy. Running time: 135 minutes; setup, 32; complicating action, 39.5; development, 30; climax and epilogue, 31 (epilogue alone, 4); end credits, 3.

COMPLEX OR CONFUSING?

The makers of *The Hunt for Red October* could hardly have anticipated the momentous events that would rapidly unfold in the USSR and its satellites during the months of the film's production and release. Sean Connery has said that when he first received a script, the front page was missing and no time frame was established.[1] By the time of the film's release, an opening title announced that it was set "In November of 1984, shortly before Gorbachev came to power." The filmmakers no doubt hoped that the ongoing disintegration of Soviet Communism would simply lend some topicality to what was essentially a traditional suspense film.

The rush of historical change, however, seems to have swept many commentators' judgments along with it. *Red October* was being reviewed in late February of 1990 for release on March 2. In 1989, the world had watched the unprecedented live broadcast of the tumultuous First Congress of People's Deputies, the Warsaw Pact states being given the right to withdraw from the alliance, the first meeting between a Soviet head of state and the Pope, Ceaucescu's execution in Romania, and the ascension to power of Dubček and Havel in Czechoslovakia. More immediately, in early February Gorbachev had persuaded the Central Committee of the Communist Party to relinquish its monopoly on power and had committed the USSR to begin destroying chemical weapons. The Central Committee issued new policies on human rights and the development of a market economy. On February 26, as *Red October*'s press screenings were being held, Gorbachev met with Havel, agreeing to a speedier withdrawal of Soviet troops from Czechoslovakia and a stop to their countries' joint cold-war intelligence operations. Small wonder, perhaps, that some reviewers had little stomach for an unrepentantly old-fashioned spy tale.

The film drew a surprising number of unsympathetic notices. The *Christian Science Monitor*'s reviewer scoffed at the film's 1984 setting: "This gives the picture a modicum of credibility, but it doesn't erase a sense of Cold War nostalgia that left a bad taste in my mouth."[2] David Denby took a similar stance:

> The picture offers a kind of nostalgia for heroic days now receding into the past. For of course *The Hunt for Red October*, based on one of Tom Clancy's techno-thrillers, has been rendered out of date by the astonishing events of the past year or so. When we see the little printed prologue explaining that the movie's action is set before Gorbachev came to power, we know that for Cold War cliffhangers, the jig is up.[3]

The *Monthly Film Bulletin*'s dismissive review remarked with little prescience that "like *Rambo III*, *The Hunt for Red October* has been somewhat inconvenienced in the marketplace by the real-life reversals of East-West relations."[4] *Premiere*'s interviewer began by trying to get Connery to express such a reaction: "I just finished reading *The Russia House* and *The Hunt for Red October*. There's an enormous difference between the two. *Red October* is a cold-war story, but the cold war is over. Do you think it is out-of-date?"[5]

More favorable reviews recognized that there was nothing inherently wrong in making a historical film about the recent past. *Variety* reviewed it favorably (and prophetically) as looking "like a b.o. smash" and remarked on its topicality:

> With a Cold War plot that could have suffered from the changes in the Western filmgoing public's perception of the USSR, the filmmakers have wisely opted to keep the story set in 1984—"shortly before Gorbachev came to power," as the opening title puts it—rather than force it into a contemporary time frame. Though Clancy's conservative slant on the Soviet threat remains strong, the essentially hopeful nature of the story has been supported by recent events and makes the film accessible to more liberal viewers as well.[6]

Another positive review referred to the "puckish opening disclaimer,"[7] recognizing it for the straightforward movie convention that it was. Indeed, there is nothing in the film that suggests that it is set in 1984. Presumably in that era even the CIA did not possess laptop computers of the type that Jack Ryan flips down during the credits.

Ordinary spectators were undoubtedly aware of recent events, but they probably recalled little of Soviet current affairs during November of 1984. Chernenko's brief, stultifying tenure in office provided an ideal void into which to slip the events of *Red October*. What audiences presumably cared about were the stars, the plot, the then state-of-the-art special effects, and so on. I saw the film in first run and simply dismissed the "1984" title as a ploy.

I suspect that the widespread assumption that the film was already outdated made many reviewers dismiss it and hence not take much trouble to understand its narrative. The severe reviews abound with comments on *Red October*'s supposedly impenetrable plot—as well as with misdescriptions of both obvious and obscure points. David Edelstein considered that "the whole movie plays like a giant, incomprehensible debriefing."[8] For David Ansen, "without detailed exposition, the elaborate strategic maneuvers of the Russian and American navies—both hunting down the renegade nuclear-armed Russian sub—whiz by in a semiconfusing blur. And Ryan's second guessing of Ramius' motivations . . . is so preposterously intuitive it seems like a form of ESP. Who are these guys?"[9] The answer is that they are parallel protagonists, and Ryan's insight into Ramius' thoughts is extensively motivated by his fascination with the man.

In fact, *Red October* is extremely tightly constructed, with motivations provided for nearly everything that happens. The usual motifs, dangling causes, dialogue hooks, and other techniques of classical narration unify this film to a remarkable degree. Yet the critics who complained of being confused were registering an important quality of the film. *Red October* contains only a few big action scenes, which are relatively easy to understand. There are, however, many conversation scenes, and these provide extensive exposition. An enormous amount of information, ranging from crucial causes to minor details, flies by. The dialogue is often delivered at a great pace, and the superimposed "printout" titles that provide vital information at the beginning of many scenes flit on and off the screen.

Red October is not only rapidly paced, it is remarkably *un*redundant, far more so than any of the other films I am analyzing here. Many names, locations, and technical terms are mentioned just once and do not return until they have important consequences, often many sequences later. So much exposition is provided that the film has little time for the usual repetitions. David Edelstein's review provides an example of such elusive motivation: "If there's one rule in thrillers, it's that there's no suspense without coherence, and 'October' manages to be both lumbering and difficult to follow. At one point a plane crashes on the deck of an aircraft carrier and people in the audience say, 'Huh?' (I still don't know where it came from.)"[10] In fact, shortly before the F14 crashes on the deck of the Enterprise, Captain Davenport rapidly explains that it has been damaged in trying to force a Soviet "Bearcat" plane off its course; only if we remember a title from several scenes earlier introducing the "Bearcat" plane that tries to torpedo the Red October will we understand the relationship of the crash to the action as a whole. And we must understand that in order to grasp Admiral Painter's impassioned reaction, "This business will get out of control! It'll get out of control, and we'll be lucky to live through it!" The crash involves the first death in the maneuverings between the two superpowers over the Red October's defection. Only a very alert viewer (perhaps one who had read the novel) could follow this on first viewing.

Indeed, I had to watch the film several times, comparing notes on various scenes, before I could tease out the causal connections laid out in this analysis. There is no doubt that *Red October* is a complicated, if extensively motivated, film. Why, then, did so many spectators obviously enjoy *Red October* when most of them must have missed so much?

One reason, I suspect, is because the most important aspects of the plot are quite obvious. No one could miss the fact that Ramius is stealing a new silent-running submarine from the Soviets, that sonar expert Jones discovers a way to track it, that desk jockey Ryan faces an uphill struggle to convince powerful American officials that Ramius is defecting, that the Soviet navy is out to sink the Red October, that there is a saboteur aboard the sub, and so on. Catching every connection and nuance may simply not be necessary to the enjoyment of a classical film, especially one based on familiar conventions of action and suspense. Not feeling professionally obliged to understand every bit of the film, spectators may not have experienced the same frustration that many reviewers clearly did.

One unifying aspect of the film, however, that is quite redundantly established is its parallel protagonists. *Films in Review*'s critic remarked of Ryan, "He knows that Ramius is made of the same stuff he is."[11] The *Monthly Film Review* called Ryan Ramius' "surrogate grandson."[12] Richard Schickel simply referred to them as "twin protagonists."[13]

Jack Ryan and Marko Ramius are clearly parallel rather than dual protagonists, as I distinguished those terms in Chapter 1. Superficially they seem to have the same general goal: arranging for the safe defection of the Red October and its officers. Yet the two men's motives differ significantly. Ramius has spent decades at sea and has become disillusioned; his wife's death during his absence impels him to take the drastic step of defecting. He knows the Red October thoroughly, and now he is obsessed with averting a Soviet nuclear strike. He is a man of action who yearns to return to his peaceful childhood occupation of fishing. In contrast, Ryan is a young armchair scholar fascinated by ships and the sea. He longs to get hold of the Red October simply because he wants to study it; he betrays no particular concern over the potential outbreak of war except insofar as it might deny him that opportunity. (He seems unfazed by risking a nuclear strike against the US on the basis of his assumption that Ramius is trying to defect.) His domestic life seems untroubled, and he can return at intervals with family and friends to his childhood home in Maine, complete with fishing. As in other parallel-protagonist films, Ryan achieves his goal through a fascination with his alter ego, Ramius—literally, in this case, spying on him. Ryan must also become progressively more like his hero, taking greater and greater physical risks until he, too, is a man of action. In the end both reach the haven of Ryan's childhood home, becoming father and son figures.

SETUP: TURBULENCE

The opening superimposed titles over a map initiate a device that will be used to introduce names, technical terms, and locations quickly. Shrill computer "printout" noise accompanies all of these titles, suggesting an objective, factual source, even though the opening title is in fact somewhat deceptive. Its statement that the Soviet sub sank, "apparently suffering a radiation problem," plus its revelation that both the Soviet and US governments have denied that the film's events "*ever happened*" leave open a possibility, later reinforced and sustained for quite some time into the film, that Ramius is actually a madman planning his own unauthorized nuclear strike against the US.

The objective narration that provides the superimposed titles can move us quickly about in space and time. In contrast to *Desperately Seeking Susan* and *Amadeus*, several sustained scenes involve neither protagonist. The titles substitute for dialogue hooks, permitting an unpredictable but broadly comprehensible movement among several locales.

The term "Typhoon-class Soviet sub" is introduced over a pan eastward across a sketchy map of the North Atlantic. Once the action begins, another title identifies the locale as the "Polijarny Inlet," a name to which reference will be made repeatedly in subsequent action, causally stitching together disparate locales and characters. The brief scene between Ramius and Captain Borodin establishes the washed-out grays and blues that will be associated with the Soviet characters and the sea. Indeed, virtually all of the action will take place indoors, at night, or on cloudy days. We glimpse sunshine only in the final brief scene.

Ramius' portentous delivery of his first line, "Cold . . . and hard," hints that he is troubled for some unknown reason. His equally foreboding declaration, "It's time. Time indeed," seems further to suggest this. The narration offers no clue as to why he is troubled, though the Cold-War ambiance might lead a spectator to infer that the Soviet Union is embarking upon some sort of threatening mission. The scene remains a dangling cause as the craft heads into the open sea.

As the credits begin, Sean Connery and Alec Baldwin are listed before the title, isolating them as central and equal characters. After the title, other actors are listed in alphabetical order, as if to avoid setting up a hierarchy among them. All play roles distinctly subordinate to the two leads. (We will see Woody Allen using alphabetical actors' credits in *Hannah and Her Sisters* for a different purpose.)

The scene in Ryan's study begins with a black-and-white engraving of a battle between sailing ships. The image picks up the idea of attack faintly suggested in the pre-credits scene. It also acts as a transition between the washed-out gray-blue tones of the opening and the orange tones associated with Ryan. These are introduced as the camera pans and tracks over the contents of his study, glowing in a warm light. The reference books and reports establish him as an expert, while the engraving and a model ship mark him as a devotee of things maritime. The blue glow of a computer screen, displaying two images of submarines, intrudes into the orange surroundings, briefly linking Ryan to the opening scene before he closes the computer.

Though technically expert, Ryan is also quickly established as somewhat impractical in everyday life. As he lingers to talk to his daughter, his wife reminds him with an impatient sigh, "Jack, you're going to miss the plane." By the end of this scene, we know that he is on a "business trip," but its nature is unclear. That line acts as a dialogue hook to the exterior scene at the airport, where the "London Heathrow" and "International Departures" signs establish where he lives and that the trip will take him abroad. Soviet choral music, which had commenced loudly with the Red October's departure, has continued softly during this scene and now wells up again. The music further suggests that Ryan is somehow causally tied to Ramius, and that Ramius' actions may be threatening.

During the trip, a major motif is introduced as Ryan tells the flight attendant he cannot sleep on planes because of turbulence. As he nervously watches his coffee cup clinking gently in a saucer, Ryan might appear almost neurotically fearful. Later a motivation for his tension will be provided, but this moment sets up a series of successively more frightening obstacles that Ryan must overcome in achieving his goal. It also sets up a motif of coffee and tea cups which will contrast the Soviet and American sides, marking moments of danger or surprise, and which will return at the end to signal the banishment of Ryan's fears.

Signs continue to establish locale. The two men who meet Ryan stand under one reading "Washington Dulles," and immediately afterward the limousine carrying Ryan pulls up to a gate labeled "Central Intelligence Agency." With this shot, the Soviet music stops, preparing the way for the moment when we learn the nature of the implied connection between Ryan and Ramius.

The seemingly trivial conversation between Admiral Greer and Ryan introduces important points. Greer mentions having vacationed with Ryan's family at their place in Maine, preparing the way for the epilogue. His close friendship with and trust in Ryan also motivate Greer's later contravention of his orders when he helps Ryan to fake the Red October's sinking. The mention of "a little brother for Stanley" brings up the teddy-bear motif, which reappears only at the final shot's track-in to the new toy.

After this peaceful chat, exposition begins to pile up. Ryan shows Greer two-day-old British Intelligence photographs of a new "Typhoon-class" sub, recalling the opening title's mention of the sinking of such a vessel. The following exchange is crucial for the parallel relationship between the two protagonists. Ryan reveals that the captain's name is Ramius. Greer inquires, "One of yours?" Ryan replies, "Yeah, I did the bio on him last year. He's taken out the lead boat in each new subclass for the last ten years. Fairly good political connection, trained most of their attack boat skippers. The Russians call him 'Vilnius *nastavnik*'—the Vilnius schoolmaster." This speech establishes that Ramius would have influence with many Soviet naval officers, that he is Lithuanian rather than Russian (a point Ryan later reiterates), and that Ryan speaks at least some Russian—something that eventually helps him gain Ramius' confidence. Greer asks about some doors visible in the photos, and

Ryan says he does not know what they are. Thus Ryan's initial goal, which will occupy the setup, is to investigate these doors. The solution will lead to the formulation of a larger goal that will sustain the narrative.

Ryan proposes consulting his friend Skip Tyler, an expert on submarines. This becomes a dangling cause picked up a few scenes later. Greer in turn picks up a dangling cause from the opening, revealing that a satellite detected the Red October's departure from the Polijarny Inlet. This dialogue hook prepares for a transition to the Dallas. As the scene at Greer's office ends, the coffee-cup/turbulence motif returns as Ryan reacts in apprehension to Greer's news, rattling his cup in its saucer.

A cut to black is bridged with the sound of whales, and a fade to blue reveals a huge sub above the camera, identified by a title as the USS Dallas, 100 miles from the Polijarny Inlet. (Polijarny, rather than the Red October, is the basis for Greer's dialogue hook, but we soon learn that the Soviet sub is also nearby.) As often happens in Hollywood films, a trainee is present to motivate exposition. Inside the Dallas, Jones, the expert, teases Seaman Beaumont, the beginner, about not being able to identify whale sounds during a sonar lesson. Jones's reference to the whale sounds as "a biologic" sets up Skip's later declaration that the Red October's caterpillar drive could sound like "whales humping." Later Jones's ability to distinguish the caterpillar's sound from natural phenomena will allow Ryan to contact Ramius. Jones's character is further established when another officer teases him about his obsessions with classical music and sonic equipment. ("This whole boat is just basically his own personal, private stereo set.") Such exposition redundantly motivates Jones's unique ability to decipher the tapes of the Red October's sound. He is also established as eccentric and self-confident, additional traits that justify his dogged search for something that others dismiss as insignificant. Soon Jones detects the Red October, still running on normal propulsion, and we meet the Dallas's captain, Bart Mancuso, who orders Jones to track it.

Since we know that the sub Jones is tracking is the Red October, the cut to the interior of that vessel is not confusing. The scene between Ramius and the political officer Putin continues to conceal Ramius' purposes. Putin is an unsympathetic character, snooping through Ramius' things unapologetically: "Privacy is not of major concern in the Soviet Union, comrade." His investigation of underlining and annotations in a Bible provides ambiguous clues as to what is troubling Ramius. Passages from the Book of Revelation, including the reference to Armageddon, have been marked, and a marginal notation quotes the *Bhagavad Gita:* "I am become death, the destroyer of worlds." Ramius' attribution of this quotation to the inventor of the atomic bomb

(J. Robert Oppenheimer) brings up the subject of nuclear war. Ramius identifies the annotations as his wife's, and Putin refers awkwardly to her death. Thus strong motivations for Ramius' actions are set in play, but what his intentions are we still do not know.

As Ramius puts the Bible away, he asks, "How many agents did the KGB put aboard my boat?" In retrospect it will become apparent that he fears having such an agent learn of his defection plan. Although there is never any further reference to the KGB, this line also implicitly prepares for the later revelation that there is a saboteur on board. The cook's assistant, who is seen at intervals and who is eventually revealed to be the saboteur, is presumably the KGB agent, fanatically willing to perish in order to prevent the sub's falling into American hands.

Ramius opens the safe and extracts their orders. The dialogue in which Putin reveals them to Ramius manages to work Captain Tupolov's name in five times, both characterizing him and ensuring that we will remember him when he becomes a major threat:

> *Putin:* We're to proceed north to grid-square reference 54-90 and rendezvous with Alpha Submarine Kanavalov—Captain Tupolov's boat.
> *Ramius:* You know Tupolov?
> *Putin:* I know he descends from aristocracy and that he was your student. It's rumored he has a special place in his heart for you.
> *Ramius:* There's little room in Tupolov's heart for anyone but Tupolov.
> *Putin:* Having made contact, we are to run a series of drills. Tupolov will hunt us while we test our ship. Having evaluated the operational readiness of the caterpillar drive, we are to return to Polijarny on or about the 16th of this month.

As Putin reads the orders, there is a close view (Fig. 8.1) showing two tea cups on the table. These at once set up the method by which Ramius will fake Putin's "accidental" death, and they link to the coffee cup motif already established for Ryan.

The reading of the orders establishes that Ramius' mission, about which he is so tense, is not part of a Soviet attack on the West. Ramius' sudden ruthless murder of Putin and his muttered "Where I am going, you cannot follow" heighten the mystery. His quotation of one of the gospels (John 13:33) suggests that he has not simply kept the Bible as a souvenir of his wife. But whether he plans to make a Christ-like sacrifice to save humanity or is delusional is unclear. We now know, however, that Ramius has some sort of secret

8.1

technology aboard the sub and that he is contravening his orders. He tosses tea on the floor to suggest how Putin met his end, reinforcing the link to the cup/turbulence motif. His call to the ship's doctor provides a dangling cause covering the scene's end.

By this point, the narrational cues would seem to imply that Ramius is a maverick setting off to launch his own independent nuclear attack. The most obvious candidate to be the film's villain has just been killed off, so perhaps Ramius will fill that role.[14] There is nothing to hint that Ramius might be defecting until Ryan expresses that opinion in the meeting with the National Security Adviser and Joint Chiefs of Staff—a scene that does not occur until early in the complicating action. The focus of the setup is to imply that Ramius is a dangerous maverick. The complicating action then reverses that impression as Ryan conceives his goal of helping Ramius to defect.

The next scene picks up on the dangling cause of Ryan's initial goal of investigating the new Soviet Typhoon submarine technology. Ryan has gone, as a title informs us, to a naval shipyard in Maryland. As he enters a hangar to the deafening sounds of a nuclear sub being built, Ryan's trait of impracticality is picked up from the credits sequence. He is fascinated by the huge shell and wanders toward it, oblivious to the danger until a worker tosses him a hard hat.

Here we encounter two of the many cases where a vital cause is mentioned only once and then picked up much later in the film. Ryan's friend Skip is dealing with a new miniature rescue sub that can attach to the hatches of most countries' submarines. He shows a diagram of the little sub attached to a big one, firmly establishing a major dangling cause that will not return until the climax portion of the film when Ryan and Mancuso use that very sub to board the Red October. Skip mentions, "We can get it anywhere in the world in 24 hours." Skip also asks Ryan, "How's your back?"—a seemingly minor line that prepares for the revelation of Ryan's helicopter accident.

Skip quickly posits that the mysterious sub doors which Ryan is investigating might be a caterpillar drive. This term was mentioned in the orders read by Putin in the previous scene, so we realize that Skip is correct. He now provides a brief explanation of this silent-running device and introduces a key premise: if sonar detected the caterpillar, "it'd sound like whales humping or some kind of seismic anomaly—anything but a submarine." (We have already been introduced to Jones, the one man who will be able to figure out that puzzle, and he has been linked to whales and sonar.) Skip also defines the danger, pointing out that the Red October could silently approach the American coast and launch hundreds of nuclear warheads.

His speech implicitly creates a dialogue hook into the next scene, as we see Ramius apparently pursuing a plan to attack. Ramius has convinced the sub's by-the-books doctor, Petrov, that Putin slipped on spilled tea and broke his neck. The scene then briefly introduces the "cook's assistant Loginov," a figure who will be glimpsed frowning in a cryptic fashion at wide intervals through the film. There is no clue as to why he reacts as he does, but at least we will recognize him by the time Ryan confronts him as the saboteur in the climactic shootout. For now, Loginov's presence is motivated by Ramius' request that he witness his appropriation of Putin's missile activation key. When the doctor objects that no one person should have both missile keys, Ramius dismisses him sharply. In fact, Ramius' control of both missile keys presumably serves simply to prevent either from falling into the hands of a KGB agent, but at this point it seems to imply that his seizure of the sub and its missiles are part of his plan to launch a nuclear attack. Ramius remarks that his address to the crew will explain matters, thus setting up a new dangling cause. The scene ends with a pan to Loginov, thus emphasizing that he will be important without our having any clue as to why. He becomes another cause that dangles for a long time.

A cut without a dialogue hook returns us to the Dallas, where an earlier dangling cause is pursued. Jones identifies the sound of the Red October as coming from a Typhoon-class sub, and the computer confirms his judgment: "Soviet Typhoon Class Submarine, Not Previously Recorded." As I have mentioned, Jones's ability to track the Red October is a crucial factor that the audience must grasp, and here his exceptional skill at interpreting sonar data is redundantly confirmed. Jones also explains to Seaman Beaumont that the Dallas can elude the Red October's sonar by staying behind it, another piece of information that will have consequences during the cat-and-mouse chases.

The next scene, in which Ramius goes to the control area and addresses the crew, seems to confirm that he is a dangerous maverick. He asks the navigator if there are any sonar contacts. The negative reply links to the previous scene by corroborating Jones's claim that staying behind the Red October makes the Dallas undetectable. Ramius then addresses the crew, as he had earlier told Dr. Petrov he would. He invokes standard Cold-War imagery, speaking of the Soviet Union's "dangerous game" with the West and appealing to the men's patriotism. He orders the silent drive mechanism engaged. Again, this is a vital cause that we must understand, and a shot shows the doors of the drive slowly opening. Ryan's quest to find the explanation for these innovative doors has put so much emphasis upon them that this scene's purport should be clear.

Ramius' speech reveals part of his true intention: "Comrades, our own fleet doesn't know our full potential. They will do everything possible to test us, but they will only test their own embarrassment. We will leave our fleet behind. We will pass through the American patrols, pass their sonar nets, and lay off their largest city." But he goes on to declare that their mission will culminate in a rest stop in Havana—something that turns out to be far from his plan. During his speech there are cuts to a number of the listening sailors, including a frowning Loginov, thus establishing the latter's presence more fully in our minds. The men then break into a patriotic song.

Aboard the Dallas, Jones reacts in bafflement as the Red October's regular propellers stop, and we return immediately to the Soviet sub as Ramius orders an abrupt change of course with a sharp left turn. Such a maneuver will later be explained as a "Crazy Ivan," the American term for a sudden turn made by a Soviet sub checking for other subs behind it. An epic extreme long shot of the Red October's exterior shows it tilting and sliding past the camera to reveal the Dallas drifting in the distance. And the scene closes with another example of Hollywood's virtuosic use of almost unnoticeable motifs to create narrative unity. Two feeble sonar peeps are heard from the American sub, emphasizing that the Dallas has lost track of the Red October. The end of the setup is fast approaching, and this motif of two peeps parallels this scene to the end of the development, where Ramius' deliberate emission of two single sonar pings will confirm his acceptance of Ryan's plan.

After the leftward swing, the Red October's sonar expert detects the presence of the Dallas, and Ramius asks whether the American sub is turning to follow them. We know that the caterpillar drive is so far untested, and the Dallas's failure to follow confirms that the system operates as planned. Back on the Dallas, Jones is mystified, but he declares to Mancuso, "I thought I heard singing, sir." Mancuso is incredulous, in keeping with the crew's general skepticism about Jones's claims. The singing, however, will motivate Jones to analyze tapes of the Red October's sounds unyieldingly until he cracks the mystery.

By now the basic situation has been established. The Soviets' new silent sub has been seized and diverted by its captain, and various Americans know parts of what has happened. The implication is still that Ramius plans to attack the U.S.

COMPLICATING ACTION: "NO LONGER A RESEARCH PROJECT"

This large-scale section lays out the obstacles that will be placed in Ramius' way and introduces Ryan's unorthodox theory that Ramius is attempting to defect. In the first brief scene, a bored Soviet bureaucrat enters his office in the Red Fleet Political Directorate and finds a letter from Ramius amid his mail. His pleased, "Ah, Marko," establishes that he knows and likes Ramius, and Ryan will soon reveal that this man, Admiral Padorin, is the uncle of Ramius' late wife. As he reads, his assistant brings him a cup of tea, which Padorin drops as he reads the letter's unrevealed contents. By this point tea has come to be linked to the Soviet leaders, coffee to Ryan; the spilled tea harks back to the death of Putin and the clatter recalls the clinking coffee cups associated with "turbulence"—scenes of fright and threat.

A straight cut returns us to Ryan, searching top secret files with Skip. A phone call summons him to rejoin Greer, who tells him: "This is no longer a research project." During the setup Ryan had continued his detached, scholarly investigations; now he will form a new goal and assume a more active role. In the elevator ride with Greer, a central element which the spectator must understand to follow the plot receives a redundant summary. Ryan says he knows what the doors on the Red October are, and Greer responds, "A nearly silent propulsion system?" revealing that a message concerning the sub's "disappearance" has been radioed in by an American captain (unnamed as yet, Mancuso on the Dallas).

Greer assigns Ryan to brief a meeting of the National Security Adviser, Jeffrey Pelt, the Joint Chiefs of Staff, and other VIPs. Greer's advice concerning Pelt is: "He's liable to ask some direct questions. Give him direct answers." This line helps motivate Ryan's unreflecting boldness in the following scene, which in turn leads to his participation in increasingly dangerous ploys to aid Ramius. (The transitional nature of this scene is reflected in part by the use of warm yellow and orange tones for the corridor conversation with Greer, followed by dark blues throughout the meeting scene.)

The first part of the meeting provides the film's longest stretch of redundant exposition, recapping much of what we've heard about the Red October's doors, its caterpillar drive, and its obvious first-strike purpose. Ryan also lays out new facts about the large number of Soviet vessels launched after the Red October changed course. An officer then reveals that Admiral Padorin had received a letter from Ramius. Ryan instantly recognizes Padorin as Ramius' wife's uncle, indicating that his biographical study of Ramius, done a year earlier, was thorough. His memory for such details hints at his fascination with Ramius, motivating his ability to intuit the Soviet captain's incentives.

One officer reveals that the Soviet fleet has sailed with orders to sink the Red October, and another exclaims, "Oh, my God, they've got a madman on their hands!" This possibility has been implicit since the scene in which Ramius killed Putin; the quotation about Armageddon, combined with his wife's death, may reflect an irrational desire for revenge. As the meeting breaks into confused babble, a series of track-ins juxtapose Ryan's intent face with an image of Ramius and his wife on the screen. Abruptly he asks Greer, "Today's the 23rd, isn't it?" The track-ins resume as Ryan stares at the image of Ramius and his wife and gets an idea, interrupting the meeting with a triumphant, "You son of a *bitch!*" This leads to the "direct question" Greer had predicted from Pelt: "You wish to add something to our discussion, Dr. Ryan?"

Ryan then puts forward a suggestion that alters the narrative's trajectory. "Well, sir, I was just thinking that perhaps there's another possibility we might consider. Ramius might be trying to defect." He goes on to describe Ramius' reasons: "And he's not Russian; he's Lithuanian by birth, raised by his paternal grandfather, a fisherman. And he has no children—no ties to leave behind." Ryan does not have to look such details up in his files, concluding, "Today is the first anniversary of his wife's death." When an officer scoffs at the idea, Ryan reveals the extent of his own fascination with Ramius: "*I know Ramius*, general. He's nearly a legend in the submarine community. He's been a maverick his entire career. I actually met him once at an embassy dinner. Have you ever met Captain Ramius, general?" His one-upmanship wins Ryan points with Pelt, but it also reveals a typical parallel-protagonist situation. Ryan is clearly part of the "submarine community" that considers Ramius "a legend."

The meeting ends with Pelt dismissing all but Ryan. Greer's parting line, "I said speak your mind, Jack, but Jesus!" confirms that Ryan has overstepped his duty—as he will continually do when trying to outmaneuver people who doubt his view of Ramius. Alone with Ryan, Pelt admits to being a cynical politician, "but it also means that I keep my options open." One of those options is to let Ryan test his defection theory. Throughout the plot, however, Ryan will contend with the fact that most of the American officials he deals with also keep their options open and can stop cooperating with him at any moment. Pelt will eventually order the Red October sunk without consulting Ryan; Mancuso will insist on carrying handguns onto the Red October despite their ostensibly peaceful mission. Only Greer and Skip will aid Ryan, despite Pelt's change of tactics.[15]

Ryan's speech to Pelt succinctly lays out three phases of his new goal of helping Ramius defect:

Well, first, we need to contact the commanders in the Atlantic *directly*. The Russians get one whiff of this through the regular communications circuits, the game is up. Second, we need to figure out, what can we do to help them? We need to devise a plan to intercede, ready to go at a moment's notice. And third, somebody's gotta go out there and make contact with Ramius and find out what his intentions really are.

When Pelt assigns Ryan to these tasks, Ryan objects, "I am not field personnel," but he will have to become more like Ramius, the man of action.[16] For now Ryan's goal is to obtain the Red October for a few days and inspect its innovatory technology. In a sense, though, Ryan never really relinquishes his research project. It just becomes much more difficult to carry through.

The three tactics laid out in Ryan's speech neatly shape the three remaining large-scale portions of the film. In the rest of the complicating action, Ryan will contact the Atlantic commanders by visiting the Enterprise and arguing his case to the skeptical Admiral Painter and Captain Davenport. The development will follow Ryan's progress in trying to contact Ramius; in the scene that ends the development, Ryan makes that contact and improvises a plan to help him. Finally, the face-to-face meeting with Ramius and his defection occur early in the climax portion. The "plan to intercede, ready to go at a moment's notice" will involve the rescue sub, already introduced by Skip as capable of being quickly deployed anywhere in the world. Pelt's final line to Ryan, "Will you do it?" becomes a dangling cause.

The next scene begins with a title introducing a new submarine, the Konovalov, and its location, grid-square 54-90, both mentioned in the Red October's original orders. Inside we meet its commander, Tupolov. Ramius' original remark about Tupolov had suggested that he is self-centered. When Tupolov first gets the order to sink the Red October, he mutters, "Seven hours. The entire fleet is after him." We might at first think that he is concerned for his old teacher's safety and might try to warn him, but as the scene ends Tupolov tells a shocked sailor, "We're going to kill Ramius." Thus his earlier aside seems to imply that Tupolov longs to sink the Red October, either for his own glory or through resentment of Ramius. At any rate, his goal of hunting down the Red October before other Soviet vessels find it suggests that he is obsessive, the "madman" that US officials suspect Ramius to be. The Konovalov will not figure prominently in the action, but it remains a dangling cause through the plot, providing the final high point.

A brief scene aboard the Dallas alludes to another dangling cause, Jones's search through the tapes of the Red October's "disappearance." We then move to the Red October for a meeting between Ramius and his fellow conspirators. A bit of suspense seems to be added by the fact that the officers disagree on how to accomplish their defection, quarreling over the murder of Putin—though in fact none of the officers will do anything but cooperate with Ramius in pursuing their goal. Ramius reveals that he has sent a letter to Admiral Padorin in order to make sure that none of the officers can back out. They realize that now the entire Soviet fleet will try to sink them—which we already know to be the case. Ramius calmly informs them that he believes they have one chance in three of escaping the Soviet pursuers.

This scene parallels Ryan's earlier meeting with Pelt and the Joint Chiefs, where it had been stressed that the Red October was designed solely to start a war. Here Ramius explains to his men his reasons for turning their defection into a political statement: "My own began the day I was handed the blueprints for this ship. A ship which had but one use." Yet the differences between the two protagonists are also stressed. Ryan was low man on the totem pole in the earlier meeting, begging for a chance to prove his eccentric theory. Ramius is thoroughly in charge, making the decisions for a group of conspirators who have little choice but to cooperate. Ryan's move toward the authority which Ramius already commands will make the two men more alike.

As the meeting winds down, Ramius, who has been drinking tea throughout dinner, offers, "More tea, anyone?" The clink of the cup is heard off-screen as the meeting breaks up, bringing up the cup motif again and recalling Ramius' murder of Putin. As with Ryan's meeting with Pelt, this one ends with two men talking. Borodin stays behind for a chat, opining that Ramius was wrong to send the letter to Padorin. Ramius' reply sets up two vital new premises of his goal: "Oh, Vasili, Moscow is not the worry, not the whole Soviet navy. I know their tactics. I have the advantage. No. The worry is the Americans. We meet the right sort, this *will work*. We get some buckaroo . . ." He shakes his head. In fact it will turn out that Ramius does not anticipate all of the tactics which the Soviets will use against him, and he will need to team up with Ryan to pull off his defection. We realize that Ryan is the only one in a position to be "the right sort" for Ramius, yet Ramius is unaware of his existence.

The word "buckaroo" provides an ironic dialogue hook into the next scene, where Ryan, dressed in an aviator's suit, is jouncing around in a fighter plane gripped by severe turbulence. His discomfort recalls his earlier fear of even the slightest turbulence on his flight to Washington. The comic copilot's casual attitude about turbulence suggests that he is precisely the sort of "buckaroo" that Ramius must avoid. Ryan mutters to himself, "Jack, next time you get a bright idea, just put it in a memo." Such asides will provide a motif that traces his reluctant emergence as a man of action.

Another superimposed title introduces the USS Enterprise, located in the North Atlantic east of Nova Scotia. This gloomy, cold northern locale is the western equivalent of Polijarny Inlet, Ramius' setting-out point. Here Ryan must convince the skeptical officers to aid him in his own hunt for the Red October, a hunt which will end with a mid-Atlantic meeting and a sudden deflection of both Ryan's and Ramius' trajectories southward. Ryan meets Admiral Painter, who demands to know what all the "hubbub" is about. Since we already know Ryan's theory about Ramius, the narration can cut away to another dangling cause, Jones's explanation of the Red October's disappearance from sonar.

Mancuso is seated at a work station next to a shelf of reference books similar to the ones in Ryan's study. Thus the potential for these two professionals to work together is set up, despite Mancuso's initial hostility to Ryan.[17] Jones describes his intensive research into the tapes, prompted in part by his curiosity about the singing he thought he heard. The computer has identified a faint background sound as "magma displacement." This phrase harks back to Skip's claim that the caterpillar's mechanism would sound "like whales humping or some kind of seismic anomaly." Speeding up the tape, Jones has discovered a regular rhythm that could only be man-made. Thus Jones has solved the problem posed at the end of the setup portion as to how to hear the "silent" sub.

Using a map, Jones provides exposition that will allow us to grasp the various vessels' geographical relations to one another. First, the Americans already know that the Soviets have extremely accurate maps of the underwater canyons, including one that begins at a formation called "Thor's Twins." Tracing sonar contact points with the Red October, Jones convinces Mancuso that the Red October is headed straight for Thor's Twins and ultimately toward the south side of Iceland. Mancuso remarks that this formation is "right in their Red Route One," a term which will come up repeatedly in the dialogue and which is crucial to our understanding the cat-and-mouse game to follow. Mancuso decides to wait at the far end of the canyon, which he cannot navigate, in order to intercept the Red October. He also declares, "This we *gotta* phone in." His message will provide the cause that allows Ryan to move from the Enterprise to the Dallas, where he finally contacts Ramius. Jones assures Mancuso that he can track the Red October. Thus the Dallas stands an excellent chance of hunting down and sinking the Red October unless Ryan can stop them—a major new dangling cause.

Aboard the Enterprise, Ryan faces considerable obstacles in trying to save Ramius and his sub—obstacles that force him to focus his goal. Captain Davenport scoffs at the defection theory, and Painter asks about Ramius' plan: "Russians don't take a dump, son, without a plan." Davenport chimes in, "What's he gonna do? Sail into New York, pop the hatch, and say 'Here I am'?" Ryan replies, "It might be just that simple, yes." In his speech to the Red October's crew, Ramius had declared that they would approach America's largest city, so we must presume that his actual plan involves something of this sort. Thus Ryan continues to have a special insight into Ramius' intentions.

Painter, however, also demonstrates that Ryan's current goal is inadequate, pointing out that a few days would be insufficient for a thorough inspection of the Red October. Ryan eagerly responds, "We have to keep it." Even this more ambitious goal is impractical, as Painter points out: "What are you gonna do with the crew? The ones that don't defect are gonna go back and say we got the boat. Or do you plan to eliminate 'em?" Ryan is shocked, and Painter introduces a vital new premise: "So the only way for this thing to work is for you to get them off the boat in such a way that they *think* we don't have it."

This obstacle will only be overcome by Ramius and Ryan working as a pair. For now, however, Ryan is baffled, murmuring only, "Yes, sir, I think I see your point," and tottering off to bed. Painter reveals to Davenport some important backstory on Ryan, describing how, despite being injured in a serious helicopter accident during his Marine training, he completed his course during a slow recovery. Painter advises Davenport to "cut the kid a little slack." Their respect for Ryan's heroism motivates their later reluctant support of his attempt to board the Dallas. Knowing the traumatic source of Ryan's fear of turbulence, we will also be prepared for him to regain that heroism.

The scene aboard the Enterprise ends with Painter wearily declaring, "Ah, Russians gonna find that sub before we get near it anyway." Thus we are left with the impression that he is disinclined to bother with Ryan's scheme. As if testing Painter's view, the rest of the complicating action will deal with the Soviet hunt for the Red October.

A dissolve reveals the Red October passing Thor's Twins as a sailor serves tea to the officers. The navigator declares, "Give me a stop watch and a map, and I'll fly the Alps in a plane with no windows." Another officer retorts, "If the map is accurate enough," injecting an element of doubt and hence suspense. Moreover, Ramius soon ratchets up the tension by unexpectedly ordering the sub to speed up. The crew's nervous reactions make it clear that this is a dangerous move. Both the peril and Ramius' skill are emphasized by the return of the tea motif, when during one of the sharp turns he catches his sliding cup without glancing at it. Presumably his motive here is to increase their chances of outrunning the pursuing Red Fleet, but the scene's main narrative function is to establish Ramius' skill, preparing us for the Soviet torpedo attack late in the climax.

During this scene, an explosion damages the caterpillar drive, forcing Ramius either to stop the sub or to proceed on normal propulsion. He orders the latter, making the Red October audible to potential pursuers. At this point, there is no indication that the damage was caused by sabotage, though that will become apparent in retrospect. One causal motivation is introduced here, however. Dr. Petrov, the only officer not in on the defection scheme, asks nervously, "Was there any core damage? Was there any radiation leakage?" Much later, Ramius will stage a fake radiation leak that will allow him to unload the crew. Petrov's nervousness over radiation will qualify him to be the dupe whom Ramius assigns the job of leading the crew off the sub.

There follows the first of three brief scenes in which the Soviet ambassador, Andrei Lysenko, visits Pelt in his office, each time lying to him about the situation. Pelt mentions recent Soviet naval activities, pointing out that "what looks like an exercise could be a prelude to war." The coffee motif returns as Lysenko nervously puts down his cup with a sharp clink and lies, claiming that the Soviet fleet is simply searching for an important sub lost at sea. He refuses Pelt's help, insisting, "We're doing everything that can be done." This exchange seems to bolster Painter's prediction that the Soviets will find the sub first—unless Ryan can come up with a plan.

The complicating action ends with a sustained suspense scene aboard the Red October. A title introduces a plane, "Bear Foxtrot #692, Soviet Anti-Submarine Aircraft, South of Iceland." Earlier Jones had predicted that the Red October was heading for this location. The plane's dropping of a torpedo and Ramius' successful evasive guidance of his sub through the underwater canyons prove his genius for pinpoint navigation and split-second timing. Thus he fulfills his earlier boast about coping with the Soviets' tactics. The scene also lays out the basics of a torpedo attack, including the release of "countermeasures" to divert the torpedo's homing system from the targeted submarine. These will prove crucial in the climactic attack by Tupolov.

Ramius' delayed turn saves the day as the torpedo rams a cliff and explodes. Borodin pretends to the crew that the whole thing was part of the Soviets' planned exercises to test the sub: "Boy, if they were really shooting at us, we'd be dead by now." This line helps to explain how the crew can come through such an attack and still believe later that the Red October is sunk by the Americans during a battle with Ramius.

This threat over, the sub's mechanic reveals how the caterpillar had been damaged: "Captain, we have a saboteur on board." Ramius realizes that it must be one of the crew rather than an officer and declares to Borodin: "We may have to put them off before we planned." This is the first indication that the officers' plot involves putting the crew off the sub at some point. It links back to Painter's declarations that the Russians always have a plan and that the Red October can only be seized by the US if the crew is removed from the sub in advance.

Up to now, Ramius has evaded his Soviet pursuers, as he predicted he could. He also has a plan to get rid of the crew. Thus it would appear he can carry through his defection plan on his own. (In fact, we will soon learn that he has not anticipated everything.) Now the saboteur jeopardizes his plan, both by forcing him to run on audible propulsion and by threatening to do additional damage. Since we have been prepared to assume that the saboteur is a KGB agent, the Soviet government now appears to have a way to defeat

Ramius. By this point the situation at the end of the setup has been reversed. Ramius, who had seemed a threat to the US, now is himself in danger and in need of help from the "right sort" of American. Ryan, who had been busy researching caterpillar drives during the setup, is now striving to figure out a way to get the crew off the Red October. This revelation that Ramius already has a plan to do so brings the two protagonists' goals a large step closer together and ends the complicating action.

DEVELOPMENT: "ALL WE HAVE TO DO IS FIGURE OUT WHAT HE'S GONNA DO"

Ramius' line, "We may have to put them off before we planned," acts as a dialogue hook into the next scene. A cut from a medium closeup of Ramius to a close view of Ryan emphasizes the links between the two. Relaxing in a sauna aboard the Enterprise, Ryan again talks to himself, parodying Painter's southern accent: "The average Russkie, son, don't take a dump without a plan." He realizes, "Well, wait a minute. We don't have to figure out how to get the crew off the sub. He's already done that. He would've had to. All we have to do is figure out what he's gonna do. So how is *he* gonna get the crew off the sub?" Again Ryan uses his fascination with Ramius to solve the problem. As he shaves, he ponders, "How do you get a crew to want to get off a nuclear sub?" A cut to the carrier's command station reveals Ryan assuring Painter that he has the answer.

Painter, however, has no time to listen, being concerned with an F14 damaged in an encounter with the Bear Foxtrot plane that fired the torpedo at the Red October. This incident serves mainly to delay Ryan's revelation of what he has intuited about Ramius' plan. Indeed, Ryan does not mention Ramius' plan again until well after it has been put in motion. Relatively early in the climax portion, Ramius will ask Ryan how he knew that Ramius was planning to stage a nuclear accident. Ryan simply says that it was logical (though how he arrived at that logical answer is clear only if one remembers the line, "How do you get a crew to want to get off a nuclear sub?").

The second half of the film draws upon a very different approach to plotting from the first half. In many cases, the causal connections among events will become comprehensible only in retrospect, especially where Ryan's and Ramius' actions are concerned. Reasoning backward, however, it will become apparent that everything Ryan does from the beginning of the development to his first conversation with Ramius stems from this moment when he realizes that the Soviet captain plans to fake a nuclear accident. In general the narration becomes far less communicative in the film's second half, and the necessity to think backward over the plot's action may have contributed to the widespread sense of confusion among reviewers. Still, nearly everything is justified, however briefly or obliquely, in the chain of causal motivations.

At this point, we are diverted from Ryan's discovery by Captain Davenport, who delivers some rapid-fire exposition. He explains that the Soviets have posted a line of attack subs along the east coast of the US and are using the rest of their fleet to chase the Red October. Ryan realizes that Ramius is heading into an ambush. Davenport responds glumly: "Your sub captain's going to make it to America, all right, Mr. Ryan. He's going to die within sight of it." His speech reaffirms the second of Ryan's goals as expressed to Pelt earlier: to find a way to help Ramius. Ramius himself had earlier claimed he could handle any threat from the Soviets, but at no point do we get any indication that he anticipates an ambush near the American coast. Now it becomes obvious that he cannot accomplish his goal without Ryan's help. Apparently Davenport and Painter now accept Ryan's premise that Ramius is defecting, but they see no way to prevent the Soviets' sinking the Red October.

The key link to Ramius that Ryan needs comes at this point. He notices the Dallas on a radar screen, and Painter tells him, "That's Bart Mancuso's boat. He's going to the bottom of Red Route One. He's had intermittent contact with what his computer calls a 'magma displacement.' He's got the idea . . ." Ryan interrupts: "'Magma displacement'? Is that like a seismic anomoly?" Painter: "I suppose so, why?" Ryan: "Admiral, is there a way you could get me on board the Dallas?" This dialogue crystallizes a number of motifs introduced earlier, providing a rare bit of redundancy that prepare us for Ryan's move to the Dallas. Painter then scoffs at Ryan's belief that the Dallas has located the Red October and says that a helicopter would have to be turned into "a flying gas can" to make it far enough to take Ryan to the Dallas. The crash of the F14 interrupts their conversation, but during the aftermath Ryan's attention shifts to the helicopters parked on deck. These act as a hook into the next scene, where Davenport outlines the premises of the helicopter flight, stressing its difficulties and dangers. As Ryan boards the helicopter, he mutters, "Next time, Jack, write a goddam memo," reprising this motif and stressing that he is still a scholar rather than a man of action.

There now begins an extended segment that alternates between the Dallas and the Red October. Aboard the former, true to his trait of dedication, Jones is sitting late into the night trying to locate the Red October. Meanwhile

Borodin informs Ramius that they have come out of the canyon route. Given that Painter has just called this "Red Route One" and mentioned that the Dallas is there, we should be prepared for Jones to make contact once more. Ramius reveals that he wants to put the crew ashore in Massachusetts or Maine, where they can be rescued. His goal strengthens the parallel with Ryan, who grew up in Maine and will eventually take Ramius there. It also confirms that Ramius has no idea that Soviet attack subs are waiting in ambush off the American coast.

Borodin then outlines his plan to live in Montana after defecting. He watches as a tea cup by the bed tilts, bringing the cup motif into play once more as we get an indication that the Red October is turning. Back on the Dallas, Jones explains to Seaman Beaumont that this sudden turn is a "Crazy Ivan" designed to detect a sub hidden in the Red October's wake. The Dallas's engines are cut, setting up the possibility that it might drift into the back of the Red October.

This scene is typical of a film's development portion, in that it mainly creates suspense and delay. (Borodin will never get to Montana, and the Dallas misses the Red October.) Its primary function is to fix the "Crazy Ivan" premise vividly in the spectator's mind in preparation for Ryan's later claim that he knows how Ramius typically executes such a maneuver. As the Dallas drifts perilously close to the Red October, Ramius expresses his own simple goal and reveals his personal motives: "I miss the peace of fishing, like when I was a boy. Forty years I've been at sea—a war at sea. A war with no battles, no monuments. Only casualties. I widowed her the day I married her. My wife died while I was at sea, you know." This revelation explains that Ramius' goal of turning over the Red October to the US is an homage to his wife's fear of nuclear war, expressed in the annotations in her Bible and her quotation from Oppenheimer. Moreover, Ramius' speech links back to Ryan's realization that the Red October set sail on the first anniversary of Mrs. Ramius' death. Thus Ryan's empathy with and understanding of Ramius are reconfirmed.

The Red October's return to course verifies Jones's diagnosis of its maneuver as a "Crazy Ivan." Here Mancuso gets a message, reporting with exasperation, "You're not gonna believe this." This dialogue hook leads to a scene of Ryan's helicopter hovering over an empty sea. Ryan demands that they use the ten minutes' worth of emergency fuel to wait for the Dallas—the first time that he has resorted to toughness rather than persuasive passion. The fuel supply creates a short-term deadline that ticks away in closeups of the control-panel clock. The dialogue among the Dallas's crew emphasizes redundantly how foolhardy the operation is, and indeed they fail to snag Ryan and bring him aboard. He takes a further step toward being a man of action by dropping into the water. Once rescued, Ryan returns to his old charm with a cheery, "How do you do, Captain? It's a pleasure to be aboard." Mancuso remains grim-faced and unwelcoming.

Across the narrative, Ryan has had to convince a series of American officials to cooperate with him as he got closer to Ramius. Pelt was relatively simple to win over, since he risked little by giving Ryan a chance. Painter and Davenport held out longer and obstructed him considerably. Now Mancuso will be the most hostile of all, and Ryan will spend the rest of the development portion winning even minor concessions from him.

A second scene in Pelt's office prepares the way for an enormous obstacle to be placed in Ryan's path. Lysenko now claims that Ramius' letter had "announced his intention to fire his missiles on the United States" and asks for help in sinking the Red October. Pelt's reaction does not reveal whether he actually believes Lysenko, but the possibility is raised that the US will join in trying to destroy the Soviet sub. This dangling cause will be picked up early in the next scene.

Upon the return to the Dallas, Ryan is handed a mug of coffee—a brief, oblique hint at the turbulence motif. Indeed, he is about to encounter serious difficulties. Mancuso reveals that he has lost contact with the Red October in order to rendezvous with Ryan; now he must relocate the sub. As Ryan briefly explains his theory about Ramius' potential defection, Mancuso receives a message and remarks, "It seems the circumstances have changed somewhat, Mr. Ryan." The US government has ordered its vessels to use force against the Red October. From now on Ryan will be up against both the Soviet and American governments—except for Greer, whose loyalty to Ryan is fundamental to both protagonists' goals. Ryan's chances now hinge solely on winning Mancuso over, and he must do so before Jones can relocate the sub and enable Mancuso to order it destroyed.

Mancuso is determined to do just that, shouting out orders as he gives Ryan two minutes to make his case. As in the meeting with Pelt, Ryan depends upon his close links to Ramius, insisting desperately, "Captain, *I know this man!*" He then pretends to predict which direction Ramius will turn in his next "Crazy Ivan" maneuver and makes a lucky guess. Mancuso agrees to contact Ramius, but he is still not on Ryan's side: "Now if that bastard so much as twitches, I'm gonna blow him right to Mars."

The development section concludes with a scene of the two subs communicating visually via Morse code. In preparation for this contact, Ramius floods his torpedo tubes but keeps their doors closed. Mancuso, impressed, remarks,

"He's a very cool customer, your Russian." The phrase "your Russian" suggests both the parallel between the two protagonists and Mancuso's dawning conviction that Ryan may actually understand Ramius. Ramius reacts in surprise to Ryan's first message, which proposes to discuss options, and in astonishment to the second, which offers to implement the defection via a rendezvous at the Laurentian Abyssal. Ramius confirms each with a single ping that echoes loudly through the Dallas's conning tower, recalling the two soft sonar pings that signaled the Dallas's loss of contact with the Red October at the end of the setup.

As so often happens in the second half of the film, only in retrospect will we be able to grasp the implications of this pivotal scene. Ramius has realized that whoever sent the messages from the Dallas has intuited his plan to stage a nuclear accident. This will be the first thing he asks Ryan during their face-to-face meeting, after recognizing him as the author of the messages. Now, as the development ends, Ryan cryptically refers to his intention to assist Ramius' scheme: "If the Russians want us to sink her, we might have to do that." Again, we have little basis for interpreting his statement at this point, but it proves that he has already grasped the basics of Ramius' plan. The contact now established between the two protagonists puts the last new premise in place, and Ryan is now in a position to help Ramius implement what has become their mutual plan. A brief scene aboard the Red October confirms that Ramius accepts Ryan's diversion to the Laurentian Abyssal. Notably, as he orders the change of course, he remarks, "We must give this American a wide berth"—not the Americans, but *this* American, just as for Mancuso Ramius is "your [Ryan's] Russian" (or rather, Lithuanian). As Ramius sits tensely reflecting during the sub's southward turn, he presumably ponders whether "this American" is "the right sort" he seeks. A cutaway to the mechanic casting Ramius a worried look from a nearby doorway reminds us that the saboteur remains a major threat. (Indeed, the cook's assistant brushes past the mechanic at this moment, though we are hardly likely to link him to the saboteur.)

CLIMAX AND EPILOGUE: THE RIGHT SORT

The climax begins with a shot of the Red October diving into deep water. A title identifies this as "The Grand Banks, just north of Laurentian Abyssal, 20 hours later." Previous titles have not mentioned temporal intervals, but this lengthy gap is important. Some major surprises will occur during the climax, and we must be able retrospectively to infer—however sketchily—that during this gap Ryan has set his elaborate scheme in motion. He must have contacted Greer, Skip, and others who unexpectedly appear in this remote spot in the Atlantic, a location chosen on the spur of the moment by Ryan as he wrote his second message for Ramius.[18]

Inside the Red October, chaos erupts, with bells, flashing lights, and escaping steam. Since the previous scene ended with a reminder of the saboteur, the spectator will almost certainly infer this to be his deed—just what Ramius wants the crew to think. Presumably Ramius intended to stage such an accident even without the added verisimilitude provided by the unexpected presence of the saboteur. The only major change is that he would have staged it near the US coast, where he could put the crew ashore. Now, however, Ramius accepts a position in which he must gamble on having contacted "the right sort" of American.

True to his character as it was earlier established, Dr. Petrov panics at the thought of radiation contamination and agrees to lead the crew in abandoning the sub. As the only officer among the evacuees, he must convince the Soviet authorities that the Red October sinks with the other officers aboard. Once the crew is outside, the American frigate appears. This is another element that has not been set up, and we will only understand how it got here when additional information is provided in later scenes. Since Ramius has had no further communication with the Dallas, he must simply react to whatever Ryan throws at him. Here he plays his part well, feigning perturbation and telling Petrov that he will scuttle the Red October to prevent its falling into American hands. Petrov's naive reply, "You'll receive the Order of Lenin for this, Captain!" adds a touch of humor and motivates the Soviets' later acceptance of the idea that the Red October was lost at sea.

Once the frigate fires a torpedo at the Red October, Admiral Greer unexpectedly appears in the control room, Skip at his side, and presses the weapon's self-destruct button. At this point, I think, the action becomes confusing. The officers of the frigate must be in on Ryan's plan to stage a fake attack on the Red October, so Greer's melodramatic secrecy ("And I—was never here") seems odd. Similarly, the rescue sub, which Skip now sends out to transfer Ryan and Mancuso to the Red October, could hardly be present on the frigate without some of the crew knowing what is going on. Nevertheless, this scene gives the first indication that during the twenty-hour gap, Ryan has contacted his friends and arranged an elaborate ruse. The rescue sub picks up on the dangling cause established as early as the setup, when Ryan visited Skip in the hangar.

The presence of the frigate provides the film's final new premise. Now the only question is whether the participants can execute the plan successfully. The narrative begins to move full circle, since all of the action after the "nuclear accident" harks back to the opening title's claim that both the Soviets and Americans have denied all of the plot's events.

Skip's order, "Get the DSRV moving," acts as a dialogue hook to shift the scene back to the Dallas. An establishing shot of the Dallas shows the rescue pod now attached to its hull. Just to reassure us that things are not necessarily going as smoothly as they might seem to be, Mancuso grouses as he boards the little sub: "There are about ten million things that can still go wrong with this stunt." (Being aware of the saboteur's presence, we know that he is right.) Mancuso's query, "How's the coffee, Ryan?" emphasizes that motif, associated with danger. And indeed Mancuso seems quite tense, checking his pistol. Given the Americans' ignorance of the saboteur's presence, Mancuso's tension must arise from his habitual distrust of the Soviets. When Ryan asserts that Ramius will not change his mind about defecting, Mancuso replies, "You willing to bet your life on that?" and persuades Ryan to accept a pistol.

Once the Americans enter the Red October, Mancuso's pistol becomes prominent during the awkward face-off between the Soviet and American officers. Spotting it, Ramius remarks to Borodin, in Russian, that Mancuso is a "buckaroo." This line harks back, after a long interval, to Ramius' claim that the defectors must find "the right sort" of American, not a "buckaroo." Mancuso, who had been eager to attack the Red October over Ryan's objections, seemingly epitomizes the gung-ho warrior who would make a disastrous contact for the Soviets. Ramius initially assumes that he is the man who had contacted them from the Dallas, yet Mancuso cannot answer Ramius' question about why the frigate fired upon the Red October. Apparently he is not fully familiar with Ryan's plan, and he tensely mutters for help, "Ryan?"

At last Ryan and Ramius make direct contact, as Ramius realizes that they are thinking along the same lines. Ryan answers Ramius' question: "It was necessary to maintain the illusion for your crew." Ramius responds, "My crew are being rescued, yes?" Ryan: "Even as we speak." The moment of Ramius' realization occurs through a subtle shift in eyelines. A close shot begins with him looking off front right at Ryan; his eyes narrow and he glances directly off right at Mancuso, then shifts his glance back to Ryan, declaring, "*You* sent the signal." Ryan: "That's correct, sir." Now Ramius realizes that it was not the "buckaroo," Mancuso, who sent the message, but a man who might just be "the right sort." Ramius further tests him: "Then how did you know our reactor accident was false?" Ryan replies, "Well, that was a guess, but it seemed logical." Logical indeed, given that the accident occurred just as the Red October reached the rendezvous point, chosen by Ryan because its extreme depth would lend credence to the idea that the "sunken" Soviet sub is irretrievably lost there. ("Abyssal" signifies one of the deepest parts of the oceans.)

Ryan's line about his logical guess seems to stump Ramius for once, as he simply replies, "Very well," and looks around. In fact he is weighing the situation, deciding that he has found the right sort of American. He then formally turns the Red October over to Mancuso, requesting asylum for himself and his crew. Mancuso drops his suspicions and declares, "It's a pleasure, sir." From this point on, he will cooperate fully with the defection plan. Now only the Soviet threat remains.

Suddenly a strange sound is heard, and one Soviet officer assumes that the Americans have fired another torpedo. But the acoustically hypersensitive Jones demurs: "Pitch is too high. The torpedo's Russian." A rapid intercutting among vessels follows as Skip and Greer, aboard the frigate, declare their bafflement at the presence of another torpedo, and Seaman Beaumont, aboard the Dallas (having apparently during the last twenty hours made a quantum leap in his ability to distinguish sonar signals), identifies it as an "Alpha-class Soviet submarine." The "Alpha-class" label harks back to the title that had introduced the Konovalov, Tupolov's sub, far back in the setup. Beaumont's line acts as a dialogue hook over cuts to the Konovalov and then to Tupolov in its control room.

Here we come to what I consider the more prominent of two unmotivated actions in the film. How does Tupolov find the Red October? He cannot initially have known the secret of tracking the caterpillar drive, since the whole point of the Soviets' planned exercise was to see if Tupolov's crew could detect the sub's new mechanism. Even if the Soviets have subsequently told Tupolov how to track the sub (something that is never suggested), he has not been shown as being in close enough range to pick up the faint sound of the Red October's caterpillar drive. (And if the Konovalov had somehow blundered into close enough range when the Dallas and Red October were south of Iceland, presumably the Dallas would have detected its presence.) Given that Ryan picked the Laurentian Abyssal on the spur of the moment, Tupolov could not have anticipated that it would be the rendezvous point and intersected the Red October there. Still, spectators are not likely to notice that the sudden appearance of the Konovalov is inexplicable, since it comes at a point of high tension. Certainly we know that Tupolov was intently pursuing the Red October, and since we have not seen the Konovalov for quite some time, the implausibility will not stand out.

The pace of the scene increases as lines of action begin to be resolved. Mancuso dispatches the rescue sub, committing himself and the others to stay and defend the Red October rather than retreat to the Dallas. Petrov and the crew conclude that "the Captain is fighting them," suggesting that they will never realize that the sub has been turned over to the Americans. Ramius orders Ryan to work some of the submarine's controls.

Ryan: I'm not a naval officer. I'm with the CIA.

Ramius (suspiciously): CIA?

Ryan: I'm not an agent. I just write books for the CIA.

Ramius (briefly nonplussed): Well, whatever. Sit down and do exactly what I tell you.

This exchange serves two functions. It confirms the pair's growing rapport, as Ramius accepts Ryan despite his CIA ties. And it provides one last assertion by Ryan that he is a scholar rather than a man of action—just before he is forced to engage the sub's resident saboteur in a gun battle.

The following action scene, in which Ramius steers the Red October directly toward the oncoming torpedo, parallels the earlier one along "Red Route One," where he had used precise timing to dodge the torpedo dropped by the Soviet plane. Here all the Soviet and American onlookers assume that Ramius has committed a colossal blunder. Yet as the moment of impact approaches, Ramius calmly resumes his earlier conversation with Ryan, asking, "What books?" For the first time he displays interest in his fellow protagonist. When Ryan says he wrote a biography of Admiral Halsey, "about naval combat tactics," Ramius replies intensely, "I *know* this book." Here Ramius, who had not remembered meeting Ryan previously, realizes that he has read his work. His line parallels two earlier scenes. In the meeting with Pelt, Ryan had emphasized, "I know Ramius," and in arguing with Mancuso he had reiterated, "I know him!" The two men's mutual fascination with naval warfare has made them colleagues by the time they meet.

Ramius signals his seniority in the relationship by declaring, "Your conclusions were all wrong, Ryan. Halsey acted stupidly." Directly after this the approaching torpedo shatters harmlessly on the Red October's hull, and Mancuso explains to Ryan, "Combat tactics, Mr. Ryan. By turning into the torpedo, the Captain closed the distance before it could arm itself."

The "combat tactics" phrase echoes both Ryan's description of the subject of his book on Halsey and, implicitly, Ramius' criticism of it. Ramius has proven himself more expert than Mancuso, Greer, and, most of all, Ryan. Ryan regresses from the expert to the greenhorn learning from the master.

Ramius declares that Tupolov will arm his next torpedo as he fires it, so the threat returns. Now the saboteur shoots into the control room, fatally wounding Borodin, and then disappears into the missile bay to destroy the sub. Here we encounter a second, less glaring causal lapse. Since the saboteur is presumably a KGB agent out to thwart Ramius' attempt to surrender the Red October to the Americans, why would he fire at the officers and draw attention to himself? Most logically, he would simply sneak into the missile bay and scuttle the ship by detonating a bomb. But again, we are not likely to notice the illogicality during this fast-moving action. The crucial plot device is that Ramius and Ryan must now concentrate on the saboteur.

The rest of the climax intercuts between the search for the saboteur and the cooperation between the Red October and the Dallas in defeating Tupolov. Ramius turns the command of his sub over to Mancuso, who redundantly signals his wholehearted acceptance of his Soviet counterpart by offering his pistol: "Captain, wait! You may need this, sir." The moment is marked by a pan to Ryan, staring in surprise at Mancuso, and by the latter's response, "Don't just stand there, Ryan, go with him!"

The hunt for the saboteur is the culmination of Ryan's progression toward becoming a man of action. We know that he had been a Marine but had been severely injured in a helicopter accident that led to a desk-bound career. During the course of the film he has begun by flying in a commercial jet and experiencing mild turbulence, then has flown in a fighter jet in severe turbulence, then dropped from a helicopter into a freezing ocean, and finally arrived in a Soviet sub where he must shoot it out with a suicidal saboteur. Once Ramius, the initial man of action, has been eliminated from the hunt with a shoulder wound, Ryan must step in for his hero and eliminate one of the two final threats to their plan. During his stealthy progress through the missile bay, Ryan picks up the motif of muttering to himself, giving a passable imitation of his double: "Ryan, some things don't react well to bullets." The vivid orange lights that play over Ryan's face through the grillwork of the bay intensify the earlier color motif associated with him and his home.

Just as Ryan fills in for Ramius in the hunt for the saboteur, Mancuso takes over the running of the sub. When Jones announces that the Konovalov has fired a live torpedo, Mancuso orders a sharp left turn. This recalls the "Crazy

Ivans" executed by Ramius in earlier scenes—one of which Ryan had successfully "predicted," fooling Mancuso into cooperating with him. The following scene is reasonably comprehensible, in that it draws upon premises laid down in the scene of the Soviet torpedo attack on the Red October that ended the complicating action. The Dallas drops "countermeasures" to draw the torpedo away from the Red October, then rockets evasively to the surface. The subsequent spectacular shot of the Dallas erupting out of the water confirms the Soviet crew's belief that Ramius is leading the Red October in a valiant underwater battle with the Americans.

After killing the saboteur, Ryan returns with Ramius to the control room. Mancuso defeats Tupolov by imitating Ramius. He orders the Red October, with the torpedo on its tail, to head directly toward the Konovalov, then turn at the last minute so that the torpedo destroys Tupolov's vessel. Late in this action, Mancuso says to Ramius and Ryan, "Hard part about playing chicken is knowing when to flinch." Ramius has never expressed such doubts, and Mancuso's possible inability to imitate Ramius—as Ryan has already successfully done—provides the film's last bit of suspense before the Konovalov is blown up.

The film's epilogue falls into three parts. During the first, Pelt meets again with Lysenko and points out, "We have ascertained the Red October's final position, but given the depth of the water and the fact that the wreckage is spread out over such a wide area, it'll be some time before anything is recovered." Lysenko's tentative inquiry about the disappearance of an Alpha sub (the Konovalov) leads nowhere, and we realize that the subject is closed, with the two countries reaching the state of mutual denial described in the opening title.

The film's final title places the Red October in the "Penobscot River, North of Searsport, Maine." Ryan and Ramius are on the conning tower, as Ramius had been with Borodin in the opening scene. Yet the cold grayish blue of that scene has been replaced with a deeper, moonlit blue, suggesting a cool spring evening. The two men now seem to be well acquainted and talk intimately, like father and son. Ryan suggests a deep relationship of this sort: "I grew up around here. My grandfather taught me to fish off that island right over there." This has been Ramius' goal—to get back to the fishing of his childhood, and now he looks wistfully at the island. Ryan opines, "When the dust settles from this, there's going to be hell to pay in Moscow." Ramius replies, "Well, perhaps. Maybe some good will come from it. [Here the Russian choral music from the credits comes up.] A little revolution now and then is a healthy thing, don't you think?" In the 1984 context of the film's plot, we must assume that Ramius is referring to his private pacifist revolt against the Soviet authorities, ironically involving a sub named for the 1917 Revolution. Most likely, his line also serves as the film's sole reference to the epochal events that were occurring in the Soviet Union as the film was being made. If we take it this way, then *Red October* bears a subtler relation to its historical context than its American reviewers realized.

Ramius then redundantly emphasizes the parallels between himself and Ryan: "Do you still like to fish, Ryan?" After Ryan's murmured "Mm-hm," Ramius continues: "There's a river, not unlike this one, near Vilnius, where *my* grandfather taught *me* to fish. 'And the sea will grant each man new hope, as sleep brings dreams [very quietly] of home.' Christopher Columbus." Ryan, in a very tight closeup, replies, with tears in his eyes, "Welcome to the New World, sir."

The epilogue is still not over, switching to a third locale, a plane in which Ryan is returning to London. A flight attendant lifts a cup and saucer from his tray table, and the resulting clinking noise concludes the cup/turbulence motif. Ryan is asleep, no longer bothered by turbulence. Through the window we see the only unclouded sunlight glimpsed in the entire film. A camera movement reveals a large teddy bear in the seat beside Ryan—reddish orange to recapitulate the color associated with his home and the daughter for whom the toy is destined. And, through the conventional association of bears with Russia and red with the Soviet Union, the Cold War threat becomes neutralized. Indeed, the most exuberant part of the Russian anthem that had accompanied the Red October's departure from Polijarny plays during this shot. Again—contra the reviewers' opinions—the traditional Cold War imagery is undercut by the film, with Soviet music celebrating the American protagonist's success.

This epilogue works intensely with parallels. Ryan's childhood home in Maine is implied to be Ramius' new home, and Ramius stresses this by emotionally quoting a passage from Columbus that mentions home. Columbus' crossing of the Atlantic has been duplicated by both men. Ryan flies westward at the beginning and eastward at the end; in between he helps Ramius complete his own pioneering journey to the "new world." The trip up the Penobscot River is contrasted with Ramius' departure from the Polijarny Inlet in the opening. Ramius' quotation from Columbus also suggests that by defecting he has found a sense of peace. Earlier in talking to Borodin, he had regretted his life at sea and his consequent absence during his wife's death. Now "the sea will grant each man new hope." His life at sea now seems ended. And

Ryan, though now headed for London and home, will presumably return to explore the Red October thoroughly, completing his research goal. His friendship with Ramius also appears to be permanent.

The Hunt for Red October is somewhat longer than the standard Hollywood film, at nearly 135 minutes. This is not long enough for it to break into five parts, and the extra time occurs in the complicating-action portion, which lays out a great deal of material.

A FINAL LESSON: ENOUGH IS ENOUGH

Though well structured in itself, *The Hunt for Red October* contains elements of a device which has become inordinately exaggerated in more recent films and which may be a symptom of the problems of mid-1990s Hollywood cinema: the tendency to pile up climaxes. I am not referring here to the final large-scale segment that I have termed the climax portion. That portion usually ends with a single high point that provides resolution to the plot, or sometimes with two high points to resolve the two plotlines. An epilogue typically follows. In recent years, however, some films in genres dependent on action and suspense have added more high points after the climax has apparently already resolved the action.

In *Red October*, the appearance of Tupolov's sub blasting torpedoes at the Red October seems to be the climactic action. It provides the means that will permit the Americans to persuade the Russians that the Red October has sunk. This action is suddenly interrupted by the shootout with the saboteur. This latter action has been prepared by several references to the saboteur and his determination to destroy the sub. Here one climactic action (the shootout with the saboteur) is intercut with another (the fight with Tupolov). This combination prolongs the intense action of the climax portion's end—but, as we have seen, at the expense of some of the narrative's otherwise tight motivation.

In his previous film, *Die Hard* (1988), McTiernan had been less successful in integrating a surprise capper into the resolution. There the spectacular death of the main villain had seemed to lead into a epilogue as McClane and his wife emerge from the building. Yet suddenly the vicious henchman Karl, whom we had earlier seen apparently fatally throttled by a chain, emerges to threaten the couple once more. His renewed menace functions to close off the subplot involving the sympathetic cop Powell, who had told McClane that he is now deskbound, unable to fire a gun as a result of accidently having killed a child. By shooting Karl and rescuing the McClanes, Powell presumably cures his phobia (a trajectory remarkably similar to Ryan's purging of his helicopter-accident trauma).

Nevertheless, the unexpected appearance of Karl sometimes raises a titter among spectators, depending as it does upon the old villain-who-will-not-die convention. That convention became an important staple of modern Hollywood cinema beginning with *Halloween* (1978), in which the intrepid Laurie seemingly kills the psychopathic Michael twice, only to have him attack her a third time; even when the psychiatrist Loomis empties a revolver into Michael, his "corpse" disappears. Such superhuman villains form the basis of the endless teen-oriented slasher cycles that followed, and a variant even figured in Martin Scorsese's remake of *Cape Fear* (1991).[19]

By the mid-1990s, however, the desire to raise the ante for each big new action film seems to have exceeded the reasonable limits on stacking up climactic scenes. Scenario adviser Thomas Pope succinctly analyzes three separate climaxes in *The Last Action Hero* (1993), necessitated by the lack of unity among the plotlines.[20] In some films the resolution of the single central plotline became arbitrary and repetitive. *Variety* reviewer Todd McCarthy diagnosed three such excessive finales in the summer of 1997 alone. Of *Con Air* he remarked:

> One can see the picture deflating right before one's eyes during the utterly overdone and needless climax-upon-a-climax, as it saps the high spirits it has maintained through most of the flight; big scene of the plane crashing into a casino is the worst in the film, with furious over cutting unable to disguise bad continuity, varying special effects techniques and inconsistent airplane speeds. Protracting things even further with the groan-inducing villain-who-won't-die gambit, and finally with a cornball reunion scene of Cameron with his family, merely makes matters worse.[21]

McCarthy found similar problems in *Face/Off*:

> Woo sets up sequence after sequence that appear intended as the climax, with Archer and Troy blasting away at each other with balletic grace, and with varying numbers of other people in the way, only to let them live for yet another confrontation. Director finally decides to end things with a speedboat chase that, even if gratuitous in feel, delivers the goods in excitement and spectacle.[22]

Regarding *Air Force One*, McCarthy identified a "piling on of an excess of climaxes."[23]

This effect of snowballing climactic events perhaps follows logically from some Hollywood practitioners' unreasonable fear of exposition that I examined in the chapter on *Back to the Future*. An imbalance induced by a lack of information and a superabundance of action runs counter to the guidelines of established classical storytelling. This is not to say that multiple climaxes constitute a trait of some post-classical filmmaking system. Rather, they seem to reflect Hollywood's traditional search for novelty within standard formulas, but taken to an occasionally ludicrous level. *The Hunt for Red October* demonstrates how to stop just short of such an imbalance.

9

Parenthood

1989. Released by Universal. Directed by Ron Howard. Screenplay by Lowell Ganz and Babaloo Mandel. Running time: 124 minutes; setup, 36; complicating action, 29; development, 30; climax and epilogue, 25 (epilogue alone, 4); end credits, 5.5.

DECEPTIVE SIMPLICITY

In any multiple-protagonist film, there is likely to be a hierarchy among the characters, with one standing out. In *Parenthood* the character played by Steve Martin, Gil, is clearly more important than his siblings, and his family's doings occupy more numerous and longer scenes. Helen's family comes second, with Susan's struggle with Nathan and Frank's with Larry being about equal. Still, with their separate goals and causal chains, each plotline constitutes a nearly self-contained narrative. Certainly Susan does not act as a "supporting player" in Gil's plot, since their two plotlines barely affect each other. Instead, they come together mainly to serve the theme, contrasting Patty's regimented, learning-oriented life and Justin's clumsy but fun-loving behavior.

Most reviewers treated the cast as "an ensemble," and David Denby remarked: "*Parenthood* has the bouncing energy of some of the kaleidoscopic Robert Altman movies of fifteen years ago, though without Altman's thicket of cross-references, without the richness and eccentricity of his atmosphere or anything like his bitter humor. Howard punches out the scenes emphatically, each making its point and then ending."[1] Certainly an ambitious film like *Nashville* creates a denser weave of many characters. Yet Howard's plotlines are not quite as self-contained and spare as Denby claims. What holds the film's narrative together are not causal links among the four lines, but parallels and contrasts which create a broad, thematic overview of the notion of parenthood.

Parenthood is an unpretentious piece of Hollywood entertainment. Yet close examination reveals considerable care and complexity in its structures. The lack of causal links among scenes gives the filmmakers even fewer chances to use dialogue hooks than would a plot centering on parallel protagonists. Dangling causes become more crucial, and sometimes we are asked to recall events several scenes back in order to follow new action. (The analysis that follows assumes, unless stated otherwise, that no dialogue hook or other local transitional device is used to move from one scene to the next.) Instead, characters are compared and contrasted in ways which demand a fair degree of alert interpretation. We are asked, for example, to register Frank's reaction to his debt-ridden son Larry's being ejected by gangsters from a speeding car and then to relate his response directly to Helen's reception of her errant daughter Julie being delivered home in a police car. At another point Frank compares Larry to Gil's son Kevin, and the precocious Patty is contrasted with Gil's awkward son Justin. Gil consciously tries to be a better father to his children than Frank had been to him, coming to sympathize with the latter only when he realizes his own failings. Todd's irresponsible obsession with race cars is compared with Frank's devotion to restoring his own classic car—both of which make them bad husbands. I cannot detail here all the resonances set up by comparisons among the characters. I can only suggest once again that a good, ordinary Hollywood narrative is not a simple thing.

SETUP: "THAT'S A PARENT?!"

The first four scenes introduce the four siblings who are the film's protagonists, roughly in order of importance. Their parents are Frank (Jason Robards) and Marilyn (Eileen Ryan); Grandma (Helen Shaw) is Marilyn's mother. We first meet Gil (Steve Martin), married to Karen (Mary Steenburgen); their children are Kevin, Taylor, and Justin. The oldest of the four siblings is Helen (Dianne Wiest), the divorced mother of Julie and Garry. The younger sister is Susan (Harley Kozak), married to Nathan (Rick Moranis); they are the parents of Patty. The black sheep of the family is Larry (Tom Hulce), unmarried but the father of Cool. Subsequent scenes move among the siblings, usually in sets of four, though in a few cases staying with Gil's plotline for two scenes in a row; all three turning points occur after, or in one case during, a scene involving Gil.

The pre-credits scene at the baseball game, Gil's memory of an "amalgam" of his childhood birthdays, establishes the action's locale. As young Gil and his father Frank enter the bleachers, a St. Louis Cardinals poster appears prominently behind them, and Cardinals programs and other fan paraphernalia proliferate here and in the modern scene once Gil snaps out of his reverie. Indeed, Gil's family hauls so many Cardinals-emblazoned objects home that one cushion gets kicked under their van and left behind. Few films establish their locales quite so insistently as this, and yet *Parenthood*'s St. Louis setting does not figure prominently in the narrative. Other cities or towns would probably do as a locale. Why the emphasis on St. Louis?

Clearly the point is to set the film in "middle America," both geographically and culturally. One might then ask why, in an era of multiculturalism, Howard has chosen to examine a white, middle-class family as typifying parenthood. I suspect it is because the film sets out to deal with family problems on a very basic level and hence presents a family which is relatively free of all the additional challenges that might be faced by minority families. In the contemporary cultural situation, the difficulties of a black or Jewish or Native American family would inevitably seem to be partly traceable to social circumstances, not merely personal ones. Moreover, it seems very likely that a director like Ron Howard, with his image as the Frank Capra of the baby-boomer generation,[2] would face a storm of criticism if he tried to attribute a similar array of problems to a minority family. The filmmakers instead chose a family that is relatively well-off and of no obvious ethnic background.[3] Indeed, for a comedy, *Parenthood* finds a surprising array of serious marital and parental problems within its microcosm of mainstream American life. If people with these advantages have trouble coping, the film seems to imply, then such problems are a universal challenge. Moreover, even Gil's apparently upscale job turns out to be at a firm corrupted by sleazy business practices—a taint which is so extreme and which is introduced so late in the narrative that it threatens to overbalance the plot a bit. Thus what we see of middle-class cultural institutions presents a different set of challenges for parents.

The film plunges immediately into exposition concerning Gil's plotline. Frank's excuse for their lateness, "I had to stop and do some business," establishes him as having been a busy, distracted father. Young Gil excuses his father's actions to the usher: "His own childhood was without a positive male influence." This is doubly odd, in that a child this age would hardly understand such a concept, and the scene seems to be set in the 1950s, while the "positive male influence" is a palpably modern term. The line prepares for the comic revelation of Gil's fantasy. It also, however, is important in establishing that Gil, while wanting to avoid Frank's mistakes, has some sympathy for and understanding of his father. This impression is reinforced by Gil's subsequent line, "His own father kicked him out when he was fifteen, so my dad was taught to see child-raising as a job, a burden, a prison, rather than a playground." Gil's tossing around of pop-psychological terms suggests that he has read books on child-rearing, trying to avoid his father's mistakes. The "playground" remark looks forward to Grandma's later anecdote comparing child-rearing to a roller coaster.

One question that arises here is whether Gil, not himself having exactly had "a positive male influence," can become the ideal father he longs to be. After revealing that he is actually 35 and a father, Gil baldly states his main goal: "I swore things would be different with my kids. It's my *dream*. Strong, happy, confident kids." During early portions of the narrative, however, parallels between Gil and Frank suggest that the former is more like his father than he realizes. Although the middle section of the film then contrasts the two, eventually their heart-to-heart talk and cautious reconciliation will form the turning point that ends the development. By the end, both will be better fathers and husbands.

Gil's belief that Frank was a bad father is central, in that he is the only one of the four siblings who expresses such a sentiment. Yet presumably all of them suffered to some extent from Frank's parenting. Susan later reveals that she had led a wild life when young, possibly in rebellion. Helen's problems are not traced to her childhood, but we must assume she married young, given that she becomes a mother again after having become a grandmother. Indeed, one would hardly expect Frank, lover of fast cars and sports, to be much interested in his daughters. Only Larry, who shares such tastes with Frank, seems to have gotten a great deal of his attention and as a result has become the family's only hopeless case. Gil's initial criticisms of Frank resonate through all four of the plotlines and cue us to speculate about why each of Frank's offspring turned out so differently.

As Karen calls Gil out of his reverie, we realize that he is with his own family on an outing to the same stadium, years later. Yet even as Gil comes to himself, he seems confused and abstracted, not having really shared the event with them. The shot/reverse shots as Karen signals that they should leave appear to place him at a distance, with the children clustered in her shot (Fig. 9.1) and with an empty seat in the foreground of his, suggesting his physical as

9.1

9.2

well as psychological separation from the others (Fig. 9.2). Thus we get a clue that Gil is not succeeding as well as he may hope in escaping Frank's influence.

The credits sequence drops hints—all elaborated later—about the traits of the family members as they clamber into their van. Karen's struggle to get Justin into his carseat prepares us for his clumsiness; the outgoing Taylor plays mischievous games with Gil; during all this Kevin leans morosely against the van. Similarly, Karen's devoted but relaxed attitude toward her children emerges as she tries unsuccessfully to clean Justin's face, then makes a gesture of resignation. In contrast, Gil pauses after finally closing the van door, registering what we will later learn is his main problem as a parent: excessive tension.

During the ride home, Gil and Karen listen, appalled, as Kevin sings "Diarrhea," which he learned the previous year at camp. Gil's ironic remark that "that was money well spent" reinforces the image of the pair as middle-class parents who try to give their children the conventional advantages. Later, while putting his sons to bed, Gil sees the nude Justin sporting only a cowboy hat, boots, and holster, and remarks to Karen, "Hey, what you say, later, when the kids are asleep—I wear this outfit." This comic seduction line introduces the film's surprisingly frank, extensive treatment of sex, both as something that parents often must forgo and as something that they confront as a major problem when their children reach adolescence. It also prefigures elements of the costume that Gil will don to portray "Cowboy Gil" at Kevin's birthday party.

The little episode in which Karen asks Gil to deal with Taylor's illness and he freezes in horror as the child vomits on him creates the first definite contrast between their parenting skills. Karen unhesitatingly rushes to Taylor's aid, snapping, "Gil, why are you just standing there?" His reply, "I'm . . . waiting for her head to spin around," evokes in a comic way parents' occasional equivocal feelings toward their children, as well as hinting once more that he is not as good a parent as Karen. (The reference to *The Exorcist* would resonate with the baby-boomer generation to which the film appeals.) The vomiting episode, coming hard on the heels of the "Diarrhea" song, quickly associates scatological imagery with young children, an occasional motif which parallels the association of sex with older ones.

Eventually Karen and Gil begin to make love, establishing that, despite the practical obstacles presented by children, their relationship is still romantic. Their passion dissolves, however, when Karen mentions an appointment to see Kevin's principal on Monday. This is the first of the film's many dangling causes; it will carry over subsequent scenes involving the three other plotlines, resurfacing in scene 5. Gil and Karen discuss Kevin's "tense face," which Gil imitates as a caricatural mask of tragedy. This grimace becomes a crucial motif, in that both Gil and Kevin will repeatedly make variants of this same face, strongly suggesting that Kevin is replicating his own father's "worries." Gil mentions that Kevin makes that same face at Little League, linking the problem to three generations: recalling how Frank had dumped him at baseball games, Gil determines to do better by his own son, and yet he will reinforce Kevin's tension by pushing him in Little League games.

The couple's reactions to the principal's concern about Kevin characterize them further. Gil gets more and more upset, denouncing teachers who label a child "problem kid" and rising to an ironic pitch of anger when he says that Kevin's next teacher should not be "one of these *hysterics!*" Karen agrees with him, but more calmly: "You know, Kevin's *great*—he can't be that much of a problem." Many comparisons and contrasts will be drawn among the various parents, who represent a spectrum of possible combinations of stable and unreliable traits. Most need to change in some way, but Karen will consistently be held up as the most adept parent, needing no improvement.

This relatively lengthy opening scene has established Gil and Karen's family as the most important and to some extent as the basis for comparison with the other plotlines. Now it ends with a contrast to a sibling's child. Consoling themselves that Kevin's problems cannot be serious, Gil remarks, "Now, if it was my sister's kid . . ." and Karen sadly replies, "Garry." This exchange, ending with Gil's line, "Now there's a kid with problems," acts as a dialogue hook into the second scene, which sets up Helen's plotline. This very explicit comparison among offspring cues us to watch for the film's pattern of comparison and contrast among the parents and among their children.

A straight cut leads to the beginning of scene 2, a close view of the aforementioned Garry furtively leaving his padlocked room. His behavior and the mysterious crumpled brown-paper bag which he carries seem to confirm Gil and Karen's belief that he has more worrisome problems than Kevin's. Helen is first seen in her bathrobe (from which we can infer that this scene takes place the morning after the opening sequence's action), paying bills; the initial implication, that she is a responsible mother who provides her children a good home, will be confirmed. Later we learn that she works in a bank—a solid, middle-class occupation. Her artificially cheery "Hi, Garry!" however, becomes a motif signaling her inability to communicate with him. His distant response establishes him as the classically withdrawn, rebellious adolescent, complete with skateboard. Helen babbles on, vainly attempting to engage him in conversation. Her speech mentions most of the family members and a big dinner that night: "Grandma and Grandpa are going to be here, and Uncle Gil and Aunt Karen, they're bringing their kids. Aunt Susie and Uncle Nathan and their kids [*sic*]." The occasion is, she says, "a big surprise." Thus another appointment and dangling cause are established that motivate the family dinner in scene 4.

After Garry's departure, we learn that Helen has problems with both her children. She knocks and enters Julie's room, asking for help with the upcoming party. Abruptly Helen asks Julie, "You hate me? . . . For making you study so much and give up all your dates and . . ." Julie, clearly not sincerely, answers, "Uh, no, you were right." Helen reveals her basic goal in regard to Julie: "Honey, I'm telling you, those SAT scores are your ticket, and Sweetie, you know, once you get to school, you're gonna . . . you're gonna meet a lotta guys that you like just as well as that Todd." Julie objects to her constant reference to "that Todd," for which Helen apologizes, adding "It's been pleasant—for a moment" as she leaves. This echoes her wistful line to the already-departed Garry, "It's nice talking to you." Thus while Helen seems to be trying awkwardly to reach her children, both are alienated.

Indeed, we immediately learn that, like Garry, Julie has turned her room into a secret domain within her mother's house. Todd emerges from under the bed, revealing that Julie has not given up all her "dates" to do well on her SATs. She plays loud music (the equivalent of Garry's lock on his door) as the two begin to make love. Todd's sophomoric gesture of producing a camera to "record our love" sets up a dangling cause that will connect this scene with the next in Helen's plotline.

This scene ends with a phone-call transition into scene 3, with Helen talking to her sister Susan. The ostensible reason is to borrow a platter for that night's dinner party, permitting a third mention of that momentous appointment. Helen also boasts about Julie's high SAT scores, permitting a transition to Susan's plotline as the latter expresses her own disappointment with her daughter Patty's work: "Math, French. Oh, everything's gone downhill. Nathan's talking to her right now." Susan is clearly younger than Helen, so we might expect her daughter to be in elementary school. As the phone call ends, we remain with Susan, who joins Nathan as he lectures the offscreen Patty: "All I'm saying is, if you want to have just an *ordinary* academic career and attend an *ordinary* university, that's your prerogative. But I must tell you, I think you're selling yourself *way* short." Susan tries a different tack: "Patty, you know we love you. Could you just give your father that little extra effort he's looking for?" A reverse shot reveals the three-year-old Patty replying, "OK, Momma." Thus far, Susan and Nathan are shown to be united in pushing their daughter beyond her years. Even here, however, Patty responds directly to Susan rather than Nathan. Soon Susan will rebel against her husband's parental plan.

Again a transition has invited us to compare children. Both Julie and Patty are being pushed academically by their parents, though their divergent ages make the parallel humorous. And already a generalization about parenthood begins to emerge: if parents push talented children too far, it may lead to other problems. Given that Nathan is a more obsessive parent than Helen, will Patty perhaps become even more alienated than Julie by the time she reaches high school?

For the first time, no transitional device moves us into scene 4, the dinner party. The shift to the evening of the same day remains comprehensible, however, because it picks up on the dangling cause/appointment established redundantly in the previous two scenes. From this point on, dangling causes become the dominant means of moving from scene to scene.

The party functions primarily to introduce Larry, the promised "big surprise," but it also reinforces characters' traits already set up. Frank asks at which of his children's weddings he was drunk: "Gil, you have a good memory." Gil, who seems to be drinking heavily himself, replies bitterly, "It was all three, Dad. Congratulations." Their edgy banter refers back to the opening, when Gil's "good memory" had summoned up Frank's neglect on his early birthdays. Now he is asked to recall Frank's bad behavior at his children's weddings. Frank's lack of shame regarding these earlier events motivates his indulgence of the wayward Larry, soon to pop up in his family's midst.

During this exchange Frank also recalls Gil's childhood: "Stayed in his room all day. Boy, you were a *moody* little son of a bitch." Again Gil responds sharply, "Gee, I wonder why?" Frank's reference to Gil's retreating to his room as a child evokes a comparison with Helen's children, Garry and Julie, who hide secrets from their mother in their rooms. This notion of childhood withdrawal creates a subtle link across a cut to the kitchen. There Helen describes Garry's unhappiness to Karen: "You remember that little guy who wouldn't leave my side? . . . Well, now, if I take a step towards him, he takes a step away." Karen's suggestion that Helen's ex-husand Ed might talk to Garry establishes Helen as the only divorced sibling; it also eliminates any possibility of help from him when Helen replies: "He won't even acknowledge he's got these kids, and he's got his *new* wife and his *new* kids. He won't even fix my kids' teeth anymore." Introducing a cause that will dangle for quite some time, Helen mentions that Garry's biology teacher has asked her out. Karen's bright response, "Biology? That's promising," seems to imply that the gentleman in question would be sexually knowledgeable and hence a desirable romantic prospect. Indeed, Helen is subsequently revealed as sexually frustrated, and she and the biology teacher eventually marry and produce the baby around whom the film's epilogue centers. For now, however, Helen dismisses the teacher as "not the type I usually go for." In a serio-comic motif that runs through much of the film, the type she does go for turns out to be disastrously wrong for her and her children.

A brief sub-scene introduces a contrast between Patty, the young prodigy, and Gil and Karen's klutzy son Justin, both three years old. Patty reads from Kafka's "The Penal Colony" and performs a mathematical feat. Though Gil declares, "Actually, Justin is quite bright," the boy seems to disprove him by eating the dots off Patty's math cards. Thus it seems possible that Gil may be failing with his younger son as well. An immediate return to the kitchen shows Susan arriving with some spartan-looking food and remarking that Nathan has his family on a "power eating" diet. This moment sets up her later rebellion by eating junk food. The scene also follows up on Helen's comment that the biology teacher is not her type. Susan remarks that she has seen Helen's ex-boyfriend. When Helen remarks, "God, what a loser, huh?" Susan continues, "in a Rolls." Helen laughs briefly and concludes, "I meant me." Thus she is established as not being able to judge men well.

Larry's entry picks up on the dangling cause of "the big surprise," established by Helen in the second scene. The three siblings' annoyance at Larry's appearance immediately characterizes him negatively. Gil specifies his drawbacks with a comic aside to Justin, "Don't give him any money," and by remarking to Larry, "You've stopped wearing your turban." Frank's delight at Larry's return suggests that the youngest son was his favorite, and the two will share the fourth plotline. Frank's ultimate realization that he has failed as a father will come from his dealings with Larry, not Gil.

Larry's dinner conversation confirms our initial impression that he is irresponsible. First he describes his affair with a Las Vegas showgirl and his recent discovery that they produced a son: "Then a couple of months ago she shows up with Cool, tells me, 'You watch him, I shot someone, I have to leave the country.' *That's* a parent?!" Cool's presence helps characterize Larry as the most hopeless of the narrative's parents, as well as the black sheep among Frank's offspring. This plot element implies that of all the interferences and pressures inflicted on children by parents—short of physical abuse—neglect is the worst. The other siblings' parenting, however misguided, sorts out into happy endings. Only Larry's story ends badly, and only Frank's intervention saves Larry from disaster.

Larry goes on to describe his pending big business deal (a scheme which turns out to be fabricated to cover up his gambling debts). Frank enthusiastically supports him: "What's wrong with getting rich quick? Quick is the best way to get rich." His attitude partially confirms Gil's earlier judgment of his father as too business-oriented. Moreover, Frank's treatment of his wife Marilyn during this scene characterizes him as a bullying husband. He insults her and her mother, the family matriarch, Grandma, and such behavior will continue until near the end of the film. In general, the narrative strongly suggests that being a good parent necessitates being a good spouse.

As if to stress this point, Larry's decision to move in temporarily with Frank and Marilyn forces Grandma to move elsewhere. Nathan and Susan volunteer to host her, and thus begins her odyssey through all the households, moving subsequently to stay with Helen's family and finally with Gil and Karen's. Grandma's relocations were clearly intended by the filmmakers as a motif that systematically reveals her dissatisfaction with each example of the younger generation of parents that she encounters. In fact, her moves are so briefly presented that most spectators probably do not notice this motif. Moreover, her appearances tend to involve her in cute-old-lady remarks that invite us to see her as a minor comic figure rather than as a wise elder. As a result, her final anecdote about preferring a life that is more like a roller coaster than a merry-go-round ends up being an unwarrantedly privileged summation of the parenthood theme.

The dinner scene ends with a sudden power blackout that provides an occasion for a redundant summary of several characters' traits. Frank gratuitously insults Marilyn: "Your mouth used up all the power." Nathan seizes the opportunity to instruct Patty: "Honey, this is a blackout. It's a temporary interruption in the electrical supply of the home." As always, Karen is more direct in reassuring the panicky Kevin: "It's OK, honey. Something's busted." The scene ends with Gil fetching what he thinks is a flashlight, only to flourish Helen's vibrator in front of the group. Everyone is shocked or embarrassed by the moment. Julie is particularly dismayed, contrasting notably with her sly delight at the discomfiture of the rest of the family when Larry's son Cool appeared. Thus we realize that Julie is not as sophisticated as she thinks she is, preparing for her eventual dependence upon Helen as "Mommy" in the climax.

The action of scene 5 quickly picks up on the dangling cause from the opening sequence, Gil and Karen's appointment with Kevin's principal. The school psychologist's conclusion has been thoroughly motivated already: "Kevin is a very sweet, very sensitive, very tense little boy. He needs some special attention." Karen seems to accept this diagnosis, explaining that Kevin's problems stem from being their first child. During her speech, Gil makes a version of "the tense face," and he and Karen briefly quarrel over who is responsible for Kevin's problems. When she says he lets their children sit too close to the television, he snarls, "So we'll throw the TVs out, we'll put the TVs in the garbage, then, and you and I, we'll—we'll perform works of Shakespeare or something." In fact Gil's idea of spending time with his son will be revealed to be taking him to a video arcade. Yet one breakthrough in their relationship will come when Gil takes the considerable trouble to perform, not Shakespeare, but at least Cowboy Gil at Kevin's birthday party. The school-conference scene ends with Gil committing himself either to sending Kevin to a private school or getting him the therapy necessary to keep him in public school. The principal and psychologist agree, and as the summer vacation is beginning, they impose a four-month deadline before the next school year. Thus Gil has a more specific goal of creating a reasonably strong, happy, and confident kid in a short period of time. His need to earn more money becomes a parallel goal linked to his primary one. For now, Karen's goals are the same as Gil's, as the final image of them holding hands in brave determination suggests.

As scene 6 begins, we quickly grasp the situation as a dangling cause from scene 2, when Todd photographed himself and Julie having sex. The pair discover that the photos they have retrieved under the name Buckman are Helen's. When Julie says, "It's the party celebrating my mother's promotion at the bank," we get both our sole indication of what Helen's job is and a confirmation that she is doing well as the family breadwinner. Julie's anxious question about who picked up the other photos provides an internal dialogue hook to switch locales to Helen's house, where she is examining Julie and Todd's sex photos.

Before Julie enters, Helen whimpers softly as she looks at each photo. Yet once her daughter arrives, she summons up a bit of humor: "I—I think this one is my favorite." When Julie tries to defuse the situation by saying, "It's just for fun, Mom," Helen replies sarcastically, "Well, I'm glad to know it's not a *job*." One of *Parenthood*'s strengths is that it manages to balance comedy with melodrama for most of its length. (As we shall see, it falters only in its climax and epilogue.) Indeed, one of its main themes is that humor is vital to parenting. The least successful parent, Larry, tries to be ingratiatingly entertaining, but he is seldom really amusing. But Helen and Gil in particular manage to salvage painful or embarrassing situations, with Gil's cowboy routine at his son's birthday party being only the most obvious instance.

Julie responds to her mother's criticism with a gibe: "Well, I thought somebody in this house ought to be having sex—I mean, with something that doesn't require batteries." Thus Helen's vibrator, set up as a dangling cause in

9.3

the previous scene, returns as a parallel to Julie's sex photos. After Julie shows herself to be hypocritically prudish in regard to her mother's sex life and locks herself in her room, Helen kicks at Julie's door: "I would just like a little respect! Not a lot, just a little. Do you know *why* I'm having sex with machinery? Because your father left to have a party and I stayed to raise two kids. And I have no life, goddammit!" In the hierarchy of protagonists, Helen ranks just below Gil, and like him, she is accorded two goals. She wants what is best for her children, but she now reveals that she also needs personal respect and, implicitly, a better romantic relationship than she had with Ed. Her main obstacle seems to be her children's failure to realize that the family's problems stem from Ed.

Julie precipitates a family crisis by moving out, declaring, "Todd's working now. We'll find a place to live somewhere." Her vaguely articulated goal of making her relationship with Todd into a viable marriage will sputter along until the climax, when Helen pushes her into achieving it. Here Helen issues an ultimatum: "If you walk out of this house against my wishes, don't ever *think* about coming back here." Just after Julie storms out, a shot in depth shows her in the yard, hesitating, while in the foreground Helen relents (Fig. 9.3), thus motivating their later reconciliation. Helen rushes out to shout after her departing daughter: "Honey, I'm always here if you need me!"—another dangling cause that will eventually result in Julie's return.

A straight cut leads to Frank uncovering his classic car in order to show it to Larry, picking up on the dangling cause of Larry inviting himself to stay with his parents. This scene also develops a growing "prodigal offspring" theme.

Larry has been away for three years, apparently without contacting his family. Only Frank has been happy to see him back. Now Julie may have flown the parental nest. Will Helen be like Frank, endlessly tolerant and forgiving? Will Julie disappear for years? The thematic and causal material becomes clearer with this juxtaposition. Frank has been willfully neglectful (with Gil and perhaps the girls) and indulgent (with Larry). Will Gil overcompensate and become suffocatingly protective? Will Helen avoid interfering in her children's lives to the point where they flee her? By extension, will Susan collaborate in Nathan's oppressive control of little Patty's childhood? In short, will they replicate or avoid their father's mistakes? (Marilyn's mistakes seem not to matter, as Frank seems to have worn her down into a doormat.)

Larry expresses delight in the car, and Frank remarks, "I knew you'd be the one who'd appreciate this," suggesting again his favoritism toward his youngest child. He also says, "Three years, every night, every weekend, I have dinner out here. You know, it was a piece of junk when I found it. First time I got laid was in a car like this." This brief speech reveals a great deal. As soon as Larry, the youngest, had left three years before, Frank apparently began to avoid his wife's company, spending all his time fixing up his beloved car. His nostalgia for his youth and especially his association of the car with his sexual initiation suggest a perpetual immaturity. Just after this line, Marilyn hails him from the house: "Frank! Cool just finished lunch." Frank responds with his usual sarcasm, "I'll call the newspapers." When she suggests, "I thought you and Larry could take him somewhere," Frank declares haughtily, "I am showing Larry my car." Larry advises Marilyn, "Just plop him down in front of the TV. It's what he always does."

These lines represent the film's height of both spousal and parental irresponsibility so far. Frank's sexual nostalgia contrasts with his gratuitously nasty treatment of his wife, and Larry's use of television as a babysitter defines his approach to parenting as benign neglect. Frank and Larry then carry on like good old boys, drinking beer and discussing sports. Larry finally reveals something of his financial troubles, claiming that a gambling debt is delaying his big deal and asking for three thousand dollars. Showing no annoyance, Frank continues to encourage him: "You're puttin' together a deal, you gotta look like you can piss with the big boys." In fact Larry secretly needs much more money, but the affinity between father and son is stressed as the scene ends on a close view of Frank winking, smiling, and swigging his beer.

A cut to a frontal closeup of Patty in martial-arts gear picks up on a dangling cause from scene 3, Patty's agreement to pursue her parents' educational demands. Yet there is also an implicit contrast with what we have just witnessed. Frank is indulging Larry's foibles to an unreasonable extent, paying his debts uncomplainingly and even almost admiringly. Here Nathan drives his daughter far beyond her years, specifying his own goal further when he explains to Grandma, "Patty studies Eastern philosophy. Our future leader's gonna have to be much more in tune with the Oriental mind." The implication, that Nathan expects Patty to be President someday, is never reiterated, but it suggests his unrealistic motivations for pushing his daughter. Grandma, who is currently staying with Nathan and Susan while Larry occupies her room, shakes her head. This understated moment provides a fleeting motivation for her moves to Helen's and Gil's houses as she avoids the unfolding parental crises.

As Susan arrives, Patty deliberately hits her father, picking up on her reluctance in scene 3 to follow her parents' program. Inside, Susan tells Nathan that she will be teaching summer school and that they can afford a vacation in Mexico. Later it will be revealed that she hopes for a romantic interlude in which she and Nathan can conceive a second child. Nathan, however, is reluctant to leave Patty for a week in Gil's household: "I'm a little concerned about his jocularity." Susan sees no problem: "She has fun over there. You know, she—she scampers, she cavorts." Here we get our first real indication that Susan is less keen on Patty's learning regimen. As we have seen, the film has quickly set up a premise that humor is a crucial ingredient in parenting, and Nathan's disapproval of "jocularity" redundantly characterizes him as oppressive. As if to confirm this, he seizes upon the idea of taking Patty to Mexico as a chance to teach her Spanish—thereby ruining Susan's plan for a romantic getaway. Susan's subsequent rebellion is set up as a dangling cause when she pulls out a secret stash of junk food and defiantly bites into a cupcake. In trying to turn his child into an adult, Nathan is driving his wife into childish behavior. Certainly she has abandoned the "power eating" mentioned in the earlier party scene, though she has not yet developed a goal of her own. Her transgression is emphasized by the fact that she is wearing gym clothes; an exercise bicycle is also prominently visible in the bedroom during the couple's argument. This emphasis on exercise provides a local motif that carries over into the next scene.

Scene 9, Gil's meeting with his boss Dave, picks up obliquely on the dangling cause introduced in scene 5, the discussion with Kevin's principal. We know that Gil needs additional money for Kevin's therapy. Dave is walking on a treadmill, setting up a subtle comparison with the exercise motif from the previous scene. We know that Nathan has tried to turn every aspect of his family life into work and that he associates success with power ("power eating," "our future leader"). Dave essentially urges Gil to do something similar, to devote himself to his job, to "dazzle" Dave and gain the partnership that seems likely to go to his rival, Phil. Phil, the boss emphasizes, works nights and weekends. Thus Gil forms a second, negatively characterized goal. Just as he must help Kevin improve over the summer, he has a new deadline: one month to "dazzle" Dave. Yet his two goals also conflict, as he points out to his unsympathetic boss: "I really have to spend a lot of extra time with my son right now." This line acts as one of the film's few dialogue hooks.

By this point, the main characters' basic goals have been formed. Gil wants to solve Kevin's problems and at the same time get a promotion. Helen wants to solve her children's problems and get a life for herself. Susan wants in some way to counter Nathan's obsessive control over Patty. Larry wants to pay his debts and make a lucrative business deal, and Frank wants to help him do both. The complicating action will serve primarily to raise the stakes within all the goals, making their accomplishment more vital.

COMPLICATING ACTION: "A WEIRD CHILD"

Gil's line about spending time with Kevin leads straight into a second scene involving this plotline. Father and son play a video game in an arcade. Thus the dialogue hook shows that Gil is trying to help his son despite the extra work his job now requires. Yet that attempt is also undercut by a parallel between this scene and the film's opening. Frank's time with Gil had actually consisted of placing the boy in the keeping of a ballpark usher. Now, having played with Kevin for a while, Gil prepares to leave him on his own at the arcade. Gil also seems still to be putting pressure on Kevin to perform; when the boy loses at a video game, his father has to reassure him. Gil's later insistence that Kevin play a key position in Little League games will further suggest that his notion of spending time with the boy is to push him into discouraging competitive situations.

Thus this scene hints that Gil may be more like his father than he would like to think. Yet when Kevin asks why he is seeing a psychologist, Gil stays to talk, showing that he is a supportive father. He comforts his son by assuring him that as a boy he had similar feelings: "If you're a kid, like *I* was, you have a lot of worries, that's all." His declaration that Kevin is "a great kid" echoes Karen's line in the opening scene's discussion of the meeting with Kevin's principal. Gil also declares: "I think this is gonna be a great summer for you." This reminds us of the school officials' deadline: Kevin must improve over the summer or attend a special school. This conversation also plants the idea of

Kevin's impending birthday, with a promised appearance by Cowboy Dan, as a dangling cause.

The scene ends with a somewhat odd exchange. Gil asks, "OK, now, what do we say when we see a cute eight-year-old girl walk by?" Kevin replies, in a deep voice imitating Gil, "Hubba hubba." Gil laughs, but adds, "Oh, don't tell your mom I taught you that. It'd be bad." This is cute enough, but it also seems inappropriate—as the remark about Karen suggests. In a sense it harks back to Frank's remark that he first "got laid" in his car. This further hint that Gil is perhaps more like his father than he realizes is rather tenuous, but it is immediately strengthened by a juxtaposition with the action of the next scene.

In scene 11, Frank shows Cool his classic car. His speech resembles the one he had given Larry, ending, "The first time I got laid was in—uh, story for another time." This juxtaposition of Gil teaching Kevin precocious sexual behavior and Frank nearly telling a small child about his own sexual adventures provides a further parallel between the two men. The scene continues as Frank and Cool see Larry being dumped out of a passing car. Larry's feeble claim that the unseen men were friends dropping him off leads to Frank's first moment of suspicion concerning Larry. This change in their relationship coincides with Frank's first expression of interest in Cool, who will in effect become his new youngest son, replacing the hopeless Larry.

The transition to scene 12 involves one of the film's most direct comparisons between situations. Like Larry, Julie is brought home in a strange car (picking up on the dangling cause from scene 6, when she left home). Larry, as we should now suspect, is in trouble over money; Julie has been picked up by the police for panhandling. Both Frank and Helen take back their prodigal offspring and struggle to solve their problems. Ultimately Frank will fail with Larry and Helen will succeed to some extent with Julie, but both illustrate Frank's big summing-up speech at the end of the development, about how your children remain your children forever. Julie's tearful criticisms of Todd lead Helen to recall some of her own experiences with men. When Julie sobs, "He told me he loved me," Helen comforts her, "Sweetie. Oh, they say that." Julie reminds Helen that one of the men she had dated had stolen their furniture and concludes, "Men are scum." Helen concurs, "I know, sweetie, men are scum," just in time for the already insecure Garry to overhear her remark.

Helen's lines remind us that her husband not only left her but has virtually disowned their children. Given that the six fathers in the four plotlines (Frank, Gil, the absent Ed, Nathan, Larry, and eventually Todd) are the sources of most of the familial problems, we might be tempted to take Helen's line as expressing the grim outlook of the film's narration—perhaps the result of 1980s liberal male angst. Yet the epilogue presents an ecstatic extended family—one seemingly becoming more extended by the month—with only Larry remaining incorrigible and disappearing forever. (Ed, who has already disappeared forever, is replaced by Helen's superior new husband.) The other men all change to various degrees, and much of the remaining action will involve their improvements as both parents and spouses. In contrast, the mothers are all reasonably good at parenting from the beginning, handicapped chiefly by their husbands' failings.

The rest of this scene, however, seems to confirm Helen's pessimism, as Todd bursts in, reveals that he and Julie are married, and coaxes her into taking him back. The scene ends with a shot of Helen's despairing face, leaving this crisis as a dangling cause to be dealt with later. The next three scenes will offer further instances of men mishandling their spousal and parental roles.

Scene 13, the first Little League game, brings back dangling causes from all of Gil's earlier scenes. Gil had mentioned Kevin's anxiety at Little League in the first scene; this game is part of the therapeutic process promised in the meeting with school officials (scene 5); in scene 9 Gil told Dave that he needed to spend time with his son; and in scene 10 he had assured Kevin of "a great summer." As Gil pushes Kevin into playing second base, his obnoxious teammate Matt groans, and Kevin makes the "tense face" we had seen Gil imitate. Gil encourages his son: "The word is 'fun.' So just go on out there, and what you catch, you catch, and what you miss, you miss, OK?" Kevin seemingly concurs, smiling as he departs for the field.

In fact, Gil's pressure on Kevin reflects his hopes for his son, not just "fun." As the boy makes a simple catch, Gil fantasizes about Kevin's graduation speech as college valedictorian, thanking his father for making him "the happiest, most confident, and most well-adjusted person in this world"—a line that repeats the young Gil's declaration of his goal in scene 1. Karen is conspicuously absent as the aged Gil rises to accept the crowd's applause. As the clapping blends into the applause of the parents present at the Little League game, Matt's father Lew, an unshaven, smoking bully, asks, "Hey, Gil! Our boys finally gonna win one game?" Gil mutters, "Way to be supportive, Lew." After Kevin misses a fly ball, his teammates, led by Matt, ridicule him: "You *stink*, Buckman!" Lew childishly raves, "He had no business being out there!" He is a caricature of a wretched father, reminding us that Gil is trying his hardest despite his problems. (The only other character who smokes cigarettes is Gil's creepy boss, Dave. Frank's cigars during the epilogue's birth scene are another matter.) Kevin's emotional devastation after his failure leads to a second fantasy, as Gil pictures Kevin becoming a bell-tower sniper while at college. The scene returns to reality with Gil assuming the "tense face," suggesting that, despite what he said to Kevin, he still pins his hopes for the boy's improvement upon his Little League performance.

In scene 13, Nathan discovers that Susan has clandestinely pierced her diaphragm. He declares that they had agreed to wait the supposedly optimum five years between "sibs," and she replies defiantly, "No! *You* agreed, and they're not 'sibs,' they're babies, and I wanna have another one." Previously Susan's rebellion has been secret; when last we saw this pair, she sneaked a cupcake—the moment that set up the dangling cause for this scene. Now it becomes clear that she has only been acquiescing to Nathan's goal, and she states one of her own: to have a second child. He stalks out, declaring, "I'm not discussing it again!" Their impasse leaves this causal line dangling.

Scene 15 presents the third and most extreme instance of fatherly irresponsibility in this portion of the film. Helen reacts with resignation as Todd gives himself and Julie silly buzz haircuts. Todd's paint-spattered pants provide the only clue that he is working at the job that Julie had mentioned. Garry declares his desire to live with his father and calls him at his office as Helen watches teary-eyed, aware that the inevitable rebuff will wound her son. As he hangs up disconsolately, Helen murmurs, "Oh, Ed, you shit." This line echoes what she had said upon Larry's first appearance, helping to parallel the plot's most irredeemable fathers, whose sons turn out to be better off without them. Garry's abrupt departure, rejecting Helen's consolation, leaves dangling her inability to cope with his problems.

Kevin's birthday party, which occupies scene 16, was introduced as a dangling cause in scene 10 (at the video arcade). This second gathering of the extended family ends the complicating action. Relatively little causal progress is made during this lengthy sequence. Instead, it primarily functions to summarize the situation in three of the four plotlines. (Larry, the *raison d'être* of the earlier dinner party, is conspicuously absent.) When Susan urges Patty to join Justin in a spinning game "just for fun," Patty replies, "It doesn't look like fun," and Nathan chimes in, "It isn't." Thus we see one way in which this plotline could continue, with Susan feebly pursuing her goal by trying to draw Patty into childish play and Nathan patronizingly overruling her. In the kitchen Helen reveals to Karen that she is clinging to her goal by letting Julie and "that Todd" live with her, hoping that Julie will still go to college. After Patty reacts in terror to Gil's "thumb trick," Susan declares to Nathan that she is "a weird child," but he again points to the klutzy Justin as hardly a role model for their daughter.

Indeed, by now Nathan has become so obnoxious that the narration offers some backstory, with Susan in the kitchen explaining to Karen that she had led a wild life in her youth. Nathan "took me in hand. I liked that. He's very manly. He got me into teaching. He got my shit together. Boy, he really turned me on." Thus her recollections help motivate her attempts to revive their romantic life and conceive a second child, as well as Nathan's eventual bid to save their marriage by singing a song from their wedding.

This conversation also includes a rare moment when a causal element from one plotline later affects another. Both cause and effect are, however, completely trivial. Susan mentions how she used to relieve Nathan's tension by performing oral sex on him while he was driving. Given that Gil's defining negative trait is excess tension, Karen mentally files this idea and later tries it on Gil—causing him to crash their van. That episode creates some comic relief after an intense scene and reemphasizes that there are no easy solutions to Gil's problems, but causally nothing further comes of her action. Thus the links between plotlines remain on the level of family relations, but major causes do not pass between them. As the two women talk, Nathan enters to tell Susan that Grandma wants to move to Helen's house. Susan agrees to drive her the next day, setting up an appointment and dangling cause to be picked up in the next scene. Very little emphasis is put on Grandma's move, and as I have suggested, the result is to undercut her role as a sage elder figure.

The bulk of the rest of the scene concerns Gil's improvised substitution for Cowboy Dan. In recent scenes, Gil has been presented as a problematic father, putting Kevin in a high-pressure situation at Little League that ended in humiliation. Now the narrative summarizes this plotline by reassuring us that Gil will go to any lengths to make his son happy. It also shows his basic understanding of kids, and especially little boys' obsessions with bodily functions and gore. The scatological motif associated with children has already resurfaced when one boy proposed, "Let's go watch the horse shit!" Now Gil wins the crowd over by describing how he has killed Cowboy Dan and slid on his blood and entrails; he then creates a messy balloon structure which he identifies as "Your lower intestines!"

During all this a series of cutaways to other family members reinforces what we already know about their traits. Nathan encourages Patty to play with him, away from the other children, watched sadly by Susan. As Marilyn reacts to Gil's performance delightedly, Frank frowns at her, and her smile fades; throughout the film we have seen him insulting and rejecting her. Yet when the group thinks Gil has seriously hurt himself by falling from the horse, Frank comes forward anxiously to watch. This will accord with his later declaration that he had been extremely worried when Gil was sick during his boyhood.

One seemingly inconsequential incident is worth mentioning. Cowboy Dan's mysterious absence is explained by a stripper who shows up because their agency had switched the addresses of their respective parties. Her grotesquely inappropriate appearance at a children's party seems merely a comic touch. It also, however, briefly introduces a motif that will return in the climax, when Gil reveals that his job advancement might depend upon providing prostitutes for clients. The juxtaposition of commercial sex and the family is pushed further in the climax, but here we get our only actual image of such an invasion of the home (though it echoes the earlier moment when Helen ironically comments that she is glad the pornographic snapshots of her daughter are "not a job").

The birthday scene ends as Gil and Karen tuck Kevin in and the latter declares that he wants to work with his father when he grows up so that "we could still see each other every day." Thus the film's first half ends with an impression that Gil's success at entertaining the group may have erased his humiliation of his son by forcing him to play second base. Kevin uses Gil's "hubba-hubba" phrase on Karen, and if it had had an inappropriate sexual overtone earlier, it now seems the sort of childish comment that Karen takes it to be. Gil appears to be making substantial progress toward his goal of bolstering Kevin emotionally over the summer. The characters in the other plotlines are having problems, but there is no impending crisis. Nathan and Susan disagree on how to raise Patty, but they are not at loggerheads. Todd is apparently working, so he and Julie may make a go of their marriage. Garry has abandoned his hope of leaving Helen to live with his father. Larry has been up to something odd, but as yet we have no indication of just how serious it is. The development, however, will ratchet up the level of the problems in all the plotlines—thus departing from the typical emphasis on delay in the third quarter of the narrative.

DEVELOPMENT: "THEN THEY GROW UP"

An abrupt cut from the serenity of Kevin's bedtime scene carries us to Garry's nocturnal vandalism of Ed's dental office (scene 17). So abrupt is the transition that we may be briefly disoriented, yet a glimpse of Ed's name on the

9.4

door and Helen's reference to him as a dentist quickly cue us. Garry's devastated reaction to his father's rejection two scenes earlier provides the dangling cause that specifies the situation. It becomes particularly clear as Garry grinds his foot on a shattered photo of Ed—our only glimpse of him—with his new wife and son. As at the end of scene 1, Kevin is contrasted with Garry, who appears to have far worse emotional problems.

Another straight cut leads to Helen returning home from work and performing another break-in, exploring the teenage mess in Garry's room. Up to now Helen has largely respected her children's privacy, to the point of letting them get away with too much within her own house. Her artificial cheeriness has kept her completely cut off from Garry. From this point on, however, she deals with her children straightforwardly. After her discovery of Garry's hidden sex tapes, she talks with him somewhat as she had with Julie upon the latter's return home. Her reassurance echoes Karen and Gil's comments about Kevin: "You're a great kid, Honey. You've just got a lousy dad. And you've just gotta learn to say, 'The hell with him.'" Although he seems to listen seriously to her, she cannot get him to talk about the tapes.

Sympathetic to Garry's reluctance to talk about sex with a woman and having no better place to turn, Helen suggests that he talk to Todd. Todd's fascination with the gadgets in Garry's room (Fig. 9.4) does not inspire confidence in him as an adviser, yet he proves surprisingly successful. Rejoining Helen for a frank discussion, he reveals that Garry's problem was simply shame over his newfound adolescent urge to masturbate frequently. After Todd's assurance that this is normal, Garry is now happy—to Helen's astonishment. Thus Garry, seemingly so much more disturbed than Kevin, improves dramatically after one brief conversation. Helen concludes, "I guess a boy Garry's age really needs a man around." Her realization forms a dangling cause that will be developed gradually until it culminates in the epilogue.

In the meantime, however, Todd gives a crucial speech that largely overturns Helen's, and our, view of him. Despite the film's obvious assumption that a boy *does* need a man around, Todd demurs, "Depends on the man," and gains Helen's sympathy by describing his own abusive father. The latter becomes the film's new limit-case, worse than any of the fathers yet seen—or, in the case of Ed, not seen. Todd's story harks back to Gil's early revelation that Frank's father had kicked him out when he was fifteen—an action that Gil uses as an excuse for Frank's deficiencies as a father. Yet despite having had no "positive male influence," Todd is revealed in this scene as redeemable. He concludes: "You know, Mrs. Buckman, you need a license to buy a dog or drive a car. Hell, you need a license to catch a fish. But they'll let any butt-reamin' asshole be a father."

Todd's sentiments also link back to Larry's earlier unselfconscious comment on how Cool's mother dumped the child on him: "*That's* a parent?!" Indeed, Todd has implicitly been paralleled with Larry in some ways. Both are essentially homeless, both had bad fathers, both seek quick money rather than steady work, and both are goofy and immature. Yet from this scene on, they are contrasted. Todd has married the girl with whom he has been carrying on an affair, and he recognizes his father's shortcomings. Eventually fatherhood will bring out the potential that Helen now begins to see in him—thus establishing the direction that this plotline will take in the film's second half.

One might wonder why the film's men should "need a license" to be parents when the women seem to do it pretty well on their own. The film seems to imply that this is because women frequently discuss motherhood (as well as dating and marriage). Karen has heart-to-heart chats with both her sisters-in-law, while Helen talks with Julie and Susan. (Surprisingly, none of these conversations lead to causal connections among plotlines, with the incidental exception of the oral-sex discussion already mentioned.) In contrast, the men seldom talk among themselves, and Nathan angrily refuses to discuss the issue of a second child with Susan. In the video arcade, Gil talks to Kevin only after the boy calls him back. When Frank asks Gil's advice late in the development, the amazed Gil responds awkwardly and hesitantly. Thus the film motivates the idea that the fathers need to improve, while the mothers simply need to get their husbands to shape up, or, in Helen's case, to find a better one. This emphasis upon mothers' ability to communicate connects to a general theme of parenting based on common sense: simple principles and normal reactions rather than elaborate theories, regimented games, or expensive therapy.

Scene 18 is not a complete scene as such but a brief initiation of a dangling cause. Entering his garage, Frank finds his vintage car missing. His initial astonishment gives way to sadness and then anger as he realizes what has happened. This segment belongs with scene 20, bookending scene 19.

Scene 19 again takes place at a video arcade. If the birthday party had confirmed Gil's devotion to Kevin, this scene displays the problems still confronting the family. When another boy robs Kevin, Frank scoffs at his timidity and Gil reacts in rage to Frank's meddling. When Kevin loses his expensive retainer and panics, Karen as usual comforts him while Gil stands by, staring in frustration at the boy. Later, as the couple search the mall's garbage for the retainer, their conversation makes even more explicit what we already know about Gil's influence on Kevin. Gil repeatedly washes his hands, complaining of his "high-strung" son, "Where does he get this obsessive behavior?" Karen replies with gentle sarcasm, "I wish I knew." She points out that the progress we thought we witnessed during the birthday party was illusory. "Gil, what'd you think? That you'd dress up like a cowboy and coach Little League and Kevin would be fine?" (Her line implicitly refers to the pat solutions of many Hollywood movies, suggesting that by stressing Kevin's continuing problems, *Parenthood* presents an unusually realistic story.) Gil eventually admits she is right and adds, "You know, when your kid is born, you can still be perfect. You haven't made any mistakes yet. Then they grow up to be like—like me." These lines later connect to Frank's speech about parenthood never ending. Both speeches in turn link to the film's overall extension of parenthood across a whole series of generations—by the end, five! Unfortunately a crucial link in this chain of parents and grandparents, Frank and Marilyn's marriage, remains largely undeveloped, with Marilyn relegated to the background.

During the ride home, Gil reveals that his goal of promotion is also going badly: "Thursday when I left for Little League, [the boss] said, 'Let's all thank Gil for stopping by.' I didn't take it as a good sign." Karen opines that "worrying isn't gonna help," a line later echoed by Frank when he says that Gil worries too much. By the end of this segment, Gil seems to be in danger of failing at both of his goals: he has obviously not dazzled his boss, and he is still creating as many problems for Kevin as he is solving. Thus by the end of scene 19, Gil has made no real progress toward his goals. There is a suggestion, however, that Karen is pushing him to become more realistic about his demands upon himself and his children. Thus the direction their plotline will take in the film's second half is also emerging.

Scene 20 picks up the action involving Larry and Frank established in the short scene 18. It begins the four segments that will close the development, each devoted to one of the plotlines. The scenes unfold neatly in the same order in which the plotlines will be resolved: Larry/Frank, Susan, Helen, and Gil. Each plotline's causal chain is brought to a state of crisis which will require resolution in the climax section.

Finding Larry in the garage, Frank for the first time becomes angry with him for having tried to sell the car. Larry reveals that he owes $26,000 to gamblers who will kill him if he does not pay. Here again we see a parallel with a previous scene. Frank had belittled Kevin for not fighting back when a boy stole his money. Now he realizes that Larry cannot fight back, and he blames his son instead for never simply having gotten a job. Larry reveals that his attitude, like Kevin's, stems from his father: "What did you always tell me, huh? 'Make your mark! Make your mark! Don't be one of the numbers. Make your mark!'" Frank wearily responds, "You misunderstood me. You weren't listening," but Larry goes on belittling work of the sort Gil does. Promising to learn from his mistakes, he makes the final appeal, "I'm your son." Thus Larry's plotline reaches its crisis: he literally depends upon his father to save his life. The scene ends with Frank pondering this. His disappointment parallels Gil's at the end of the previous scene, when the latter had realized that children grow up "to be like me." Frank's similar realization creates a dangling cause that soon returns when he asks Gil's advice.

Scene 21 brings Susan and Nathan's plotline to a crisis, picking up on the dangling cause from the last two scenes involving the pair. As Nathan uses flashcards to test Patty on the table of elements, Susan interrupts, using similar cards to announce that she is leaving Nathan. As he reads the simple phrases, Nathan at first fails to recognize what is going on and declares, "Honey, this is really basic stuff. She's way beyond this." His obtuseness brings forward the theme of parenting and being a spouse as involving straightforward common sense. The scene ends abruptly on the dangling cause of Susan's threat to leave Nathan, picked up again in the climax.

The move to scene 22 contrasts Susan's and Helen's situations. While Susan's marriage seems to be disintegrating, Helen, the only family member to have divorced so far, is revealed to be dating Garry's biology teacher, mentioned during the dinner party in scene 4. The last time we had seen

Helen (scene 17), she had realized that Garry needed a father, a cause developed and left dangling here. Mr. Bowman makes a joke as he brings her home, and she responds, "You're pretty funny for a biology teacher." Given that humor has been established as a vital component in parenting, this brief exchange marks Mr. Bowman as a potentially suitable mate. Helen reveals that Grandma had advised her to date Mr. Bowman. This is the one of Grandma's two significant causal contributions, demonstrating, if understatedly, that even at her age she occasionally goes on parenting. Helen also mentions that Grandma is moving the next day to Gil's place, setting up another dangling cause that will complete Grandma's odyssey through the siblings' houses.

This plotline's crisis emerges when Todd and Julie squabble about his return to race car driving. His revelation that his partners in the painting business have absconded with their equipment harks back to Julie's mention of Helen's former boyfriend who had stolen their furniture. Thus again a parent's mistakes threaten to be repeated by a child. The revelation of Julie's pregnancy comes just as her marriage seems to be falling apart. Helen's panic at the prospect of becoming a grandmother may also threaten her new relationship with Mr. Bowman, though his unflappable attitude again suggests that he is an admirable candidate for marriage and parenthood.

Scene 23 reveals that the one-month deadline for Gil's attempt to dazzle his boss Dave has passed and that the partnership has gone to his rival. Dave explains: "Phil has just brought in three new multi-million dollar clients. He has spent the last month wining and dining these guys, gettin' them laid. He doesn't tell me about problems with his kids. I'm not even sure if he *has* kids. If this man's dick fell off, he would still show up for work. He is an animal. That's what dazzles—not the *work*. You can't do what he does. You hate that shit." Dave seems not to be a family man; the scene begins with a shot of a photo of him standing next to a sleek race horse (Fig. 9.5) which contrasts with the pony Gil had ridden while trying to make Kevin's birthday party a success. Another photo shows Dave by a race car, suggesting a parallel with the irresponsible husbands Todd and Frank. Dave's office apparently contains no family portraits.

In an unusual move for a classical narrative, this late scene introduces a major new premise. Initially Dave had told Gil to put in time and he might get the partnership. The idea of wining, dining, and even pimping for clients injects a new factor into Gil's job. He is being asked to do things that not only take him away from his family but that are against his principles; as he quits in disgust, he says, "Don't make me a party." This whole issue of corruption at

9.5

Gil's firm muddies the narrative waters. Up to now, the job-versus-family issue had merely been one of balancing time between the two. Presumably even if he were single, however, Gil would object to working at a firm with such practices. Yet eventually, in order to support his family and expected fourth child, he will return to this job. Are we to conclude that only partners or prospective partners have to entertain their clients with prostitutes, and therefore that it is acceptable for Gil to pursue his lower-level job and wink at the activities of his superiors? As we shall see, the issue of the corruption Gil must endure in his job will cause motivational problems in this central plot-line from now on.

Once Gil returns home, the dangling cause of Grandma's final move is picked up when Karen mentions it in her fast opening speech—thus preparing the way for Grandma's one big intervention in the plot. Trying to explain why he quit his job, Gil provides background on his rival: "Phil Richards! This is a guy who leaves his wife and kids and then puts all his money in his girlfriend's name so they can't touch it for child support." Thus Phil is comparable to Helen's ex-husband Ed, a man who dumps his family. Karen's revelation that she is pregnant causes Gil angrily to lay out what appears to be his new goal: "Whether I crawl back to Dave or I get another job, it's obvious now I'm gonna have to spend less time at home. I'm gonna have to have 'business dinners,' and I'm gonna have to play racquetball, and I'm gonna have to get guys laid, so I hope you don't mind if I bring a few prostitutes home, honey, because that's what it takes to get anywhere, and I'm not getting anywhere."

Here the new notion of Gil's job as a threat to the family is taken to an extreme point, as earning a living is reduced metaphorically to pimping. Admittedly we must take the idea of Gil literally bringing prostitutes home as angry hyperbole, but the point is that his work will taint his family. Indeed, when Karen asks whether he wants her to have an abortion, the narration implies that Gil's pressures at work have driven him to want to kill their expected child. This dark twist added to Gil's desire for a partnership pushes this plotline distinctly off balance, raising issues so serious that they cannot be resolved so late in a film that has up to now carefully balanced humor and drama. Indeed, despite tidy resolutions for the other siblings, Gil's plotline never reaches a really satisfactory conclusion.

This scene ends with Gil's bitter declaration, "My whole life is 'have to.'" He turns this pressure against Kevin, summoning him to a Little League game. When Kevin protests, "You said I didn't have to play any more!" Gil responds, "I know what I said, but now I'm changing my mind. If I have to go, you have to go. Move it!" With Kevin's revelation that Gil had stopped pressuring him into playing but now is reverting to his old ways, this plotline reaches its crisis. Karen reacts sadly to this exchange, which provides a dialogue hook into the next scene.

Scene 24, the last Little League game, presents a relatively rare case where one large-scale narrative portion ends and the next begins within the same scene. (We saw the same situation in Chapter 3, where the transition between the setup and complicating action of *Back to the Future* occurred in the scene at the Twin Pines Mall.) As the team warms up, Frank appears to ask Gil's advice about Larry's predicament, explaining to his astonished son, "Because I know you think I was a shitty father. Thank you for not arguing. And I know you're a good father, so tell me—what would you do?" Coming on the heels of Gil's realization of his own failings as a father ("Let's see how I can screw the fourth one up!"), this question causes Gil at last to converse seriously with Frank. Frank belatedly reveals that his goal had been to retire the next year, something that will not happen if he gives Larry $26,000. He also reveals that he had been so distraught as to hate Gil when at two years of age he had been misdiagnosed with polio. Frank proceeds to his key speech: "There is no end zone. You *never* cross the goal lines, spike the ball, and do your touchdown dance—ever! I'm 64, Larry's 27. And he's *still* my son, like Kevin is your son. You think I want him to get hurt? He's my son." Gil's awkward embrace to comfort Frank constitutes a tentative reconciliation. For a moment it appears as if one plotline (Gil's) may have a causal effect on another (the Larry/Frank situation). But in fact Gil gives no advice, and Frank turns away, saying "Ah, I'm all right. I'll figure it out." Gil's line, "Who's to say who's a shitty father?" and his summary of his own family's problems lead to the end of the development. Frank grins and says, "You worry too much. You always did." This, of course, is exactly Gil's problem, and his reluctant smile soon turns into the tense face. Still, Frank's line seems not to have any causal impact on Gil's eventual epiphany in the climactic school-play scene.

CLIMAX AND EPILOGUE: "THE WONDERFUL AND AFFECTING ROLLER-COASTER STORY"

Although the Little League scene continues, an ellipsis moves us well into the game, when a crucial out is needed. Gil's pep talk, "Come on, just relax, relax and concentrate!" suggests that he may be trying to heed Frank's advice. Yet as a fly ball soars toward Kevin, both he and Gil make exaggerated versions of the tense face, and it is clear that the outcome is still vital for both of them. The result is no doubt emotionally satisfying, as Kevin catches the ball not once, but twice, when the obnoxious Matt knocks it out of his grasp. Yet as an apparent solution to Gil's family problem, it does not follow from anything that has so far been motivated. Gil's reconciliation with Frank, while signaling a transition into the plot's resolution phase, could hardly have a causal impact on Kevin's sudden success. (His skillful catch is only motivated retrospectively in the next scene when Karen mentions that Gil has spent a lot of time hitting pop flies to his son.) And given that the previous scene had treated Gil's pressure on Kevin as a bad thing, this action seems to contradict the narrative's own premises. Here we have, I think, one indication of the wobbly footing upon which Gil's plotline has been placed as a result of the new premises raised in the previous segment. I suspect that the film spins into a mode of greater sentimentality in order to compensate for the introduction of corrupt business into the family. Coming directly after Frank's semi-despairing speech about never escaping parenthood, Kevin's catching the fly ball almost seems like another of Gil's fantasies about his son.

Scene 25 picks up on the dangling cause of Frank's declaration that he will solve Larry's problem. He presents his reasonable plan to pay the gamblers in installments and to put Larry to work in his plumbing-goods company, and Larry proposes instead to go to South America in pursuit of another big deal. The plotline is quickly resolved as Frank gives up on Larry, stakes him to the

South American trip, and volunteers to take care of Cool. Frank's declaration to the boy that Larry is never coming back disposes of that character and launches Frank and Marilyn into a new lifelong commitment to parenting. We are to assume that Frank's realization of how badly he had raised Larry will make him a better father this time around. Thus the fourth and last plotline introduced is the first one resolved.

The third plotline to be introduced is settled next. Nathan confronts Susan in summer school—the job that was to provide them with a romantic Mexican vacation. His first reason for asking her to return home is characteristic: "This is very bad for Patty. She can't concentrate." When Susan rejects this, Nathan assures her, "I can compromise. I can change." He convinces her by abasing himself and singing a song in front of her class. This not only goes against his previous character traits but also recalls their wedding, when their romance was still flourishing. True to form, the girls in the class delight in this emotional display, while the boys are embarrassed and join in the applause reluctantly. We must assume that Nathan and Susan's separation has truly modified his character.

Scene 27 resolves Helen's plotline, though with a bit less finality than the previous two. Picking up the dangling cause of Todd's return to racing, the scene presents a new threat. Todd may not only break up with Julie, but he may even kill or maim himself. After his crash, Julie begins to leave: "I can't! I can't! This is too intense!" Helen, who has come a long way from her hesitant, strained conversations with her children, snaps, "This is marriage!" pushing Julie to join Todd. (Luckily, he has emerged from the crash unscathed. The narrative never confronts the notion of a burned and scarred Todd as a father to Helen's grandchild.) When Todd is offered a job crashing cars nightly for the spectators' entertainment, he reveals an awareness of his own stupidity: "That's a good job for me. Crash dummy!" Helen assures him that he is important "because you're gonna be the father of my grandchild." Her simple statement mends Julie and Todd's marriage, as the awestruck Garry points out. Helen resignedly says the marriage will probably only last six months, explaining that she patched it up "because Julie wants Todd. Whatever you guys want, I want to get for you. That's the best I can do." This declaration harks back to the film's theme song, "I Love to See You Smile," but in a bittersweet fashion. Garry approves of Helen's dating Mr. Bowman: "Well, he's funny. And he's the kind of guy that'd be nice to you. Somebody *should* be nice to you." His line recalls the theme of humor being necessary to parenting and reconfirms Mr. Bowman's acceptability as a father. Helen's response, "I'll tell you, kid, I could stand that," leaves open the distinct possibility that she will marry Mr. Bowman. Thus her personal goals from scene 6—"I would just like a little respect!" and "I have no life!"—seem likely to be fulfilled. Garry respects her and believes that Mr. Bowman would as well. Some small loose ends are left dangling, but they will be tied up in the epilogue.

The climax's lengthy last scene, centering around Taylor's school pageant, resolves Gil's plotline—though not in a thorough or entirely motivated fashion. Early in the scene, Justin's head-butting behavior leads Kevin to joke, "And *I'm* the one in therapy"—suggesting that he is developing a sense of humor about his plight and hence is improving. Gil reveals that he has his job back: "Dave called. He was crying. He actually cried. He said if I'd come back he'd give me a corner office with new furniture and a raise. Like that's supposed to make up for everything. Anyway, I took the job. I couldn't think. I was still high from the Little League game." Why the apparently callous Dave should suddenly show such contrition and generosity remains unexplained. (Here we encounter a rare case of a character behaving inconsistently with his established traits.) Do Gil's new office and raise imply that he is promoted and hence is closer to having to provide prostitutes to clients? Does his speech imply that Gil's quitting and returning resulted simply from mood swings rather than his disgust at the nature of the job? Must he now spend more time at work and less at home? Thus Gil's goal of higher pay resolves unsatisfactorily by classical narrative standards.

The plot shifts to Gil's second goal, coping with his children's problems. By now Karen also has a goal, helping Gil to do that and hence reconciling him to the idea of another child. He reacts badly: "And you wanna have four. And the fourth one could be Larry. And they're gonna do a lot of things. I mean, baseball's the least of them. And of all those things, sometime, they're gonna *miss*." Karen insists that sometimes they will not miss: "What do you want me to give you? Guarantees? These are kids, not appliances. Life is messy." Gil declares: "I hate messy." Karen, the perfect mother, is of course right, and she is backed up by Grandma, now staying with them, who tells about preferring the excitement of roller coasters to the blandness of merry-go-rounds. The narration seems to undercut her clichéd allegory of parenthood and life with Gil's frustrated reaction, "Yeah, a minute ago I was really confused about life, and then Grandma came in with her wonderful and affecting roller-coaster story, and now everything's *great* again." But it soon will be, and Grandma's story will play a big part in the resolution. (Again the film displays an awareness of pat movie conventions and then embraces them.)

The school pageant returns Gil and Karen's other two children to prominence, as Taylor acts in "Snow White and the Seven Dwarfs" and Justin ascends the stage and wreaks havoc. Most of the audience members, including Karen, react with amusement. One woman, clearly as tense as Gil, declares, "He's ruining the play! He's ruining the whole play!" Gil fumes, and then, framed with a rolling camera and accompanied by roller-coaster sounds, he goes into an anxiety attack. In some unexplained way, he apparently realizes that he does worry too much. Given the sound effects, we must assume that Grandma's "affecting roller-coaster story" contributed to this change of heart. Gil grins broadly at his chaotic surroundings, then caresses Karen's pregnant belly.

The choice of Taylor's school play as an occasion for Gil's epiphany is an odd one, given the trajectory of his plotline up to the end of the development. He had been characterized as pushing Kevin too much in Little League, and Frank's line about Gil worrying too much ended the development. Yet Gil's new ability to enjoy his children despite their mistakes comes in a scene that does not directly involve Kevin (who is glimpsed videotaping the disorder after Justin invades the stage). It is notable that none of the children and only one of the parents blames Justin for the play's breakdown; in contrast, the Little League players and Lew had excoriated Kevin for missing the crucial catch. Here universal amusement and tolerance reign, and so Gil has no real reason to become tense over Justin's behavior. Kevin's psychological problems, so crucial to both of Gil's goals, have simply vanished with one outstanding catch—the sort of isolated event that Karen has emphasized could not instantly solve their son's problems. Indeed, Karen's declaration that "life is messy" had seemed a privileged moment, the very thing that Gil needed to learn, and yet his plotline is anything but messy in the film's late scenes.

Had the filmmakers stayed with the original implications of Gil's plotline, the new issue of the corrupt nature of his job would not have been introduced. Instead, he might have continued to divide his time between his job and helping Kevin. The climactic scene might have come at a third Little League game where Kevin again botches a crucial play. Gil's realization of what he has done to his son could then lead both of them to resign from the team and spend time together at less competitive, tension-filled activities. Gil might also accept his lack of advancement at his job as simply the cost of his desire to spend more time with his family. (He might even, in a neat turnaround, take the humble job in Frank's plumbing-goods store that Larry had spurned.) Such a sequence of events might not provide the current buoyantly happy ending. Still, the frequent reservations expressed by reviewers concerning the film's late scenes suggest that it is possible for a Hollywood ending to be *too* happy, especially if it is not thoroughly motivated.[4] In contrast, the teary-eyed, cautious optimism that had resolved Helen's story (the plotline most praised by reviewers) followed well from the motivations introduced throughout its scenes. Perhaps we can also conclude that a resolution that mixes bitter and sweet elements will leave the audience with the impression of a happy ending if the sweet elements come last—as with Garry's praise for his mother and the suggestion that her romance with Mr. Bowman is flourishing.

Compared to this problematic resolution of Gil's plotline, the epilogue's giddy celebration of babies has been thoroughly motivated. All the men who have needed to reform have done so. Nathan carries Patty piggyback and makes a silly face at her—carrying through his willingness to behave foolishly to win Susan back. Having become a doting father to Cool, Frank now treats Marilyn tenderly, picking up the film's frequent implication that adults can only be good parents as long as they are also good spouses. (As usual, men bear the brunt of this moral lesson; Helen is a more effective parent once she remarries, but it had not been her fault that she became a single mother.) Todd and Julie are still together after what is presumably about a year (and have grown their hair after their impetuous buzz cuts); the fact that they have survived Helen's pessimistic six-month estimate and are devoted to each other and their baby suggests that Helen has saved their marriage. Gil, once terrified at the prospect of being a bad father to a fourth child, casually diapers his new baby while carrying on a conversation. Helen's new husband, Mr. Bowman, is ecstatic over their baby girl, and he has become a loving father to Garry.

To its credit, the film undercuts the overall sentiment when Taylor is seen cuddling a doll. We might at first simply think that she represents a future mother—yet the doll's head falls off, and Kevin immediately picks it up and treats it as a ball, tossing it into his baseball mitt to the amusement of Taylor. That baseball mitt, however, suggests that Kevin is now a confident, devoted player, his former tensions banished by his breakthrough catch. Here we have a last retrospective attempt to motivate the simplistic resolution of Gil's plotline.

The film's depiction of an extended family burgeons during the epilogue. Grandma, who is the great-grandmother of the story's children from Julie on down, has recently become a great-great-grandmother upon the birth of Julie's baby. That event also made Frank and Marilyn great-grandparents just after they entered renewed parenthood by taking in Cool, their seventh grandchild; Helen's third go at motherhood gives them an eighth grandchild.

All this gives a new meaning to Frank's speech about parenthood being lifelong.

Like so many well-constructed Hollywood films, *Parenthood* returns to its beginning. Gil watches Frank kiss Marilyn, and, though a bit embarrassed, he shows something of the understanding of his father that he had expressed in his initial memory/fantasy while talking with the baseball-field usher. Moreover, Justin peruses a photograph of a row of naked babies seen from the rear, labeled, "A healthy bottom line." He twists backward to compare his own (clothed) bottom, harking back to the whole scatological motif associated with children—beginning with the song "Diarrhea" in the first scene. Though Justin had been too young to join in the song, we must assume that he and the plethora of new family members will soon be challenging their parents with similarly distasteful childhood foibles.

Parenthood's four sections fall into roughly proportional parts. The relatively lengthy setup (36 minutes) includes the credits-sequence action of going home from the stadium, which adds little new information. The complicating action and development are well-balanced at just under half an hour each. The climax and epilogue last only 25 minutes, and we might suspect that the slight disproportion results from neglected opportunities to work out problems in the plotline concerning Gil, Karen, and Kevin.

A FINAL LESSON: STILL A CHARACTER-BASED CINEMA

In an interview with the scriptwriting team Lowell Ganz and Babaloo Mandel (*Parenthood* and other Ron Howard films), Ganz described their basic approach:

> We usually think of the situation first. But then, in the development process before we actually sit down to write, we want to know what the structure is, we want to have a basic sense of the beginning, middle, and end. But in developing it, almost all of the conversation will be about characters and our attempt to hear them, hear their voices, to be able to recognize their sound when they start talking.[5]

His description provides a helpful reminder that the New Hollywood, like the old Hollywood, is based on consistent, unambiguous characters whose goals provide the main narrative momentum.

Ron Howard, currently one of the most powerful directors in Hollywood,[6] has built a career on character-oriented films. Despite the fact that reviewers had some reservations about *Parenthood*'s plot when it appeared, along the lines that I have already discussed, the film is still remembered with affection on the basis of its characters and dialogue. (When the same writing team's film *Fathers' Day*, directed by Ivan Reitman, appeared in 1997, Gene Siskel turned his thumb down, recommending that audiences rent a tape of *Parenthood* instead.) Similarly, when Howard ventures into other genres, he is praised for creating intriguing characters, as in the thriller *Ransom* (1996).

The work of Howard and his screenwriters surely provides a modern exemplar of a very traditional Hollywood value. Compare Ganz's statement above with this one by Wells Root, who worked during the studio era on such films as Hawks's *Tiger Shark* (1932) and Sirk's *Magnificent Obsession* (1954):

> I believe in the classical story form, not disjointed and unstructured. But generally speaking, the most successful stories are those of human character. The most important thing in a script is how to have strong leading characters. Plot and structure and the rest are really secondary. It's how your characters behave and what they say that really makes a film live.[7]

He cites *The African Queen* (1951) and *Casablanca* (1942).

The question of whether the modern Hollywood cinema is plot-driven or character-driven is in most cases misleading. It is both, with strong plots being based on strong characterization. Even an action-oriented film will, according to classical ideals, depend to a considerable extent upon character psychology. Of all the films I have analyzed thus far, *The Hunt for Red October* is the most action-driven, yet all of the maneuvering between the two protagonists depends upon their respective traits. Similarly, in a more formulaic entry in the genre, *The Rock* (1997), the filmmakers take the trouble to outline the Nicholas Cage character's shifting reactions to the news that his girlfriend is pregnant and the Sean Connery character's attempts to reestablish contact with his estranged daughter. Neither subplot is vital to the big action scenes. Moreover, Ed Harris's character is not simply a crazed villain who is seizing Alcatraz to demand money; his motivation is to right injustices he witnessed through his Gulf War experiences. Such efforts are somewhat mechanical in *The Rock*, but they typify Hollywood's attempts to avoid characters who are mere pawns in a series of chases, explosions, and shootouts. This continued reliance on character traits as the main source of motivation for narrative events points again to the endurance of the classical system of storytelling.

10

Alien

1979. Released by 20th Century-Fox. Directed by Ridley Scott. Screenplay by Dan O'Bannon. Story by O'Bannon and Ronald Shusett. Running time: 116.5 minutes; opening credits, 2; setup, 31; complicating action, 24; development, 27; climax and epilogue, 29.5 (epilogue alone, 1); end credits, 3.

Which members of the semi-star-studded cast will die before the final credits?

—CNN review of *Independence Day*, 3 July 1996

A SHOOTING-GALLERY IN SPACE

Those of us who saw Ridley Scott's *Alien* shortly after its initial release in the spring of 1979 experienced it in a way that most likely will never again be possible. We had no clue as to which member of the Nostromo's crew—if any—would survive the alien's onslaught. (Clues we thought we had soon proved unreliable.) Sigourney Weaver was an unknown quantity to the vast majority of spectators. Moreover, the film's conventions seemed so different from those of "prestige" science fiction predecessors like *2001: A Space Odyssey* and *Star Wars* that I distinctly remember discarding assumption after assumption in trying to hypothesize about what the outcome could possibly be. As a result, the film was probably far more frightening to watch than it is to a new viewer today. In part, this chapter is an attempt to reconstruct the way a 1979 viewer like myself reacted to the film, for that experience was closely linked to the skill with which the narration balanced the multiple protagonists against one another.

Along with drawing on conventions of both science fiction and horror films, *Alien* exhibits that cross-genre narrative phenomenon of action movies (and other media), the shooting-gallery plot. In such narratives, a group of characters is introduced, usually in a limited locale, and then killed, one by one or in small groups, by a hostile force. The shooting-gallery plot might be used in a war film, as with *The Lost Patrol* (1934), where soldiers surrounded at a desert oasis are gradually picked off by their enemies. It might be part of a mystery, as with *And Then There Were None* (1945), where guests at an island estate are murdered at intervals. More recently it has become quite common as the basis of many of the ubiquitous, multi-sequeled teenage slasher films. (I am not talking here about related films where very minor characters are randomly killed or attacked, as in *Jaws*.)

The shooting-gallery plot presents a challenge to filmmakers, in that audience involvement depends to a considerable degree on both suspense and surprise. That is, we know from experience with such films that people will be killed off, so we feel suspense concerning when and how each killing will occur. But such films generally give few clues as to which character will succumb next, so a carefully crafted narrative will surprise us each time.

Alien presents its characters as group-based protagonists. Although we seek to discover which are the most important characters (for example, will Dallas and Ripley form a romantic couple and defeat the alien?), the film performs a careful juggling act, refusing to single any one out for more than a brief period. The narration uses several strategies to maintain the balance among the characters so that we will continue for most of the film to believe (or at least we could do so in 1979) that Ripley is as vulnerable as any of the others, if not more so, to an attack by the alien. In the next chapter, I will suggest that a remarkably similar strategy is at work in *Hannah and Her Sisters*, a film which, though striving for a different sort of surprise, also balances characters against one another and prevents our singling out one protagonist.

Alien's primary strategies for maintaining its characters as multiple protagonists are two: the casting, and the introduction of a gritty realism in place of the gleaming high-tech look and glamorous missions of the standard big-budget science fiction film.

The casting is quite ingenious, in that it avoids using any stars who would obviously be expected to survive to the end. All the actors had had some film experience, but none was noted for major leading roles. All are listed at the beginning of the credits in the same size letters, one by one, in an order that gives scant sense of their relative importance or how long they will survive. Moreover, as each name appears, a white horizontal, diagonal, or vertical bar fades in at the top of the screen, eventually spelling *Alien*. Thus the spectator may not even be paying much attention to the cast's names. Indeed, the science fiction film often features special effects over stars as its major draw, as *2001* and *Star Wars* demonstrated.

Tom Skerrit's (Dallas) name comes first, and he was probably the most prominent "star" in this lineup. Although he had worked in films since 1962, Skerrit's biggest successes had been supporting roles in *M*A*S*H* (1970) and

The Turning Point (1977). Nevertheless, in comparison with the other actors in *Alien*, he seemed to a 1979 spectator the most likely to survive.

Sigourney Weaver's (Ripley) name appears next. She had had a lead role in a minor Israeli-produced thriller, *Madman* (1976), and appeared momentarily in a long shot as the main character's date in *Annie Hall* (1977). Certainly neither of these roles had made her known to the general public (and indeed, until recently, publicity material often touted *Alien* as her first film). Of all the cast, she was the most obvious cannon fodder. A plausible assumption from the start was that her role would be to provide some cheesecake and/or romance before either succumbing to an alien attack or nearly doing so before being rescued by the "hero."

In 1979, Veronica Cartwright (Lambert), whose character is now notorious as the whining counterpart to Ripley's strong female protagonist, was in fact more plausible as a prominent science fiction character. Vaguely familiar from her childhood TV roles and her part in Hitchcock's *The Birds*, she was then fresh off a supporting role in the 1978 remake of *Invasion of the Body Snatchers*.

Harry Dean Stanton (Brett) is named next in the credits. Stanton was less famous then than he has become since his leading role in *Paris, Texas* (1984) and subsequent smaller roles in films like *Repo Man* (1984), *Pretty in Pink* (1986), and *The Last Temptation of Christ* (1988). Still, he was a well-established character actor, having appeared in *Cool Hand Luke* (1967), *The Godfather, Part II* (1974), and other reasonably prominent films. Given his essentially supporting-role function, however, he was, along with Weaver, one of the most likely early victims.

John Hurt (Kane) was in the process of gaining a wider reputation in the late 1970s. Few probably remembered him from his supporting role in *A Man for All Seasons* (1966), but he had been nominated for a Best Supporting Actor Oscar for *Midnight Express* (1978); the awards ceremony occurred only about a month (9 April 1979) before the May release of *Alien*. Thus informed viewers might have expected him to play a fairly important role. Dedicated horror fans might also have recognized him from his prominent supporting role in the 1975 British film *The Ghoul*. Fellow Britisher Ian Holm (Ash), though well established as a stage actor in England, was essentially unknown to the American moviegoing public in 1979. Because of his character's secret mission of supporting the alien against the crew, however, Ash never gets into a position where he seems in danger of becoming a victim of the alien (though he is always there, available to get into such danger later on).

Finally, there is a credit for "Yaphet Kotto as Parker." This phrase seems to single Kotto and Parker out, but the "and So-and-so as So-and-so" credit is so frequently used, and for such a variety of reasons, that it offers little help in anticipating narrative events. Kotto had appeared in supporting roles in such films as *The Thomas Crown Affair* (1968) and *Live and Let Die* (1973). Hence Parker, like Brett, seems distinctly (as the computer, Mother, puts it) "expendable." It is also notable that none of the characters appeared in the poster art, which centered on an alien egg.

The unconventional realism of the film also thwarts expectations about the course of the action. The ship itself is aging, with rusty equipment, dangling chains, and leaking water in its depths. The characters are divided into two classes, the specialized officers and the working-class support crew, bickering over wages. Gone are the stewardess, the exercise treadmill, and the bright corridors of *2001*. This crew prefers hypersleep to the dubious attractions of the Nostromo. Parker remarks that the only good thing on the ship is the coffee. (The gritty realism follows the approach taken in the previous year's remake of *Invasion of the Body Snatchers*.)

With this realism comes the jettisoning of notions of super-heroism. Some of these characters might survive through reluctant cooperation, by blind luck, or, as we eventually learn, by displaying unsuspected strengths. I clearly remember thinking at one point while first watching the film (I believe it was shortly after Ash's "death") that this might be a film capable of letting the alien kill all the humans and win in the end. That eventuality did not occur, of course, but *Alien* was innovative enough to allow such a hypothesis to seem temporarily plausible.

THE SETUP: "A TRANSMISSION OF UNKNOWN ORIGIN"

Unlike many of the films I have examined, *Alien* does not use its credits sequence to introduce much information. We know only that we are somewhere in space. The credits lead to an extreme long shot of the ship with a superimposed title:

commercial towing vehicle "The Nostromo"
crew: seven
cargo: refinery processing
20,000,000 tons of mineral ore
course: returning to earth

This title establishes several things. First, the film opens with an objective, omniscient narration. *Alien* will be far from the sort of film we examined in the section on single protagonists, where the narration largely structured itself by attaching to one character—Michael Dorsey, Marty McFly, Clarice Starling, or Phil Connors. Rather, the narrative moves freely among all the characters. (Interestingly, *Hannah and Her Sisters* also uses titles, in that case throughout the film, to establish a similarly omniscient narration that balances several major characters.)

The characters are initially presented simply as a crew of seven on a mundane mission. Mineral ore is being processed in a way which, as we soon discover, does not necessitate any of the crew members being awake. Hence they have no initial goal except getting back to earth. The subsequent goals they do conceive—finding the source of the transmission, getting rid of the alien—are thrust upon them rather than initiated by the crew members. Indeed, *Alien* is a rare case of a Hollywood film in which the most basic causes that generate the action are institutional—the institution being the Company, which has apparently planned to investigate the alien for its potential military use. (We do not learn this directly; late in the film Ripley posits this as a plausible reason why the Company is so keen to acquire the alien.) Even here, however, a human-like character, the robot Ash, has been programmed to cooperate with the Company's computer. Ash is given traits and motives just like the others, so he can act as a palpable embodiment of the malicious intentions of the Company.

The sequence of tracking and panning through the ship's interior further establishes the narration as being free of links to the characters (though once they appear it skips among them rather than, say, moving off to reveal the alien on its own). The scene also shows off the design and establishes the long corridors and many potential hiding places where the alien might later be lurking. Sideways tracking shots close to the furniture and equipment reveal a limited amount of space onscreen at any given moment. The tone here is of mild tension, with "eerie" music, dim lighting, and barely glimpsed objects and movements, such as a bit of paper that flutters in the lower foreground at one point. (Indeed, the conventions are borrowed from the haunted-house horror film, and *Alien* is not above exploiting harmless objects to startle us, twice using the yowling-cat trick.)

As the computer screens flick on, we see them reflected in the surfaces of the empty space helmets that face them. This moment introduces the motif of non-human sentience controlling the ship and thus prepares us to grasp that Mother, along with its ally, Ash, will be the source of many crucial causes.

As the crew members wake from their hypersleep, the scene singles out Kane, one of the three characters who will seem to be slightly more prominent than the others during the first half of the film (the others being Dallas and Lambert). I suspect his waking first is also a way of making sure we can recognize him, since he spends most of his time in a space suit or in the concealing grip of the face-hugger.

The meal scene that follows is handled in a style popularized by Robert Altman's 1970s films, with simultaneous and overlapping dialogue. Most of the lines are insignificant, since there are no goals and no line of action yet in place. We do, however, get bits of characterization. Brett and Parker engage in an elaborate hand-slapping ritual, suggesting their working-class solidarity. Lambert whines, "I am cold," and she will remain a complainer. (Later, while outside exploring the moon, she reiterates this trait redundantly: "I like griping.") Ripley is largely ignored here, being offscreen, blocked by other characters, or in the background in most shots; she barely speaks and then only to make an inaudible comment about the food. Ash is also less prominent than the others.

The conversation soon turns to Parker and Brett's demand for full rather than half shares of the money paid for the mission. Given that they have contracts, it seems odd that they hope to get more pay at this late stage, especially since none of the other characters presumably has the authority to grant them extra money; indeed, nothing ever really comes of their goal. Still, it serves to set up the relatively realistic environment of the ship's miniature society, with its class conflict. It becomes clear that this industrial ship will not foster a flashy, military-type science fiction plot à la *Star Wars* (or even *Aliens*). The argument also sets up the almost constant bickering among the crew, who ultimately form a common goal only through necessity and then argue about how to accomplish it.

In the midst of this conversation, the computer starts beeping. Only Ash notices it, immediately saying to Dallas, "Mother wants to talk to you." From the start he is characterized as alert and attuned to the computer system; here in a minor way he helps further Mother's aims. Dallas, on the other hand, appears laid back and a bit casual about his job, making a semi-audible joke about "for my eyes only."

As the characters move to their instrument panels, Ripley and Ash are again kept largely in the background or offscreen. The conversation is mostly between Lambert and Kane as they try to determine the ship's location. Not surprisingly, given the later revelation of her competence, Ripley is the first to recognize that "It's not our system"—yet she speaks this line offscreen, not being accorded one of the close framings that are used on Kane, Lambert, and, less often, Ash. (Note Ash's crisp "Thank you" to the computer when it comes on.) Even when Ripley begins her radio message, there is a cut to the exterior of the ship rather than to her face. (There is one brief closeup of Ripley when she repeats, "That's not our system.")

During this scene the narrative action begins to progress. We gradually learn that this mid-voyage awakening is not routine and that something is apparently wrong. The information we piece together comes from brief lines spoken by various characters, so again we are blocked from focusing on any one of them.

A short scene follows in the bowels of the ship. Parker complains to Brett that the others never come "down here." This moment functions similarly to the tracking shots through the upper corridors at the beginning, establishing the space of part of the ship's labyrinthine support section, where some of the encounters with the alien will occur.

The crew then reassemble around the table, and Dallas explains the basic situation: Mother "has intercepted a transmission of unknown origin; she got us up to check it out." This is the narrative's most fundamental cause, though we will not learn its true nature until the end of the development portion of the film, when Ripley will conceive a short-term goal of using the computer to investigate the nature of the signal.

None of the crew members seems eager to adopt Mother's goal. There is little scientific curiosity evident here (though Kane displays some later and thus gets himself in trouble); no one expresses any altruistic hope of rescuing someone. We must assume that most go along, like Parker, only because a clause in their contract deprives them of all pay unless they comply. Ash is the one who explains this, as he is presumably programmed to do. This is his first moment of real prominence; he has been downplayed in this early part of the film almost as much as has Ripley. Such balance makes sense, since the two will eventually emerge as the antagonist and the primary protagonist.

The scene of the detachment from the main ship and the landing on the moon provides the first big display of special-effects action. Little important narrative information is revealed except that the ship is damaged in the turbulence. Parker and Brett are upset, but Dallas insists on continuing—a further indication of his casual approach and lack of caution. More damage occurs on landing. Characteristically, it is Ripley who first leaps up to fight the small fire that breaks out, but she does so in the background of the shot. With such techniques, the narration is able to make her seem adept without making her also seem a central character.

The damage caused in the landing leads to an apparent deadline. Parker and Brett demand 25 hours to fix the ship, causing Ripley to come down and confront them angrily. The deadline never really comes to anything, as it is not used to generate suspense, and we never learn how much time elapses before the ship is readied for takeoff. Indeed, *Alien* largely avoids genuine deadlines, saving the few it employs for the climactic abandonment of the ship. Still, the characters are all focused on the same powerful but simple situation, and the action seems to occur over a relatively short time span. Given that the "get it before it gets us" premise generates a great deal of suspense, specific deadlines are hardly necessary. The argument scene ends with Ripley stalking away, while the camera lingers with Brett and Parker—seeming again to imply that she is a minor character.

After the landing, the foul weather discourages Kane and Dallas, but Ash goads them on by saying in a slightly optimistic tone (something that in itself sets him off from the rest of the griping crew): "Well, Mother says the sun's coming up in twenty minutes." Kane expresses interest in walking to the source of the transmission, and Ash fosters his enthusiasm by reading, in a fascinated tone, a description of the atmosphere's chemical composition. Kane then volunteers to be in the landing team. That he is by nature curious and venturesome is confirmed by Dallas's reply: "Yeah, that figures." This exchange motivates Kane's later incautious examination of the alien egg. Lambert is considerably less eager but obeys Dallas's order to join them. Thus Lambert, Kane, and Dallas, the three officers who have been given the most prominence in the staging and dialogue (as well as being played by the three marginally most prominent actors), now seem to affirm their roles as the main sources of causal action.

Once they have gone outside, Ripley and Ash are alone in the control portion of the ship. Here they finally become more salient, though they primarily are hanging around monitoring the more active crew members. The narration must maintain a fine balance between Ripley and Ash. To favor one of them would be to diminish the moment when Ash opens the door and lets the face-hugger on board against Ripley's express command. At that point, suspense will be enhanced by our not knowing what Ash's motives are or which of them is right.

The focus on Ash starts with him doing a brief, tense run-in-place. In retrospect we will realize that this scene is the real beginning of his part of the mission and the accomplishment of his separate goal. Apparently he has been programmed to be emotionally involved in his duty. His excitement is further conveyed by his odd smile and double-handed wave to the departing team. When Ripley asks, "How's it going?" he responds in a deliberately casual tone, "Oh, all right." This is the first time anyone has said anything is going well on the mission—and it is, for him and Mother.

Ripley undertakes to decipher the transmission's meaning, a task which again suggests her abilities but leaves her on the sidelines for much of the rest of this scene. From this point the narration emphasizes the three explorers and the design of the derelict spaceship, with occasional cuts to Ash, who does little but observe their progress. Up to this point, the film had relied on extensive intercutting except when the group was assembled in the dining area. Now the editing pace slows down considerably, and we stay with the landing team, with shots from the video cameras in their helmets providing something akin to optical POV (point-of-view) shots. Again these three characters seem to be treated as the most important. In traditional science fiction films, women tend to be around to provide a minor love interest. We might posit at this point that the trio represent de-glamorized, grittily realistic versions of the stalwart captain, his girlfriend, and the overly curious scientist who disturbs the monster—as indeed Kane will.

The discovery of the fossilized creature inside the ship provides some exposition about how the aliens reproduce parasitically. Dallas remarks: "Bones are bent outward—like he exploded from inside." This is of course what will happen to Kane, but at this point the reference is unclear. Indeed, the scene has confused some commentators, who refer to the creature as a dead alien, that is, as being of the same species as the monster that invades the Nostromo. Yet logically this is a member of a third species, neither human nor "Giger" alien, which long ago died in a manner similar to Kane's upcoming demise. Presumably its fellows, after setting up a repeating radio warning, either died elsewhere or fled the planet and the cavern of alien eggs. Only in *Aliens* will we get some clues about how the eggs must have gotten there.[1]

At the point where the team examines the dead creature, there is no specific threat of immediate danger—despite the considerable suspense generated by the design, lighting, music, genre expectations, advertising ("In space no one can hear you scream"), and so on. The corpse seems simply to be the remains of an ancient calamity. Yet the track-in on its empty eye after the team moves on is distinctly creepy, and there is a straight cut to Ripley, who announces that Mother has translated part of the transmission and that it looks like a warning. (Mother's cooperation with Ripley is unmotivated, given that it defies her in subsequent scenes. Certainly this cooperation runs counter to the Company's secrecy with anyone but Ash.) Ash discourages her from going out to fetch the explorers back, but his arguments seem reasonable, and we are not likely to suspect that he has a hidden motive.

From this point the narration becomes strongly attached to Kane for a while, abandoning intercutting and giving true POV shots for the first time as he approaches the egg. Given the genre, we might expect that such treatment means that Kane is (1) being revealed as a more important character or (2) about to die. Neither is in fact the case, but the final POV shot—the face-hugger leaping toward the camera—pretty much renders Kane null and void as a POV figure from then on. The setup ends on a shot of Kane falling back. The imposed goal of investigating the transmission has been accomplished, with disastrous results that will transform the plot premises and the characters' goals.

COMPLICATING ACTION: "YOU DON'T DARE KILL IT"

The next section of the film begins with an extreme long shot zooming back from the derelict spaceship—a pause to mark an unexpected turn of events and emphasize that the crew must cope with it. There follows an argument between Dallas and Ripley. He demands that the explorers be let into the ship immediately; she orders them into quarantine for 24 hours. Ash's decision to open the hatch might be seen as a gesture of mercy—as Dallas points out, Kane could well die as a result of the delay. To a 1979 spectator, the film might seem to question Ripley's judgment, suggesting that she might be sticking to the rulebook at the expense of the others, while Ash is willing to flout regulations to help a colleague. We do not know Ripley well yet, though we are also unlikely to dismiss her worries. Just as important, however, the plot would grind to a halt with a quarantine, so we are likely to accept the fact that she is disobeyed. Moreover, these people are constantly bickering anyway, and female characters were, at the time, not likely to be vindicated in such matters.[2]

Our attention is immediately diverted from this issue as the new communal goal and main line of action of this section of the film begin: a new investigation, this time into the nature of the face-hugger. The question of Ripley's competence, though not emphasized, runs through this section as well. If Kane can be saved and the creature disposed of, then she was presumably wrong. If not, she was right.

Ash seems to cooperate with the others, testing ways to remove the face-hugger. Parker's twice-stated question, "How come you guys don't freeze him?" is ignored. His suggestion raises a causal issue never resolved in the film. We do not know what the state of technology is at this point, but even a non-specialist seems to think that freezing would be a viable option. Indeed, shortly before the baby alien is "born," Parker again asks why Kane was not frozen, though a digression forestalls any reply. In that same scene Brett refers to the sleeping pods as "freezerinos," suggesting that the crew are put into hypersleep through some sort of freezing technology. Yet the opening did not suggest that they were frozen; quite the contrary, they seemed simply to wake from a very deep sleep induced by electrodes attached to their bodies. Indeed, the idea of freezing Kane with the face-hugger on him and taking him to earth might fit well into the Company's plans to obtain the alien. Yet Ash, though cooperating with the Company, ignores Parker's suggestion. (The film gives virtually no clue as to how much Ash or the Company knows about the nature of the alien, so perhaps he cannot risk freezing the face-hugger.) The whole issue of freezing remains a dangling cause that is never picked up, explained, or motivated.[3]

In retrospect, we can realize that in this examination scene Ash is beginning his investigation, on behalf of the Company, into the nature of the creature. He calmly explains that the hugger has inserted something down Kane's throat and is feeding him air, but he seems startled when the hugger bleeds acid.

The race to trace the acid's progress in eating through a series of floors marks a shift in the crew's attitude. Parker commands urgently, "Don't get under it, don't get under it!" as Ripley moves past him to examine the hole. From this point on the class conflict which had prompted Parker's quarrel with Ripley largely disappears. Increasingly the dwindling crew will cooperate with one another by necessity. Parker also remarks: "It's got a wonderful defense mechanism. You don't dare kill it." This motivation is crucial, since we need a plausible explanation as to why so small a creature should pose an ongoing threat to the crew.

As this scene ends, a new situation is established. Ripley asks, "What about Kane?" and Brett similarly asks, "Well, what'll we do now?" Dallas responds: "[Leave?] Kane to Ash. [To Brett] You get back to work." (This is one of the film's rare dialogue hooks.) Thus the others' attempts to help Kane are dismissed, and he and the hugger pass into Ash's charge. Parker and Brett do go back to work. Now their complaint is not about money. Parker says they should not have landed and adds, "This place gives me the creeps" (a classic line of the haunted-house genre). Fear has supplanted class oppression.

The following tense conversation between Ash and Ripley reaffirms their opposition. (The scene is emphasized by being the film's first conventional shot/reverse-shot passage.) He acted against the rules to save Kane; she emphasizes that she was senior to Ash and that she was going by the book. One bit of important, if vague, causal material is dropped in here. Ash remarks on how quickly the creature replaces its cells with "polarized silicon." This statement is the only suggestion we ever get as to how the alien grows so quickly from the small version we see burst out of Kane's stomach to a roughly human-sized monster. (The time elapsed is vague, but it certainly gives the impression of being at most a few days.) By the end of the scene, we are likely to suspect that Ripley is right and Ash wrong, but this is still only a hypothesis.

Shortly after this argument, the face-hugger detaches itself from Kane, and after a suspenseful hunt, Ripley, Dallas, and Ash find its remains. Ash insists that "it has to go back, all sorts of tests have to be made." Ripley wants to eject it into space: "This *thing* bled acid. Who knows what it's going to do when it's dead?" As with her earlier insistence on putting the landing team in quarantine, Ripley again comes down on the side of caution for the good of the ship and crew. Ash, like Kane, seems to be willing to take risks in order to gain knowledge. In retrospect, we will realize that his eagerness serves the Company's interests, not the crew's or humanity's.

Here we get our strongest cue yet that Ripley is right in opposing Ash's doings. In the hall she has a key conversation with Dallas, asking why Ash can decide to retain the hugger. Dallas explains that the Company wants it that way. When Ripley asks if that is standard procedure, he replies, "Standard procedure is to do what the hell they tell you to do." He reveals that the Company inexplicably replaced his regular science officer with Ash two days before departure. Ripley remarks, "I don't *trust* him," and Dallas replies, "I don't trust anybody." Thus Dallas will prove useless in Ripley's struggle against Ash, being resigned to corruption and reluctant to buck the Company's system. Presumably Ripley figures among the "anybodies" he doesn't trust.

Up to now, there has been only one apparent plotline in the narrative: the crew struggles to cope with the transmission and then with the face-hugger. No secondary line of action, romantic or otherwise, has emerged. Yet there is a secondary plotline, also directly related to the alien: the Company is secretly and callously manipulating events. The revelation of Ash's mysterious last-minute assignment to the ship provides our first clue that this other line of action is under way.

This conversation ends with another disagreement. Dallas wants to take off from the moon before the repairs are completed. Ripley is again more prudent: "You think that's a good idea?" His final statement, "Look, I just wanna get the hell out of here, all right?" provides a dialogue hook into the lift-off scene. All goes well, and Dallas's decision seems justified at this point. The narration has to walk a fine line with Ripley. She has to be smart and tough enough to be a plausible survivor at the end, but in order to prevent us from guessing that outcome too soon, the film again hints that we should doubt her. Perhaps after all she is just overly wary. The presence of the much-maligned Lambert is, I think, important in that it hints that Ripley might be another timid female, albeit a less whiny one, out-guessed by her more daring male colleagues.

The discovery of Kane awakened from his coma returns Ripley, who had become quite prominent during the complicating action, to the periphery of the plot. The action seems to be taking a different turn, with the crew again having no apparent goal except to get back to sleep and return to earth. As in the opening, the meal scene places Ripley primarily in the background or offscreen. And if Kane is really going to recover from the face-hugger's attentions, that would suggest that Ripley has been too rigid in her by-the-books stances. The overlapping dialogue of the opening meal scene also returns. We catch trivial banter primarily involving the bad food, leading to Parker's crude joke about oral sex. We might expect to see Ripley's response to this joke (as we do during the more extended sexual braggadocio at the breakfast table in *Aliens*), but instead we see a reaction shot of Lambert's shocked, then reluctantly amused response.

The infant alien's bloody emergence from Kane's stomach and its flight into the depths of the ship mark the end of the complicating action. This action occurs about 80 seconds before the film's temporal center—as clear an example as one could wish of a central turning point. The crew's goal of fighting this new and even more threatening creature will sustain the rest of the plot. The scene continues with a brief pause during which the characters stare in shock and bafflement in various directions (Fig. 10.1), reflecting the midpoint's complete change of plot premises. A final closeup of Ash's enigmatic face ends this portion, prefiguring his later prominence.

DEVELOPMENT: "CREW EXPENDABLE"

The disposal of Kane's body continues this brief caesura at the film's center. This perfunctory funeral prefigures a basic premise that will soon be set up

10.1

concerning the alien: that it should be ejected from the ship into space, thus killing it while preventing its acidic blood from destroying the crew and the Company's precious spaceship.

Now the action cranks up again as Brett shows the others how to use an electric prod. Lambert sums up the new goal straightforwardly: "Now we just have to find it." Ash then demonstrates a motion sensor that he claims will help them do so. In fact, Ash's motion sensors are treated quite inconsistently in the film. He claims the device has a range of a mere five meters and reacts to "micro-changes in air density." When he demonstrates, it gives off a humming noise. Yet later, when Dallas crawls through the air shafts, he carries only a bright light and a flame thrower. It is Lambert who monitors his movement and that of the alien, using the motion sensor from a distance and through walls; it gives off beeping noises and provides an electronic-grid readout. This inconsistency is perhaps the most obvious, if not the most causally significant, gap in an otherwise fairly thoroughly motivated plot.

Further details of how the alien is to be netted and ejected through the air lock are given, with the characters assuming that it is still small. Indeed, the suspense early in the second half will be based on the premise that the razor-toothed little creature could be lurking just about anywhere in the ship. During this conversation, Dallas points out that the "channels" on all decks are open and that the crew members are constantly to communicate with each other. (They in fact do so only in the scene of Dallas' fatal venture into the air shafts, and then by using radio headsets.)

The characters are divided into teams of three, so that again no individual is singled out. At this point we move into the sort of delaying scene that is typical of development sections. Ripley, Brett, and Parker edge through the depths of the ship. Ripley wanders on her own, and eerie music cues us to expect that she might become the next victim. Instead, the trio use the tracker to locate movement in a locker. It turns out to be Jones, the feline mascot—making us jump with a clichéd shock-cut yowl. (How Ash's detector senses movement through a closed door and how the cat, seen earlier in the dining room, has made its way into a closed locker are never motivated.)

Now the film moves into an attached POV with Brett as he searches for Jones. The sequence resembles the way the camera had stayed with Kane just before the face-hugger got him. And as in that earlier scene, the leisurely buildup of suspense is motivated by a display of the set design. We explore the ship's depths, with rusting heavy equipment, dripping water, and swaying chains. All this is accompanied by the tense heartbeat throb of the engine. Brett becomes the mature alien's first victim. His death was predictable, in that he had seemed mainly to be the sidekick of the more dynamic Parker. Thus his early demise insinuates that *Alien* will indeed follow a fairly conventional shooting-gallery pattern.

The next scene picks up on the hook provided by Brett's dispatch with Parker's anguished face as he declares, "Whatever it was, it was . . . it was *big!*" So now the characters understand that the threatening creature has grown, yet the ship is still big enough for it to be hidden anywhere. They conclude that the alien moves about via the air shafts. (How they infer this is not mentioned. A trail of Brett's blood?) Ash suggests using fire to drive the alien into the air lock and then expel it from the ship.

Dallas's instructions to the crew create a dangling cause that lingers over the next brief scene. In the computer control center, Dallas questions Mother about his tactics for destroying the alien. The computer refuses to respond, hinting to us that the whole system is working against the crew.

During Dallas's passage through the air shafts, the narration moves freely among the characters, now creating a continuous conversation via their radio headsets. The tracking device provided by Ash turns out not to protect Dallas at all. It shows the alien as a dot moving toward him on a two-dimensional grid, but when Lambert urges Dallas to move away, he goes down a shaft and discovers that the alien was hiding on a lower level. Thus Ash has provided a crude and misleading tool. There is a cutaway during the height of the danger to his undisturbed, even smug face (Fig. 10.2). Again, retrospectively we may realize that he has deliberately sent Dallas to his death.

I suspect that for 1979 spectators, the death of Dallas was a more disconcerting moment than it might be to first-time viewers today. The most likely

10.2

survivor, played by the most prominent actor, had been killed at a relatively early point, and the effect reversed the assumptions we may have formed when Brett was killed. Traditional science-fiction conventions came to seem unreliable guides as to what might happen next.

In the discussion that follows Dallas's death, most of the basic premises for the last third of the action are outlined. Ash, whose identity is one of the few new premises to be revealed later, remains out of focus in the background during most of this scene. With Ripley now the new captain, the camera sticks closer to her, no longer placing her consistently in the background or off-screen. Still, in the light of Dallas's fate, this is far from a guarantee that she will not herself fall victim to the alien.

The characters resume their earlier bickering. Lambert wants to escape in the shuttle, Parker furiously demands that they kill the alien, and Ripley insists on pursuing Dallas's plan to force it into an airlock and eject it into space. Ash has no opinion, being, he claims, still "collating" data. Ripley points out that the shuttle will not take four people, though we never learn exactly how many it will accommodate. The group works together out of desperation, but they never really mesh into a unit.

Ripley now asserts her authority and confronts Mother. She gains access to "special order 937": "Nostromo rerouted to new coordinates. Investigate life form. Gather specimen. Priority one. Insure return of organism for analysis. All other considerations secondary. Crew expendable." Again, why Mother cooperates with Ripley by revealing the special order is unmotivated. Earlier Mother would not share information with Dallas, but by now we may assume that Ripley is simply more adept at working the computer. Revealing the special order to any of the crew except Ash, however, would seriously jeopard-ize the mission—and indeed this bit of information is the crucial cause that allows Ripley to confront Ash and ultimately to defeat the Company's efforts to bring the alien to earth.[4]

Ash offers to explain the special order, but Ripley pushes him aside and leaves. Here we have the most explicit explanation of the plotline that has been operating covertly throughout the film. The crew have been struggling to protect themselves and the Company's property, while all along the Com-pany has been using them for a purpose that could threaten not only them but also human life on earth.

The violent struggle between the remaining crew members and Ash ends the development. Ash's initial attack on Ripley is staged in dual terms, as both a confrontation between human and robot and a pseudo-rape scene. As it begins, Ripley has a slight nose bleed, suggesting her human nature, while Ash is "sweating" a drop of the white liquid that he seems to have in place of blood. (He was seen drinking a glass of what appeared to be milk at the end of his first argument with Ripley.) Her blood also perhaps suggests a sexual violation, while his white fluid hints at a pre-orgasmic drop of semen.

Ash makes a twitchy head gesture as this scene begins, suggesting that he has gone out of control. He picks Ripley up and tosses her down easily, revealing his inhuman strength for the first time. He then slams her onto a desk surrounded by soft-core porn photos and tries to force a rolled-up magazine into her mouth. This scene has been interpreted in a way that takes no account of the context, as "relating pornography to violence against women."[5] Undoubtedly the narration invites us to read the magazine as a phallic substitute in an oral sexual assault. Yet the obvious question is why the scene is handled this way, since Ash's ultimate purpose is presumably to kill Ripley to prevent her from telling the others about the secret order, and it would seem to be to his advantage to do so quickly. As it is, he allows the others time to intervene, bringing on his defeat.

I would suggest that the moment is connected with the other scenes where a character has a tube-like object inserted down his throat: Kane in the grip of the face-hugger. That more successful penetration is also related to sex—though in a less sensational fashion, more concerned with the physiology of alien procreation.[6] In the CAT-scan sequence, we see computer-screen im-ages that give us only a vague sense of what has been done to Kane. Dallas asks, "What's it got down his throat?" but Ash does not reply. The "what" must be some sort of tube emanating from the underside of the face-hugger.

10.3

Once the hugger is dead, Ash places it in a tray and we get a close look at the side that had been pressed against Kane's face (Fig. 10.3). Except for the clutching "fingers" with which it grips its prey, the object is clearly a grotesque amalgam of caricatural female and male human genitalia. At the right side of the central portion, hairless *labia majora* frame a complex moist central section representing in a chaotic, unspecific way the vulva. This center is flanked by two bulbous swellings like testicles, and in this framing the top of the "tail" that had circled Kane's neck resembles a penis. There is no sign of the tube that had penetrated his throat. There has been academic discussion of the alien's gender,[7] but the face-hugger seems to be presented as equally male and female. The design of the hugger may be calculated to hint ominously at the true purpose of the creature's parasitic attachment to Kane, since we do not yet know that he carries an alien embryo.[8]

Thus Ash's assault on Ripley with the magazine appears to imitate the behavior of the alien, which he admires and seeks to protect. At this point we do not yet know the precise nature of Ash's villainy, and the bizarre mode of his attack hints at his inhuman quality, about to be revealed when Parker discovers he is a robot. We learn little about what sorts of instructions Ash has received from the Company; possibly they never intended that he kill any of the other crew members. Certainly the face-hugger's penetration of Kane's throat had ended in Kane's death, and perhaps this has become Ash's notion of how to kill a human being. (I should add, however, that this interpretation is certainly not likely to occur to any spectator upon first seeing the film.)

The dismemberment of Ash ends this section of the film.

The climax portion begins with Ripley giving us the closest thing to an explanation for the Company's actions that we will get until the sequels: "All I can think of is they must've wanted the alien for their weapons division. It's [Ash] been protecting it right along." Now there is no issue of loyalty to the Company. After questioning Ash's briefly revitalized head and discovering that he knows of no way to kill the alien, Ripley articulates the new and final goal: "We're gonna blow up the ship. We'll take our chances in the shuttle."

As we have seen in other films, characters' crucial goals often change over the course of the film. Clarice Starling forms her goal of trying to save Katherine Martin after she has already made considerable progress in her dealings with Hannibal Lecter. Salieri decides to revenge himself upon God by killing Mozart only after repeated frustrating run-ins with his rival. In *Alien*, the four large-scale parts can be generally defined by the crew's distinct goals: investigate the transmission; investigate the nature of the face-hugger; seek to eject the alien into space and save the Company's ship; seek to escape into space and blow up the alien inside the Company's ship.

The main premises for this last goal are quickly introduced as Parker reveals that the ship's self-destruct system will go off ten minutes after activation. The narration emphasizes this crucial plot point by using redundant dialogue. Ripley replies to his statement, "No bullshit?" and he responds, "We ain't outa here in ten minutes, we won't need no rocket to fly through space." (Again we have a minor unmotivated point. Why, in an age of routine space travel, could they not set off the ship's self-destruct system by remote control once they had reached a safe distance in the shuttle?) In the meantime, Ripley gives Parker and Lambert an interim deadline of seven minutes to fetch coolant tanks. The action then intercuts for a while between the pair loading coolant while Ripley first prepares for departure and then goes in search of Jones.

By now we must suspect that if anyone survives, it will be Ripley. Yet here she wanders through the ship in the same way that previous victims had—and again, the first time I saw the film, it seemed to me quite possible that all the humans would be killed. Odd though it may sound today, the film's consistent unpredictability made Ripley still seem as expendable as the other two. Her frivolous gesture of going back for the cat seems to place her in danger—after all, a similar search for Jones had led to Brett's death. The roaming camera creates gloomy areas of offscreen space that could harbor the alien. Once again the sudden spring of the yowling cat creates a startle effect that, clichéd though it is, heightens the suspense.

The deaths of Parker and Lambert resolve the question of who will be the last to survive, but not the question of whether anyone will survive at all. At this point the style changes considerably. The intercutting virtually disappears, and the POV will be spatially attached to Ripley for the rest of the film (with the exception of a shot of the alien staring down at Jones in the carrying case that Ripley has dropped). Her optical POV is repeatedly shown, and the fast cutting contrasts with the many long, slow tracking shots used in earlier scenes. As Ripley activates the self-destruct system, the written instructions and the voice of Mother both clearly establish that the ship will explode in ten minutes and that the failsafe switch will not abort the process after five minutes. In preparation for what will apparently be the grand finale, the plot doubles the dangers threatening Ripley. Even if she escapes the alien, she might get caught in the explosion of the ship. The lack of earlier deadlines is here balanced by a relentless countdown after Ripley arms the system. The computer's voice loudly announces the passage of time, pumping up the suspense as the alien blocks Ripley's way to the shuttle.

When the self-destruct countdown begins, sirens, flashing lights, and gushing steam create a chaotic atmosphere for Ripley to navigate. Indeed, the chaos may provide a motivation for the alien's move into the shuttle. It seems unlikely that the creature is so intelligent that it can anticipate that Ripley is heading for the shuttle. Hence we might ask why the alien hides there—if not through sheer coincidence. Perhaps it goes there to escape the tumult within the main ship. The film carefully shows that all the hatches between the shuttle and the place where we had last seen the alien in the ship are open, since Ripley's flight involves only closing hatches behind her, not opening any. (We also know that the crew have been closing off the ship's corridors and ducts in their search for the alien, so perhaps its options are limited.) None of this is made explicit in the narrative, but at least it is possible to find a rationale for the alien's presence in the shuttle.

In general the climax portion of the film emphasizes the characters' panting and sweating. Ripley pauses to tie up her hair at one point, and after Mother refuses to reverse the self-destruct process, Ripley unsuccessfully orders it to turn on the cooling system. Thus we have moved from a steely, cold atmosphere in the opening sections, with the characters (frozen?) in dry, sterile sleeping pods, to a hot, steamy milieu—rather like the cave where the alien eggs had been. Indeed, Mother may have turned up the heat to suit the alien better.

After the shuttle departs and the ship explodes, an apparent epilogue begins, with Ripley preparing a sleeping pod for herself and Jones. The narration plays fair here, insofar as the cat's hisses and yowls suggest that it senses the alien's presence.

After Ripley has suited up to fight the alien, she belts herself into a seat and makes her arrangements, softly singing "You are my lucky star" over and over. As we saw with Clarice Starling in *The Silence of the Lambs*, putting a woman into a traditionally male role in a suspense film allows the character to express terror more openly, even as she takes steps to defeat the menace. That heightened sense of fear cues what the spectator should appropriately feel. At any rate, Ripley's singing suggests simultaneously her apprehension and her determination. Her dart then penetrates the alien's body at an appropriate place, the midriff—the same spot on Kane's body from which it had erupted. And like Kane, the alien is ejected into space.

The true epilogue begins with Ripley recording a report on the Nostromo's fate. She recites items in the same order as in the original superimposed title over the first post-credits shot. Where the title had begun with the ship's name, she also names the Nostromo in beginning the report. Next the title had mentioned "seven" crew members. Ripley now lists her six dead colleagues, in no particular order. The third item of information in the title had been the nature of the cargo. Ripley goes on to say that the ship and cargo have been destroyed. The title had ended with the ship's course as "returning to earth." Ripley gives her destination as "the frontier." But while the title had ended there and remained anonymous and objective, Ripley adds, "This is Ripley, last survivor of the Nostromo, signing off." Thus the trajectory of the film's action ends with a move from a completely objective narration dealing evenhandedly with all its characters to a tight concentration upon Ripley, now our sole source of information. The main function of that trajectory, as we have seen, was an effort to maintain suspense as long as possible about which characters would be killed. Yet by the end the attachment to Ripley became so strong that audiences seemingly have an unflagging interest in sequels to the original film (provided Sigourney Weaver plays Ripley)—despite the long intervals between the sequels and the fact that the third film was widely considered a disappointment. The fourth is even worse, but its epilogue threatens a further sequel.

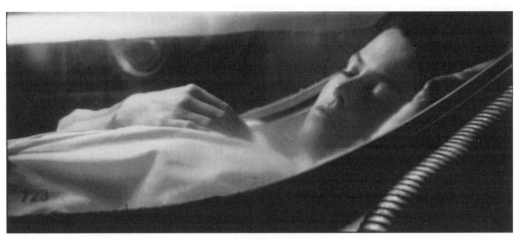

10.4

Indeed, the last shot of *Alien* seems, intentionally or not, to prefigure Ripley's future. Her brightly lit hand is posed rather oddly and prominently (Fig. 10.4). It looks a bit like a face-hugger lying on her chest. At just the point where we might be likely to notice this resemblance, a dissonant trumpet note joins the soothing string music. Thus the narrative ends on a slightly portentous moment, hinting that Ripley might again be threatened by aliens. Indeed, in a decade when sequels were becoming increasingly common, it would make sense for a film like *Alien* to hint at that possibility, however subtly.

A FINAL LESSON: RAISING THE STAKES

While watching the films mentioned in this book—both the ten main examples and the subsidiary ones—I was occasionally struck by the question, "Could this film, now considered a classic, be made today?" It is certainly hard to imagine even some fairly recent titles being greenlighted in current Hollywood. Could *Witness* make it to the screen? The second and third quarters have almost no big action, being concerned mainly with John Book's uneasy settling into the Amish community. Although the crime plotline ends with the defeat of the villains, Book's final parting from Rachel brings the romance to an unhappy resolution. *The Fugitive* (1993), with its lack of a second, romantic plotline, seems a more typical 1990s vehicle.

Similarly, *Chinatown* (1974) would appear an unlikely candidate for production in the late 1990s. Its convoluted plot and ambivalent protagonist, along with lengthy sections lacking violent action, result finally in a sordid and grim climax. Its modern equivalent is perhaps *Se7en* (1995), the central premise of which delivers shocking crimes at regular intervals; an unabashedly sentimental friendship between the Morgan Freeman character and his young partner's pregnant wife leads up to a more sordid and grim climax. Still, Harrison Ford and Jack Nicholson probably have enough power to get a film like *Witness* or *Chinatown* made today, though they might have to fight a little harder.

Oddly enough, of the ten main films I am analyzing in this book, one of the least likely to be produced in the current climate may be *Alien*, which is, after all, the oldest among them. *Alien* may be a prototype of the modern film blending horror and science fiction; it may enjoy cult status among sci-fi fans and a more general respect among the broader public; yet would it have enough action to get made today? It had no stars to go to bat for it—a fact that was, as I have suggested, part and parcel of its basic suspense strategy.

In the opening chapter I mentioned that one source of the recent Hollywood doldrums might be the fact that action films, which dominate the most prominent genres, depend upon a constant ratcheting-up of the stakes. This snowballing effect perhaps began back in the 1960s with the first James Bond films. Richard Maibaum, who co-scripted the first twelve Bond films, described the trend thus:

> Penelope Gilliatt once said that Bond films were "modern mythology." In my opinion, they started this whole larger-than-life aproach to action-adventure pictures. There have been others, of course; and Burt Lancaster always ribs me about imitating the style of *The Crimson Pirate* [1952]. But I do think the Bond pictures started this whole cycle, and then everybody else climbed on the bandwagon. That's not generally accepted. I think *Raiders of the Lost Ark* [1981] was, except for having a wonderful gimmick (the ark itself), a kind of Bond picture. The action, the villains, the unexpected!
>
> You know, Hitchcock once told me, "If I have thirteen bumps in a picture, I think I've got a picture." A bump is something like someone says, "I'm looking for a man who has a short index finger," and a totally unexpected guy says, "You mean like this?" That's in *The 39 Steps*. After *Dr. No* Cubby, Harry, and myself decided that we weren't going to be satisfied with thirteen bumps in a Bond story, we wanted thirty-nine.[9]

"Bumps" in this sense clearly means important plot twists, whether they are quiet but dramatic revelations or more action-oriented moments.

In more recent years, however, the bump has grown into the "wham," simply a moment of high action. The producer Art Linson, describing a discussion with a scriptwriter, suggests how formulaic this notion has become:

When you've run out of theories, and you can sense that the writer's eyes are getting glassy, you can always pull out the "Whammo Chart." Supposedly Joel Silver got this from Larry Gordon, who got it from some Egyptian who worked at American International Pictures (AIP) many years ago. As the legend spreads, it is a scientifically tested theory that requires each action script to have a "Whammo" every ten pages. This would be a big-action set piece, something that would kick you in the groin and wake you up. If a script wavers a bit, spending a little too much time on nuance and character, it violates the theory. According to the natural laws of physics, without a bang the audience is buying popcorn by the twelfth page and looking for the exit signs if you stretch it to page twenty-five.

So the script gets tested against the Whammo Chart, and the script meeting goes like this: "Go back to your laptop and don't come back until something explodes every ten pages. Come on, give me a wham." I am starting to notice this theory even creeping into comedy scripts.[10]

How widespread this notion of "whams" really is is difficult to judge,[11] but the reviewer Richard Schickel claims to find it part of the formulaic quality of *First Knight* (1995): "There are well-staged, smartly edited bursts of action at the approved modern intervals (every 10 minutes or so), the scenery is always pretty, and aside from Ben Cross's villain, everyone is terribly nice, terribly agreeable."[12]

The action-packed, overblown, and inexplicably overrated third sequel to *Alien, Alien Resurrection* (1997), suggests that the exponential need to raise the level of action with each successive season of filmmaking has by the late 1990s reached absurd heights. As I suggested in Chapter 1, big moments of action do not equal turning points. A constant barrage of high action leaves little room for exposition, motifs, humor, subplots, character development, and the many other components of well-balanced classical narratives. Such concentration on action does not represent a "post-classical" approach so much as incompetence. Despite its unpretentious simplicity, *Alien* contains nuances that put to shame much modern Hollywood filmmaking.

11

Hannah and Her Sisters

1986. Released by Orion. Directed by Woody Allen. Screenplay by Allen. Running time: 106.5 minutes; setup, 18; complicating action, 33; development, 29; climax and epilogue, 24 (epilogue alone, 4); end credits, 3.

"BOY, LOVE IS REALLY UNPREDICTABLE"

At first glance, *Alien* and *Hannah and Her Sisters* would seem to have virtually nothing in common. Yet they share one major underlying strategy. In each, the narration seeks to prevent the spectator from figuring out who the main character or characters are. *Hannah*'s refusal to single out a protagonist, however, has quite a different purpose than in *Alien*. In the latter film the narration seemed to equate the characters' importance in order to preserve suspense by making it difficult to predict who would survive the monster's onslaught. *Hannah and Her Sisters* has no need to generate such suspense, being oriented instead toward the characters' traits, changes, and interactions.

A clue to the film's pattern comes in the scene where Mickey remembers how his marriage to Hannah ended. His final remark is, "Boy, love is really unpredictable." After this line, a cut shifts the scene to the opera, where Hannah's sister Holly is sitting in a box with the architect, David. The last time we had seen her, she was upset because she thought David was more attracted to her friend April than to her. Now it turns out she was wrong, and for a while it seems that her relationship with David is progressing well. Later, however, David abruptly switches his attention and begins dating April. Indeed, all the main characters' relationships demonstrate the validity of Mickey's remark about the unpredictability of love.

Just as the unpredictability of sudden death had provided suspense in *Alien*, the motif of love's unruly turns creates a unity among *Hannah*'s lines of action. During much of the film, Hannah's husband Elliot debates whether to leave her for her sister Lee. Since Lee receives more screen time than Hannah, it might seem plausible that Elliot and Lee could end up together. That plausibility is reinforced by Lee's deteriorating relationship with Frederick. Yet Lee eventually marries another man, a professor about whom we know almost nothing, and Elliot stays with Hannah. Similarly, the final romance between Mickey and Holly comes as a surprise, since the two have barely been seen together; the flashback to their one disastrous date apparently precludes a romance between them. Thus, by centering on a group of characters of roughly equal prominence, the narration fosters unpredictable action. Moreover, each character's goals change radically, making it even more difficult for us to sense how each line of action will turn out.

Most, possibly all, Hollywood films depend to some degree on unpredictability. Ordinarily, however, we have a rough sense of what the basic outcome will be. In *Back to the Future*, Marty McFly will certainly get back to 1985; in *Groundhog Day*, Phil Connors will undoubtedly end up romantically attached to Rita; in *Jurassic Park*, the children will not be killed by dinosaurs; in *The Silence of the Lambs*, Clarice will eventually figure out who Buffalo Bill is. Our involvement comes in following or anticipating the twists and turns in the achievement of these outcomes. *Hannah and Her Sisters*, however, makes unpredictability the central focus in its narrative, and it does so by balancing protagonists against one another.

The film's style reinforces the idea that several of the characters are of roughly equal importance. The framing and editing tend to emphasize them as groups, keeping the characters present in a scene together onscreen. Rather than using shot/reverse shots between the characters as they converse, most scenes employ relatively little editing. When the characters are stationary, the camera usually keeps them together in a balanced framing, and when they move, it pans to keep them onscreen. During the opening party, for example, a single shot shows Hannah and Holly talking as they set the table, and the only cut during this part of the scene occurs when April enters; she immediately moves to the table, with the camera panning to frame all three women. Later, the dinner is handled in one long take, as the father, mother, and Hannah give brief speeches. This tactic continues through most of the film, as in the scene where Elliot takes his rich client to look at Frederick's art; there the four characters are lined up during a long-take conversation (Fig. 11.1).

11.1

11.2

Much later, during the second Thanksgiving scene, Hannah discusses Holly's play, and the camera simply pans back and forth as the two women move around the kitchen. Even in scenes with only two characters present, where one would expect a shot/reverse-shot technique, the action often occurs in a long take. During Elliot's crucial action of pleading his love to Lee, he faces slightly away from the camera (Fig. 11.2), and there is no cut to his face until after she leaves. In such cases, the ordinary Hollywood film would use editing to underscore certain lines or facial reactions.

This stylistic refusal to single out characters is enhanced by a dense sound mix with their speeches overlapping frequently, especially during the party scenes. Hence important causal material is dropped casually into conversa-

11.3

tions. Such a technique enhances the realism of the action. Realism in turn helps motivate the theme of unpredictability, by appealing to the notion that real life is less predictable than most movie plots.

Indeed, the only scenes that depend extensively upon cutting and especially shot/reverse shots are the early ones involving Mickey. The fast editing displays his series of medical tests in brief montage sequences, and the shot/reverse shots show him talking with minor characters: his doctors or his colleagues at the television office. This stylistic treatment sets Mickey apart as being a more isolated character, since most of the people with whom he interacts are minor figures. Usually when he is with other major characters, the scenes are handled in longer takes and balanced framing, as in the single-shot flashback when Hannah and Mickey discuss artificial insemination with their friends or in the final lengthy shot of the film (Fig. 11.3). Thus in general the film's style helps to avoid emphasizing a single character.

The main exception to this equalizing treatment comes in those moments when the narration links us very strongly to individual characters by allowing us to hear interior monologues. These come only rarely, and because all five major characters get this treatment, no one of them is singled out by it.

The film's unusually large group of protagonists and prominent secondary characters could create problems in moving from scene to scene. In *Alien*, the crew of the spaceship were all involved in the same line of action, which occurred within a limited locale. In *Hannah and Her Sisters*, however, the characters participate in several lines of action, and they are often in different places. Moreover, Holly's concerns overlap only slightly with those of the rest of Hannah's family, and for the bulk of the film, Mickey's subplot seems to have only a tangential connection to any of the other characters.

As a result, the narrative uses four distinctive strategies for switching among the characters and lines of action. First, the repetition of the Thanksgiving parties allows the characters to interact and exchange crucial information. Second, the intertitles that open many scenes pique our curiosity and draw us into a game of figuring out how they relate to the action's significance. Third, the order of the scenes moves us among characters in a cyclical fashion. Finally, recognizable musical passages are associated with the various lines of action, signaling at the beginnings of most scenes which line will be featured.

The first strategy involves the narrative action, which lasts for two years. Three of the twenty-one segments take place at Thanksgiving parties, thus bringing several of the characters together at intervals through the film. In contrast to *Parenthood*, these family gatherings set up important causal influences of one plotline on another. The opening scene occurs at one such party, and here we meet all the protagonists except Mickey. The resolution of the Lee-Elliot-Hannah triangle takes place at another, one year later. Finally, the epilogue is set at the third party, and here all five protagonists are present for the first time. Thus the cycle of holidays unifies the narrative's disparate plotlines. Holly emphasizes this use of holidays in her banter about the lack of attractive men at the party: "Yeah, really, we mustn't get discouraged. Hannah will invite some men over that *don't* look like Ichabod Crane—if not this Thanksgiving, you know, maybe at Christmas, you know, or if not Christmas, New Year's—if not this New Year's, next New Year's." The repeated holidays also reinforce the film's thematic equation of happiness with domesticity.

The second strategy for switching among the characters consists of a series of intertitles. Of the twenty-one segments in the film, sixteen begin with such titles, somewhat in the style of silent films. These are of various sorts, so that it is usually difficult to predict how they will relate to the action. The first title, "God, she's beautiful," leads into the opening party scene; the same line is spoken immediately by Elliot as we hear his thoughts on the sound track. As the second scene begins, a title appears, reading, "We all had a terrific time." Here the line is not spoken until well into the scene between Lee and Frederick, when she says it aloud. Later intertitle texts are not spoken at all, as when "The anxiety of the man in the booth" leads into the scene of Mickey undergoing a series of tests in a hospital. One intertitle is a quotation from a poem that Lee reads aloud near the end of the scene; another quotes Tolstoy, but no one ever speaks the text. These intertitles create a set of variations, a formal device of interest in itself. They also, however, help signal shifts to different lines of action.

In the third strategy, scenes throughout the film tend to move among the characters in a patterned way. Most notably, Mickey usually appears in every third scene. The film's first scene involves the party, the second shows Lee at home with Frederick, and the third introduces Mickey at the television studio where he works. Next comes the scene with Holly and April catering a party; the fifth scene consists of Elliot pretending to meet Lee by accident in the street and going with her to a bookshop. Then, in the sixth, Mickey visits his doctor. This pattern continues through the film, with one scene dealing with Mickey followed by two scenes (or in one case three) with some combination of the other characters:

1. Elliot and Lee most centrally, also Holly and Hannah (first Thanksgiving party)
2. Lee and Frederick (in their apartment)
3. Mickey (at the television studio and doctor's office)
4. Holly (catering, meeting David)
5. Elliot and Lee (bookshop scene)
6. Mickey (doctor's office, his apartment), Holly briefly (at opera with David)
7. Elliot, Lee, Frederick (at the latter's apartment and in the street outside)
8. Hannah visits her parents (their apartment)
9. Mickey (clean bill of health, but quits job)
10. Elliot and Lee (hotel room)
11. Lee and Frederick break up (their apartment)
12. Elliot, Hannah, and Lee (their respective apartments)
13. Mickey and Holly (flashback to their failed date)
14. Elliot and Lee, then Elliot and Hannah (the affair continues, Elliot and Hannah quarrel)
15. Holly and Hannah (quarrel while shopping)
16. Mickey (trying to become Catholic)
17. Hannah, Holly, and Lee (quarrel while lunching together)
18. A series of brief scenes covering the summer's passage: Elliot (with

11.4

psychiatrist), Mickey (still seeking religion), Lee (on wharf), Holly (on phone with Hannah)
19. Hannah, Holly, Lee, and Elliot (second Thanksgiving)
20. Mickey and Holly (her play; story of his recovery)
21. Epilogue at third Thanksgiving: Elliot, Hannah, Lee, Holly, and Mickey all present

At least one of the three sisters appears in every scene in which Mickey is not present. Thus, although a scene may not relate directly to the ones that precede and follow it, we still develop a sense that the action is moving among the main characters in turn and that the plotlines are progressing in a parallel fashion. The film's title points up this strategy.

Finally, musical passages signal the shifts among plotlines. For example, Elliot and Lee's romance is linked to the music that accompanies the opening of the first Thanksgiving party, a slow jazz version of "I Think I've Heard that Song Before." Mickey has a faster-paced jazz passage that suits the frenetic quality of many of his scenes. This use of leitmotifs adheres to a standard pattern of classical Hollywood scores.

Some of the film's devices, particularly the intertitles, are not typical of the classical Hollywood cinema. Such art-cinema touches have made Allen's films popular with intellectual audiences. The opening title and first shot of Lee (Fig. 11.4), with the actress's disconcerting stare into the camera, prepare us immediately for this art-film patina. Yet unusual though these devices may be, they are hardly confusing. Alongside these patterns, *Hannah* draws upon

Cast
(in alphabetical order)

Woody Allen   Lloyd Nolan
Michael Caine   Maureen O'Sullivan
Mia Farrow   Daniel Stern
Carrie Fisher   Max Von Sydow
Barbara Hershey   Dianne Wiest

11.5

many of the same classical strategies that we have seen in the other nine films. It uses clear causal relations to create a progression among scenes, and its characters have clear-cut traits and pursue personal goals. Appointments and dialogue hooks often stitch scenes together. What is even more important for this particular film, many dangling causes are established, and some of these linger across several scenes or even the whole film. Thus, although we may concentrate in turn on several characters' widely differing concerns, we will be prepared from segment to segment to recognize events and traits that had been referred to earlier. Moreover, information is often presented redundantly, as when Mickey's hypochondria comes up over and over. In this sense *Hannah* is not that far removed from *Parenthood*.

SETUP: "BEWITCHED . . ."

As in *Alien*, the cast credits refrain from cuing us about the relative importance of the characters (Fig. 11.5). Here ten actors' names are given in alphabetical order. Moreover, several of the actors are well known; the film has a "star-studded" cast. To confuse matters, Daniel Stern, a supporting player whose main role to date had been in 1982's *Diner*, is listed among the ten actors even though he plays only the minor role of Elliot's client, Dusty. And the better-known Sam Waterston appears uncredited. As the narrative unfolds, we eventually discover that five of these actors play the main roles, and they are not always the most famous performers of the group. Dianne Wiest, as Holly, had previously played dependable mothers in a few films of the early 1980s. She was certainly not well known when she made this film, though she gained fame when she won an Oscar for it. On the other hand, some actors who had played leading roles in previous films portray relatively minor characters here: Carrie Fisher, heroine of the *Star Wars* series, has a small role as Holly's friend April, and the distinguished Max Von Sydow, as Frederick, appears in only three scenes and drops out of the action relatively early. Maureen O'Sullivan and Lloyd Nolan, stars from Hollywood's studio age, take fairly minor roles as Hannah's parents.

Even once the narrative proper begins, we have to wait for a considerable time before we start to discern the five protagonists: the three sisters, Hannah's current husband, and her ex-husband. We gradually realize that they are the main characters partly because they appear in more scenes than the minor characters do and partly because they are the ones whose thoughts we occasionally hear as voice-overs. Their shifting goals also govern the unpredictable outcomes of the romances and the film's divisions into large-scale parts.

Even though we must work hard to sort out the protagonists and supporting characters, they are not assigned the sorts of ambiguous traits typical of many art-film characters. Each actually has only a few traits and behaves in a fashion consistent with those traits. The protagonists all have goals and struggle to achieve them. They seem complex, I think, partly because there are so many characters and partly because the protagonists all change their goals unpredictably in the course of the narrative—although in every case the change is clear and thoroughly motivated. But because the characters spend a great deal of time talking or thinking about their attitudes and desires, we gain a sense that they possess unusual psychological depth.

One might argue that Mickey emerges as the single most prominent character, especially late in the film. True, his viewpoint ultimately seems to be the one privileged by the narrative (in his "love is unpredictable" line and his epiphany while watching *Duck Soup*). Similarly, the major breaks between the large-scale portions of the narrative come at crises in Mickey's life. Still, the balance among the five main characters is sustained quite well. Moreover, Mickey fails to function as a central, sole protagonist. For one thing, he has no connection whatsoever to the major portion of the plot concerning Elliot and Lee's affair and the latter's relationship to Frederick. As the title suggests, Hannah functions as the one character who ties together the various strands of action, even though she appears somewhat less frequently than any of the other four protagonists. Moreover, she has no strong long-term goal, reacting mainly to fend off the problems created by Elliot and Holly. Yet this is precisely the point. Hannah is the fulcrum, and she fosters her domestic life over any career ambitions. By the end, all five of the protagonists are in stable marriages, and Mickey has been drawn into the fold by becoming the successful husband and father that he had failed to be with Hannah.

The opening party scene assigns one or more basic traits to nine major and secondary characters. (The only significant character not seen or mentioned is David.) These traits will remain consistent or will result in motivated character development. Yet unpredictability will result because all except Hannah are ambivalent about the goals that they conceive or incapable of achieving them. As the film begins, Elliot is expressing his desire for Lee, but also struggling to convince himself that this desire should be suppressed. Indeed, Elliot's voice-over thoughts are usually given as a sort of interior argument with himself. Throughout the film his major trait will be his indecision, which he sums up in the much later scene with his psychiatrist. Ultimately it will be Lee who ends their affair and convinces Elliot to stay with Hannah. Elliot's voice-over concerning Lee also mentions his desire "to take care of her," and his later complaint about Hannah is that she is too self-sufficient; his reconciliation with her will come when she reveals her need for his support. Lee herself is characterized partly by her beauty, on which both Elliot and Hannah remark. At one point she mentions, however, that she enjoyed a book Elliot had loaned her. This line sets up her most crucial trait, her attraction to men who teach her about art and culture. Frederick has been an intellectual mentor for her; Elliot seduces her with poetry and music; and she ultimately marries a Columbia literature professor. More generally, then, Lee's main trait is a desire to learn. She speaks of possibly taking courses at Columbia, a plan which she eventually will execute: "sociology, psychology maybe—I've always thought I might like to work with children." Thus she is linked to the film's central focus on family.

Holly's traits are set up with dizzying speed: her cooking ability, her desire to act, and her flightiness, the last trait linked to her history of cocaine use. Both she and April talk about having come to the party hoping to meet attractive single men, and they later compete for David's attentions. (Of these traits, only her desire for marriage could give us the slightest clue as to how she will end up.) The parents are characterized as nostalgic, reliving their past theatrical glories; the flirtatious mother has a drinking problem. Hannah is revealed to be competent, domestically oriented, and a successful actress and mother. The first time we see her, she wanders through rooms lined with family pictures. As dinner begins, her parents reveal that she has cooked the huge meal and has recently acted in Ibsen's *A Doll's House*. April's desire to act and her interest in attractive men set her up as a later rival to Holly.

Even the two absent characters are discussed, with their basic traits laid out. When Lee mentions having seen Mickey, Hannah remarks, "God, Mickey's such a hypochondriac! I wonder how he'd handle it if there was ever anything really wrong with him." Her speculation sets up the later action, when we witness Mickey's panic at the possibility that he has cancer. Similarly, Holly points out to Hannah that Frederick has not accompanied Lee to the party, adding that he is "angry" and "depressive." Shortly thereafter, Lee mentions to Elliot that Frederick has sold a painting. When we eventually see Frederick, we know his essential traits, and he acts in accord with what has been said of him. Virtually all of the film's action harks back to character traits introduced rapidly at this party.

I have suggested that *Hannah* depends heavily upon dangling causes to achieve clarity while shifting among unconnected lines of action. The early scenes rapidly provide quite a number of dangling causes that are picked up later—in some cases much later. For example, early in the first party scene, Lee remarks to her sisters that their mother has not been drinking. Nothing more is said about this here, but the dialogue sets up the later scene where Hannah has to visit her parents when her mother has gone on a binge. That scene in turn helps to suggest why Lee has been an alcoholic in the past and why Holly has had problems with cocaine. Similarly, Holly says that she and April plan to start a catering business, and three scenes later we see them working at a party. (Holly also remarks that seeing the "adorable" children at the party makes her feel lonely; this dangling cause is only picked up in the very last line of the film when she announces that she is pregnant.) Holly says she had thought Lee was going to leave Frederick—as she later does. Elliot tells Lee that he has clients who might buy art from Frederick. Lee mentions to Hannah that she had recently run into Mickey in the street, on the way to the doctor; Hannah remarks on what a hypochondriac Mickey is, and two scenes later we see Mickey, again consulting a doctor. This sequence in turn ends with Mickey making an appointment for some medical tests. The next time we see him, he is undergoing the tests. Thus the narrative progression skips among several lines of action, but dangling causes link these scenes quite comprehensibly.

Neither Mickey nor Frederick is present at the first party. The film ends with a party in which Mickey has been reincorporated into Hannah's extended family. In contrast, Frederick is rejected and disappears. Initially Mickey and Frederick seem equally dysfunctional. Frederick cannot bear being with people other than Lee; for him, love seems to consist of teaching Lee about high art. (Lee remarks in their last scene together that their relationship no longer involves sex.) The notion of a man as a romantic and artistic mentor is true as well of David, the architect, who invites women to his box at the opera in order to seduce them, and Elliot, who romances Lee with Bach recordings and e. e. cummings poetry. Among the men, Mickey is the one fan of popular art—and by implication, the most sincere. He works in television and likes Bobby Short. Yet because of his cancer scare, he risks ending up isolated and bitter, like Frederick. He avoids this fate by becoming integrated into Hannah's family.

While the opening scene had shifted among characters, the second focuses primarily on Lee. In the taxi, we hear her thoughts, as we had heard Elliot's at the beginning. It becomes evident that we will not concentrate on one character but will have access to the thoughts of several. Her final reflection, "It's funny, I still feel a little buzz from this flirting," motivates her later decision to begin an affair with Elliot. Lee's difficult relationship with Frederick, hinted at in the opening scene, is further revealed when she reaches home. She offers him tea, coffee, and food, all of which he rejects. Thus his austere, isolated life is contrasted with Hannah and Elliot's apartment, packed with people and food.

The first two scenes, the party and Lee's return home, are relatively calm in tone and rhythm. The introduction of Mickey suddenly initiates a frantically fast pace, and indeed the segment focusing on him consists of three short scenes in rapid succession.[1] An opening title, accompanied by the fast, jazzy music that will be associated with Mickey, reads "The hypochondriac," seeming to offer an objective confirmation of Hannah's earlier characterization. An elaborate tracking shot follows him through a corridor, with people bursting in and out of the frame to hector him. Mickey exasperatedly glances up and asks, "Why me, Lord?" preparing for his later quest to find a meaning for his life through religion. He further confirms Hannah's remark that he is a hypochondriac by mentioning his ulcer. During the course of the film, Mickey's character change will be signaled by a gradual replacement of the fast pace of his early scenes with a much calmer tone. By the end he fits into the quiet group at the final Thanksgiving party.

Late in Mickey's first scene, we hear his voice-over, recalling his ex-partner's success in California. We are thus confirmed in the belief that the narration will allow us access to several characters' thoughts. Mickey's scene ends with a combined dialogue hook and appointment as he remarks that he has to visit his ex-wife the next day. A straight cut reveals Mickey entering

Hannah's apartment to deliver birthday presents to their twins. No dialogue hook ends this brief scene, but the subsequent visit to a doctor follows from the dangling cause of Mickey's hypochondria, with the doctor remarking, "So what's the problem *this* time?" Mickey's hearing loss turns out to be actual rather than imagined, and we witness the beginning of a series of answers to Hannah's speculation about how Mickey might react to a real health problem. He objects that he is "perfectly healthy," then belittles his weakness in hearing high decibels by saying, "I won't go to the opera." This remark links doubly to Holly, in that there are hints that her love for loud rock music may have damaged Mickey's hearing and that she also may have become interested in opera through dating David. (She is carrying some opera recordings near the end when Mickey encounters her in Tower Records.) Mickey's telephone conversation with a second doctor ends with the possibility that he might have a brain tumor, providing a dialogue hook into Mickey's panicky conversation with his colleague at the office. Here we learn that his real response to a possible health problem is a typical hypochondriac's escalation of the situation.

By the end of this scene, the characters' salient traits have been introduced, and we know all that we need to about their initial situations. Mickey's line, "I was happy, but I just didn't realize I was happy," ends the setup portion.

COMPLICATING ACTION: ". . . BOTHERED . . ."

This new section of the film begins with another title, "The Stanislavsky Catering Company in action." Holly and April's cooking abilities had been mentioned twice in the opening scene, both when Elliot and Hannah praised some of Holly's hors d'oeuvres and later during the dinner when Hannah gave part of the credit to Holly and April. Holly had also mentioned their desire to run a catering business. Thus, although this is the film's fourth segment and we have not seen Holly and April since the opening, spectators should have no trouble in grasping what is going on. This is the first time any of the characters has taken a step toward achieving a goal (albeit in this case a short-term one), and so we are in a new phase of the film. The two women's real, long-range goal is reiterated redundantly when April reveals that she has failed an acting audition and Holly replies encouragingly, "You'll get five jobs next week!"

We also know from the first scene that both women are looking for an attractive man, and their efforts to impress David motivate the rivalry that will end their friendship. Similarly, his mention of his private box at the Metropolitan Opera provides a dangling cause for the later brief scene showing him and Holly together there. His friendly conversation with the two women makes him seem an attractive figure, one who might well become central to the action and a plausible mate for Holly. David's line, "What time to do you get off?" creates a dialogue hook into the next scene, a conversation and montage sequence of him taking the pair on an architectural tour of Manhattan.

Like Frederick and Elliot, David uses intellectual conversations about art to achieve his romantic ends. From this montage, we are evidently to understand that his taste in architecture is impeccable; the sequence is essentially an homage to Manhattan by Woody Allen. Yet David turns out to be fickle. Thus he fits in with the film's general pattern of making characters unpredictable.

After the tour David drives the two women home, and we hear the fourth voice-over monologue as Holly reflects on her apparent failure to attract David. This scene parallels Lee's earlier monologue in the cab, pondering Elliot's attraction to her. Once again the film balances the characters, giving us access to their thoughts in turn. Indeed, we have had one voice-over passage in each of the film's segments so far, every one spoken by a different character. Yet even within these scenes the narration is subjective for only part of the action. Each scene also has shots with groups of characters talking, putting no emphasis on any particular one. Thus the film manages to move briefly into the minds of major characters while still stressing the group as a whole. Holly's ruminations betray that she feels inferior to her mother and to Hannah, both of whom she thinks can tell jokes better than she can. She also reveals that she needs an extra Secanol to get to sleep; her drug-taking has not wholly stopped.

No dialogue hook leads into the next segment of the film, where Elliot and Lee visit a bookshop, followed by a brief scene in which Lee reads a poem from the book he buys for her. Only at the end is it revealed that the opening title, "nobody, not even the rain, has such small hands," is a quotation from e. e. cummings. Yet again, as with the catering scene, this segment picks up on a dangling cause from the opening party. Elliot is exploring the possibility of starting an affair with Lee by pretending to meet her coincidentally in the street. Thus he, like Holly, is moving toward the accomplishment of a goal established during the opening party. The musical motif, "I Think I've Heard That Song Before," also harks back to the earlier scene.

Here Lee reveals that she is a recovering alcoholic, creating a parallel with Holly's previous cocaine use. When Elliot expresses bafflement about her drinking, Lee remarks, "Don't let me get started on my childhood!" Thus clues planted in the opening scene are becoming more explicit, and we might suspect that all three sisters experienced problems with their celebrity parents. How Hannah has apparently avoided the substance abuse into which her two sisters fell becomes a mystery, and it hints at motivations for Holly's and Elliot's resentments of Hannah's apparent perfection.

Other narrative information that had been introduced earlier is recapitulated and developed more explicitly. Lee remarks on how much she learned from Frederick in visiting an exhibition on Caravaggio, and we know already that their alliance is based on his intellectual mentoring. Elliot immediately vies with his rival by buying Lee a book on cummings: "Maybe we could discuss it sometime." That his tactic is successful is revealed through a dialogue hook. As they part, Elliot reminds Lee to read the poem on page 112. A cut leads to her at home that night reading it and reacting emotionally. A cutaway to Elliot wandering about his own apartment sets up a false shot/reverse shot between the two, suggesting a rapport that will motivate Lee's willingness to start an affair.[2]

The sixth scene returns to Mickey, using his jazzy music and a title, "The anxiety of the man in the booth." The doctor reveals that his X-rays warrant a CAT scan. This brief scene ends with a comic reverse dialogue hook, as the doctor says "Don't panic," and there is a straight cut to Mickey jolting awake in bed: "I'm dying!" Mickey's goal so far has been less clear than those of the characters in other scenes, but now he gains a general goal of sorts: "Look, I'll make a deal with God. Let it just be my ear. I'll go deaf, I'll go deaf and blind in one eye, maybe. But I don't want a brain operation." Thus his immediate goal is to survive. This speech also brings in the religious motif a second time, providing further motivation for Mickey's later spiritual odyssey.

Mickey's ruminations lead to a flashback in which it is revealed that during his marriage to Hannah, he was told that he has a small sperm count and cannot father children. This in turn leads into information about how Hannah was artificially inseminated and bore twins. Mickey assumes that this problem was one factor in his breakup with Hannah, and he remarks, "Boy, love is really unpredictable." His final line acts as a thematic rather than a causal dialogue hook into the brief scene of Holly and David at the opera. In effect, this moment serves as the end of Mickey's segment, since it forms a confirmation for his remark.

Once again there is no dialogue hook between the opera scene and the segment in Frederick and Lee's apartment. The title, "Dusty just bought this huge house in Southampton," is not very helpful, but Elliot speaks it immediately as the scene begins, adding, "and he's in the process of decorating it." Here another dangling cause, mentioned in passing in the opening party scene and again when Lee returned home to Frederick in the second scene, returns. This scene serves in part to reinforce the idea that Lee might be better off leaving Frederick. For one thing, the potential client, Dusty, is presented as naive but enthusiastic and friendly. Frederick has the option of at least treating him courteously but instead angrily refuses to sell anything to him; after Lee behaves politely to Dusty, Frederick criticizes her. We also see several nude sketches of Lee arranged around the apartment. In the opening party she had expressed some discomfort at having such images in strangers' homes, yet Frederick offers one to Dusty. The implication may be that Frederick is exploiting Lee by selling drawings she would rather keep private.

The scene also introduces information about what Elliot calls "a conflict" between himself and Hannah: her love for their woodland country house and his dislike of nature. His conversation with Lee reiterates some of the film's goals as Lee mentions Holly's romance with David. Elliot remarks, "I'd like to see her end up settled. She's a tense one." He then reveals his own goal by impulsively kissing Lee and declaring his love. After Elliot leaves the apartment and Lee meets him in the street, he claims that "Hannah and I are in the last stages" and will split up. When Lee says she does have some feelings for Elliot, he replies with a remark that echoes his earlier desire to take care of Lee: "OK, OK, you've said enough. It's *my* responsibility now. *I* will work things out." In fact he never makes any decisive move, and it will finally be Lee who breaks off their affair. Indeed, Lee also ends her long-term relationship with Frederick against his will. Thus we must eventually question our assumption that she passively accepts men who seek to control her through teaching her about art.

The next scene stands apart from all the others in the film, concentrating largely on Hannah. It begins without an intertitle, though a piano version of "Bewitched, Bothered, and Bewildered" harks back to the song her parents had played and sung at the opening party. Indeed, Hannah is visiting them in order to solve a crisis that has arisen through her mother's flirting with a young man and going on a drinking binge. The mother criticizes her husband and remarks, "It's a good thing we had a talented daughter." This line follows up on hints dropped at the opening party, suggesting that Hannah, before having children, had supported her family with her acting. We now hear Hannah's inner monologue—the fifth of the five protagonists whose thoughts are presented in voice-over. She and her mother discuss Holly and Lee's lack of theatrical success, offering further hints as to why they are still struggling to overcome problems. By the end of the scene, we can understand why there was no introductory intertitle, for this is where the film's title proper, "Hannah and Her Sisters," is explained most fully. A cut to a brief scene of Lee sitting on a wharf reinforces the idea that she is troubled and confused.

The ninth segment, heralded by the intertitle "The abyss," ends the complicating action. Here we go the farthest into one of the characters' minds, as Mickey fantasizes about a doctor telling him that he has inoperable cancer—followed by a cut to the real doctor entering and giving him a clean bill of health. This moment seems to satisfy Mickey's goal as he formulated it earlier, since he has indeed lost some hearing but has no brain tumor.

The previous scene with Hannah and this one with Mickey mark the section of the film at which the characters' initial goals seem at least in part to be accomplished, and now they begin to shift. Elliot wanted Lee, and now he seems to have her. Holly seems to be doing well in her romance with David. Hannah has averted another crisis with her parents and preserved the family. Mickey has no serious health problem. All these plotlines could continue along the same courses, yet all now begin to take unpredictable new directions. First Mickey swings suddenly from joy to despair, deciding to quit his job and seek meaning in his life. His final line to his colleague at the TV station establishes his new goal: "I gotta get some answers. Otherwise, I tell you, I'm gonna do something drastic." His line contrasts with Elliot's ebullient final line the last time we had seen him, just after Lee admitted she had some feelings for him: "I have my answer. I *have* my answer. I'm walking on air." Yet while Elliot thinks he has his answer, in fact he soon will begin to equivocate about leaving Hannah for Lee and eventually will abandon that goal altogether. Mickey now wants answers but will only be able to pull out of despair when he realizes that there are none.

DEVELOPMENT: ". . . AND BEWILDERED"

In the second half of the film the family increasingly expresses feelings of inferiority to Hannah. In the hotel scene between Elliot and Lee that begins the development, she remarks after they have made love, "I was so worried I wouldn't compare with Hannah," and Elliot incredulously replies, "You really do have those thoughts, don't you?" Lee's feelings will emerge as mounting guilt over her affair with Elliot, while Holly and Elliot will express resentment over Hannah's self-sufficiency and high standards. These tensions will eventually collapse as the romantic couples unexpectedly realign. The characters' resentments fit in with the fact that here, as in many classical films, the development portion consists largely of delays in the accomplishment of goals. Hannah embodies the domestic bliss that all the major characters will achieve, but at this point they resist her and what she stands for.

No intertitle opens the hotel scene, but the Bach music associated with Elliot and Lee's romance quickly suggests that their affair is progressing. Elliot reiterates his previously established desire to love a woman he can take care of, saying of Hannah, "Yes, she's very warm and giving. But it's *me* that wants to be giving to *you*. I want to do things for you. Hannah doesn't *need* me as much." Lee affirms that "I *want* you to take care of me," so we may assume that the romance will continue and lead to Elliot's divorcing Hannah.

The next scene presents the opposite side of the affair—a distinctly un-glamorous view as Lee walks home through the rain and has a painful confrontation with Frederick when he realizes she's been with another man. His bitter criticisms of American culture and the revelation that their sex life has atrophied continue to suggest that Lee might leave Frederick for Elliot. She finally states a fairly concrete goal: "I want a less complicated life, Frederick. I want a husband, maybe even a child, before it's too late." Thus the domestic urge that eventually solves all the protagonists' problems is attached to Lee as well. She makes it clear, however, that a marriage to Frederick would not work. The scene ends without the couple breaking up definitively, leaving this cause to dangle for some time.

Another straight cut reveals Hannah reading in bed. There is no dialogue hook, but the two scenes are linked by contrast. Frederick had immediately realized that Lee was having an affair, while Lee refused to accept guilt concerning it. Here Hannah remains placidly ignorant of Elliot's infidelity, while he begins to feel tormented about betraying her. There has been no voice-over since the fourth scene back, Hannah's visit to her parents. Now Elliot describes his joy over the meeting with Lee and then his self-hatred for his betrayal of Hannah. He refers to the afternoon of lovemaking as living out "a great dream" and adds, "There's something very lovely and real about Hannah." The voice-over is parallel to his thoughts in the opening, when he both desired Lee and castigated himself for it. Now again he thinks, "God, I'm despicable!" and concludes, "I'd rather hurt Lee a little than destroy Hannah." That line sums up his attitude for much of the rest of the action, as he continues the affair without having any strong desire to leave Hannah. Thus his goal essentially becomes to make up his mind, as he later tells his psychiatrist. Yet Lee's phone call, in which she says she feels very close to him, suggests that now she will be the one to provide the impetus for keeping their affair going. Apparently she loves him, and this line strongly implies that her goal is to marry him.

Once again there is no dialogue hook into the following scene with Mickey. The intertitle, "'The only absolute knowledge attainable by man is that life is meaningless.' Tolstoy," is the one least explicitly related to the scene that it introduces. It looks forward, however, to the later moment when Mickey grasps this idea by watching *Duck Soup*. Mickey has been in the library at Columbia University, and he has failed to find the answers he has been seeking; ironically, Lee will find the solution to her own romantic quest at Columbia by marrying one of her professors.

The literary reference of the intertitle is picked up indirectly in Mickey's voice-over musings: "Maybe the poets are right. Maybe love is the only answer." This line echoes his statement of his goal the last time we had seen him: "I gotta get some answers." He immediately dismisses the idea of love being the answer by recalling his divorce from Hannah and his subsequent disastrous date with Holly. The extensive flashback to the latter episode seems to support the idea that love is not the answer—yet it will prove to be so for both Mickey and Holly. Thus the "love is unpredictable" theme is further motivated.

Mickey and Holly's incompatibility is demonstrated by the pair of musical performances to which each drags the other. While listening to Holly's pre-ferred form of entertainment, loud punk rock, Mickey shouts, "I can't hear, I can't hear anything. I'm gonna lose hearing in my ear." There may be a hint that this concert really is the "loud noise" that has caused Mickey's partial hearing loss. Yet the date had taken place years before, and the doctor in-quires about whether Mickey has been subjected to a loud noise recently. So there may be no causal connection, but we are at least left with the ironic possibility that Holly could be both the indirect cause of Mickey's existential crisis and part of the solution to it.

After Holly fails to appreciate Bobby Short's rendition of Cole Porter, Mickey sends her off in a cab. His voice-over, from the present, ends by remarking, "Too bad, too, 'cause . . . I always have had a little crush on her." This phrase echoes Lee's voice-over in the taxi in the second scene: "Is it my imagination, or does Elliot have a little crush on me?" The Elliot-Lee rela-tionship had initially looked serious but has perhaps started to unravel. The Mickey-Holly relationship, in contrast, seems to have died aborning. Still, love is unpredictable.

No dialogue hook leads into the next scene, which begins with the intertitle "Afternoons." Yet there is only a brief daytime scene of Elliot and Lee dancing and sipping wine during what we must now assume is a habitual hotel rendezvous. The bulk of the scene, however, deals with an evening talk between Hannah and Elliot. Dinner ends with Hannah explaining a camera to one of their two adopted Asian children, telling him to try it when they get to the country. This line recalls Elliot's earlier comment to Lee that Hannah likes their country home and he does not. Thus we are prepared for their subsequent quarrel, in which she declares her desire to have a child by him and he complains about her attempts to regiment his life. Again his voice-over reveals his inner debate: "Tell her you want out and get it over with. You're in love with her sister. You didn't do it on purpose. Be honest, it's always the best way." Thus the narrative still holds out the possibility that Elliot will leave Hannah, but their embrace makes it seem more likely that he will not.

The shift to the next segment involves no dialogue hook, but a title announces "The audition," a motif associated with Holly. Two earlier dangling causes are developed, by means of the two outfits for which Holly is shopping as she chats with Hannah. Initially Holly says she needs some-thing to wear to the opera with David, confirming that their romance is progressing. So far we have had no indication of David's flaws. Now we learn that his wife is institutionalized and that he will eventually leave her when their daughter goes to college the next year. While Holly is sympathetic to him, we should suspect that this may be the classic adulterer's rationaliza-tion. (Hannah's remark, "You found all of this out on *one date?*" is a further signal that David is using this as a seduction ploy.) Holly is also looking for an outfit to wear to an audition for a musical, and Hannah's surprise at her attempt to sing should signal to us that Holly will fail yet again. This scene leads directly into the audition, where Holly's weak voice confirms Hannah's worries that her sister is setting herself up for continual disappointment. Holly's failure in turn motivates her eventual decision to abandon acting. Similarly, April's revelation outside the theater that David has asked her to the opera brings Holly's romantic goal to an abrupt halt. Now even her relationship with April is imperiled, motivating the collapse of their catering business.

No dialogue hook leads into the next scene, but it is Mickey's turn, so an intertitle announces, "The big leap." Again we have typical development-section delay, with Mickey continuing his search for answers by attempting to convert to Catholicism. He declares to his parents, "I need a dramatic change in my life." The comedy in the brief scenes with his parents and with his shopping bag full of religious objects and groceries suggests that his goal is not taking him in the right direction.

The three sisters' luncheon meeting brings them together without the others for the only time, and it ends the development. The transition to this scene is accomplished without a dialogue hook or intertitle. Again dangling causes serve to orient us quickly. Aside from emphasizing again the tensions among the sisters, the luncheon serves to set up Holly's sudden change of goals. Her repeated failures and the collapse of the Stanislavsky Catering Company have prompted her to abandon acting and try writing: "I've gotta, you know, latch onto something in my life. Something with a future." Lee's guilt over her affair with Elliot surfaces for the first time, motivating her later decision to break with him. (The scene also briefly confirms that she has left Frederick.) Hannah's reluctant agreement to fund Holly's writing project introduces the last new cause necessary to allowing the film to move toward resolution.

CLIMAX AND EPILOGUE: "IN LOVE AGAIN"

By this point, all the characters' goals demand that the narration give us a sense of considerable time passing. Most obviously, Holly must have an interval in which to write something that we could believe is worthwhile. (At lunch, Hannah told her to take six months or a year, and she clearly takes something approximating the former.) Elliot must drag his feet on deciding which woman he loves long enough to provoke Lee into taking action. Mickey must continue his search for meaning long enough to drive him nearly to suicide. Thus the climax portion opens with a cluster of brief scenes entitled "Summer in New York," which function as a montage sequence of passing time. Elliot tells his analyst about his inability to decide between Hannah and Lee. His voice continues over scenes of Lee at Columbia, accompanied by the professor whom she eventually marries—even though Elliot presumably does not know about this new situation. At any rate, we get a hint that she is moving to resolve their affair without Elliot's help. Returning to the analyst's office, we see Elliot conclude: "But it's *my* fault," recalling his earlier assurance to Lee that working out their relationship would be his responsibility.

Elliot's wistful conclusion, "For all my education, accomplishments, and so-called wisdom, I can't fathom my own heart," creates a sort of dialogue hook to a scene of Mickey getting recruitment literature from a Hare Krishna follower. He mentions that he has failed to become a Catholic. Now we hear Mickey's voice-over, ending with "God, I'm so depressed!" Earlier he had declared that he would find answers or do something drastic. Now he is close to despair.

A title, "Autumn chill," once more suggests the passage of time. Hannah's two sisters are shown, both having made distinct progress toward their goals. First Lee sits again on the wharf where we had earlier seen her looking bleak and lost. Now she is cautiously optimistic, revealing in a voice-over that she has gone out with her literature professor: "Funny, I feel like I'm betraying Elliot, but that's ridiculous. Why shouldn't I see Doug? Elliot's not free. Just go one step at a time. Let's see what the next few months bring." Thus Lee has made her first steps toward breaking off with Elliot, and the film indicates the further passage of time to make this change plausible.

The final brief time-passing scene shows Holly on the phone to Hannah, revealing that she has the first draft of a play. Her arrangement to give it to Hannah and get her comments at the Thanksgiving party set up the first definite appointment and dialogue hook in quite some time, suggesting the accelerated resolution of plotlines that is beginning. In passing, Holly mentions Lee's romance with a man she met at Columbia, reiterating that that plotline is progressing. She concludes, "We'll talk at Thanksgiving," leading directly into the second party scene.

During this party, dangling causes are picked up almost as quickly as others had been established in the opening segment. The parents again entertain the guests with tales of their past, revealing no hint of their earlier quarrel; indeed, the father boasts of how his wife's beauty used to dazzle men. In the kitchen, Holly opines that Lee is in love with her new boyfriend. The sisters' and Elliot's resentments concerning Hannah come out when Hannah comments on Holly's play: "You make it sound like, you know, I have no needs or something. You think I'm too self-sufficient." Hannah's reaction motivates Holly's later abandonment of this play in favor of writing another one which ultimately impresses Mickey.

In another room, Lee terminates her affair with Elliot, despite his urging her to continue it. Thus her line of action is the first one resolved, and thereafter she disappears, except for the confirmation in the final scene that her goal has been achieved through marriage to her professor. Elliot's subsequent argument with Hannah brings their relationship to its crisis as he declares: "Jesus! I've told you, I need someone I can matter to." This line harks back to his desire, expressed in the first scene and subsequently, to find a woman he can take care of. Hannah replies, "You matter to me—completely." Elliot: "It's hard to be around someone who gives so much and needs so little in return." Hannah: "I—I have enormous needs." Elliot: "Well, I can't see them and neither can Lee or Holly!" As Hannah walks down the dark hallway after this conversation, there still seems a real possibility that Elliot will leave her, despite the failure of his affair with Lee.

This possibility is immediately reversed, however, in the short scene between the two in bed. Hannah at last betrays some need for Elliot's support by declaring, "It is pitch black tonight. I feel lost." Elliot replies, "You're not lost," and kisses her. With this simple exchange their individual goals are achieved.

Hannah's sudden, uncharacteristic declaration of need ties in with the theme of unpredictability. Through much of the film, her rock-like stability has allowed other characters to pursue their willful goals. Elliot could enjoy his indecisive fling because he always had the option of staying with her. Holly receives financial support from Hannah to pursue her dreams. Both sisters obviously depend on Hannah to patch up their parents' occasional problems, and Lee is willing to have an affair with Elliot without his first leaving Hannah (for which she accepts blame in breaking off with him). Yet none of them can detect that Hannah has needs, and by assuming that she does not, they collectively manage to drive her to the edge of crisis.

As Elliot and Hannah embrace in reconciliation, the piano version of "Bewitched, Bothered, and Bewildered" comes up and acts as a bridge into the next scene, introduced with the intertitle, "Lucky I ran into you." Earlier in the film Mickey had always been associated with jazz, but now his scene with Holly is introduced with the music associated with the parents and their daughters. His cheery meeting with her in Tower Records contrasts completely with the last time we saw him, depressed and near despair. Thus a dangling cause seems to be contradicted; something is missing that would explain Mickey's new attitude, and it will soon be supplied. Holly is carrying some opera discs, suggesting that her old interest in punk rock is dead. He remarks that she looks great, and indeed she looks healthier than in earlier scenes. His agreement to listen to her play that could be revised into a TV script sets up a dangling cause. Mickey also remarks that although he has not worked in nearly a year, he needs to get back into television because his funds are dwindling. Their mutual improvement since their last major scenes is confirmed in the dialogue. Holly: "You OK, though?" Mickey: "Yes, yes, I'm fine. How are you?" Holly: "Oh, I'm fine."

Her appointment to come and read the play to him the next day acts as a dialogue hook into the next scene, which begins as she finishes reading. His enthusiastic reaction leads him to offer her lunch. This action is accompanied by a jazz version of "You Made Me Love You," the music which had been heard over the credits and which has not returned until this point. Thus this scene is singled out as the pair walk in Central Park (locale of one of Mickey's earlier moments of despair) and he tells Holly about his low point. His epiphany during a screening of *Duck Soup* had led him to renounce his old goal of finding answers (his voice-over being juxtaposed with scenes from the film): "You know, what the hell, it's not *all* a drag, and I'm thinking to myself, jeez, I should stop ruining my life, searching for answers I'm never gonna get and just enjoy it while it lasts." Mickey asks Holly to dinner as the climax portion ends. The trumpet version of the song provides another bridge into the final scene.

A title, "One year later," introduces the epilogue, which takes place at the third Thanksgiving party. Again the dialogue quickly sums up the successes of the various characters: Lee and her father mention how good Holly's new play is, and the mother asks if Hannah will play Desdemona in a PBS production of *Othello*. The techniques of the opening return, as we get one final voice-over from Elliot, accompanied by the same song that had played in the first scene. He reflects on his affair with Lee, clearly still a bit in love with her despite her now being married, but also still castigating himself over it: "What did I put us both through? And Hannah, who, as you once said, I love much more than I realized."

Holly's arrival is greeted, appropriately, by a new tune, "Isn't It Romantic?" played offscreen by her father. Mickey arrives, now married to Holly. His speech as they embrace recaps the theme of the unpredictability of love: "I was talking to your father before, and I was telling him, it's ironic, I used to always have Thanksgiving with Hannah, and I never thought I could love anybody else, and here it is years later, and I'm married to you, and completely in love with you. The heart is a very, very resilient little muscle." He then suggests that she write a story based on that idea, adding, "How're you going to top that?" She responds, "Mickey, I'm pregnant," adding one more surprise to the plot. The music that the father is playing offscreen on the piano is "In Love Again," the same song that Bobby Short had sung during Mickey and Holly's first date. At that time Holly had disliked it; now it returns as a motif to link the two scenes, stressing again how unpredictable it had been that these two would ever fall in love.

The final credits present the cast in order of appearance, again refusing to rank the actors and their characters.

As we have seen, *Hannah* falls into the standard four parts and epilogue. Its unusually short setup is possible because character traits and dangling causes are introduced at such a breakneck pace during the opening party scene (rather as they are in *The Shop Around the Corner*, mentioned in Chapter 1). The leisurely complicating action then sorts out and advances several of the dangling causes established earlier. The development and climax/epilogue are reasonably balanced at a fairly standard length.

A FINAL LESSON: AMBIVALENT AUTEURS

Interviews with screenwriters are full of complaints about the effects of the auteur theory in the American film industry. Too much credit, they say, is now given to the director at the writer's expense. In a discussion recorded in about 1971, the writer David Giler (*The Parallax View*, 1974) dismissed the theory but acknowledged that it had enhanced directors' power: "It seems strange that a bunch of French critics could have had as much effect on the giant corporate establishment over here as they have. André Bazin and all those guys at the *Cahiers* in the fifties."[3]

Screenwriters annoyed with the auteur theory not unnaturally except directors who write or collaborate on the scripts for their films. The notion of the writer-director tends to be a European one. In the studio era, American directors seldom worked on scripts until the last stages of pre-production. In Europe, however, the art cinema was to a considerable extent a product of writer-directors such as Ingmar Bergman and close author/director teams such as Cesare Zavattini and Vittorio De Sica. Given such control, a body of work bearing a personal stamp could accumulate.

By this criterion, Woody Allen is as close to an auteur as anyone who has worked in the American cinema during recent decades. He controls his films to a remarkable degree, and his stylistic experiments and autobiographical concerns have given his oeuvre a unique quality. To some extent he has followed the new Hollywood tactic of alternating daring "art-cinema" projects (such as *Shadows and Fog*, 1992) with more commercial ones (like *Bullets over Broadway*, 1994), though both types bear his imprint. His reputation as an actor's director (backed up by several Oscars and nominations for past cast members) has allowed him to continue to attract the sort of all-star cast we have seen in *Hannah*. Such star-power has undoubtedly been crucial in his ability to work with relatively little compromise.

Clearly the auteurist directors who emerged in the 1970s aspired to a similar independence from studio interference. In their cases, the recent see-sawing between personal and money-oriented projects has been more extreme. Scorsese's credits include *The Color of Money* (1986) and *The Age of Innocence* (1993), so he can occasionally make a film of artistic aspirations but limited appeal such as *Kundun* (1997). When *John Grisham's The Rainmaker* was released in 1997, Coppola was forthright in saying that he made it in the hope of moving on to an unnamed personal project:

> All of the directors in the Bob Altman category—if I may allow myself to be in that category—Martin Scorsese, Brian De Palma, all of these directors are in a state of anxiety that they're not going to be able to make the kinds of movies they're capable of unless their Friday-night grosses are big. We're all on borrowed time, hoping we can be viable in this new setup so that we can go on in the time we have left to make a few personal films.[4]

Such personal films, one must suspect, are ones which would come close to the ideal of the European art film, as *The Conversation, Kundun,* and many of Altman's and Allen's films do.

There is a certain irony in this, in that the auteur theory was designed precisely to call attention to mainstream commercial Hollywood directors. The argument was that, although they did not have the extensive authorial control apparent in many European films, certain directors managed to impose a personal style and outlook even upon ordinary genre pictures. The work of John Ford in Westerns and Howard Hawks in romantic comedies would be exemplary here. In an interview in the mid-1970s, Scorsese discussed how important Andrew Sarris's promotion of auteurism was to him when he took film history courses at New York University:

> "They told us in film school that we had to like only Bergman," Scorsese says. "Now Bergman's good, but he isn't the only one. I discovered that I had liked most of the films those auteurist guys were talking about. I found there were many other things to do, that you didn't have to reject totally the films you liked as a child. For three years I hadn't looked at American movies. I found that very damaging."[5]

Yet the attitudes of the auteurist directors have remained surprisingly ambivalent about what they aspire to make—and what they are proud of and what they downplay in their own filmographies. Spielberg clearly considers some of his best work, most notably *Jaws*, as a vaguely embarrassing necessity along the path to his more respectable middlebrow projects, such as *The Color Purple* (1985) and *Schindler's List* (1993). Of course John Ford thought that *The Informer* (1935) and *The Fugitive* (1947) were important films, but it is for *Stagecoach* (1939), *The Quiet Man* (1952), and other comparable films that he is revered today.

The same ambivalence crops up among other aging auteurists. Coppola still deplores his masterly film *The Godfather*, yet working essentially without restraints, he apparently felt that *One from the Heart* (1982) was the direction in which Hollywood should move. In a surprising development, Coppola's 1998 award of 80 million dollars in a lawsuit against Warner Bros. seemed to rekindle his 1970s ambitions to use American Zoetrope to defeat the Hollywood studio system. According to *Variety:* "Coppola brushes aside suggestions that Zoetrope will be mowed down once again by the studio juggernauts. 'Their days are numbered,' he insists. 'Art studios will replace them. This is my dream.'"[6] Such quixotism recalls the claims of the auteurists in the heady days of the early 1970s (see Chapter 1. The subsequent reduction of the award by 60 million dollars has presumably rescued the Hollywood studios).[7]

Without downplaying the undoubted talents of Coppola and the other auteurist directors of his generation, one wonders why they are so reluctant to embrace the kinds of genre-based filmmaking that made the master auteurs of the studio age great. The paradox here is that the auteurists were the directors who helped revivify the genre filmmaking of Hollywood's past. The very films of which they seem ashamed—most tellingly *The Godfather* and *Jaws*—are those that are most comparable to, say, *Scarface* (1932) or *King Kong* (1933). It is as if the auteurists long simultaneously to be Michelangelo Antonioni and Howard Hawks—a bizarre and, one might think, contradictory goal indeed. A review of two films directed by auteurists and based on the work of John Grisham hints at this paradox:

It may be a coincidence, but there's an undeniably pungent irony to the fact that Altman and Francis Ford Coppola, two of the artistic titans of '70s Hollywood, have, within three months of each other, joined creative forces with Grisham, whose name has rarely, if ever, been linked to the word *art*. Tempting as it is to interpret the coincidence cynically, as proof that filmmakers like Altman and Coppola must, in the bottom-line '90s, knuckle under to the clout of the box office, such is the magic of movies that the cynicism seems misplaced. *John Grisham's The Rain-*

maker, Coppola's recent courtroom drama, was the director's most re-laxed and craftsmanly work in years. Now comes *The Gingerbread Man*, a trickier and even more satisfying entertainment.[8]

Relaxed, tricky, satisfying craftsmanship. That's not a complete description of the great auteurs of Hollywood's past, but it's not a bad start. It is also not a bad description of the ten films I have analyzed here. Although they may not equal the very best that the "golden age" of the studios produced, they admirably carry on its tradition.

12

Hopes and Fears for Hollywood

Wasn't this supposed to be the age of Tarantino?

—DAVID ANSEN, "Our Titanic Love Affair," *Newsweek*

The ten principal analyses in this book have avoided the sort of thematic interpretation that prevails in academic film criticism. Most analysts concentrate on the messages, overt or hidden, which a film purportedly sends. And it is true that many of the films I have examined could be read in just such ways. Many of them purvey clichés of American values: "Be yourself" *(Tootsie)*, "Your future is yours to make" *(Back to the Future)*, "Jealousy is self-destructive" *(Amadeus)*, and so on. Noting the presence of such messages, however, does little to explain how popular cinema provides viewers with engaging experiences. Even homilies must be woven into artistic form, and the sorts of classical principles and devices we have been considering add up to a powerful system for doing so. Narrative analysis (which has been my principal concern here), along with stylistic analysis (which has not), shows how films operate as coherent wholes, shaping and developing their subject matter in ways that hold audiences.

In addition, though they may replay cultural clichés, films are never reducible to them. There are always other aspects to be considered, such as *Amadeus*'s overarching ironic narration or *Desperately Seeking Susan*'s clever play with visual parallels. Hollywood craftsmanship forces creators beyond the bare-bones themes, not least by encouraging them to devise intricacies and details which, though unnoticed by most of the audience, subtly unify the film and give nuance to its central action. By analyzing principles of large-scale structure and local texture, we can reveal a cinema which prizes an accessible, enjoyable form of coherence and complexity—the kind of coherence and complexity we find, say, in a well-made play or a Cole Porter song. Hollywood filmmaking, contrary to the voices announcing a "post-classical" cinema of rupture, fragmentation, and postmodern incoherence, remains firmly rooted in a tradition which has flourished for eighty years and shows every sign of continuing.

HOLLYWOOD DOLDRUMS

The tradition, however, seems to be continuing at a lower level of quality, at least temporarily. I must admit that the mid-1990s have witnessed a dearth of really good American films. Hollywood is making enormous amounts of money and expanding its hold on world markets following the breakup of the Soviet Union and the strong trend toward multiplexing in Europe and Asia. The growing urge on the part of studio executives to make films that can appeal to virtually any person on the planet has apparently reduced some of the flexibility in the classical system. This bid for universal appeal is often cited as evidence of a "post-classical" approach, but I would argue that such tactics are only used for a limited number of films, and where they have been used, they have simply fostered an exaggeration and simplification of older techniques.

Richard Corliss eloquently remarked upon this negative trend during the summer of 1997, the season when big action films are customarily released:

> A manic roteness now envelops action films; the need to thrill has become a drab addiction. Isn't there more to moviemaking than having a finger on the pulse of the world public? Can't the megalomelodrama be infused with passion and ingenuity? The answer so far, and with just one exception, is no—not this season. For this is Hollywood's Summer of Dumb.[1]

Hollywood, as I have suggested, has been using formulas for several decades, but they have never seemed so consistently enervated.

The result has been a tendency to seize upon any halfway interesting film as a major event. Corliss's "one exception" in the passage quoted above was John Woo's *Face/Off* (1997), which critics seem to me to have overrated—perhaps beginning to despair that the Hong Kong auteur would find his sea legs in Hollywood and so hailing this slight improvement as a return to form. The critic Ty Burr has commented on a similar phenomenon in relation to the entertaining 1997 kidnap thriller *Breakdown:*

It's a comment on the remarkably flea-bitten state of commercial American moviemaking that *Breakdown* was greeted by critics as a Great Film when it was released last May. It's not—it's a very, very Competent Film. But since such rudimentary skills as sentient plotting, intelligible dialogue, and coherent characterizations are apparently beyond Hollywood's grasp in the '90s, reviewers and audiences can be forgiven their enthusiasm.

Fact is, the studios used to churn out movies like this every other week back in the '40s—only then they called them B movies. The factory system specialized in engaging professionalism, and it's so shocking to see at this late date that if you caught *Breakdown* in a theater, you might have been tempted to drag out the Howard Hawks comparisons in regard to director-cowriter Jonathan Mostow.[2]

Even when a critic is more enthusiastic about a major studio production, similar reservations may arise. José Arroyo remarked of *Titanic:*

Arguably one of the best big-budget films of the past year, *Titanic* is certainly enjoyable. But it's impressive and depressing in about equal measure: it's of a quality Irwin Allen always aspired to and fell short of, for example, yet to be praising one of Hollywood's most imaginative and proficient filmmakers for having made a film better than *The Poseidon Adventure* or *The Towering Inferno* is to have lowered expectations into the realm of the tawdry and the absurd. In this sense *Titanic* is emblematic of the state of contemporary Hollywood film-making.[3]

Such comments point up the fact that the classical approach to narrative has not been replaced by a new model; it has just not been as well applied recently as it had been in years past.

One problem is that the big producers have actually increased the traditional redundancy of Hollywood narratives in order to compensate for a supposed short attention span among spectators. In reviewing *Washington Square* (1997), Richard Schickel commented on the heavy-handedness of the acting and suggested that the fault resulted from "the '90s notion, endemic among studio types, that audiences no longer have the patience to endure subtle, psychologically indirect interchanges between characters or delicate exfoliations of complex relationships."[4] It is perhaps even more disturbing that intelligent and educated people who would never read a trashy best-seller or listen to bubblegum pop music seem quite willing to watch teenage-oriented hits simply because a film's box-office success has been so thoroughly linked to its "importance" by the Hollywood publicity machine.

The prominence of the action genre has contributed to the formulaic, overblown quality of many recent films. I personally like films such as *Terminator 2: Judgment Day* and *The Hunt for Red October*. But there do not seem to *be* any films like *Terminator 2: Judgment Day* and *The Hunt for Red October* appearing in the late 1990s. Even fanzines oriented to the action genre have complained. In early 1998, *Cinescape* offered an intelligent analysis of the situation:

> At some point within the past few years, it became evident that the action genre's quality is sinking as quickly as Sandra Bullock's ship in *Speed 2: Cruise Control*. Gone are the suspense-filled thrills, memorable characters and infectious charm of *Die Hard*, the original *Speed*, *Raiders of the Lost Ark*, and the early James Bond films. In their place is a veritable army of mega-stupid mega-movies—loud, bloated ActionChaseExplodoRamas brimming with Unabomer-style subtlety and all the wit and character development of a Simon and Simon episode.[5]

And this from a journal which exists mainly to publicize new movies to fans.

There has been some suggestion that the plethora of screenwriting manuals and courses has begun to have a harmful effect, influencing the studios' methods of choosing or revising scripts (see Appendix B) and making narratives more formulaic. Art Linson, producer of *The Untouchables* and *Fast Times at Ridgemont High* (1982), ridicules executives (and writers) who depend upon rigid guidelines:

> I have sat in many meetings where an executive or a producer, right out of one of those colleges, would sound real smart, but what he was saying just wasn't important. It wasn't from the heart. It was a mechanical approach from a bad handbook. Rhetoric. It became more important to sound impressive than to help the script get better.
>
> This usually manifests itself in the "three-act talk," which seems to be a language everyone but me understands.

"The third act needs to be goosed." "Makes the first act funnier." "The second act is too long."[6]

There is even evidence that some screenplay authors may use the three-act formula as a way of manipulating studio script readers. Lew Hunter, who actually advises a very strict set of page numbers on which act breaks should fall, reveals that these apply only to the spec script, not to the finished film: "Ignore the actual third act film-running times, which reflect neither eleven nor sixty-four minutes. These numbers are 'selling draft' rather than 'shooting draft' page counts. These were the scripts that persuaded people to put down money. That's your goal for now and will keep you alive as a writer."[7] Similarly, a writer with a script in pre-production at a major Hollywood firm assured me that while it is necessary to pitch a film as if it conforms to Field's model, the writer can then create the actual script to suit him- or herself.

Remarkably, a group of people, almost none of whom have ever authored a major feature film, have propagated a set of guidelines that anxious producers and writers alike seem to have taken as inviolable formulas.[8] No doubt some of these scenario manuals are very useful in defining basic techniques of classical storytelling, but as I have suggested here, in the past Hollywood's approach has always been quite flexible—especially in comparison to today's rigid rules. One can only hope that the rising complaints and the occasional small-budget sleeper will eventually lead to a greater balance between the formulaic side of the classical cinema and its parallel quest for originality.

HAVE MAVERICKS AND INDEPENDENTS CREATED A POST-HOLLYWOOD CINEMA?

Critics and pundits, however, have already sought for signs of possible revivification of the American cinema through changes in its fundamental approach to storytelling. Such a renewal might come through foreign influence or through the success of modest, innovative films. At intervals through the history of Hollywood, films in an alternative style have been released in the American market without bringing about the collapse of the classical storytelling approach. In the 1920s a few prestigious German films caused a minor stir. Hollywood adopted German camera movement and hired famous stars like Emil Jannings and Pola Negri; somewhat later the studios, especially

Universal, copied Expressionistic set designs for atmospheric horror and crime films. After World War II, the realism of wartime documentaries and more naturalistic feature films from Italy led to increased location shooting in movies like *Call Northside 777* (1948). The playful techniques of the French New Wave also had some impact on Hollywood, though mainly as filtered through such English-language hits as *Tom Jones* (1963) and *A Hard Day's Night* (1964). In all cases, the Hollywood system has culled those techniques it found useful from each movement or trend, ignoring elements that are too challenging to the classical system.

More recently, commentators and critics have seized upon the relative commercial successes of a few maverick filmmakers as evidence that the Hollywood system is tottering and might give way to a more innovative, quirky approach. The general commercial rise of independent filmmaking in the 1990s has stimulated much hopeful speculation that the formulaic mainstream cinema is finally passing into a more personal, low-budget phase. I would argue that in fact the rise of "independents" has created a situation similar to that of the auteurist directors of the 1970s "movie brat" generation. Such filmmakers are not reforming Hollywood in any fundamental way, though they are having some influence on it. Rather, the mavericks and independents succeed to the extent that their films make money, and the mainstream longevity of any one filmmaker depends upon some adaptation to the Hollywood system. Consider briefly two films by the maverick directors most widely hailed as saviors of Hollywood.

David Lynch's *Blue Velvet* (1986), financed with a small budget by producer Dino De Laurentiis, made back a bit more than its cost. Quentin Tarantino's *Pulp Fiction* (1994) grossed over $200 million worldwide on an $8 million budget. Both films clearly are non-classical. For one thing, they linger over ambiguities. Indeed, in *Blue Velvet*, although Jeffrey seems to have the standard goal of solving a mystery (the cut-off ear), his motivation becomes increasingly cryptic, as Sandy notes: "I don't know if you're a detective or a pervert." Jeffrey replies: "Well, that's for me to know and you to find out." Much of the dialogue in both films, and especially in *Pulp Fiction*, exists to create atmosphere and explore the idiosyncratic characters rather than to further the story. *Blue Velvet* juxtaposes its bizarre and violent action with a caricatural small-town cheeriness. It even parodies classical devices, as when the coroner's grotesque dialogue hook, "It looks like the ear was cut off with scissors" is followed by a closeup of a pair of scissors cutting a plastic crime-scene tape. *Pulp Fiction* introduces a startling shift in temporal order without warning or motivation, and it brings its two main characters (played by Bruce

Willis and John Travolta) together only for one fleeting encounter in a bar before the long-delayed moment when one kills the other.

Yet these two films have had little influence on the form or style of Hollywood cinema. Lynch and Tarantino imitators have skimmed off the obvious traits of shocking sex and violence without picking up on the non-classical elements that made *Blue Velvet* and *Pulp Fiction* appeal to intellectuals as well as to teenage boys. At the moment, Lynch and Tarantino seem to be following paths similar to those of the auteurist directors of the 1970s. Lynch has pursued a route similar to that taken by Robert Altman and has achieved a cult status that is increasingly outside the mainstream of Hollywood, as the financial disaster of *Lost Highway* (1997) demonstrates; reportedly it cost $16 million and grossed well under $4 million.[9] After lengthy speculation on whether Tarantino could even direct another film after *Pulp Fiction*, *Jackie Brown* (1997) turned out to be a creditable blending of a classical-style narrative with his distinctive touches. The dialogue still rambles, but not so far afield as in *Pulp Fiction* or in directions so little integrated into the plot. The multiple repetitions of one scene toward the end are motivated by its obvious function of showing a crime from different characters' viewpoints, a convention with precedents in film noir. In sum, despite all the critical acclaim and fan excitement that films such as *Blue Velvet* and *Pulp Fiction* deservedly generate, they are blips on the radar screen when seen within the history of Hollywood.

The 1990s rise of the independent film is undoubtedly more significant. Established in 1984, Robert Redford's Sundance Film Festival has become an important venue for independent filmmakers to premiere and market their works; its later expansion into exhibition via the Sundance cable television channel undoubtedly brought independent film a higher profile.[10] Moreover, independently produced films became more commercially important during the 1990s. Art cinemas that had previously revived classic films and shown subtitled imports increasingly focused on acclaimed Sundance items like *Welcome to the Dollhouse* (Grand Jury Prize winner in 1996). This trend attracted widespread attention in early 1997 as a result of the widespread furor in the mainstream media over the fact that four of the five 1996 films nominated for best-picture Oscar were "independents." *Jerry Macguire*, the only big-studio nominee, lost to *The English Patient*, produced by Saul Zaentz (who also underwrote *Amadeus*). Was Hollywood about to be rendered irrelevant by outsider films replete with artistic integrity?

Not exactly. By August *Variety* was declaring that the independent phenomenon was declining:

But few observers expect a repeat of last year, when summer releases including "Lone Star," "Trainspotting," and "Emma" as well as fall pics like "Secrets & Lies" and "Big Night" turned critical acclaim into box office success.

That commercial success—which some see as a fluke, others as a cyclical peak—along with copious Oscar noms, inspired the consumer press to dub 1996 "The Year of the Independents."

It also strengthened the resolve of two studios to stake their claim in the specialized arena: Witness Universal's acquisition of October Films and Paramount's ongoing search for an arthouse guru to run its classics division.

But so far, this year has offered specialized distribbers—whether they be well-heeled studio divisions or struggling indies—little to cheer about. Recent casualties include Fox Searchlight's "Star Maps" and Trimark's "Box of Moonlight."[11]

By early 1998, the popular press was widely discussing the ironic contrast between the 1996 "independent" Oscar race and *Titanic*'s record-tying fourteen nominations.

As some commentators had pointed out all along, the reason for the success of the independent films was not so much that they were taking over Hollywood as that Hollywood was taking them over. The mainstream industry had noted that some independent films were quite successful. Hollywood could profit from skimming off the most promising films and marketing them to that segment of the audience interested in slightly offbeat fare. They could also sign promising young independent filmmakers to create more standard movies. Even the Sundance Institute has fairly close ties to the Hollywood establishment, as the organization of its Screenwriters Laboratory indicates. Screenwriters, mostly beginners, come to the Institute in Utah for intensive artistic sessions where they can discuss their work with established screenwriters—usually mainstream authors who clearly enjoy the experience of encountering more personal, offbeat work. Yet an eyewitness account of such a laboratory suggests that few of the scripts are radically removed from the commercially acceptable norms and that writers with a more experimental bent may be guided in more conventional directions.[12]

Such tendencies are reflected in the ambiguity of the term "independent." In recent years the big Hollywood companies have purchased some of the key independent distributors, which are now subsidiary firms. Disney purchased Miramax in 1993, while Universal acquired a majority interest in October

Films in 1997. Fine Line is the art-house distribution wing of New Line.[13] As Robert Redford, creator of Sundance, declared: "The majors have always been predatory. They'll scoop up anything they can if they think they can make money with it. It's only recently that independent films suddenly showed a side that Hollywood felt they could make money off of, so they're now buying up these companies."[14] During 1997, several companies, including Sundance in association with General Cinemas, were building or refurbishing chains of art houses.[15] By early 1998, *Variety* reported that many truly independent films with multi-million-dollar budgets produced without a prior deal with an American distributor were finding no takers.[16]

Unquestionably, the big Hollywood-owned distributors were still buying high-profile independent films for distribution. At the 1997 Toronto Film Festival, executives from Miramax and October left in the middle of the screening of Robert Duvall's *The Apostle*, keeping in touch with their representatives in the auditorium via cell phone as they bid against each other for the distribution rights. October won with a $6 million bid for a film made on a $5 million budget.[17] The 1998 Sundance Film Festival saw similar fees paid for its top films.[18] More typical bids, however, range below $3 million. *Pulp Fiction* aside, the grosses on such independent films, while often representing a profit in relation to their small budgets, are tiny in comparison with the mainstream hits.

Indeed, quite often the big firms do not buy low-budget independents because they expect them to be profitable. Rather, they wish to sign up a talented first-time director. Distributors' representatives at the 1998 Sundance Film Festival were quite candid about this, including Miramax's Mark Gill:

> "The main reason to be in on these deals is to get the filmmakers' next films." Similarly, LIVE Entertainment deflected criticism of its purchase of the quirky π by describing the expenditure as a long-term investment to director Darren Aronofsky that cost "a fraction of $1 million." Says LIVE president Amir Malin, "He has the goods to become a great filmmaker."[19]

Given the huge scale of Hollywood budgets for mainstream films, such expenditures are quite small.

In such an environment, what can the term "independent" mean? In early 1998 the journal *FilmMaker*, aimed at independent filmmakers, editorialized on what it meant to apply that term indiscriminately to aspiring mainstream

Sundance directors and politically and/or experimentally inclined filmmakers who would never touch a Hollywood contract.[20] At the same time, *Variety* mused on a parallel star system that was emerging to support independent filmmaking:

> Pity the poor indie film director. His debut feature that he financed by maxing out his credit cards nabbed honors at Sundance and played for a week at the local multiplex. But his auteur days are numbered.
>
> He's going to have to cast an ensemble of recognizable names in his sophomore effort if he wants to raise money from conventional sources. As the cost of P[rints] & A[dvertising] rises, fewer banks are willing to gamble on a film—regardless of its budget—unless its cast offers marquee value.
>
> While helmers at the studios must adjust their films (and schedules) to accommodate Tom Cruise, Mel Gibson or Demi Moore, their indie counterparts are learning to live with the demands of "boutique casting."
>
> Besides such independent icons as Harvey Keitel, Lili Taylor, John Turturro, Rosie Perez, Steve Buscemi and Parker Posey, the talent pool for low-budget films includes models, aging rockers, former A-list stars looking to re-invent themselves the way John Travolta did in "Pulp Fiction," and TV sit-com regulars trying to make the jump to the big screen. Foreign stars such as Julie Delpy and Stellan Skarsgard can help guarantee pre-sales in key overseas territories.[21]

In short, the commercial end of the "independent" spectrum essentially represents a source of additional profits and upcoming talent for the big Hollywood firms.

THE NOTION OF POST-CLASSICAL CINEMA

In the opening chapter, I suggested that the primary traits ascribed to "post-classical" filmmaking are the breakdown of coherent plot development and character traits by the increasing dominance of spectacular action and special effects. My analyses of representative films have shown that this breakdown is far from widespread. Why then have a number of critics and historians come to believe that narrative has fallen apart?

The most common explanation given for the rise of "post-classicism" is an assumed "fragmentation" of audiences since the Divorcement Decrees of the late 1940s. Faced with unpredictable returns and the pivotal role of the youth audience, Hollywood has used increasingly varied means to attract spectators for both theatrical and video presentations. Thomas Schatz's summary of the Hollywood industry since World War II, "The New Hollywood," is widely quoted in this context. He claims: "It has become virtually impossible to identify or isolate the 'text' itself or to distinguish a film's aesthetic or narrative quality from its commercial imperatives." He credits a "blockbuster mentality" with giving rise to "fragmented" films, especially in "high-cost, high-tech, high-stakes blockbusters," and declares that "this emphasis on plot over character makes a significant departure from classical Hollywood films."[22] In the recent anthology *Contemporary Hollywood Cinema*, a number of the authors pick up on the notion that a fragmented audience appeal produces equally fragmented narratives. Richard Maltby states: "In this New Hollywood the major companies, acting primarily as financiers and distributors, have gradually come to terms with a fragmentation of the audience, a concern with ideas of demographics and target audiences derived from market research, globalized markets and new delivery systems."[23] Scriptwriter/producer James Schamus elaborates on the same idea:

> The supposed "identity" of the filmic text comes increasingly under the dissolving pressures of its various revenue streams. Do *Volcano* (1997), *Mission Impossible* (1996) or *ID4* [*Independence Day*] (1996) need "classical Hollywood" narrative construction, when it is precisely the fragmentation of their narratives into soundtrack albums, somatic theme-park jolts, iconic emblems stuck on T-shirts, and continuous loops of home entertainment that are really what is being sold? I don't think so.[24]

These assumptions are also tied in with Justin Wyatt's emphasis on "high concept," which I have discussed in Chapters 1 and 5 and which is also seen as impinging on traditional narrative coherence.

There is a slippage in logic in the application of the notion of "fragmentation" in this context. The old monolithic family audience of the pre-Divorcement days never really existed, given that boys and men tended to go to action matinees, that studios categorized certain films as "women's pictures," and so on. But assuming the audience did break up into a greater number of "niches" beginning in the 1950s, that is one sort of "fragmentation." The idea of a narrative being comparably fragmented, however, is quite a different thing, perhaps more metaphorical. So far no argument has been bolstered with historical evidence to show that a product being marketed in a greater variety of ways to different audiences should itself fall apart as a result. Indeed, one model of car can be marketed to college kids and to young professionals using different ads, but the individual vehicles do not cease to run as a result. Selling a song on a soundtrack album does not "fragment" it like a jigsaw-puzzle piece out of its original narrative function within the film. And the possibility that a family member might someday slip away to the refrigerator during a video viewing at home does not imply that he or she will cheerfully accept plot holes during a viewing of the same movie in a theater.

One might claim that the notion of the blockbuster that appeals to a wide variety of audiences causes creative strains, forcing scriptwriters into longer and more convoluted pre-production processes that create fragmentation. Yet such a claim would necessitate case studies comparing the creative processes behind a set of spectacle films with sloppy narrative structures to those of a set of tightly plotted films. I do not believe that truly representative films could be found to support such a claim. Indeed, as we have seen with *Tootsie* (and *Casablanca*), lengthy development periods involving dueling writers can still result in unified, complex films. The very fact that classical standards have endured in most well-made, well-regarded films despite the pressures of the need to appeal to niche audiences strongly suggests that the classical paradigm remains robust.

The issue of fragmentation is largely illusory for at least three reasons. First, planning for a set of niche audiences can be done in quite a systematic way. Just because Hollywood cannot predict how successful any one film will be does not mean that it has no effective guidelines for minimizing its risks. This is how large businesses work.

Second, one could argue, as my coauthors and I did in *The Classical Hollywood Cinema*, that the mode of production is a key buttress of narrative form. Note that the mode of production does not equal "the film industry" or its conglomerate identity. Hollywood's mode of production has not changed all that much since the studio days. Although personnel are now usually hired on a film-by-film basis rather than kept under long-term contract, they still are fitted into the same basic division of labor used in the studio era. The tasks of the various filmmakers are still coordinated from development to post-production via the use of a numbered continuity script used as a blueprint. The many people who work together on Hollywood films still share a set of craft assumptions inherited from older generations; indeed, these are now explicitly taught in film schools. (The main difference is that many more of these workers now receive on-screen credit.)

Third, considerable evidence suggests that recent popular cinema, including Hollywood's blockbusters, appeals to a quite homogeneous audience.

Peter Kramer has argued convincingly that many of the biggest box-office successes of all time (all of which have come in the 1970s and after) are precisely those that appeal to a wide age range. He terms these "family adventure" films and sees them as a revival of the family-oriented films of the 1930s and 1940s. He cites *E.T.*, *Jurassic Park*, *Forrest Gump*, *Star Wars*, *The Lion King*, *Mrs. Doubtfire*, *Aladdin*, *Back to the Future*, and *Terminator 2* as examples.[25] The fact that enormous numbers of people from ten-year-olds up to senior citizens attended *Titanic*, often several times each, seems to bolster Kramer's claim. Few of these films would attract children much under ten, but films appropriate primarily to young children have always been exceptional. (During the early 1930s, when my mother was about ten, her favorite movie star was Harpo Marx.)

Beyond this wide age-span in the audience, Hollywood's geographic appeal has expanded enormously during the 1990s, following the disintegration of the Soviet Union and the economic reformations in China. Far from being made for local niche audiences, most of Hollywood's biggest films are increasingly aimed at the largest, broadest international market.[26] Such films appeal in the most unlikely places. For example, although American culture is officially banned in Iran, a bootleg market for Hollywood videos flourishes there. According to the *Washington Post*, "Noushabeh Amiri, an Oxford-educated journalist who edits an Iranian film magazine, attributes part of the fascination with American movies to Hollywood special-effects wizardry. 'You have great techology,' she says, citing Steven Spielberg's 'Jurassic Park' as an example. 'You make dreams, and those dreams can be understood anywhere.'"[27] Note that Ms Amiri stresses not the spectacle in Hollywood films but their comprehensibility.

Could "fragmented" Hollywood films appeal to audiences even in countries such as Iran, which nominally have cultures totally opposed to U.S. values? The fact that such films are so easily comprehensible makes them more accessible. One need only imagine young Americans watching French films, Iranian films, and so on, to grasp the astonishing appeal of American movies. The films of countries like France or Iran are, for better or worse, the niche-audience product. And that does not make them disunified, as the beautiful, intricate films of Abbas Kiarostami demonstrate.

Why has the notion of fragmented, incoherent, spectacle- and action-laden films taken such hold in academia recently? For one thing, most commentators have too quickly equated all of Hollywood cinema with its blockbusters. Most films made in any given year are medium-budget comedies, romances, action pictures, and children's fare. As the foregoing chapters indicate, such genres tend to be built on principles of classical construction. Even if special-effects extravaganzas were as fragmentary as critics claim, they would not constitute the norm.

In fact, the claims of fragmentary construction do not hold up well with respect to blockbusters either. Rather than accepting loose generalities about plot being more important than character or action reducing psychology to incoherence, we should scrutinize the big-budget hits in detail. I know of no case where a critic has shown through a close analysis that *Batman* (1989) or *Jurassic Park* or *Speed* is merely an assemblage of fragmentary scenes. In fact these films have highly wrought plots, full of conflict, goal-orientation, long-term mysteries, dangling causes, and surprising twists. My short analyses of *Jaws* and *Terminator 2* in Chapter 1 and the longer ones of *The Hunt for Red October* and *Alien* (surely blockbusters by any standards) show them to be just as coherent as the other films discussed in this book.

Granted, Hollywood has always explored a spectrum ranging from mildly episodic forms (such as the musical and the slapstick comedy) to tightly woven ones (such as the classic mystery or suspense films). And occasionally we find contemporary films which are fairly episodic, but these seem to me actually quite rare. There are undoubtedly relatively incoherent blockbusters (such as *Stargate*, 1994), but these are not part of some systematic new practice. As I have emphasized earlier, such films have narrative problems as measured by modern Hollywood's own standards.

Thus Schamus's suggestion that blockbusters like *Mission Impossible* (1996) and *Independence Day* (1996) have "fragmented into" lines of merchandising does not logically entail that the films have as a result somehow become fragmentary in their storytelling. *Mission Impossible* is a characteristic spy film: it alternates suspenseful undercover operations with games of hidden identity and double-bluff. *Independence Day* is a highly linear, fairly unoriginal science fiction invasion movie with a plot that children can easily follow. True, there are slips of causality (most notoriously, how could Jeff Goldblum's character patch his Apple laptop into the alien ship's mainframe?), but these pose little threat to the overall flow of goal-orientation, cause-and-effect, and motivic unity. Schamus's description makes it sound as if such films have literally splintered into soundtrack albums, T-shirts, and "continuous loops of home entertainment" (whatever that may be). Set all those ancillary markets and products aside, however, and the film experience itself involves a remarkably coherent narrative. Those who believe otherwise must confront the burden of proof.

Historians who posit the decline of narrative and character in modern Hollywood might also do well to read popular and trade reviews of films. These almost invariably talk about plot and character more than about spectacle. Where special effects draw heavy attention, the result is not always positive; reviews of the box-office disappointment *Starship Troopers* (1997) were full of charges that the overwhelming special effects had rendered the characters mere ciphers. In the summer of 1998, reviewers often complained that *Godzilla* lacked interesting characters comparable to those in *Independence Day*. *Variety*'s reviewing formula usually involves devoting most of its space to narrative and character, with relatively brief attention to design elements at the end.

The enormous success of *Titanic* led to some revealing attempts to fathom its appeal. One newspaper story focused on repeat viewership. A 23-year-old computer librarian summed up the typical view that the Kate Winslet and Leonardo DiCaprio characters were the key draw: "Fifteen hundred people drowning can't be experienced emotionally. It's too much. But through two people you can absorb it. It's an emotional window." An industry commentator described why adults as well as teenagers were returning to see it over and over:

> There have been other movies that have attracted adults who go back again, something like "Sleepless in Seattle." But "Titanic" is different. It has a romance that's geared to the ladies, but it also has all these other elements that give it an appeal to young and old.
>
> You've got Leonardo DiCaprio and Kate Winslet, and you've got Gloria Stuart (a 1930s film star now 87 years old). And then you've got the spectacle and effects for the science-fiction crowd.

Thus niche audiences such as "the science-fiction crowd" (interestingly, the main group assumed to be fixated on special-effects spectacle) unite in the cliché of studio-era publicity: "an appeal to young and old." *Titanic*'s producer, Jon Landau, explicitly stated that spectacle does *not* overwhelm the central plotlines even in epic films: "Basically it's these two characters. People didn't go to 'Gone With the Wind' to watch Atlanta burn. They went for Scarlett and Rhett, who are lovers at the center of big events and a larger tapestry."[28] Simple common sense would suggest that there is much truth to such claims. Even actual spectators, part of the supposedly fragmented audience, seem to agree. One reader of *Entertainment Weekly* responded thus to an article on *Titanic*'s success:

> Hollywood, please take the hint: Don't underestimate your audience. We're not impressed by the blow-up-in-your-face effects, pointless story lines, and flaky characters. We can handle complex story lines and deep, interesting characters. In fact, we love them! *Titanic* is so successful because it had a well-written, well-paced plot with moving characters.[29]

Such a request suggests that the classical aspects of Hollywood cinema still hold enormous appeal.

There is also evidence that the action-packed special-effects film may have been one of Hollywood's usual cycles rather than a new approach that has permanently replaced classicism. Sketching the history of the "event" film, *Variety*'s Leonard Klady suggested that 1989 was the year of the "seminal summer" that made blockbusters a warm-weather phenomenon. By 1995, there were twelve such event films in one summer. And by 1996, some industry commentators seem to have reluctantly concluded that the summer season at least was doomed to be dominated by mindless action films.[30]

Yet by 1998, a reversal of this trend was widely trumpeted. While the production cost of the five top-grossing films released in the first six months of 1998 had jumped a remarkable 75 percent over the comparable figures from 1997, the overall domestic box office for the same period had risen only 8 percent (and the average gross for films in wide release had actually fallen 11 percent).[31] In that year, only three or four summer releases could count as "tent-pole" or event films—and only one of them, *Lethal Weapon 4*, was a sequel. The average negative cost for Hollywood films in general had risen by 34 percent to $53.4 million.[32] Extensive special effects, mostly in the form of computer-generated shots, were not only driving up direct costs but were causing many films to miss their scheduled opening dates, thus shortening runs and adding interest to production loans. For example, the Robin Williams star vehicle, *What Dreams May Come* (1998), was delayed from the summer to the fall.[33] Director Richard Donner and the stars interviewed on television to publicize *Lethal Weapon 4* stressed the fact that the film was finished on schedule because all of the car crashes, explosions, and other stunts were actually executed rather than created through special effects.

The biggest 1998 event films, *Armageddon* and *Godzilla*, both made a great deal of money, but not as much as was expected. The success of such fare as *The Truman Show* and *Saving Private Ryan*, films of types not usually associated with the summer season, caused much comment. *Godzilla* came in for considerable derision as a result of its publicity slogan, "Size does matter." Before its release, *Variety* cautiously noted, "The general consensus is that 'Godzilla' delivers top-notch special effects and non-stop action, but some complain it lacks such niceties as emotion, humor and convincing characters."[34] Once the film had opened, *Variety* ridiculed it for its use of the tactic that most historians argue is the cornerstone of all "post-classical" Hollywood filmmaking—excessive merchandising tie-ins: "To many, 'Godzilla' has become the ultimate example of a marketing campaign in search of a movie. The movie was seemingly made, not to entertain audiences, but to help sell tacos and T-shirts."[35] Fittingly, one wag at Lucasfilm (a bastion of classical filmmaking) posted a message on the *Star Wars* Web site, designed to publicize the upcoming prequels to the original trilogy: "Plot Does Matter."[36]

By July, *Variety* noted that many of the successful films were remarkably old-fashioned: not only *Lethal Weapon 4*, but also the remakes of *The Mask of Zorro* and *Dr. Dolittle*, the slapstick comedy *There's Something About Mary*, and the war film *Saving Private Ryan*. It declared: "Indeed, all the movies on the 'retro slate' have been received warmly by critics and audiences alike. It's almost as if moviegoers want to end the 'tyranny of the techies.'"[37] As the 1998 summer wound toward its end, *Variety* commented:

> After years of hand-wringing over summer blockbusters' apparent disregard for plot, character development, and innovation, industry critics should be upbeat about the past three months at the box office. . . . Though some execs claim the more challenging films represent a conscious aesthetic decision, Hollywood may simply have discovered that plotless, effects-driven thrill rides can't be counted on to attract a large enough audience to justify their enormous production costs. . . . In fact, the summer B.O. results follow a trend that began during the 1997 holiday season, when character- and story-driven features such as "As Good as It Gets" and "Good Will Hunting" outperformed seemingly more commercial fare.[38]

Hollywood will undoubtedly go through its customary cycles of genres and will continue to agonize over the question of whether big-budget films are more profitable than modest sleepers. That's what the industry did in the late 1960s, too, when big-budget musicals like the first *Doctor Dolittle* failed.

I do not wish to be an apologist for the Hollywood film industry. In recent years it has indeed displayed serious problems, and these are not going to disappear with a few successful plot- and character-driven films. More important, there is no doubt that Hollywood has increasingly dominated world markets, which means that many alternative sorts of filmmaking are confined to the festival circuit. The unquestionable result is that the few and precious filmic masterpieces that are made today are accessible only to a tiny audience. Still, there is much to be valued in the Hollywood system. The best examples are complex and well-crafted. If the classical storytelling system is still with us, then the successes of that system's past suggest that there is hope for improvement in the future. Moreover, the international cinema in general has lost much of the heady excitement of the "new waves" and other trends of the era from the 1950s to the 1970s. In recent years, more than ever, we need good cinema wherever we can find it, and Hollywood continues to be one of its main sources.

Appendixes

Notes

Index

APPENDIX A

Large-Scale Portions of
Classical Films

Credits and end titles of less than a quarter of a minute are not listed.

* indicates a film with three large-scale parts, ** a film with five large-scale parts.

All silent films were watched on videotape, where the projection speeds could not be determined precisely. I have noted cases where a film meant to be projected at 16 or 18 frames per second (fps) was clearly recorded at 24 fps. Whatever the speed, the proportionate times among the large-scale parts would not be affected.

1910s (films for this decade rounded off to nearest minute)

* *Alias Jimmy Valentine* (1915): Running time, 65 minutes; setup, 17; complicating action, 27; climax, 19 (epilogue missing).

* *The Avenging Conscience* (1914): Running time, 56 minutes; setup, 20; complicating action, 19; climax and epilogue, 20 (epilogue alone, 2).

* *Civilization* (1916): Running time, 85.5 minutes (not counting modern replacement credits); setup, 28.5; complicating action, 32; climax and epilogue, 25 (epilogue alone, 5).

The Italian (1915): Running time, 60 minutes (at 24 fps); setup, 15; complicating action, 14; development, 16; climax and epilogue, 15 (epilogue alone, .5).

Male and Female (1919): Running time, 94 minutes; setup, 21; complicating action, 26; development, 30; climax and epilogue, 19 (epilogue alone, 2).

* *Regeneration* (1915): Running time, 61 minutes; setup, 19; complicating action, 19; climax and epilogue, 34 (epilogue alone, .5).

The Social Secretary (1916): Running time, 62 minutes; setup, 14; complicating action, 15; development, 18; climax, 14 (brief epilogue).

* *Traffic in Souls* (1913): Running time, 71 minutes; setup, 23; complicating action, 25; climax and epilogue, 23 (epilogue alone, 4).

* *The Wishing Ring* (1914): Running time, 45 minutes (at 24 fps); setup, 17; complicating action, 12; climax and epilogue, 16 (epilogue alone, 1).

Young Romance (1915): Running time, 58 minutes; credits, 1; setup, 13.5; complicating action, 13.5; development, 15.5; climax and epilogue, 15.5 (epilogue alone, 1).

1920s

The Big Parade (1925): Running time, 136 minutes; credits, 1.5; setup, 40; complicating action, 31.5; development, 35; climax and epilogue, 27.5 (epilogue alone, 3).

Flesh and the Devil (1927): Running time, 111.5 minutes; credits, 1.5; setup, 29; complicating action, 25.5; development, 34.5; climax, 21.5 (no epilogue).

* *Girl Shy* (1924; the Thames Television unabridged version): Running time, 87.5 minutes; credits, 1; setup, 30; complicating action, 32.5; climax, 24.5 (no epilogue).

The Mark of Zorro (1920): Running time, 89 minutes; credits, 1; setup, 22; complicating action, 23.5; development, 22; climax and epilogue, 22 (epilogue alone, 2.5).

* *Miss Lulu Bett* (1921): Running time, 64 minutes; setup, 22; complicating action, 23; climax and epilogue, 20 (epilogue alone, 1).

* *Our Hospitality* (1923): Running time, 72 minutes; credits, 1.5; setup, 25.5; development, 22; climax and epilogue, 24.5 (epilogue alone, 1.5).

The Phantom of the Opera (1925): Running time, 114 minutes; credits, 1; setup, 22.5; complicating action, 34.5; development, 27.5; climax and epilogue, 28 (epilogue alone, .5); end credits, .5.

7th Heaven (1927): Running time, 115.5 minutes (not counting modern replacement credits); setup, 29.5; complicating action, 26.5; development, 35.5; climax and epilogue, 24 (epilogue alone, 1.5).

Tramp, Tramp, Tramp (1926): Running time, 61.5 minutes; credits, .5; setup,

15.5; complicating action, 18; development, 13.5; climax and epilogue, 14 (epilogue alone, 2).

Wings (1927): Running time, 138.5 minutes; credits, 2; setup, 33; complicating action, 29.5; development, 37; climax and epilogue, 37 (epilogue alone, 8).

1930s

* *The Bat Whispers* (1930): Running time, 84 minutes; credits, 1.5; setup, 30; development, 26.5; climax and epilogue, 26.5 (epilogue alone, 2); end title, .5.

Grand Hotel (1932): Running time, 113 minutes; credits, 1.5; setup, 24; complicating action, 32; development, 27.5; climax and epilogue, 27 (epilogue alone, 2.5).

The Mummy (1932): Running time, 72 minutes; credits, 1; setup, 17.5; complicating action, 19.5; development, 17; climax, 17.5 (no epilogue); end credits, .5.

A Night at the Opera (1935): Running time, 87 minutes; credits, 1; setup, 19.5; complicating action, 33.5; development, 16.5; climax and epilogue, 18.5 (epilogue alone, .5).

The Prisoner of Zenda (1937): Running time, 101 minutes; credits, 2; setup, 23; complicating action, 22; development, 29; climax and epilogue, 24.5 (epilogue alone, 1).

Queen Christina (1933): Running time, 97 minutes; credits, 1; setup, 23.5; complicating action, 27.5; development, 24; climax and epilogue, 23 (epilogue alone, 1.5).

Stagecoach (1939): Running time, 96 minutes; credits, 1; setup, 21; complicating action, 24; development, 21.5; climax and epilogue, 26 (epilogue, 2.5).

The Thin Man (1934): Running time, 88.5 minutes; credits, 1; setup, 21; complicating action, 22; development, 26; climax and epilogue, 18.5 (epilogue alone, 2).

Top Hat (1935): Running time, 97 minutes; credits, 1.5; setup, 26; complicating action, 23; development, 26; climax and epilogue, 22 (epilogue alone, .5).

You Can't Take It With You (1938): Running time, 125.5 minutes; credits, 1; setup, 27; complicating action, 31.5; development, 39.5; climax and epilogue, 26 (epilogue alone, 1); end credits, .5.

1940s

* *Adam's Rib* (1949): Running time, 101 minutes; credits, 1.5; setup, 31.5; development, 35; climax and epilogue, 33 (epilogue alone, 3.5); end credits, .5.

Casablanca (1942): Running time, 102 minutes; credits, 1; setup, 24; complicating action, 26.5; development, 24.5; climax and epilogue, 27 (epilogue alone, 1.5).

Citizen Kane (1941): Running time, 119 minutes; title, 20 seconds; setup, 29; complicating action, 41; development, 27.5; climax and epilogue, 19 (epilogue alone, 47 seconds); end credits, 2.

The Ghost and Mrs. Muir (1947): Running time, 104 minutes; credits, 1; setup, 28; complicating action, 28; development, 27; climax and epilogue, 20 (epilogue alone, 1).

His Girl Friday (1940): Running time, 92 minutes; credits, 1; setup, 23.5; complicating action, 22.5; development, 22; climax and epilogue, 23 (epilogue alone, .5).

The Lady Eve (1941): Running time, 94 minutes; credits, 1.5; setup, 23, complicating action, 26.5; development, 22; climax and epilogue, 20.5 (epilogue alone, 16 seconds); end credits, .5.

The Little Foxes (1941): Running time, 116 minutes; credits, 1; setup, 27; complicating action, 33.5; development, 24; climax and epilogue, 30.5 (epilogue alone, 1); end credits, .5.

Out of the Past (1947): Running time, 97 minutes; credits, 1.5; setup, 23.5; complicating action, 22; development, 25.5; climax and epilogue, 24 (epilogue alone, 2); end credits, .5.

The Shop Around the Corner (1940): Running time, 97 minutes; credits, 1; setup, 17.5; complicating action, 31.5; development, 21.5; climax, 27.5 (no epilogue).

T-Men (1947): Running time, 92 minutes; credits, 1.5; setup, 20; complicating action, 25; development, 27; climax, 18.5 (no epilogue); end credits, .5.

1950s

* *The Big Heat* (1953): Running Time, 89.5 minutes; credits, 1; setup, 35; development, 26; climax and epilogue, 27.5 (epilogue alone, 1).

The Egyptian (1954): Running time, 140 minutes; credits, 1.5; setup, 33.5; complicating action, 41.5; development, 38; climax and epilogue, 25.5 (epilogue alone, 1.5).

In a Lonely Place (1950): Running time, 92.5 minutes; credits, 1; setup, 23; complicating action, 16.5; development, 26.5; climax, 26 (no epilogue).

Invasion of the Body Snatchers (1956): Running time, 80 minutes; credits, 1.5; setup, 23; complicating action, 18.5; development, 17.5; climax, 20 (no epilogue).

Journey to the Center of the Earth (1959): Running time, 129 minutes; credits, 2; setup, 34; complicating action, 32; development, 35; climax and epilogue, 26.5 (epilogue alone, 4.5).

Land of the Pharaohs (1955): Running time, 103.5 minutes; credits, 1.5; setup, 25; complicating action, 25; development, 29.5; climax and epilogue, 22.5 (epilogue alone, 1).

The Pajama Game (1957): Running time, 102 minutes; setup, 25.5; complicating action, 27.5; development, 22.5; climax and epilogue, 26 (epilogue alone, 2).

River of No Return (1954): Running time, 91 minutes; setup, 17; complicating action, 26; development, 29; climax and epilogue, 19 (epilogue alone, 20 seconds).

Some Like It Hot (1959): Running time, 120 minutes; credits, 1.5; setup, 27.5; complicating action, 30; development 29; climax, 32 (no epilogue).

The Wrong Man (1957): Running time, 105 minutes; prologue and credits, 4; setup, 21; complicating action, 35; development, 24; climax and epilogue, 25.5 (epilogue alone, .5).

1960s

Bells Are Ringing (1960): Running time, 125.5 minutes; credits, 2; setup, 28.5; complicating action, 43; development, 36.5; climax and epilogue, 16 (epilogue alone, 2).

Butch Cassidy and the Sundance Kid (1969): Running time, 110 minutes; credits, 3; setup, 28.5; complicating action, 29.5; development, 33; climax and epilogue, 16 (epilogue alone, .5); end credits, .5.

Dr. Strangelove (1964): Running time, 94.5 minutes; crawl title, .5; setup, 22 (including pre-credits and credits); complicating action, 21.5; development, 20; climax and epilogue, 29 (epilogue alone, 1.5).

The Graduate (1967): Running time, 106.5 minutes; setup, 24.5; complicating action, 30; development, 18.5; climax and epilogue, 33.5 (epilogue alone, 1.5).

The Miracle Worker (1962): Running time, 109.5 minutes; credits, 2.5; setup (including pre-credits prologue), 27.5; complicating action, 33; development, 27; climax and epilogue, 17 (epilogue alone, 2).

* *The Pink Panther* (1964): Running time, 114.5 minutes; credits, 3.5; setup (including pre-credits prologue), 52.5; complicating action, 31; climax and epilogue, 27.5 (epilogue alone, 2.5).

* *The Producers* (1968): Running time, 89 minutes; setup, 26; development, 31.5; climax and epilogue, 32 (epilogue alone, 3).

** *The Sound of Music* (1965): Running time, 172.5 minutes; setup (including pre-credits and credits), 35; complicating action, 43; first development, 25.5; second development, 34.5; climax and epilogue, 35 (epilogue alone, 1), end credits, .5.

To Kill a Mockingbird (1962): Running time, 128.5 minutes; credits, 3; setup, 29.5; complicating action, 34.5; development, 31.5; climax and epilogue, 30 (epilogue alone, 4).

What Ever Happened to Baby Jane? (1962): Running time, 132 minutes; credits, 2; setup, 33 (including pre-credits portion); complicating action, 33; development, 33.5; climax, 34 (no epilogue).

1970s

* *Assault on Precinct 130* (1976): Running time, 91.5 minutes; credits, 2.5; setup, 29.5; development, 30; climax and epilogue, 28 (epilogue alone, 2); end credits, 1.

The China Syndrome (1979): Running time, 121.5 minutes; setup, 30 (including pre-credits and credits); complicating action, 31.5; development, 29; climax, 28.5 (no epilogue); end credits, 3.

Chinatown (1974): Running time, 130.5 minutes; credits, 2; setup, 29; complicating action, 35.5; development, 37; climax and epilogue, 27 (epilogue alone, including credits, 2).

Deliverance (1972): Running time, 109 minutes; setup, 32.5; complicating action, 24.5; development, 26; climax and epilogue, 26.5 (epilogue alone, including end credits, 3).

The French Connection (1971): Running time, 103.5; credits, 1; setup, 30; complicating action, 24; development, 22.5; climax and epilogue, 25.5 (epilogue alone, 1); end credits, .5.

** *The Godfather* (1972): Running time, 171 minutes; title, .5; setup, 35; complicating action, 34.5; first development, 27; second development, 42.5; climax, 33.5 (no epilogue); end credits, 2.5.

Klute (1971): Running time, 113.5 minutes; setup, 29.5; complicating action, 29; development, 30; climax and epilogue, 24.5 (epilogue alone, 2); end credits, l5.

The Poseidon Adventure (1972): Running time, 117 minutes; setup, 30; complicating action, 26; development, 32.5; climax 26.5 (no epilogue); end credits, 1.5.

Semi-Tough (1977): Running time, 107 minutes; setup, 35; complicating action, 19; development, 27; climax and epilogue, 26.5 (epilogue alone, including end credits, 3.5).

Three Days of the Condor (1975): Running time, 117 minutes; setup, 32; complicating action, 28; development, 28.5; climax, 28 (no epilogue); end credits, .5.

1980s

The Big Chill (1983) Running time, 105 minutes; setup, 28; complicating action, 24.5; development, 25.5; climax and epilogue, 24 (epilogue alone, 4); end credits, 3.

The Dead Zone (1983): Running time, 103 minutes; credits, 3; setup, 23; complicating action, 29; development, 26.5; climax and epilogue, 18.5 (epilogue alone, 1); end credits, 3.

The Elephant Man (1980): Running time, 123 minutes; credits, 1.5; setup, 29.5; complicating action, 33; development, 30.5; climax and epilogue, 25.5 (epilogue alone, 7); end credits, 2.5.

The King of Comedy (1983): Running time, 109 minutes; credits, 2.5; setup (including pre-credits prologue), 29.5; complicating action, 29; development, 23.5; climax, 19 (no epilogue); end credits, 4.

Nine to Five (1980): Running time, 109 minutes; credits, 2.5; setup, 28.5; complicating action, 26; development, 23.5; climax and epilogue, 26.5 (epilogue alone, 1.5); end credits, 2.

Scrooged (1988): Running time, 100.5 minutes; setup, 24.5; complicating action, 26.5; development, 22; climax and epilogue, 20.5 (epilogue alone, 2); end credits, 5.5.

Somewhere in Time (1980): Running time, 103 minutes; setup, 25.5; complicating action, 21; development, 28; climax, 25 (no epilogue); end credits, 3.

The Untouchables (1987): Running time, 119 minutes; credits, 2.5; setup, 31; complicating action, 28.5; development, 29.5; climax and epilogue, 26 (epilogue alone, 4); end credits, 3.5.

* *When Harry Met Sally* (1989): Running time, 95 minutes; credits, 2; setup, 32.5; development, 32.5; climax and epilogue, 25 (epilogue alone, 1); end credits, 3.5.

Witness (1985): Running time, 112 minutes; credits, 2; setup, 27; complicating action, 27.5; development, 26.5; climax and epilogue, 26.5 (epilogue alone, 4.5); end credits, 3.

1990s

The Bodyguard (1992): Running time, 129 minutes; setup, 31.5; complicating action, 29; development, 31; climax and epilogue, 38.5 (epilogue alone, 6); end credits, 4.5.

Demolition Man (1993): Running time, 114.5 minutes; setup, 32.5; complicating action, 31; development, 18; climax and epilogue, 29.5 (epilogue alone, 2); end credits, 5.5.

Edward Scissorhands (1990): Running time, 105 minutes; credits, 2.5; setup, 21; complicating action, 24; development, 24; climax and epilogue, 28 (epilogue alone, 3); end credits, 5.

Falling Down (1993): Running time, 112.5 minutes; setup, 29.5; complicating action, 30; development, 24.5; climax and epilogue, 25 (epilogue alone, 2.5); end credits, 3.5.

* *The Frighteners* (1996): Running time, 109.5 minutes; setup, 30.5; development, 41.5; climax and epilogue, 24 (epilogue alone, 1.5); end credits, 4.5.

Jerry McGuire (1996): Running time, 139 minutes; setup, 33.5; complicating action, 32; development, 33; climax and epilogue, 36 (epilogue alone, 3.5); end credits, 5.

Liar Liar (1997): Running time, 86.5 minutes; setup, 20.5; complicating action, 21.5; development, 20; climax and epilogue, 18.5 (epilogue alone, 1.5); end credits, 6.

The Rock (1996): Running time, 137.5 minutes; setup, 38; complicating action, 35; development, 28; climax and epilogue, 31 (epilogue alone, 6); end credits, 5.5.

Se7en (1996): Running time, 127 minutes; setup, 29; complicating action, 32; development, 30; climax and epilogue, 30.5 (epilogue alone, 1); end credits, 5.5.

Sleepless in Seattle (1993): Running time, 104.5 minutes; setup, 25; complicating action, 25.5; development, 27.5; climax and epilogue, 23 (epilogue alone, 1.5); end credits, 4.

Bombs, or What Makes Bad Films Bad?

The main point of this book is to demonstrate classical Hollywood norms by analyzing films that have been reasonably successful and critically praised, but readers may also want to know how films widely perceived as bad use those same norms.

In their book *Hollywood Cinema*, Richard Maltby and Ian Craven have claimed that Hollywood's profit orientation makes its leaders oblivious to quality. They attack the characterization of such cinema by Bordwell, Staiger, and myself as "classical" because the Hollywood industry, they claim, "functions according to what we have called a *commercial aesthetic*, one that is essentially opportunistic in its economic motivation."[1] That is, "Hollywood's commercial aesthetic is too opportunistic to prize coherence, organic unity, or even the absence of contradiction among its primary virtues."[2] Yet the most common complaint lodged against the Hollywood establishment has to do with its insistence on formula. Since incoherence, disunity, and the presence of contradiction can hardly be formulized, it seems very likely that Hollywood's dependence on the tried-and-true stems from a shared assumption that a comprehensible narrative is more commercially viable than a chaotic one. The real issue becomes how industry officials judge the quality of the scripts they must greenlight for production.

The first line of "quality control" for Hollywood production companies is typically the script reader, who composes a brief "coverage" summarizing the script and ranking it as to the degree of consideration it should be afforded.[3] It is common knowledge that in recent years, Syd Field's formula of ¼ - ½ - ¼ has dictated the first move that many such overburdened readers make: skim pages 25–30 and 85–90 to check whether something resembling a "Plot Point" occurs. If it does not, the script may receive no further attention. One anonymous script reader has said: "When you look at a script, you instinctively know where everything is supposed to fall. With a feature script, if your first Act is under 20 pages, you know there's going to be a problem. That's why you keep going back to structure."[4] I have delivered lectures based on portions of this book and had film students who had worked as script readers (both in the United States and England) confirm that their instructions were to commence by checking for turning points at those page ranges. This practice is, however, probably not universal. T. L. Katahn's *Reading for a Living*, perhaps the only manual for script readers, sets forth a three-act model while stating that the turning points do not need to occur on certain pages.[5]

Given that producers risk such large sums on films, it is understandable that they might yearn to quantify the quality of a screenplay. Indeed, such an attempt is probably not new to the post-Field era. Allan Scott, who wrote most of the Astaire-Rogers musicals at RKO, has described an interview with studio head Pandro S. Berman in the 1930s:

> But I remember—and this will give you an idea of how they looked at scripts back then—the first time I was called to the front office after I'd done *Top Hat*. I was sent up alone to meet with Pandro. I didn't have any particular trepidation because we all loved what we had done, but still, I thought, "Oh shit, who did I fall over? What did I do?" And Pandro said, "Allan, I like this, but there are fourteen more speeches in this than in the last picture." They used to number the speeches. And that was the extent of that conversation.[6]

Counting speeches or page numbers would seem an absurd way of judging the quality of a script. Common sense would suggest that bad films can result from any of a wide variety of reasons that have nothing to do with large-scale proportions.

In a spirit of scholarly inquiry, I decided to test this hypothesis by watching a body of films that are widely considered bombs. The criteria for inclusion within that category were simple: the film had to have been universally disparaged upon its initial release and certified as a "BOMB" in Leonard Maltin's *Movie & Video Guide*.[7] It also had to be a mainstream film with at least vague pretensions to respectability (reasonably well-known actors, big budget, and so on), rather than a cheap exploitation film. I limited my sample to five films; the specific choices were dictated by what I could find in my local video outlets. These are the resulting titles and their claims to fame: *Howard the Duck* (1986), produced by George Lucas; *Myra Breckinridge* (1970), from a novel by Gore Vidal; *Nothing But Trouble* (1991), directed by "Saturday Night Live" alumnus Dan Aykroyd and starring Chevy Chase and Demi Moore; *Once Bitten* (1985), with established star Lauren Hutton and star-to-be Jim Carrey; and *Return to the Blue Lagoon* (1991), a postcard-pretty sequel to the Brooke Shields hit.

I think it is safe to claim that one thing these works have in common is that the best way of predicting their ghastliness would not be by scanning script pages 25–30 and 85–90. Indeed, most tend to break into reasonably well-proportioned large-scale segments. Instead, each failed in its own special way.

In *Howard the Duck*, the character goals are initially unclear, and once they are articulated, they provide little guidance for the action. Moreover, Howard never looks like anything but a small human in a duck suit. Worst of all, the film provides a steady stream of lame jokes (for example, when a gang surrounds Howard in a dark alley, he says, "I'm a dead duck!"). Still, this 110-minute film has turning points 27.5 minutes in and 26 minutes before the credits, and so those points would greet the eye of a script reader scanning the requisite sections of the text.

Myra Breckinridge (called by Maltin "as bad as any movie ever made") perhaps occupies category all its own. It is clearly a misguided product of the art-cinema-influenced "youthquake" of the early 1970s. In addition to its self-important incoherence and pointless bad taste, its central character's goal ("My purpose in coming to Hollywood is the destruction of the American male") is too vague to serve as the basis for a plot and is unattainable to boot. The incoherence leads to many short, choppy scenes. The dreadful acting seems almost beside the point, since it is hard to imagine performers being able to do their jobs well under the circumstances. In a film running 94 minutes, the first turning point (which I take to be the end of Myra's first acting class) comes 27 minutes in. The climax is distinctly short, at 18 minutes—the most seriously disproportioned major segment in any of the bombs surveyed. One would hope, however, that an unduly short climax would not be the main reason a modern script reader might reject *Myra Breckinridge*.

Nothing But Trouble is a rather interesting case, in that the bulk of the setup portion is merely mediocre. The arrest of the main couple by the constable played by John Candy and the subsequent drive into Valkenvania are faintly intriguing and could have led into a plot dealing with an isolated, anachronistic community—a sort of grimly comic *Deliverance*. Instead the appearance of Judge Valkenheiser suddenly plunges the film into a willfully immature and revolting situation that continues relentlessly to the end. When Chevy Chase and Demi Moore spend their time reacting bug-eyed to each new revelation, one knows that the plot has fallen out of control. Yet, clocking in at 93 minutes, *Nothing But Trouble* falls into three neatly balanced parts of 29, 31, and 28.5 minutes.

Once Bitten follows all of the Hollywood rules, but with a notable lack of energy. Its hero has a goal: to lose his virginity. The villainess, a female vampire, also has a goal and a deadline as well: to remain youthful-looking, she must suck the blood of a virgin man three times by week's end. The bald simplicity of these goals and deadlines is matched by a clumsy exposition and minimal complications. As with *Howard the Duck*, lead-balloon jokes abound (as when the mincingly gay vampire assistant asks the villainess, "Did we get up on the wrong side of the coffin this evening?"). Again, however, the film breaks nicely into thirds, at 34, 30, and 30 minutes.

Finally, *Return to the Blue Lagoon*, despite its impressively lush images of nature in the South Seas, manages to create a narrative with virtually no momentum. Once the widow and the two children wash up on an uninhabited tropical island, their goal is simply to wait for a ship to find them, something they can actively work toward only by building the obligatory signal beacon. The apparent danger caused by the periodic visits of a native tribe to conduct mysterious rituals suggests a threat which, amazingly, never materializes. The film is instead structured mainly around the cycle of the children's lives, which is treated in extraordinarily clichéd terms.

The film's breakdown into large-scale segments would not have raised any red flags with a script reader. Indeed, the filmmakers may have been trying to follow Fieldian proportions. In a film that totals 102 minutes, the setup ends 25.5 minutes in, at the fade-out that covers the children's growth from toddlers to something like eight-year-olds. The climax, which I take to begin with the arrival of the ship, lasts 29 minutes (including the epilogue). The remaining central portion of 42.5 minutes may be a somewhat truncated version of the Fieldian hour-long "Act Two," yet there are in fact two events within it that are as important as the initial growth of the children that ends the setup: a second time gap when the children grow to adolescence (marked by another fade-out at 43 minutes) and the moment at which Lili gets her first period and tells Richard that she is a woman (at 56 minutes), an event which has earlier been emphatically anticipated. Thus the middle "act" breaks into nearly equal thirds of 16, 13, and 13.5 minutes. This atypical breakdown still creates a reasonable balance among the film's large-scale parts and hence is not a symptom of the film's problems, which lie elsewhere. Instead, the tripartite structure of the central portion may provide a bit of additional evidence that a long "second act" in a plot is difficult to maintain without at least one turning point. Here, without momentum supplied by an active goal, two more key stages of the protagonists' life cycle have been used to move things along.

These five examples suggest that most bad films are probably bad because they have dumb premises and/or characters with lifeless or poorly defined goals. A skewed balance of large-scale portions may occasionally signal a problem, but it seems an odd place to start looking. Daniel Pyne, scriptwriter of *Doc Hollywood*, has summed up the problem with such a narrow approach: "As I've said, I don't go by act one, two, and three. Sometimes I wonder if that's even relevant. Maybe only for studio story editors who are reading the scripts and breaking them down. Maybe that's who's taking all these screenwriting courses."[8]To put it another way, no bad film has ever been saved by having its turning points in the "right" places.

One final point on the notion of script length as a means of quality control is worth making. The widespread assumption that one page of script equals one minute of screen time probably only works when there are further constraints at other stages of the production process. Most notably, there are good indications that if the director does not cooperate, the page/minute equation means little. The proliferation of long films (that is, over two and a half hours) in the late 1990s has led to considerable comment. One such comment is that a film is most likely to go over its planned time when the director has the right of final cut.

Take the case of *Meet Joe Black* (1998), a film widely lambasted by critics, who almost universally pointed out that it was about three hours long even though it was a remake of a 78-minute film (*Death Takes a Holiday*, 1934). *Entertainment Weekly* stated: "According to Kevin Wade, one of *Meet Joe Black*'s screenwriters, what looks like a a two-hour movie on the page can balloon once the director gets behind the camera or into the editing room." The various drafts of the script ran about 135 pages each, only slightly over optimum length. The timing was in the control of the director: "Simply put, if Martin Brest has the right to the final cut and he wants *Meet Joe Black* to be three hours long, all the powerhouses in the Hollywood universe either can't—or won't—do a thing about it."[9] Actress Mary Kay Place has recalled how Lawrence Kasdan (who did not have final cut) worked on *The Big Chill*:

"Larry timed all of the scenes. If our scenes went longer than the time allotted per page, we had to do it faster. During *Body Heat*, he'd had to cut a lot of things. This time, he didn't want to lose anything."[10] Thus the script can only provide one way of controlling film length, and the idea that its most crucial dramatic moments can be pinpointed well in advance solely by page number seems dubious.

Notes

1. Modern Classicism

1. Thomas Elsaesser, "The Pathos of Failure: American Films in the 70s—Notes on the Unmotivated Hero," *Monogram*, 6 (1975): 14.
2. Justin Wyatt, *High Concept: Movies and Marketing in Hollywood* (Austin: University of Texas Press, 1994), p. 8.
3. For a particularly successful use of tie-in products in the 1920s, see John Canemaker, *Felix: The Twisted Tale of the World's Most Famous Cat* (New York: Pantheon, 1991).
4. Douglas Gomery, "The American Film Industry in the 1970s: Stasis in the 'New Hollywood,'" *Wide Angle*, 5, 4 (1983): 52–54.
5. Jim Hillier, *The New Hollywood* (New York: Continuum, 1994), p. 18.
6. Eddie Dorman Kay, *Box-Office Champs: The Most Popular Movies of the Last 50 Years* (New York: Portland House, 1990).
7. Michael Pye and Lynda Myles, *The Movie Brats: How the Film Generation Took Over Hollywood* (New York: Holt, Rinehart and Winston, 1979), p. 83.
8. Ibid., p. 9.
9. Ibid., p. 10.
10. See Dale Pollock, *Skywalking: The Life and Films of George Lucas* (New York: Harmony Books, 1983), pp. 118–120.
11. Jeff Giles and Kendall Hamilton, "The Joys of Summer," *Newsweek* (11 May 1998): 76.
12. Chris Nashawaty, "A Coppola Things," *Entertainment Weekly* (21 November 1997): 62.
13. *Wired*, 6, 2 (February 1998), cover and accompanying story, Paula Parisi, "Lunch on the Deck of the Titanic," pp. 148–159.
14. David Ansen and Corie Brown, "Lights, Camera, Oscars!" *Newsweek* (26 January 1998): 58–63.

15. Jack Kroll, "Knock on Woody, He's Doing Fine," *Newsweek* (20 July 1998): 68.

16. Rebecca Ascher-Walsh, "Tough Cookie," *Entertainment Weekly* (30 January 1998): 16.

17. Warren Buckland, "A Close Encounter with *Raiders of the Lost Ark:* Notes on Narrative Aspects of the New Hollywood Blockbuster," in *Contemporary Hollywood Cinema*, ed. Steve Neale and Murray Smith (London: Routledge, 1998), p. 167.

18. Thomas Elsaesser, "Specularity and Engulfment: Francis Ford Coppola and *Bram Stoker's Dracula*," in *Contemporary Hollywood Cinema*, ed. Neale and Smith, pp. 191–208.

19. There is some indication that the studio contract writer is enjoying a comeback. *Variety* has reported that big firms like DreamWorks are securing prominent screenplay authors for original scenarios and rewrites. See Andrew Hindes, "Studios Struggle to Build Scribe Tribe," *Variety* (9–15 December 1996): 1, 119.

20. For a more extensive account of these principles during the studio era, see David Bordwell, Janet Staiger, and Kristin Thompson, *The Classical Hollywood Cinema: Film Style and Mode of Production to 1960* (New York: Columbia University Press, 1985), chaps. 2 and 3.

21. Joe Leydon, "*Flubber*," *Variety* (24–30 November 1997): 64.

22. Todd McCarthy, "Star Wattage Brightens 'Twilight,'" *Variety* (2–8 March 1998): 83.

23. Todd McCarthy, "Noisy 'Armageddon' Plays 'Con' Game," *Variety* (29 June–12 July 1998): 37.

24. Dana Cooper, *Writing Great Screenplays for Film and TV*, 2nd ed. (New York: Macmillan, 1997), p. 121.

25. David Howard and Edward Mabley, *The Tools of Screenwriting: A Writer's Guide to the Craft and Elements of a Screenplay* (New York: St. Martin's, 1993), p. 45.

26. Eugene Vale, *The Technique of Screenplay Writing* (1944; rev. ed., New York: Grosset and Dunlap, 1972), pp. 38–39.

27. Information provided by David Bordwell.

28. Vale, *The Technique of Screenplay Writing*, p. 194.

29. Owen Gleiberman, "Executive Action," *Entertainment Weekly* (25 July 1997): 49.

30. David Bordwell, *On the History of Film Style* (Cambridge, Mass.: Harvard University Press, 1997), p. 260.

31. William Lord Wright, *Photoplay Writing* (New York: Falk, 1922), pp. 60, 82. For a discussion of early manuals' models of Hollywood narratives, see my "Narrative Structure in Early Classical Cinema," in *Celebrating 1895: The Centenary of Cinema*, ed. John Fullerton (Sydney: John Libbey, 1998), pp. 225–238.

32. Constance Nash and Virginia Oakey, *The Screenwriter's Handbook: What to Write, How to Write It, Where to Sell It* (New York: Barnes and Noble, 1978), pp. 2–3, 21. An unrevised paperback edition was published by HarperCollins (New York) in 1993.

33. Todd Coleman, "The Story Structure Gurus," *The Journal of the Writers Guild of America, West*, 8, 6 (June 1995): 15. This article offers interesting insights into

the modern history of scenario manuals, the careers of the most successful scenario advisers, and the controversies over such issues as the "three-act paradigm."

34. Syd Field, *Screenplay: The Foundations of Screenwriting* (New York: Delta, 1979), pp. 8–9.

35. Ibid., pp. 9–11.

36. Ibid., p. 8.

37. See, for example, Raymond G. Frensham, *Screenwriting* (Chicago: NTC Publishing, 1996), p. 48; Andrew Horton, *Writing the Character-Centered Screenplay* (Berkeley: University of California Press, 1994), p. 95; Linda Seger, *Making a Good Script Great* (New York: Dodd, Mead and Company, 1987), pp. 4–5; Michael Hauge, *Writing Screenplays That Sell* (New York: Harper Perennial, 1991), pp. 86–87.

38. William Froug, *The New Screenwriter Looks at the New Screenwriter* (Los Angeles: Silman-James, 1991), p. 20.

39. Karl Schanzer and Thomas Lee Wright, *American Screenwriters* (New York: Avon, 1993), pp. 247–248.

40. Gary Walkow, "Ernest Lehman: An Interview with a Legendary Screenwriter," *Screenwriter Quarterly*, 1, 1 (Spring 1996): 21–22.

41. Seger, *Making a Good Script Great*, p. 46. For similar opinions, see Frensham, *Screenwriting*, p. 187, and Katherine Atwell Herbert, *Writing Scripts Hollywood Will Love* (New York: Allworth, 1994), p. 96.

42. Mary J. Schirman, "*Bull Durham* and *Tin Cup*: An Interview with Ron Shelton," *Creative Screenwriting*, 3, 2 (Fall 1996): 64.

43. Viki King, *How to Write a Movie in 21 Days: The Inner Movie Method* (New York: Harper and Row, 1988), p. 8.

44. William Froug, *The Screenwriter Looks at the Screenwriter* (1972; reprint, Los Angeles: Silman-James, 1991), pp. 208–209.

45. For more on the typical confusion over "plot points" and their timings, see Allen B. Ury, "Off to See the Wizard," *Fade In* (Fall 1998): 78–79.

46. Syd Field, *Four Screenplays: Studies in the American Screenplay* (New York: Dell, 1994), p. xviii. Field introduced and discussed what he at that point called "the midpoint" in *The Screenwriter's Workbook* (New York: Dell, 1984), pp. 131–145.

Field's description of analyzing the midpoint of *Chinatown* in the latter book (pp. 131–135) is interesting, in that he started by looking at p. 60 in the script rather than timing the film itself; he finally hit upon an action that occurs on p. 66, where Gittes sees a photo of Evelyn Mulray and Noah Cross together, revealing that they are related. I would suggest that the turning point between the complicating action and development portions of *Chinatown* is the end of Gittes' meeting with Noah Cross, when he agrees to take the latter on as a client (a moment that comes 66.5 minutes into a 130.5-minute film). This action means that he will seemingly accept Cross's claims that Mrs. Mulray is unbalanced and that the girl she is protecting was her husband's mistress. These ideas in turn will determine Gittes' fatal misunderstanding of later actions, including his belief that Mrs. Mulray was involved in her husband's death.

47. Todd McCarthy, *"Deep Impact,"* *Variety* (11–17 May 1998): 58. See also McCarthy's review of *The Siege*, where he notes that an apparent resolution of the plot takes place 50 minutes into a 116-minute film but then is soon followed by a massive explosion that sets a new train of events into motion. "'Siege': Terrorism Gets a Quick Hit From Zwick," *Variety* (2–8 November 1998): 49.

48. Robert McKee, *Story: Substance, Structure, Style and the Principles of Screenwriting* (New York: HarperCollins, 1997), pp. 218–220.

49. William Froug has recently campaigned against the three-act paradigm. In his *Screenwriting Tricks of the Trade* (Los Angeles: Silman-James, 1993), he declares: "However, the idea that all screenplays are written in three 'acts' is nonsense. The truth is many screenplays use *five* acts, six acts, two acts, or any number of large, developmental story sections" (p. 72). But Froug offers no guidance as to what function these various acts might serve. As with so many advisers, he assumes that the lengthy middle is problematic but offers only broad advice: "create more problems for your characters" (p. 104) and "add new elements as needed" (p. 109). See also Froug's *Zen and the Art of Screenwriting* (Los Angeles: Silman-James, 1996), a combination interview and advice book that attempts to loosen up the increasingly rigid guidelines offered by the majority of recent manuals.

50. Field, *Four Screenplays*, pp. 79–154.

51. One might wonder whether the true turning point does not come when Sarah has her dream of the nuclear holocaust and decides to assassinate Dyson. I would not quibble with that segmentation, since the main point is to note that during this section the film moves in a completely new direction as a result of Sarah's realization. The scene in the car seems to me to mark the main shift, since Sarah's demand to know everything about Dyson suggests that she decides at this point that he must be eliminated or at least persuaded to abandon his work. She has no short-term deadline for dealing with Dyson, and we might infer that she will move ahead with the plan to hide John and the Terminator somewhere in Mexico. She would then presumably return at some unspecified time to deal with Dyson. Her wrenching dream of the nuclear blast then drives her to try and kill Dyson immediately.

52. In the question sessions after lectures dealing with large-scale parts, I have several times been asked whether these breaks are dictated by the commercial pauses anticipated during the film's showings on television. This is in fact not the case, since the filmmakers have no knowledge of where those commercial breaks will fall. Indeed, they fall at different points during different broadcasts. The network premiere tends to space the commercial breaks far apart early on, then increase their frequency in the second half. Subsequent late-night screenings often contain far more such breaks. By contrast, two-hour TV movies are routinely divided into seven large-scale parts, building in the standard quarter-hour prime-time commercial breaks. One interesting source on this topic relates to Danny Rubin's original intent to write *Groundhog Day* as a TV movie; see Tod Lippy, "Writing *Groundhog Day*: A Talk with Danny Rubin," *Scenario*, 1, 2 (Spring 1995): 51.

53. Joel Engel, *Screenwriters on Screenwriting: The Best in the Business Discuss Their Craft* (New York: Hyperion, 1995), p. 105.

54. On the Academy of Ancient Music recording of the Opus 9 violin concerti, the first and third movements tend to run between three and four minutes, the second movements between two and three. (L'Oiseau Lyre CD 421 366-2).

55. Susan Bullington Katz, "A Conversation with Ted Tally," *The Journal of the Writers Guild of America, West*, 9, 1 (December/January 1996): 49. In the original novel, Jack Crawford is a far more prominent character than in the film, and many scenes where Clarice is not present are told through his point of view.

56. An exception to this generalization would be *His Girl Friday*, where parallel protagonists Walter and Hildie are well acquainted but have opposing goals: he wants to remarry her, while she is determined to marry Bruce. These opposing goals do, however, keep them in separate spaces for a long stretch in the middle.

57. Douglas Brode presents a similar claim concerning *Amadeus:* "This, then, was a film with two heroes and no villains: Salieri may at first seem a cynical, manipulative Iago to Mozart's naïve, trusting Othello, but under Milos *(Ragtime)* Forman's firm though delicate directorial hand, something quite special transpired. Despite what Salieri does, he wins our sympathies. He may be weak, but he is not evil." See Brode's *The Films of the Eighties* (New York: Citadel, 1991), p. 132.

58. Cooper, *Writing Great Screenplays for Film and TV*, pp. 95–102.

2. *Tootsie*

1. Syd Field, *Screenplay: The Foundations of Screenwriting* (New York: Delta, 1979), p. 31.

2. Linda Seger, *Making a Good Script Great* (New York: Dodd, Mead, 1987), p. 118.

3. Michael Hauge, *Writing Screenplays That Sell* (New York: Harper Perennial, 1991), p. 12.

4. Erik Bauer, "The Mouth and the Method," *Sight and Sound*, 8, 3 (NS) (March 1998): 8.

5. Hauge, *Writing Screenplays That Sell*, p. 57.

6. Quoted in my *Wooster Proposes, Jeeves Disposes, or Le Mot Juste* (New York: James H. Heineman, 1992), p. 63.

7. Slightly less eloquently than Wodehouse, Dustin Hoffman has described this process in relation to *Tootsie:* "So we started talking about a movie about a guy. What would make a guy wanna be a woman, that wasn't a turn-off, you know, that was something you could understand? What happens when you're, by circumstances, just because you want to work as an actor, *forced* into women's clothing, and you pull it off so that people think you're a woman, and then what happens? What happens to you? What happens? What happens when people start to relate to you differently?" See *The Making of Tootsie*, documentary directed by Rocky Lang, 1982. Voyager Co. laserdisc of *Tootsie*, 1991, side 4.

8. This is an example of what in cognitive psychology is referred to as the primacy effect. Frequently information we learn at the beginning of a text will be particularly memorable and will shape how we construe later information. For more on

the primacy effect, see David Bordwell, *Narration in the Fiction Film* (Madison: University of Wisconsin Press, 1985), esp. pp. 38, 150–151.

9. Leonard Klady, "*My Giant*," *Variety* (6–12 April 1998): 47.

10. The very notion of a play about Love Canal parodies the avant-garde "high art" theater Michael seeks to promote—in much the same way that Michael's temperamental acting parodies reports that Dustin Hoffman is notoriously "difficult" on the set.

11. According to Sidney Pollack, this scene was devised late in the script revision process: "Then Barry Levinson and Valerie Curtain came on one week into shooting, to help smooth it out. They didn't do much writing. By that time the film was already on a railroad track. They did help remove a stumbling block in the plot: how Dustin would get into bed with Teri Garr. Levinson and Curtain had Teri emerge from her shower while Hoffman's undressing because he wants 'Dorothy' to try on Teri's clothes." (See Michael Sragow, "Ghostwriters," *Film Comment*, 19, 2 [March–April 1983]: 15.) The scene is still weakly motivated, but apparently we must assume that it improves on whatever happened in earlier drafts.

12. Sandy's presence at the party recalls Jeff's earlier line in the birthday party scene that he has invited ten people who each invited ten people. George has invited Michael, who has in turn taken Sandy as his date. No stress is laid upon the fact that here Michael has apparently made and kept a date with Sandy (though he attempts to abandon her for Julie). This party thus provides a slight motivation for the fact that Sandy continues to assume that her affair with Michael is ongoing.

13. Actually the producer says "another year." It is hard to believe that Michael has been playing Dorothy for a full year by this point, despite the montage sequence of magazine covers. Michael has put off Sandy several times since their inadvertent affair began, but there is little sense of more than a month or two passing in that line of action. The vague sense of temporal relations across the film as a whole is one of the few flaws in *Tootsie*'s structure, and it is not a particularly important one.

14. To a slight extent, this moment echoes the acting exercise in the credits sequence where Michael has two actors wordlessly mimic each other's facial expressions. In this late scene, his gesture may express his depression over his situation—but to the spectator, it surely reflects more strongly the fact that most sensible people find street mimes annoying.

15. Judy Brennan, "Eraser Heads," *Entertainment Weekly* (21 June 1996): 6–7.

16. Sragow, "Ghostwriters," p. 10.

17. This quotation and other information on the project's writing history are from Chapters 4 through 6, Side 3 of the Criterion laserdisc, which condenses material from Susan Dworkin's *Making Tootsie* (New York: Newmarket Press, 1983).

18. Sragow, "Ghostwriters," p. 9.

19. Pat McGilligan, "Julius J. Epstein: A King of Comedy," in McGilligan, ed., *Backstory: Interviews with Screenwriters of Hollywood's Golden Age* (Berkeley: University of California Press, 1986), pp. 183–185. For a similar situation at MGM, see

Todd McCarthy and Joseph McBride, "John Lee Martin: Team Player," in the same volume, p. 251.
20. Sragow, "Ghostwriters," p. 15.

3. *Back to the Future*

1. Oddly, *Variety*'s primarily positive review denigrated the entire setup section, referring to "a shakey opening overloaded with frenetic exposition" and opining that "the filmmakers scramble too furiously here and the film doesn't find its control and its feet, and what a relief it is, until the hero is dropped into the same town in 1955." *Variety Film Reviews 1985–1986*, vol. 19 (New York: R. R. Bowker, 1988), n.p. By a decade later, however, the scene was offered as a model of script exposition by Allen Ury: "If it's science fiction, either establish your arena in broad strokes (the skull-crushing robot juggernauts in 1984's *The Terminator*) or do so subtly (the tour of Doc Brown's lab in 1985's *Back to the Future*). Your opening should tell your reader what kind of story to expect, and how far one is expected to suspend belief." See Ury's "The First Page," *Fade In*, 1, 2 (1995): 46.

2. Actually, given how the time machine works, it is hard to imagine how the clocks lost time. They would presumably have to have all been in the time machine traveling at 88 miles per hour—since later Einstein's trip one minute into the future ends with his clock, rather than Doc's, being slow. (Moreover, Doc labels the tape of this trip "Temporal Experiment Number One," suggesting that he has never tested the time machine before.) The moment's functions are to hint further that Doc has invented a time machine and to make Marty late for school.

    Similarly, it is unclear why the powerful audio equipment has been sitting turned on throughout Doc's absence and why it experiences a power overload. The narration might have provided some motivation, such as Doc's having tested the plutonium's potency as a power source for the equipment, but in fact the surge remains unexplained.

3. Ironically, the failure of Crispin Glover to reprise his role in the two sequels meant that George is not present as an anchor of the family. (Indeed, he spends much of Part II dead!) The continued use of the time machine and the popularity of Doc as a character also made it inevitable that he would return to his role as surrogate father.

4. One might simply pass over this as a pleasant paradox, but it would have been possible for the film to motivate it quite simply. Had Marty arrived to find Doc exulting over his discovery of the key component (i.e., the flux capacitor) of a potential time machine, Doc would not need to get any ideas for building that machine from Marty. He would not be able actually to build the time machine between 1955 and 1985, since he would lack the ability to generate the necessary 1.2 gigawatts of power until he finally gets access to plutonium. (Knowing that a lightning bolt could supply the necessary energy would do him no good, since he would never again know in advance exactly when and where lightning would strike.) Granted, Marty's 1955 contribution to Doc's invention of the time machine creates a deeper emotional bond between the two, which Doc later ex-

presses as Marty is about to leave for 1985. Still, such a bond could have been motivated in other ways.

5. The many comic reversals of the early scene with the family demand an unusually long epilogue, which runs 6.5 minutes. To accommodate it, the development portion is unusually short, at 18 minutes. Together the climax and epilogue run nearly twice this long, at 35 minutes.

6. Eugene Vale, *The Technique of Screenplay Writing* (1944; New York: Grosset and Dunlap, 1972), p. 81.

7. Lew Hunter, *Lew Hunter's Screenwriting 434* (New York: Putnam, 1993), pp. 100, 129.

8. Linda Seger, *Making a Good Script Great* (New York: Dodd, Mead, 1987), p. 13.

9. William Goldman, *Adventures in the Screen Trade* (New York: Warner Books, 1983), pp. 181–185.

10. Tim Purtell, "Credits Where Credit Is Due," *Entertainment Weekly* (1 December 1995): 43.

11. Todd McCarthy, "Redford Lassos Powerful Saga," *Variety* (4–10 May 1998): 83.

4. *The Silence of the Lambs*

1. This may seem a bit bizarre, but one need only contrast the characterization of Lecter with that of Miggs or any of the other inmates of the same row of high-security cells; we cannot imagine Clarice interviewing them, let alone playing mind games with them in such a complex way.

2. There is no possible causal connection between the two Belvederes. Lecter's sketch cannot be a subtle clue that he has planted for Clarice, since initially he does not know who Buffalo Bill is or where he lives. He gives Clarice only psychologically derived clues. Indeed, Lecter is not even aware that Clarice is connected to the Buffalo Bill case when he first meets her, yet the sketch is already on his wall.

   By the way, there is no town named Belvedere in Ohio.

3. One might imagine that Clarice's desire to transform herself from small-town girl to FBI agent could be parallel to Gumb's desire for transformation. (In fact, the clichéd metaphors of the awkward girl's transformation into beautiful womanhood as either an ugly duckling's growth into a swan or a caterpillar's emergence as a butterfly are perverted and gender-reversed by the moth imagery related to Gumb.) Yet the film provides no imagery, causality, or other devices to suggest that Clarice is in any way like Gumb.

4. This salubrious notion of a woman who helps prevent other women from becoming victims of crime was quite a novelty at the time, but it has become a bit more routine for Hollywood, as witnessed by such films as (the ironically titled) *Copycat* (1995), where a small, feisty female detective (Holly Hunter) consults a female psychologist ("Ripley" herself, Sigourney Weaver) who specializes in serial killers. (The psychologist in this case is not an incarcerated serial killer, but she is traumatized and unable to leave home.) As *Entertainment Weekly* put it, "*Copycat.* Nothing

at all like *The Silence of the Lambs*. This time *two* women chase a serial killer." Jim Mullen, "Hot Sheet," *Entertainment Weekly* (3 November 1995): 12.

5. By now the idea that *The Silence of the Lambs* was a feminist reshaping of the crime-thriller genre has become common currency. For example, an article claiming that Kathryn Bigelow criticizes genres from a feminist perspective praises *Blue Steel* as "predating *The Silence of the Lambs* in its scrutiny of a woman's place in the genre." See Lizzie Francke's "Virtual Fears," *Sight and Sound*, 5, 12 (NS) (December 1995): 12.

6. The novel *The Silence of the Lambs* ends lamely with Clarice in bed with one of the entomologists. Generally, the film improves upon the book's characterization of Clarice—unlike the treatment of the protagonist in the often overrated *Manhunter*, based on Harris's earlier (and better) novel, *Red Dragon*. *Manhunter* even substitutes a happy ending for the original grim one—ironically, featuring the hero in bed with the woman he loves.

7. The original novel develops the idea of Gumb's training as a tailor more extensively; the film uses this motif so little as to make it almost unnoticeable upon first viewing.

8. Clarice's habitual truthfulness is demonstrated again when she avoids lying outright to the police guarding Lecter in Memphis; when asked if she is part of Dr. Chilton's group, she hesitates, despite the importance of her getting in to see Lecter. She then says, quite accurately, "I just saw him outside," allowing the officers to infer that she is with Chilton.

9. For a sampling of the controversy that attended the film's release, see the comments by a variety of writers and artists collected by Lisa Kennedy as "Writers on the *Lamb*," *Village Voice* (5 March 1991): 49, 56, 58–59, and responses in the letters column (19 March 1991): 6. The film was both widely touted as feminist and denounced as a potential cause of anti-gay violence.

10. For Jonathan Demme's insistence that Gumb is not a transvestite, see Gavin Smith, "Identity Check," *Film Comment*, 27, 1 (January/February 1991): 37. The film's producer's and production designer's comments on Gumb's not being gay, a transvestite, or a transsexual appear in Dan Persons, "The Making of 'Silence of the Lambs,'" *Cinefantastique*, 22, 4 (February 1992): 35–36, 38.

11. Syd Field takes this scene between Chilton and Lecter to be the "Mid-Point" of *Silence*. See his *Four Screenplays: Studies in the American Screenplay* (New York: Dell, 1994), pp. 205–206.

12. The photos might initially lead us to suspect that they were taken by a lover who subsequently murdered Frederica. Given that there is no later suggestion that Gumb and Frederica were lovers, the photos seem in retrospect misleading in this sense. Moreover, Stacey declares quite emphatically that she would have known if Frederica had a boyfriend and that she had none. Thus the photos remain narratively unmotivated.

   They do, however, help slightly to characterize Frederica as having had romantic impulses unknown to her father or friend. Thus her death briefly becomes vividly pathetic as, for the only time with any of Bill's victims, we catch a glimpse of her past life.

13. David Ansen's review of *Ransom* (1996) suggests how unusual such emotional expression is for male action stars: "Unlike most rugged, square-jawed action-hero movie stars, Mel Gibson doesn't play it cool. He's the least afraid of showing wild emotion (think of his suicidal ravings in "Lethal Weapon," his rants in "The Bounty"), and in *Ransom* he gets to emote like mad." See Ansen, "Money for Nothing," *Newsweek* (11 November 1996): 74.

14. After writing this passage, I read the script of *The Silence of the Lambs.* There Gumb's gesture is described in this way: "His free hand reaches slowly out, covetously, as if to stroke her skin—his fingers floating delicately through the air, just an inch or so away from the side of her face." (Ted Tally, "*The Silence of the Lambs*," *Scenario*, 1, 1 (Winter 1995): 193.

   This passage seems to imply that Gumb does simply covet Clarice's skin. Yet he has been established as preying on "size 14" women. Moreover, in the actual film his hand hovers over her hair rather than her skin during much of the gesture. From a viewer's standpoint, I prefer my interpretation—and indeed, the screenplay's designation of this as a "covetous" gesture could also imply that Gumb simply wishes he were like Clarice.

15. Dan Cox, "H'wood Hunts 'The Great Idea,'" *Variety* (2–8 February 1998): 1.

5. *Groundhog Day*

1. Tod Lippy, "Writing *Groundhog Day:* A Talk with Danny Rubin," *Scenario*, 1, 2 (Spring 1995): 183.

   At one point, the producers wanted to add motivation to the film: "Both Ramis and Rubin groaned over the studio's insistence on an explanation for Phil's predicament. As Ramis related, 'The problem was that any explanation seemed completely arbitrary. Maybe it would have worked if the thing were set in India, but there was nothing indigenous to the place that made it sensible. To try and tie it to the groundhog legend destroyed the mundanity of the whole thing, which was very important to the tone of the movie.' Rubin's famous 'gypsy curse' scene was cut only after a new studio head, Mark Canton, came on board while the film was in development, and remarked after reading the script, 'You don't need this curse thing, do you?'" Tod Lippy, "Harold Ramis on *Groundhog Day*," *Scenario*, 1, 2 (Spring 1995): 53. Thus while some producers might find the lack of motivation for the central premise to be disturbing, others apparently would not—suggesting that it is not strongly disruptive to a classical film.

   The published draft of Rubin's script contains a reference to *It's a Wonderful Life*, which is playing at the Punxsutawney movie theater; Phil remarks with annoyance, "I've seen it a jillion times!" (See this issue of *Scenario*, p. 24.)

   More recently, *Sliding Doors* (1998) presents a warped time scheme in which two story lines develop simultaneously from a single initial situation. Here the moment when the two plots split comes as an overt narrational intervention, with the action of one scene freezing and then running back to start again with a slight difference in causality that precipitates a different string of effects. No motivation beyond the playfulness of the filmmakers is offered for this device, and yet the film played to moderate success (and apparent enjoyment, at least during the screening when I saw it) in mainstream commercial theaters.

2. Many days are indicated by a brief depiction of incidents (be it only one slap in the montage of Rita rejecting Phil day after day). The days of which we definitely see at least one shot total 34. Phil's description of his suicide attempts (at the beginning of the development portion) seemingly mentions six methods not shown, putting the total days to roughly 40. If we assume that the scene of Phil feeding the old beggar in the café and the scene of the beggar dying at night in an alley take place on two different days, the number of days rises to 41. (This is, I think, the only ambiguous case.) If we count the final, nonrepeating day, February 3, the total becomes 42. I am grateful to David Bordwell for suggesting this possibility.

3. This has been raised in Phil's opening forecast, in his smart-aleck response to the radio broadcast in his room on the morning of February 2, and in his replay of his weather forecast to the hostess of the bed-and-breakfast.

4. The main reason for this may be that virtually all spectators probably have some knowledge about the premise of *Groundhog Day* before seeing it.

5. The Danny Rubin draft published in *Scenario*, 1, 2 (Spring 1995) makes the time scheme much more explicit. Rubin envisioned Phil as spending many years in his temporal limbo, even becoming a doctor in his quest to do good. The final film makes duration far less explicit. Rubin's doctor notion may have survived in the party scene, in which Felix and his wife stop Phil to thank him for healing Felix's back. It is the only good deed mentioned at the party that has not been shown earlier.

6. Oddly enough, the film's presentation of this final day lacks the usual care in making its events match earlier repetitions. There is no sign of the blizzard that should be hitting Punxsutawney as Phil saves the boy falling from the tree and changes the tire (scenes that takes place in bright sunlight). Apparently the blizzard now hits during the evening, since the establishing shot of the hotel exterior that begins the party scene shows no snow on the ground, but the cut outside to Phil sculpting an ice bust of Rita reveals a snowy landscape. This anomaly is one of the film's few flaws. It is not an insignificant one, since there is no motivation as to why Rita and Larry do not drive back to Pittsburgh or at least ask Phil to go with them. (There is also only patchy snow on the ground in the earlier scene when Phil goes driving with the two drunks from the bowling alley.)

7. One might ask why Phil bothers doing the good deeds when he assumes they will just need to be done over and over. The point is that Phil is building his ideal day. In effect, he is practicing being a decent guy, just as he practices the piano and ice carving, because he enjoys this new approach to coping with the repeated days.

8. The death of the beggar, once one begins to think about it, haunts this part of the film. Presumably during the Groundhog Day party he is out dying in that alley. Phil has tried repeatedly to save him and accepted the fact that it was indeed simply the old man's time to die. Yet one cannot help feeling that a man so nice as Phil has become would have kept trying despite everything. The film depends upon our forgetting about the beggar by this point in the climax so that we will not be wondering at the end whether Phil should be partying with Rita or trying

over and over in vain to save the old man. This problem could have been remedied by showing Phil rushing to the beggar at the beginning of the last repeated day and immediately checking him into a hospital, thus doing his best for him.

9. Appropriately, it now starts with "Hey, I got you, babe," rather than "Then put your little hand in mine," as it had previously.

The choice of "I Got You, Babe" as the signal for the beginnings of new days fits in with the other irritating motifs that add up to make the repetitions so gratingly annoying to Phil: being accosted by Ned Ryerson, stepping in the puddle, getting the cold shower, and so on. It is also a very simple and repetitive song, and hence alert viewers can recognize on the morning of February 3 that it starts on a different passage.

Other musical pieces are used cleverly in the film to refer to love stories with fantastic time schemes: the Rachmaninov piano piece that Phil learns was a central motif in *Somewhere in Time* (1980), and "It's Almost Like Being in Love" comes from *Brigadoon* (1954).

10. Murray's performance is not unerringly this convincing. The smart-alecky side of his star persona seems to inhibit his delivery of some lines, as when Rita urges him to look upon the repeating days as a blessing. His "Gosh, you're an upbeat lady!" sounds ironic at a point when Phil is actually supposed to be gaining real inspiration from Rita. (Admittedly it is not a very good line to begin with.) Still, Murray is quite convincing in this final scene, and hence we are likely to accept Phil's transformation.

11. After I had written this chapter, Thomas Pope's *Good Scripts, Bad Scripts* (New York: Three Rivers, 1998) appeared, including an interesting brief analysis of *Groundhog Day* (pp. 119–124) as based on a script containing unpredictable yet clearly comprehensible actions. Pope also treats the old beggar's death as a crucial moment in Phil's maturation process.

12. Quoted in Justin Wyatt, *High Concept: Movies and Marketing in Hollywood* (Austin: University of Texas Press, 1994), p. 13.

13. Wyatt, *High Concept*, p. 190.

14. Ibid., p. 8.

15. "Fall Movie Preview," *Entertainment Weekly* (21/28 August 1998): 52.

16. Richard Corliss, "Shading the Past," *Time* (26 October 1998): 92.

17. Lisa Schwarzbaum, "In Living Color," *Entertainment Weekly* (30 October 1998): 78.

6. *Desperately Seeking Susan*

1. Pam Cook, "Desperately Seeking Susan," *Monthly Film Bulletin*, no. 620 (September 1985): 276. Though there are quite a few minor similarities between *Smithereens* and *Susan*, the former hardly seems a "dry run" for the latter, and the differences go beyond the smoothing over of "rough edges." Indeed, *Smithereens* offers an interesting contrast with *Susan*, in that it owes little to the classical narrative model. Its heroine, Wren, is unable to formulate a single goal, let alone

two that she could conceivably attain. She is defiant but pitiable and slides into homelessness and despair—in contrast to Susan, who is savvy and triumphs in the end. Wren's only goal (articulated quite late in the film) is to accompany a minor rock singer to Los Angeles and somehow become famous—something she never makes a bit of progress toward achieving. The vision of New York life presented in *Smithereens* is far bleaker than in *Susan*. *Susan* offers a fascinating example of how a director can take a kernel of an idea from a downbeat, mildly avant-garde film and transform it completely to create a cheerful, thoroughly classical narrative.

2. The earrings are also a fantasy, since not a single piece of jewelry known to have belonged to Nefertiti survives—let alone a matched pair of intact earrings. Indeed, almost none of the many extant images of Nefertiti show her wearing earrings (though, like all royalty of the Eighteenth Dynasty, her ears were pierced for them). Given the style of the earrings in the film, one might add that Nefertiti would not be caught dead in them—and could not be, since her mummy has never been found.

3. Alert readers might be wondering at this point how Nolan found out about the Battery Park rendezvous. We must infer that Susan left behind the newspaper with the heart-encircled ad in the Atlantic City hotel room. Nolan must have found the ad and watched for a second one in the personals. Ordinarily a classical film would establish such an event by showing either a big closeup of the ad as dropped by Susan in the hotel room or a shot of Nolan noticing the discarded paper.

4. A device like a character hitting her head and losing her memory recalls the casual but powerful motivation we find in screwball comedies of the 1930s. Carole Lombard needs to find a tramp as part of a scavenger hunt, setting up her hiring of William Powell as her valet in *My Man Godfrey*. Katharine Hepburn receives a leopard, so she has an excuse to drag Cary Grant all over Connecticut in *Bringing Up Baby*. Indeed, the name Susan may well be an homage to the latter film, which could have easily been titled *Desperately Seeking Baby*. One comic director who has used amnesia as a device in his films is Sir Charles Chaplin, in *The Gold Rush* (1925) and *The Great Dictator* (1941). The heroine of the 1933 Depression musical *Hallelujah, I'm a Bum* also develops amnesia and falls (temporarily) in love with her rescuer.

5. This scene concludes with a delightful parody of the clichéd Hollywood portrayal of eroticism. In the 1960s and 1970s, sex scenes often involved suggestive saxophone music. During this scene, saxophone music plays over. As Roberta remarks, "You're not quite what I expected, either," they both look off, and there is a cut to a man playing a saxophone in a nearby apartment. (See also the "Girl Hunt" number in *The Band Wagon* [1953] for a similar gag with a trumpet player.)

6. Quoted in Jim Hillier, *The New Hollywood* (New York: Continuum, 1994), p. 122.

7. Ibid., p. 138.

8. Phil Gallo, "Sex and the City," *Variety* (8–14 June 1998): 27.

7. Amadeus

1. That the film's artistic aspirations made its commercial success doubtful is evidenced by Richard Corliss's comment in his favorable *Time* review: "One wonders: Can this galloping metaphysical thriller find an audience? For the vast majority of today's moviegoers, the 18th century is far more remote than the sci-fi 25th; Salieri is a loser from Loserville, and Mozart, he's the guy who wrote *Elvira Madigan*, and his first name is Mostly, isn't it?" "Mozart's Greatest Hit," *Time* (10 September 1984): 75. Most moviegoers had probably never heard of Salieri. The subsequent mild revival of his music has done far less than the film to bring his name before the public.

2. Pauline Kael, "The Current Cinema: Mozart and Bizet," *The New Yorker* (29 October 1984): 123. Some other reviewers misconstrued the plot in a similar way; see, for example, David Edelstein, "Wolfiegate," *The Village Voice* (25 September 1984): 63.

3. Milos Forman and Jan Novak, *Turnaround: A Memoir* (New York: Villard, 1994), p. 259.

4. David Denby, for example, dismissed *Amadeus* as a "middlebrow problem film." Quoted in an unsigned entry on Milos Forman in John Wakeman, ed., *World Film Directors* (New York: H. W. Wilson, 1988), vol. II, "1945–1985," p. 355.

5. Shaffer's stage version uses the nickname "Wolferl," a specifically Austrian diminutive. This would have been both difficult for American actors to pronounce and impossible for most viewers to appreciate. Thanks to my colleague Sabine Gross of the Department of German of the University of Wisconsin-Madison for helping to clarify these nicknames.

6. For another positive view of the brief musical analyses in the film, see Robert L. Marshall, "Film as Musicology: *Amadeus*," *The Musical Quarterly*, 81, 2 (Summer 1997): 173–179.

7. Cavalieri says that Turkish clothes—presumably inspired by Mozart's upcoming opera—are the latest rage, and she has had time to acquire this elegant outfit. Yet Salieri considers that she has learned of his meeting with Mozart quickly: "News travels fast." This lapse is one of the few flaws in the film's causality. In general, the chronology of the narrative is too indefinite to give rise to serious mistakes.

8. Oddly, this is the only moment in the film when Salieri fails to appreciate Mozart's music. In every other case he is fully comprehending and achingly envious. I can find no motivation for this one failure of vision—especially since Salieri's own lesson involving scales segued directly into the aria. A solution to this problem would have been to portray Salieri as *pretending* to his friends to be put off by the virtuosic aria.

9. This brief excerpt from the Mass is one of the few passages of Mozart's religious music which the film contains, and it is not here identified as his own composition.

10. Here we have an elaboration of the "too many notes" line. It seems reasonable to assume that Orsini-Rosenberg (who used the phrase twice in previous

scenes) means that Mozart's music is too dense, presenting too many notes too quickly. Now Salieri (who himself wrote lengthy operas) accuses Mozart of creating too long an evening of listening—too many notes over too long a time.

11. Until I had finished the first draft of this analysis of *Amadeus*, I delayed reading any version of the script of Shaffer's original play in order to avoid inadvertently imposing structures from the play on the film's narrative.

12. Version 2 was published in *The Collected Plays of Peter Shaffer* (New York: Harmony Books, 1982); references to page lengths in my text are to this edition. Version 3 is available as *Amadeus*, ed. Richard Adams (Harlow, Essex: Longman, 1984). Shaffer's Preface in the latter (pp. xxvi–xxviii) is quite interesting, in that it suggests how important his stage directors had been in leading him repeatedly to rewrite *Amadeus*. I suspect that Forman contributed considerably to the extensive revisions for the film.

13. This theme goes back to Alexander Pushkin's brief drama, *Mozart and Salieri* (1832); the forgiveness theme is not present there. See Alexander Pushkin, *Mozart and Salieri: The Little Tragedies*, trans. Antony Wood (London: Angel, 1982), pp. 35–44.

14. Although he does not mention the forgiveness theme or the use of parallel protagonists, Mark Ringer offers some brief, insightful comments on the film's improvements over the play in *"Amadeus:* From Play to Film," *Eighteenth Century Life*, 9 (October 1986): 119–120.

15. Adams, ed., *Amadeus*, p. xvii.

16. Rick Marx, "How Screenwriters Can Read the Minds of Hollywood's Gatekeepers: Insight from Professional Script Reader Doug Michael," *MovieMaker*, 24 (March/April 1997): 52.

17. William Goldman, *Adventures in the Screen Trade* (1969; New York: Warner Books, 1983), p. 106.

18. William Froug, *The New Screenwriter Looks at the New Screenwriter* (Los Angeles: Silman-James, 1991), p. 170.

19. Joel Engel, *Screenwriters on Screenwriting: The Best in the Business Discuss Their Craft* (New York: Hyperion, 1995), pp. 176–177.

8. *The Hunt for Red October*

1. Robert Scheer, "Back in the USSR," *Premiere*, 3, 8 (April 1990): 96.

2. David Sterritt, *The Christian Science Monitor* (12 March 1990), reprinted in *Film Review Annual 1991* (Englewood, N.J.: Jerome S. Ozer), p. 714.

3. David Denby, *New York* (19 March 1990), reprinted in *Film Review Annual 1991*, p. 717.

4. Kim Newman, *"The Hunt for Red October,"* *Monthly Film Bulletin*, 675 (April 1990): 108.

5. Scheer, "Back in the USSR," p. 96. Connery was starring at the same time in an

adaptation of *The Russia House* which incorporated *glasnost* into its plot. That topicality has not made it a classic.

6. Mac., *"The Hunt for Red October,"* *Variety* (28 February 1990), reprinted in *Variety Film Reviews 1989–1990* (New Providence, R.I.: R. R. Bowker, 1991), n.p.

7. Sheila Benson, *Los Angeles Times* (2 March 1990), reprinted in *Film Review Annual 1991*, p. 715.

8. David Edelstein, *The New York Post* (2 March 1990), reprinted in *Film Review Annual 1991*, p. 718.

9. David Ansen, *Newsweek* (5 March 1990), reprinted in *Film Review Annual 1991*, p. 720.

10. Edelstein, *Film Review Annual 1991*, p. 718.

11. Marcia Garcia, *Films in Review* (June–July 1990), reprinted in *Film Review Annual 1991*, p. 714.

12. Newman, *Monthly Film Bulletin*, p. 108.

13. Richard Schickel, *Time* (5 March 1990), reprinted in *Film Review Annual 1991*, p. 721.

14. It is difficult in retrospect to determine just how seriously viewers in 1990 would have taken this possibility. The *Variety* review suggests that such a suspicion would fit a Hollywood precedent. It describes Ramius as "an enigmatic seaman whose actions cause intense debate in the inner circles of Moscow and Washington as the action proceeds inexorably to a fail-safe point. Is he a madman planning to launch his own preemptive nuclear strike on the U.S.? Or is he a conscientious would-be defector trying to turn over his advanced new sub in order to prevent Soviet hardliners from being able to start World War III?

"At first 'Red October' leads the audience to believe that Connery, with his secretive and sometimes ruthless behavior, is the Soviet equivalent of Sterling Hayden's deranged Gen. Jack D. Ripper in 'Dr. Strangelove.' The film gradually shifts the viewer's perspective to consider the other alternative, urged on by Baldwin, who knows more than any other American about the character of Ramius."

See *"The Hunt for Red October,"* *Variety Film Reviews*, n.p.

15. The cynical behavior of Soviet and American officials alike saves *Red October* from falling into the traditional us-versus-them Cold-War ideology decried by several reviewers quoted above.

16. Pelt gives Ryan three days to prove his theory, seeming to set up a classic deadline. In fact, changes in the plot premises will render this deadline irrelevant, but it temporarily provides a sense of urgency.

17. Early in this scene, Mancuso sends his assistant for a cup of tea. This is the film's only violation of the contrasting association of tea with the Soviets and coffee with the Americans. Yet we never see the tea or hear a cup clinking, as in earlier scenes. Perhaps the suggestion here is simply a mild parallel between Mancuso and Ramius, as two sub captains; during the climax, despite all his suspicions, Mancuso will accept Ramius as an equal and even lend him his own pistol.

18. Grasping any more than the bare bones of the plot is probably unnecessary for a

basic understanding of what follows, and even a close analysis cannot uncover all the details of Ryan's actions.

19. Leonard Maltin sums it up, "*Cape Fear* for the Freddy Krueger generation." See his *1998 Movie & Video Guide* (New York: Signet, 1997), p. 198.

20. Thomas Pope, *Good Scripts, Bad Scripts* (New York: Three Rivers, 1998), pp. 99–100.

21. Todd McCarthy, "A Mostly Lean, Mean Flying Machine," *Variety* (2–8 June 1997): 53.

22. Todd McCarthy, "*Face/Off*," *Variety* (23–29 June 1997): 97.

23. Todd McCarthy, "U.S. Prexy as Last Action Hero," *Variety* (21–27 July 1997): 37.

9. Parenthood

1. David Denby, *Film Review Annual 1990* (Englewood, N.J.: Jerome S. Ozer, 1990), p. 976. In this same volume, Sheila Benson claims that Howard's "fine touch with ensembles ('Cocoon') reaches real maturity here" (p. 973); Renee Tajima comments that "the story's structure, as in '80s television dramas like *Hill Street Blues* or *L.A. Law*, shifts in and out of the four households" (p. 980). See pp. 978 and 979 for similar comments.

2. A 1997 survey of moviegoers' interest in film directors placed Howard second overall after Steven Spielberg, but first "among baby boomers and mature adults." "People Meter: Directors' Marquee Power," *Variety* (19–25 May 1997): 72.

3. The inclusion of Larry's black girlfriend and their mixed-race son does little to disrupt the overall concentration on the white characters. Although the family is shocked when Larry presents Cool to them, they seem to react more to the fact that their unmarried son has a child rather than to the child's race; certainly the grandparents accept Cool as their own. The unseen mother is irresponsible not because she is African-American but because she is a Vegas showgirl, which is linked to Larry's equally irresponsible gambling obsession.

4. *Variety* opined, "Pic sometimes dives into the sentimental, but Howard usually pulls its nose up with deft comedy. Not so in the last reel, when all loose ends get tied up in bright packages." Daws, "*Parenthood*," *Variety's Film Reviews 1989–1990* (New Providence, R.I.: R. R. Bowker, 1991), n.p. See also the dossier of reviewers' comments in *Film Review Annual 1990*, pp. 971–981. John Pym, for example, singles out the school play as "the one unabashedly indulgent sequence," p. 974.

5. Karl Schanzer and Thomas Lee Wright, *American Screenwriters* (New York: Avon, 1993), p. 162.

6. As of 1998, Howard's independent production company, Imagine Entertainment (which produced *Parenthood*), was supplying a large portion of Universal's release schedule and co-producing five new series with the Disney channel. See Jenny Hontz and Dan Cox, "Imagine Revs Twin Engines," *Variety* (13–19 July 1998): 1.

7. Lee Server, *Screenwriter: Words Become Pictures* (Pittstown, N.J.: Main Street Press, 1987), p. 185.

10. *Alien*

1. In *Alien*, another possibility is that the derelict ship had crashed on the planet with a queen alien implanted in this creature, and that the latter managed to set up a warning before his death. We must then ask, however, how the queen managed to create the huge cavern, apparently fashioned from alien secretions, in which to lay her eggs. In general, the means by which aliens travel through space and set up their colonies do not bear too much causal scrutiny, especially in the sequels after *Aliens.*

2. Carol J. Clover has linked Ripley to the figure of the "Final Girl," conventional in slasher films since 1974's *The Texas Chainsaw Massacre.* In such films, the Final Girl manages actively to resist the villain(s), killing him or being rescued in the end even though her comrades have succumbed during the course of the action. To some extent Clover's interesting analysis is valid, and it is quite possible that the filmmakers might not have decided to turn the originally male character Ripley into a woman had it not been for the relatively active Jamie Lee Curtis character in *Halloween* the year before (1978). Yet even though the Final Girl was becoming a convention by 1979, she was primarily confined to low-budget—though sometimes very successful—horror films, and it seems unlikely that it would occur to most 1979 viewers to anticipate that Ripley, an apparently minor character in a fairly prestigious science fiction film, would conform to this convention. (Indeed, *Alien* was presented to 1979 audiences almost as an "art" version of the sci-fi film, with some spectators being more familiar with Scott's previous feature, *The Duellists,* than with *The Texas Chainsaw Massacre.*)

   Moreover, Clover characterizes the victims in slasher films using the Final Girl figure as succumbing to the menace relatively quickly, without long anticipating their demise, while she claims that the Final Girl suffers and resists for an extended period before earning her triumph. In *Alien,* all the characters are equally aware of the threat facing them, and, with the exception of Ash, they cooperate in fighting it. Ripley's final solitary escape from the ship and conflict with the alien in the shuttle may owe something to the travails of the Final Girl. And indeed, by the time that Ripley becomes the sole human survivor, we will probably expect that she will manage to defeat the alien somehow. My point here is that the Final Girl convention is only used in *Alien* to a limited extent near the end of the film. A 1979 viewer would most likely not have drawn upon it earlier on, to hypothesize that one of the female characters might be the sole survivor. See Clover's *Men, Women, and Chain Saws: Gender in the Modern Horror Film* (Princeton, N.J.: Princeton University Press, 1992), pp. 35–41, 46.

3. In *Aliens,* Ripley's speech describing Burke's plot to smuggle alien embryos back to earth says that hers and Newt's "impregnated" bodies would be frozen for the return voyage and that Burke could thus slip them through quarantine. Assuming the filmmakers were trying to make the sequel conform reasonably well to the premises of the original, this would seem to suggest that, despite appearances, hypersleep does involve freezing (or perhaps hypersleep technology has evolved in the interval). Ash does not take this approach of freezing Kane while the alien

embryo is still inside him, but presumably he does not realize yet how fast the creature develops (something he remarks on later). He seems nearly as astounded as the others when the little alien is born.

4. One would expect that the scriptwriters would solve such a problem by having the remaining crew members discover by other means that Ash is a robot. They could then use this discovery in some way to penetrate Mother's data bank, pretending to be Ash by plugging part of him into the computer or using a special code found in his database and uncovering the special order that way.

5. James H. Kavanagh, "Feminism, Humanism and Science in *Alien*," in Annette Kuhn, ed., *Alien Zone: Cultural Theory and Contemporary Science Fiction Cinema* (London: Verso, 1990), p. 78.

6. Charles Packer's brief but interesting analysis, "Classic of the Month: *Alien*," also makes this connection: "This discovery provokes a form of oral rape, with a rolled up 'girlie' magazine mirroring the alien's pseudo-sexual assault on Kane." *Dreamworks*, 17 (January 1996): 45.

7. See, for example, William Paul, *Laughing, Screaming: Modern Hollywood Horror and Comedy* (New York: Columbia University Press, 1994), pp. 391–392.

8. In *Aliens*, the physiology of alien reproduction becomes much more explicit. The face-huggers have a similar design, but the central portion of the underside more closely resembles female human genitalia, and in a few brief shots a phallic tube comes forth from the vagina—striving initially to seize onto Burke (Hicks remarks to Burke, "It looks like love at first sight to me"). Later it similarly tries to enter Ripley's mouth and "impregnate" her (or "whatever you call it," as she says). Like the face-hugger as a whole, this tube combines male and female sex organs. It is a miniature version of the large tube used by the "queen bee" alien mother to lay her noxious eggs. Thus we must apparently assume that the aliens reproduce by an elaborate system in which the distinctly female queen lays eggs bearing face-huggers; these dual-sex parasites then penetrate the bodies of humans (or other hosts) with a tube that resembles a long but flaccid penis extended from a vaginal opening, depositing an embryo in the stomach. finally, the creature that emerges is a small (seemingly male) alien that rapidly grows to menacing size.

Presumably the tube does not simply "ejaculate" something into the stomach that joins with something else in the host that creates the baby alien. Nevertheless, in an early version of Dan O'Bannon's script there was a notion that the alien's DNA was mixed with that of its human host. (See side 5, frame 248 of the Foxvideo 1992 laserdisc.) That idea was dropped, but it seems to linger in Ash's mysterious line, in the scene before Dallas's death, that the alien is "Kane's son."

This idea of mixed human and alien DNA was picked up in *Alien Resurrection* (1997), although there it somehow resulted from the ludicrously represented "cloning" process.

9. Pat McGilligan, "Richard Maibaum: A Pretense of Seriousness," in McGilligan, ed., *Backstory: Interviews with Screenwriters of Hollywood's Golden Age* (Berkeley: University of California Press, 1986), p. 287.

10. Art Linson, *A Pound of Flesh: Producing Movies in Hollywood—Perilous Tales from the Trenches* (New York: Avon, 1993), p. 64.

11. David Bordwell has determined that there is little if any empirical evidence that high points come at such regular intervals. Personal communication to the author.
12. Richard Schickel, "Jaunty Ride," *Time* (international edition, 7 August 1995): 45.

11. *Hannah and Her Sisters*

1. Mickey is the last of the film's major characters to be introduced, roughly eleven minutes in. Of course we know that he is played by the film's director and is likely to be a central character. Still, the delay helps to balance Mickey against the others, since we know more about them by this point than we do about him.
2. This kind of deliberate confusion of spatio-temporal relations reflects the influence of 1950s and 1960s European art cinema in Hollywood. It is not common, but certainly films occasionally use cuts that make such relations unclear. For example, the montage sequence in *The Graduate* that covers time passing during the early stages of Benjamin's affair with Mrs. Robinson cuts several times between him at home and him with her in their hotel room, with Benjamin wearing similar clothes and assuming similar postures. Moreover, as we saw in *The Silence of the Lambs*, the intercutting between the raid on the house in Calumet City and the doorbell ringing in Jame Gumb's cellar initially tricks us into thinking that the police have found Gumb's lair. Such deceptive editing, however, is used only locally and does not become a systematic practice in classical narrative films.
3. William Froug, *The Screenwriter Looks at the Screenwriter* (1972; reprint, Los Angeles: Silman-James, 1991), p. 237.
4. Chris Nashawaty, "A Coppola Things," *Entertainment Weekly* (21 November 1997): 62.
5. Michael Pye and Lynda Myles, *The Movie Brats: How the Film Generation Took Over Hollywood* (New York: Holt, Rinehart and Winston, 1979), p. 191.
6. Benedict Carver, "New Dreams for Zoetrope," *Variety* (20–26 July 1998): 7.
7. It is perhaps worth noting that within weeks of Coppola's windfall, Jack Valenti, head of the Motion Picture Association of America, revealed that the average cost of producing and marketing a studio film was $75.6 million, just a bit less than the award. Leonard Klady, "Boom and Gloom in B.O. Cume," *Variety* (29 June–12 July 1998): 53.
8. Owen Gleiberman, "Above the Law," *Entertainment Weekly* (23 January 1998): 38.

12. Hopes and Fears for Hollywood

1. Richard Corliss, "One Dumb Summer," *Time* (30 June 1997): 47.
2. Ty Burr, "Median Cool," *Entertainment Weekly* (10 October 1997): 78.
3. José Arroyo, "Massive Attack," *Sight and Sound*, 8, 2 (NS) (February 1998): 19.
4. Richard Schickel, "Misplaced Affection," *Time* (20 October 1997): 103.
5. Annabelle Villanueva, "Action Dissatisfaction," *Cinescape* (March/April 1998): 46.
6. Art Linson, *A Pound of Flesh: Producing Movies in Hollywood—Perilous Tales from the Trenches* (New York: Avon, 1993), pp. 57–58. For a similar view, see Richard

Walter, *The Whole Picture: Strategies for Screenwriting Success in the New Hollywood* (New York: Penguin, 1997), p. 3.

7. Lew Hunter, *Lew Hunter's Screenwriting 434* (New York: Putnam, 1993), p. 269.

8. There can be no doubt that many studio script readers use the three-act formula as a basic criterion for plot structure. Katherine Atwell Herbert's *Writing Scripts Hollywood Will Love* (New York: Allworth, 1994) was written by a professional script reader and quotes from interviews with other readers and industry executives. Her advice includes the following:

> Chris Meindl [a reader at MGM and other studios] believes that for the purpose of breaking-in, in Hollywood, writing scripts in three acts is necessary. "After you are established and you have mastered the form, then you can experiment." The director of development at a large production company feels that sticking with the three-act structure isn't always necessary, "but most commercial projects are written that way and development executives and readers look for it." She goes on to say, "Writers should master the conventional structure first, then deviate."
>
> Many analysts don't necessarily notice or want to notice the act breaks, but feel, as one reader does that, "for lack of a better option" taking the three act approach is the best. Another reader at one major studio agreed but added that while he appreciated "writers trying to do otherwise, it's a hard sell if a script doesn't follow the standard approach. [Ted] Dodd [script reader at Columbia] summed it up best when he said that while screenplays should follow the three-act structure, writers "don't have to be fanatics about it."
>
> Those that dissent from the three act convention felt that the whole concept of acts ran counter to the way movies operate, but until you are a master of the craft, you are probably better off if you stick with the three act approach as a way to organize your material into workable chunks. (pp. 90–91)

Given this stress on three acts and the dearth of actual three-act films which I found, I can only suspect that such three-act scripts form the bulk of the many sitting in studio files, optioned but unproduced.

9. "1997's Sundance Domestic Box Office Chart," *FilmMaker*, 6, 2 (Winter 1998): 49.

10. For a good brief summary of Sundance, see Gregg Kilday, "The Festival," *Entertainment Weekly*, special issue, "The New Hollywood: Inside the World of Independent Films" (November/December 1997): 26–32.

11. Andrew Hindes and Leonard Klady, "Niche Pix Notch High Profile: Specialized Fare Crowds Fall Skeds," *Variety* (13–24 August 1997): 7.

12. Patricia Troy, "A Week in the Life of the Sundance Screenwriters Lab," *The Journal of the Writers Guild of America, West*, 9, 1 (December 1995/January 1996): 20–26.

13. For an excellent summary of the independent business and its relationship to the big studios, see Monica Roman and Benedict Carver, "Ya Gotta Have Art," *Variety* (4–10 May 1998): 1, 103. Tom Garvin suggests that the financial success of independent films tends to move their makers toward the mainstream industry

in "Independents Find Money's Available, For the Right Price," *Variety* (2–8 March 1998): 80–82.

14. Patricia Troy, "Robert Redford Talks Scripts, Independent Film, and Sundance," *The Journal of the Writers Guild of America, West*, 9, 1 (December 1995/January 1996): 30

15. Leonard Klady, "Niche Pix Notch High Profile: Exhibs Enter Arthouse Building Fray," *Variety* (18–24 August 1997): 7.

16. Andrew Hindes and Benedict Carver, "Distribs Roll Out the Un-welcome Mat," *Variety* (9–15 February 1998): 1, 87.

17. Bruce Fretts, "Face of the Oscars: Robert Duvall," *Entertainment Weekly* (13 February 1998): 24.

18. Monica Roman and Andrew Hindes, "Sundancers Scale the Loftier Height$," *Variety* (26 January–1 February 1998): 5.

19. Gregg Kildry, "Reeling & Dealing," *Entertainment Weekly* (6 February 1998): 31. *Entertainment Weekly* was one of the co-sponsors of the Sundance Film Festival in 1998; see Chris Nashawaty, "Shall We Dance?" in the same issue, p. 30.

 In fact π confounded predictions and made back its million-dollar cost in its first month of release, being declared a hit (by independent-film standards) by *Variety* and ironically earning its directer a contract to direct a big-budget action film. See Leonard Klady, "How Hot Is Hot Enough?" *Variety* (17–23 August 1998): 49.

20. Jim Moran and Holly Willis, "The War of Independents," *FilmMaker*, 6, 2 (Winter 1998): 22.

21. Monica Roman, "Star-powered Pix, Indie Style," *Variety* (5–11 January 1998): 11.

22. Thomas Schatz, "The New Hollywood," in *Film Theory Goes to the Movies*, ed. Jim Collins, Hilary Radner, and Ava Preacher Collins (New York: Routledge, 1993), pp. 9–10, 12–13, 23.

23. Richard Maltby, "'Nobody Knows Everything': Post-classical Historiographies and Consolidated Entertainment," in *Contemporary Hollywood Cinema*, ed. Steve Neale and Murray Smith (New York: Routledge, 1998), p. 23.

24. James Schamus, "To the Rear of the Back End: The Economics of Independent Cinema," in *Contemporary Hollywood Cinema*, ed. Neale and Smith, p. 94.

25. Peter Kramer, "Would You Take Your Child to See This Film? The Cultural and Social Work of the Family-Adventure Movie," in *Contemporary Hollywood Cinema*, ed. Neale and Smith, pp. 294–295, 305–306. Evidence supporting Kramer's view appears in Laura Shapiro and Corie Brown's "Hollywood Family Values," *Newsweek* (3 August 1998): 66. The authors deal with the prominence of family-oriented films like *Dr. Dolittle*, *Mulan*, *The Mark of Zorro*, and *The Parent Trap* in the summer season of 1998. (All but the last were among the top ten grossers of the summer.)

26. For a summary of this trend, see Sharon Waxman, "Letting Exports Write the Script," *The Washington Post National Weekly Edition* (7 December 1998): 8–9.

27. John Lancaster, "Embracing the Great Satan's Culture," *The Washington Post National Weekly Edition* (14 December 1998): 9.

28. The three quotations in this paragraph are from Desmond Ryan and Daniel

Rubin, "A Loyalty of 'Titanic' Dimensions," *Wisconsin State Journal* (1 March 1998): 1F (Knight Ridder Newspapers wire service).

29. Eun Young Park, untitled letter in "Mail: The Unsinkable," *Entertainment Weekly* (6 March 1998): 4.

30. See Benjamin Svetkey's pair of insightful, vituperative, and (perhaps) overly pessimistic articles, "Who Killed the Hollywood Screenplay?" *Entertainment Weekly* (4 October 1996): 33–39, and "Has Hollywood Lost It?" *Entertainment Weekly* (14 March 1997): 22–31.

31. Leonard Klady, "Boom & Gloom in B.O. Cume," *Variety* (29 June–12 July 1998): 1, 53.

32. Leonard Klady, "Budgets in the Hot Zone: The Sum Also Rises," *Variety* (16–22 March 1998): 1, 80.

33. Paul Karon, "H'wood Dreads Tech Wreck," *Variety* (6–12 April 1998): 1, 61.

34. Andrew Hindes, "Size May Not Matter Enough For Exhibs," *Variety* (11–17 May 1998): 5.

35. Peter Bart, "Lessons From the Lizard," *Variety* (1–7 June 1998): 4.

36. Carrie Bell, "Flashes," *Entertainment Weekly* (19 June 1998): 18.

37. Peter Bart, "Are Moviegoers Going 'Retro'?" *Variety* (20–26 July 1998): 4.

38. Andrew Hindes, "Summer Sums: A Summary," *Variety* (17–23 August 1998): 9, 13. See also David Hochman, "The Summer About 'Mary,'" *Entertainment Weekly* (11 September 1998): 28–30.

Appendix B

1. Richard Maltby and Ian Craven, *Hollywood Cinema: An Introduction* (Oxford: Blackwell, 1995), p. 7.

2. Ibid., p. 35.

3. Raymond G. Frenshaw's *Screenwriting* (Chicago: NTC Publishing, 1996) discusses the script reader's assumptions on pp. 13–15. On the evaluation system, see Rick Marx, "How Screenwriters Can Read the Minds of Hollywood's Gatekeepers: Insight from Professional Script Reader Doug Michael," *Moviemaker*, 24 (March/April 1997): 51–53. For a cynical view of the script reader as "the enemy," see Charles Zucker, "A Reader Confesses," *The Journal of the Writers Guild of America, West*, 8, 8 (August 1995): 39.

4. Frenshaw, *Screenwriting*, p. 96.

5. T. L. Katahn, *Reading for a Living: How To Be a Professional Story Analyst for Film and Television* (Los Angeles: Blue Arrow Books, 1990), pp. 57–61.

6. Lee Server, *Screenwriter: Words Become Pictures* (Pittstown, N.J.: The Main Street Press, 1987), p. 194.

7. Published annually (New York: Signet).

8. William Froug, *The New Screenwriter Looks at the New Screenwriter* (Los Angeles: Silman-James, 1991), p. 133.

9. Rebecca Ascher-Walsh, "When Longer Is Less," *Entertainment Weekly* (4 December 1998): 21.

10. Jeff Gordinier, "A Time to Chill," *Entertainment Weekly* (6 November 1998): 38.

Index

Froug, William, 23, 211, 372n49
Fugitive, The (1947), 333
Fugitive, The (1993), 33, 304

Gale, Bob, 77
Ganz, Lowell, 248, 281–282
Garland, Robert, 75
Gelbart, Larry, 50, 75
Ghost and Mrs. Muir, The, 39
Ghostbusters, 134
Ghoul, The, 285
Giler, David, 331
Gill, Mark, 343
Gilliat, Penelope, 305
Gingerbread Man, The, 8, 334
Goals, 14–15, 27–29, 35, 41–42, 45, 51–52, 74, 76, 103, 155, 281, 348
Godfather, The, 5–6, 8, 30, 47, 333
Godfather, Part II, The, 285
Godzilla, 349–351
Goldman, William, 100–101, 211
Gold Rush, The, 381n4
Gomery, Douglas, 4
Gone with the Wind, 349
Good Will Hunting, 8, 351
Gordon, Larry, 306
Gorillas in the Mist, 23
Graduate, The, 15, 25, 388n2
Grand Hotel, 48
Great Dictator, The, 381n4
Groundhog Day, 45, 101, 131–154, 308, 372n52
Guber, Peter, 153

Hair, 47
Hallelujah, I'm a Bum, 381n4
Halloween, 246
Hammett, 5
Hannah and Her Sisters, 45, 48, 218, 284, 287, 307–331
Hanson, Curtis, 8
Hard Day's Night, A, 340
Harper, 100–101
Harris, Thomas, 103–106
Hauge, Michael, 51–52
Hawks, Howard, 282, 332–333, 337
Heat, 37–38, 47, 212
Henry, Buck, 25
High concept, 3, 152–154, 345
Hillier, Jim, 4
His Girl Friday, 16, 130, 373n56
Hitchcock, Alfred, 7, 39, 285, 305
Hook. *See* Dialogue hook
Horse Whisperer, The, 101

Howard, David, 15
Howard, Ron, 248, 281–282
Howard the Duck, 365–366
How Green Was My Valley, 10
Huillet, Danièlle, 182
Hunter, Lew, 99–100
Hunt for Red October, The, 43, 45–46, 155, 213–247, 282, 338, 348

Independence Day, 348–349
Independent films, 2, 175–176, 339–344
Informer, The, 333
Invasion of the Body Snatchers, 285–286
Italian, The, 38
It's a Mad, Mad, Mad, Mad World, 40
It's a Wonderful Life, 3, 131–132, 378n1

Jackie Brown, 51–52, 341
Jaws, 5–6, 8, 13–14, 21, 33–36, 43, 50, 78, 130, 284, 333, 348
Jeanne Dielman, 23, Quai du commerce, 1080 Bruxelles, 16
Jerry Macguire, 341
John Grisham's The Rainmaker, 7, 332–334
Jurassic Park, 32, 308, 347–348

Kael, Pauline, 180
Kasdan, Lawrence, 367–368
Kaufman, Bob, 75
Kay, Eddie Dorman, 5
Kazan, Nicholas, 23–24
Keaton, Buster, 38
Kiarostami, Abbas, 347
King Kong, 333
King of Comedy, 20
King, Viki, 25
Klady, Leonard, 350
Koch, Howard, 75
Kramer, Peter, 347
Kundun, 332

L. A. Confidential, 8
Lady Eve, The, 38
Landau, Jon, 349
Landscape in the Mist, 16
Large-scale parts, 21–44, 85, 129, 151–152, 180, 209, 211, 275, 364–366
Last Action Hero, The, 246
Last Boy Scout, The, 17
Last Laugh, The, 10
Last of the Mohicans, The, 211
Last Picture Show, The, 6
Last Temptation of Christ, The, 285
Last Year at Marienbad, 23